A Special Foreword
for *Wall Street Journal* Subscribers

On April 9, 2002, *Wall Street Journal* subscribers awoke to find that their familiar *Journal* contained a brand-new section—Personal Journal. Introducing coverage of what we now call "the business of life," Personal Journal immediately captured the interests of readers everywhere. In the days, weeks, months and years that followed, we have received volumes of correspondence from readers asking questions, commenting on stories and suggesting topics of their own.

Personal Journal's popularity came in the wake of Weekend Journal's resounding success and has led to the coming launch of the much-anticipated Weekend Edition, which promises to deliver a sharp focus on events of the week past—as well as perspective on the week ahead—while expanding *The Journal*'s "business of life" approach into weekend activities.

The amount of interest our readers have expressed in Personal Journal, Weekend Journal and our plans for a Weekend Edition comes as no surprise to those of us who know *Journal* readers well. Together, their popularity makes one fact obvious to all: *Wall Street Journal* readers lead well-rounded lives.

The book you hold in your hands, *The Wall Street Journal Guide to the Business of Life,* contains all-new material on the topics that have made Personal Journal so popular. Culled from the expertise of *Wall Street Journal* reporters and their sources, *The Wall Street Journal Guide to the Business of Life* provides insightful information on everything from work and family to health and fitness, from personal finance to personal technology, with cars, clothes, real estate, relaxation and much more covered along the way.

The Wall Street Journal Guide to the Business of Life is intended to serve as a valuable reference as well as an enjoyable read. I hope you find it to be both.

I want to thank you for subscribing to *The Wall Street Journal* and for your loyalty to the paper.

MICHAEL F. SHEEHAN
Senior Vice President
The Wall Street Journal

"Today was my first visit to your Subscriber Services Web site—
I think this is an excellent service and is what I have come to expect
from The Journal. *Thank you."* —St. Louis, MO

HAVE YOU VISITED SERVICES.WSJ.COM?

he Wall Street Journal would like to introduce you to Services.WSJ.com, the ultimate, secure customer service site, with all the convenience and features you need to make your life easier. Think of it as your personal *Wall Street Journal* assistant, connecting you with a wealth of resources 24 hours a day, seven days a week.

Visit Services.WSJ.com to:

- Temporarily stop your subscription while you're away
- Resolve a delivery problem
- Renew your subscription
- Update your delivery address
- Search for recent articles
- Contact *The Journal*

Your Online Customer Service Resource makes it faster and easier than ever for you to connect to the resources you need. Log on today!

THE WALL STREET JOURNAL
GUIDE TO THE
BUSINESS OF
LIFE

NANCY KEATES

CROWN PUBLISHERS NEW YORK

Published in the United States by Crown Publishers, an imprint of the Crown Publishing Group, a division of Random House, Inc., New York.
www.crownpublishing.com

Crown is a trademark and the Crown colophon is a registered trademark of Random House, Inc.

This title may be purchased in bulk at a discount for business or promotional use or for special sales. For information, please write to: Special Markets Department, Random House, Inc., 1745 Broadway, New York, NY 10019 or e-mail: specialmarkets@randomhouse.com.

Library of Congress Cataloging-in-Publication Data
Keates, Nancy.
    The Wall Street Journal guide to the business of life / Nancy Keates.—1st ed.
    Includes bibliographical references and index.
    1. Finance, Personal—Handbooks, manuals, etc. 2. Life skills—Handbooks, manuals, etc. 3. Success—Handbooks, manuals, etc.
I. Title: Guide to the business of life. II. Wall Street journal. III. Title.
    HG179.K433 2005
    650.1—dc22   2004027467

ISBN 1-4000-8159-9

Printed in the United States of America

Design by Robert Bull

10 9 8 7 6 5 4 3 2

First Edition

CONTENTS

CHAPTER EDITORS

GETTING THERE: SECRETS OF THE SAVVY TRAVELER
NANCY KEATES

With contributions from: Scott McCartney (Beating the Game: The Scoop on Lost Luggage)

CREATURE COMFORTS ON THE ROAD
NANCY KEATES

GETTING PAMPERED, HAVING FUN AND ROUGHING IT: LEISURE AND ADVENTURE TRAVEL
NANCY KEATES

With contributions from: Raymond Sokolov (Scenes from the Cruise Frontier)

LOGISTICS: THE NUTS AND BOLTS OF TRAVEL
NANCY KEATES

AFTER HOURS
KATY McLAUGHLIN (contributing editor) writes about the food industry, cuisine and restaurants for Personal Journal. She joined *The Wall Street Journal* in 2002 after a stint as freelance journalist and a writer and producer of television, film and theater, including a stint at Home Box Office.

With contributions from: Katy McLaughlin and Suein Hwang (The Double Dip); Eileen Daspin (The Savvy Diner: Decoding Restaurant Costs); Dorothy J. Gaiter and John Brecher (The No-Brainer Way to Order Wine in a Restaurant); Ken Wells (Confessions and Advice of a Hophead; Beer Geek Speak)

GADGETS: LEARNING TO SPEAK GEEK
LEE GOMES (contributing editor) has worked at *The Wall Street Journal* since 1996, writing about technology from the San Francisco bureau. Prior to joining the *Journal*, he reported for the *Oakland Tribune* and the *San Jose Mercury News*.

With contributions from Jason Fry (Using the Internet Smartly to Research Consumer Products); Peter Grant with Martin Peers (The War for Your Remote: Satellite Gains on Cable); Walter S. Mossberg (A Primer on Buying a Digital Still Camera); Nancy Keates (When Good Gadgets Go Bad: The Repair Conundrum in a Throwaway Society)

THE GREAT GAME: BUYING, FINANCING AND KEEPING A CAR IN SHAPE

NANCY KEATES

With contributions from: Reed Albergotti (Wheel Life: We Go Shopping Online); Jim Carlton (Sell Your Car on eBay!); Joseph B. White (Inside FICO; Technology: The Car Gadgets You Can Have Now); Alex Frangos (Putting the Brakes on Teen Expenses); Joseph B. White (The Future Is Now in Car Audio); Michelle Higgins (Technology to the Rescue); Sharon Begley (Smart Cars Can Kill Traffic)

REAL ESTATE: BUYING, SELLING AND UPGRADING YOUR HOME

DANIELLE REED (contributing editor) covered business travel and real estate for Weekend Journal from 1996 to 2004. She began her career in journalism at the *New York Observer* and later worked at the *New York Daily News.* She currently writes about the bond market for Dow Jones Newswires.

With contributions from: Ruth Simon (What Type of Mortgage?); Christopher Oster (How Much [Homeowner's Insurance] Is Enough); Jeff D. Opdyke (Houses with Checkered Pasts); Paula Szuchman (A Really Moving Experience); Elizabeth Bernstein (The High-Tech Home; Bright Lights, Big Systems); Asra Q. Nomani (The Three-Decorator Experience); Alexandra Peers (Finding Great Art for Your Home); June Fletcher (More Things Worth Doing)

HEALTH AND FITNESS: TAKING CONTROL OF YOURSELF

TARA PARKER-POPE (contributing editor) is a twelve-year veteran of *The Wall Street Journal,* having worked in London and New York covering consumer products, marketing, advertising and health. She currently writes the Health Journal column for Personal Journal and is the author of a book on the tobacco industry.

With contributions from: Laura Landro (The Informed Patient: How to Check Up on Your Doctor); Andrea Petersen (His and Her Sex Drugs)

EDUCATION: THE LONG HAUL

ELIZABETH SEAY (contributing editor) is a feature writer and editor who joined *The Wall Street Journal* in 1992. She edits home and family coverage for Personal Journal and is the author of a recent book on Native American languages.

With contributions from: Anne Marie Chaker (Little Kids, College Methods; Do You Need a Financial-Aid Counselor?; A Back-Door Route to College); Michelle Higgins (Playing Hide-and-Seek with Financial Aid); Elizabeth Bernstein (Feeder Mania; The New Safety Schools; Your Tuition Dollars at Work)

LIFE IS A TIGHTROPE: BALANCING WORK AND FAMILY

CAROL HYMOWITZ (contributing editor) oversees *The Wall Street Journal*'s management and workplace coverage, and writes a weekly column, In the Lead, about leadership issues. A senior editor, she also reports and writes frequently about top executives and work and family matters.

With contributions from: Jeffrey Zaslow (Belly Talk and Womb Music: Does It Work?); Sue Shellenbarger (The One Promise You Should Never Make; The Brave New World of Eldercare)

FINANCING YOUR LIFE: THE NEW REALITIES

E. S. (JIM) BROWNING (contributing editor), a *Wall Street Journal* reporter since 1979, covers investment and financial markets out of New York. He previously served as a *Journal* correspondent in Paris, Tokyo and Hong Kong.

With contributions from: Jonathan Clements (Staying Unconfused; Picking a Broker)

SHOPPING: THE NATION'S NEW SEX?

NANCY KEATES

With contributions from: Katy McLaughlin (Groceries: Things Supermarkets Won't Tell You); Anne Marie Chaker (Do You Need a Pill to Stop Shopping?); Kelly K. Spors (Virtual Models: A Fit Over Online Swimsuits); Anne Marie Chaker (Wedding Help Online); Mei Fong (Tips for Women); Robert Frank (Shopping? It's My Job—Really!); Walter S. Mossberg (Rating Some Internet Music Stores); Charles Passy (Better Clothes for Bigger Guys); Jennifer Saranow (A Fashionista's Dry-Cleaning Tips)

SUPERVISING EDITOR

KEN WELLS joined *The Wall Street Journal* in 1982 and served stints in the San Francisco and London bureaus before moving to New York in 1993 as a Page One editor. A novelist and author of a recent book on the U.S. beer industry, he is now editor of the *Journal*'s book-publishing enterprise.

CONTRIBUTORS

Reporters contributing to chapters 1–4: Scott McCartney, Melanie Trott-man, Stephen Power, Ron Lieber, Kortney Stringer, Nicole Harris, Rob Turner, Susan Carey, Evan Perez, Eleena de Lisser, Peter Meyers, Katy McLaughlin, Jane Spencer, Daniel Machalaba, Paula Szuchman, Lisa Miller, Michelle Higgins, Paul Glader, Melanie Trottman, Christina Bink-ley, Motoko Rich, Brooks Barnes, Lauren Lipton, Eric Wee, Lisa Kalis, Anne Marie Chaker, Albert R. Hunt, Sara Calian, J. Lynn Lunsford, Sam Schechner, Andrea Petersen, Joseph T. Hallinan, Lisa Gubernick, Eliza-beth Bernstein, Robert J. Davis, June Fletcher, Everett Potter, Suzanne McGee, Avery Johnson.

Reporters contributing to chapter 5: Eileen Daspin, Lorraine Farquhar-son, Ken Wells, Dorothy J. Gaiter and John Brecher, David S. Thompson.

Reporters contributing to chapter 7: Alex Frangos, Josef Federman, Bart Ziegler, Karen Lundegaard, Nick Wingfield, Joseph B. White, Terri Cullen, Jonathan Welsh, Lisa Kalis, Kelly Greene, John R. Emshwiller, Stephen Power, Timothy Aeppel, Michelle Higgins, Sholnn Freeman, Alex Frangos, Christopher Oster, Jane Spencer, Gregory L. White, Jane J. Kim.

Reporters contributing to chapter 8: Reed Albergotti, Patrick Barta, Jonathan Clements, Terri Cullen, June Fletcher, Nancy Ann Jeffrey, Nancy Keates, Jeff Opdyke, Danielle Reed, Ruth Simon.

Reporters contributing to chapter 9: Laura Landro, Tara Parker-Pope, Kevin Helliker, Sarah Rubenstein, Kelly Greene, Barbara Martinez, Ron Winslow, Christopher Windham, Robert J. Davis, Lucette Lagnado, Eleena De Lisser, Eileen Daspin.

Reporters contributing to chapter 10: Ronald Alsop, Johanna Bennett, Elizabeth Bernstein, Anne Marie Chaker, Jonathan Clements, Kathy Chu, Terri Cullen, Kemba J. Dunham, Daniel Golden, Michelle Higgins, Jane J. Kim, June Kronholz, Elizabeth Seay, Kaja Whitehouse.

Reporters contributing to chapter 11: Sue Shellenbarger, Hilary Stout.

Reporters contributing to chapter 12: Anne Marie Chaker, Jonathan Clements, Terri Cullen, Alex Frangos, Tom Herman, Michelle Higgins, Zachery Kouwe, Ron Lieber, Jeff D. Opdyke, Christopher Oster, Rachel Emma Silverman, Ruth Simon and Kelly K. Spors.

Reporters contributing to chapter 13: Joseph Pereira, Mei Fong, Teri Agins, Eleena de Lisser, Ann Zimmerman, Jennifer Saranow, Jane Spencer, Reed Albergotti, Sally Beatty, Katy McLaughlin, Sarah Robertson, Lauren Lipton, Lauren Mechling, Eileen White Read, June Fletcher, Danielle Reed, Alexandra Peers, Michelle Higgins, Rick Brooks, Vernon Clement Jones, Karen Mazurkewich, Sarah Ellison, Francesco Fiondella, Andrew Blackman, Ron Lieber, Kathy Chu, Jeremy Wagstaff, Carl Bialik, Jeanette Borzo, Martin Peers, Nick Wingfield, Kelly K. Spors, Jane J. Kim.

FOREWORD

JOANNE LIPMAN

The last time I flew across country, I paid too much for my ticket and sat crammed in the back of coach. I lost all feeling in my legs after five hours wedged into a middle seat between two sniffling road warriors with sharp elbows and a propensity to nod off, drooling, on my shoulder.

Next time, you can bet I'll pay less and get a better seat, besides.

How do I know?

Because I just read this book.

You'd expect *The Wall Street Journal* to help you in business and, of course, it does. But perhaps you didn't know the *Journal* is just as authoritative on the "business of life." It can help you avoid life's little indignities—cramped seats and overpriced tickets among them—and navigate life's biggest challenges, from finding the best medical care to helping your child get into the college of his or her choice.

For sure, our reporters know personal finance and give excellent advice when it comes to investing, financing or refinancing a home or paying down credit card debt. But they're also experts in health and fitness; cars and travel; fashion and food; gadgets and education; and entertainment and shopping.

That's where this book comes in. *Journal* editor Nancy Keates, with the help of some of our most seasoned staffers, has taken the best of our business-of-life coverage, much of it distilled and updated from the paper's Personal Journal and Weekend sections. But Nancy went a step further, asking reporters to contribute the "trade secrets" of the areas they cover, everything from when stores are most likely to mark down merchandise, to a list of the secret "VIP" phone numbers at the nation's most exclusive restaurants. And she has shaped it into a clear, highly organized compendium of first-rate consumer advice.

The result is the ultimate reference book, one that will save you money as well as time. It will help you make the best, most informed decisions about matters ranging from travel to shopping and health. And it will cut through the frustrations life tends to throw our way. In short, it's an instruction manual for living life to the fullest.

Our travel reporters will tell you the best way to cash in on frequent flier miles and the best times to fly. Our retail reporters are shoppers extraordinaire who know how to find out when the sales start before anyone else and how to separate out the fads from the classics. Our Pulitzer Prize–winning health team offers unparalleled coverage of health issues, including useful advice on diet, fitness and state-of-the-art treatment for illnesses. Our food reporters can tell you how to get a reservation at the hottest restaurant of the moment (and, by the way, how to do it at a discount). In a world in which the Web, the personal computer, the cell phone and a plethora of high-tech devices are rapidly changing the way we communicate, shop and entertain ourselves, our tech reporters not only give smart advice on what to buy: they tell you *how* to shop for high-tech gadgetry while demystifying tech trends that will make you a more informed user and consumer.

Of course, no *Wall Street Journal Guide to the Business of Life* would be complete without our unparalleled advice about how to manage your money and investments, and you'll find plenty within these pages as well. We've got a primer on how to pick a broker, plus how to understand—and minimize—investment fees. We've got specific advice on what to do with your 401(k) if, as most people do, you change jobs.

I've saved two of my favorite pieces of advice for last:

On a recent morning, after reading chapter 13's advice on online shopping, I bought a present for my daughter and was able to get an unadvertised deal on free shipping. I whooped out loud as I learned that I can get a discount almost each and every time I shop on the Web. Thanks to this book, I will never have to shop online without a "promotional code" discount.

Only minutes later, on a more serious note, I heard news of a dear friend's illness. But I was able to jump into action, using Chapter 9's authoritative advice to help her research her disease, check out doctors and even find clinical trials she may be eligible for.

Those two extremes—the delight in getting a discount versus the serious need to find information when a life hangs in the balance—are both a part of the business of life. That's why this book is so essential. Whether you're facing major life decisions, planning a vacation, buying a car, or just want to be entertained, *The Wall Street Journal Guide to the Business of Life* helps you get there.

So read on, and enjoy the business of living.

Joanne Lipman is a deputy managing editor of The Wall Street Journal *and founding editor of its Weekend and Personal Journal sections.*

THE WALL STREET JOURNAL

GUIDE TO THE

BUSINESS OF
LIFE

CHAPTER ONE

GETTING THERE

SECRETS OF THE SAVVY TRAVELER

To travel well you must travel smart. To travel smart you must travel informed. And being informed isn't just being up on sources and methods, though we have plenty of advice for you in that regard in the pages that follow. It's also understanding that when it comes to airfares, time is money. Some people, though, never get it.

THE ART OF THE FARE CHASE

You know the type: Those compulsive deal-finders whose self-esteem depends on getting an absolute rock-bottom price and crowing about it, never mind that they wasted all day Saturday, missing the kids' soccer game, to save $11.25 on a round-trip to Cleveland. In our opinion, a key factor in booking air travel is knowing when to *stop* the search. For the search can often be a frustrating and complex endeavor that's akin to shopping in the dark—imagine groping about blindly in Wal-Mart without being able to see the merchandise (and all the while the prices are shifting). Airlines, you see, price tickets not on what it costs to provide the service, but rather on how much money the carrier thinks it can get at any given moment. That means a ticket for the same flight can cost $200 or $2,000, depending on when you inquire. So, yes, some endeavor can lead to big savings. But too much can be a huge waste of time. So how do you strike a reasonable balance? Knowing a few basic rules about airfares is a must.

1. Watch carefully for airline announcements of new routes or flights. New service often means—initially, at least—empty seats. To fill those planes, airlines often offer fares at garage-sale prices.

2. Keep an eye out for fare wars, which happen all the time. When one airline announces price cuts, wait a few days to see if the other carriers are matching it (they often do). Then find out from the airlines what time of day they load their computers with new fares. This is easier to do than you think: Airlines routinely list all this information on their Web sites. (And we run new service announcements in *The Wall Street Journal*.)

Beyond that, several travel Web sites offer fare alerts—they keep track of airlines' fare sales, and will send you free e-mails to keep you up to date. Travelocity's Fare Watcher (**Travelocity.com**) will e-mail you if a specific itinerary you requested goes on sale; you can enter a number of cities and choose to be e-mailed either when a price falls by $25 or if it falls below a threshold you specify. Orbitz (**Orbitz.com**) will show when the lowest prices are available and has a "Deal Detector" that lets you register a price you want, then alerts you if it shows up. **SmarterTravel.com** offers weekly newsletters with various deal alerts—fare sales from major carriers as well as last-minute weekend deals from your hometown. Last-minute deals are sent to you on the Wednesday before the weekend that's on sale (Monday for international flights). The newsletters also offer travel tips and news, and **SmarterTravel.com**'s site has links to the airlines so you can buy directly from them. A few other tips:

3. Connections are usually cheaper than nonstop flights. You may not like the hassle of a longer trip or the risk of missing a connection, but a few hours of extra travel may be worth saving enough to afford, say, a bottle of really nice champagne when you arrive.

4. Don't be a snob and rule out package deals. Yes, we know that "package travel" often conjures up images of noisy vacationers in baggy Bermuda shorts waiting in endless queues. But one of the industry's best-kept secrets is that packages increasingly are a tool for snagging airfare bargains, not only for last-minute romps but also for business travelers, routine trips and even family emergencies. The idea is essentially to buy the package for its parts, since the airfare is often a bargain—and there isn't a penalty if you ditch the hotel. For most domestic travel, a trip with a Saturday-night or at least a three-night stay will get the best deals. The opposite is true for leisure destinations like Las Vegas or the Caribbean, where midweek travel is the best bet for a cheap package.

And bear in mind:

5. Timing is everything. It helps to know when the peak travel times are for where you want to go, since booking the last or first day of the new season can save hundreds of dollars without changing your schedule too drastically. For example, tickets are usually more expensive to the Western United States from June through August and January through March, while on the New York–Boston route it is June through September and the month of December. Peak to European cities is May through September, but the Riviera and Greece are less expensive in September. Also find out what your airline's peak travel times are; in general the most expensive times to fly are between 7 A.M. and 7 P.M. There's an old trick frequent fliers use: If they want a peak-hour flight but don't want to pay the peak rate, they make a reservation on a cheaper flight right after it—and then show up at the airport early. Assuming there's room, most ticket agents will let you on the earlier flight without changing the fare. But call first and ask for the airline's policy.

A little-noticed rule change is making it easier for travelers to get cheaper tickets on some international flights. Under the new procedures, it is possible for travelers to benefit from the fact that some tickets cost substantially less when bought overseas. Previously, airlines had a system that kept many of these lower prices off-limits for travelers trying to book overseas flights—you had to physically go to, say, Thailand to get the cheaper Thai price. But on January 15, an airline trade group discarded that system, putting the new ticketing guidelines into effect. For example, the lowest price on American Airlines for a Dallas-Istanbul business-class round-trip via Zurich used to be $6,946, not including taxes. Now, however, a traveler can book the same trip as two one-way tickets (instead of one round-trip), and pay $6,047, undercutting the listed round-trip price by about $900. That wasn't possible before, because travelers buying outside Istanbul would have been charged the higher Zurich-Dallas fare by default.

However, it still can be tricky to take full advantage of the changes. For starters, some travel agents don't know about them yet. In addition, some of the airlines' own Internet sites won't yet process bookings for points of origin that don't match the credit-card address. As a result, calling an airline's 800 number and talking to a human to make a booking may be the best bet. For travelers flying out of the United States, the best deals come on itineraries that include a connection at an airport abroad. That's partly because previously, itineraries that made connections through large hub airports in high-priced markets (say, London), automatically took on the higher fare prices associated with that market—even if the flight was continuing on to a low-fare market such as India. Now, that is no longer the case. (One exception: The higher fares still automatically kick in on flights with a layover of 24 hours or more.) Travelers can benefit by pricing a trip as two one-way tickets because, for the first time, they will have access to the cheaper price formerly intended for sale in the low-fare market.

Also, keep in mind two other money-saving tips:

1. **Flying to an international destination from a hub airport is likely to be more expensive than flying out of a non-hub city.**

2. **Foreign partners in airline code-share agreements usually have cheaper tickets for the same flight.**

Now you can start the buying process. Here's what to do:

Armed with an Official Airline Guide (OAG), which lists all the flights to every airport in the world, start online by downloading sidestep.com.

The service will appear on the left half of your screen and will sift through airline Web sites and lots of other travel vendors you wouldn't normally search that aren't in the big centralized reservation systems. Then check the Big Three ticket-buying Web sites—**Expedia.com, Travelocity.com** and **Orbitz.com.** Route by route, these can be quite different because they have different pricing negotiated with different carriers. All offer packages of airfare and hotel bookings that can yield savings. And they'll search alternative airports near your destination—a key money-saver. Don't spend more than half an hour trying to find a bargain this way and—unless you really do have all the time in the world, we recommend skipping all the other, smaller sites. Our long experience shows that the return for this extra effort is usually quite slim. On the other hand, beware of hype on the big sites. For example, Travelocity's "Good Buys" simply aren't always the best deal. Orbitz may have good fares but it doesn't negotiate proprietary deals with airlines—meaning other sites may well have deals Orbitz doesn't.

1. **That's why the next stop is the airlines' own sites,** where they often sell fares that aren't widely available and list last-minute deals. Booking through the sites can also net incentives, like bonus frequent-flier miles, and lets you avoid fees charged by the Big Three. Don't just look at the big carriers—every airline has its own site and the less-known ones don't show up elsewhere.

2. **Finally, go on Hotwire** (www.hotwire.com) and bid 10 or 20 percent lower to see what you get—if you don't like it, you have an hour to cancel the results.

BONUS TIP: KEEP LOOKING AFTER BUYING

Just because you already bought a ticket, don't stop looking at prices. Even with the airline industry's financial woes, most carriers will still refund you the difference between the two prices—as long as you qualify for the new fare's rules and restrictions. And here is the big surprise: Generally you *do* qualify. The best way to make sure is to call the airline. Refunds either come in the same form in which you paid, or as travel vouchers, depending on the carrier.

When would you not qualify? One example: You hear about a lower fare four days before your departure but it has a 14-day advance-purchase requirement. Because that is a common requirement, check published fares at least two weeks before you leave. The caveat: Most airlines have exceptions. For instance, Delta won't issue refunds if the lower fare is an Internet-only one.

Finding Scarce Air Tickets

The Problem: The plane tickets you want for the holidays are already sold out.

The Solution: Stay up late.

Every night at midnight, new plane seats go back onto the system. That's when airline reservations made but never confirmed expire, freeing up space on many flights. Airlines typically "reload" at midnight in the time zone where they are based—in all, hundreds of new seats are fed back into the system every night. On a recent evening, for example, American Airlines' Web site showed three nonstop flights from New York to Orlando, Florida, an especially busy route, with seat availability for the coming Friday. But at midnight CST, seats on a fourth flight (one with an earlier departure) popped up as well.

Tracking Flight Delays

The Problem: What can you do to cut down on future waits at the airport?

The Solution: Most major airlines have flight-tracking services, which provide the latest information on arriving and departing planes, and some have special features.

Delta (**delta.com**) and Northwest (**nwa.com**) will e-mail you with gate information and any schedule changes. American (**aa.com**) will call or page you. These sites are now updating their information more frequently. Even if you don't know the exact itinerary, often you can input what you do know and a list of possible flights will pop up. Some sites have a few extra features. **Flightarrivals.com** tells you about delays at the airports themselves. **Trip.com** even shows the plane moving across a map in real time, and its speed and altitude.

The Joys (and Benefits) of Delay

The Problem: What to do if you get bumped.

The Solution: If you can handle the hassle of a delayed trip, getting "bumped" from a flight can reap big rewards.

The Department of Transportation requires that airlines compensate bumped passengers, and the rules officially apply only if the flight leaves from the United States and if the carrier can't find a way to get you to your destination within an hour of your scheduled arrival. You typically get around $300 in vouchers for future tickets, but if too few people raise their hands, airlines will sweeten the deal—sometimes up to $800 or more in perks—until they get enough takers.

Always ask for a seat reservation on another flight before agreeing to get bumped—for common routes, you could end up departing just 15 minutes later, but for tropical islands, the next available flight may not leave for two days. Airlines should put you on another carrier's flight if one is available. If you get stranded overnight, ask the airlines to pay for extra expenses such as hotel rooms, transportation and meals.

Want to improve chances of a bump? Check in as early as possible. Once at the gate, ask the agent if the flight is oversold, and volunteer on the spot to give up your ticket. Airlines bump on a first-come, first-served basis, so those who get their names in first are guaranteed to be left behind if the airline determines volunteers are needed. If you check in 30 minutes or less prior to departure, you could get bumped without compensation.

AIRLINE MILES AND MILES AND MILES AND MILES . . .

Obsession? Frustration? Confusion? Followed by periods of enlightenment and elation?

No, we're not talking about your last trip to your analyst. We're talking about airline frequent-flier programs and people's relationship to them.

As with airfares, it's hard not to feel like everyone else is figuring out the game while you're left foundering. The rules change all the time. Accruing lots of miles is no guarantee you'll be able to use them (more about expiring miles later). Worse, airlines have diluted the programs by linking them together in alliances, raising the mileage cost of awards and imposing fees—it can cost you $100 these days to change a free-travel booking.

Here's our no-nonsense advice on how to get a handle on the system and maximize your miles:

1. Start by signing up for every airline program. It doesn't cost anything and you will get better treatment all around.

2. Pick just one airline to fly on as much as you can. You'll build miles faster and you'll more quickly achieve elite status, which takes a minimum of 25,000 miles a year. But such status comes with lots of benefits (typically a 25 percent to 100 percent mileage bonus each time you fly, early boarding, better seats, free upgrades and exclusive lines at check-in and security).

3. If more than one carrier flies your favorite route, study each elite requirement carefully to figure out which one is most advantageous— the object **being to obtain the highest possible status for the fewest possible miles.**

4. Study airline alliances, which may let you earn miles on your favorite carrier by flying someone else.

5. Work the ground hard. You know all those ads for long-distance providers and credit cards that offer frequent-flier miles? Very annoying. But it turns out that half of all miles are earned on the ground, through retailers, hotels, car-rental companies, restaurants, financial-services companies and long-distance providers. (And the bonus: This is money you would spend anyway.) So pay attention and take advantage of getting miles wherever you can. All of the big programs now have tie-ins with mortgage lenders and moving services, and they're trying to take advantage of that. But the advice is the same: Be sure not to overpay for the miles when purchasing a service. Also be careful with airline credit cards: They earn miles, but can come with annual fees from $50 to $100, which can be the price of a one-way ticket.

BONUS TIPS:

1. Try adding an extra stop. Instead of flying nonstop between Minneapolis and Washington, route through Detroit and Houston. It will take more time but the two extra legs won't cost much more (in fact, sometimes accepting more than one stop will cost you *less*). And it will have the beneficial effect of depositing a couple of thousand miles to your account.

2. **Consider "mileage runs"**—journeys just to rack up miles to qualify for elite levels. These involve choosing cheap flights and flying them long distances in a short period of time. Some of the best deals can be had during slow travel seasons—like Europe in the winter—when empty seats mean cheap fares. By buying a $200 ticket, you can earn enough miles for a more expensive ticket later. When the deals are good enough, mileage-runners can arbitrage airline tickets, paying less than two cents for each mile, but cashing them in for first-class tickets or upgrades that would cost far more per mile. FlyerTalk.com has a message board devoted to mileage runs, where frequent fliers post great deals that maximize miles for minimal dollars, and where travelers post predicaments and ask for help from the community of expert frequent fliers. If you play mileage runs right, you can even use mileage collected from runs to upgrade future mileage runs, constantly churning accounts with added bonuses from airlines.

3. **Cash miles in wisely.** When it comes to using your miles, there's an old rule of thumb: Every mile is worth two cents, which in theory makes a 25,000-mile award worth $500. So smart consumers will aim for a ticket that costs at least that much. On the other hand, the airlines say their actual experience is that most awards are cashed in for round-trip tickets that cost about $300. Our advice: If the ticket is under $300, you're better off buying it and saving your mileage for a pricier trip.

4. **The restricted-ticket gambit.** For most mileage plans, that 25,000-mile award is actually for a *restricted* ticket, a class that's often sold out even when the plane isn't full. The wrinkle: If you still must go or want to go, you can usually get an unrestricted ticket for 40,000 to 50,000 miles. Check first to see how many miles a restricted business or first-class seat requires—surprisingly it's actually sometimes *less*. Obviously, the best way to get an unrestricted seat is to book early. But the last-minute gambit can also pay off if you're willing to take the risk that seats will open up.

RATING THE REWARDS PROGRAMS

 Here are the winners in *InsideFlyer Magazine*'s "Freddie Awards" given to airline frequent flier clubs announced in 2004:

BEST CUSTOMER SERVICE
Americas: Southwest
International: Virgin Atlantic Airways
The scoop: Upstart Frontier Airlines came in second while Alaska Airlines was third.

BEST BONUS
Americas: Southwest
International: Swiss International Airlines
The scoop: Swiss Air offered a credit card welcome bonus of 30,000 miles with an annual bonus as a chaser.

BEST AWARD
Americas: Southwest Airlines
International: TAP Portugal
The scoop: Southwest bumped Alaska Airlines, which held the prize for the past two years, because of a promotion it offered with a credit card partner, Diners Club Rewards.

BEST AWARD REDEMPTION
Americas: Southwest
International: Emirates
The scoop: Southwest has no limit on seats available for awards. Emirates offers business-class upgrades starting at 5,000 miles.

BEST ELITE LEVEL
Americas: America West Airlines
International: KLM Royal Dutch Airlines
The scoop: America West offers unlimited complimentary first-class upgrades on all published fares; upgrades confirmed anytime on full coach fare.

5. Don't forget: Free means flexible. With frequent-flier tickets, almost all major airlines let you make a free layover. Don't even think about doing this on most paid tickets.

BUYING, SELLING, TRADING AND DONATING MILES

What if you don't have enough miles to get that unrestricted ticket?

Some programs allow you to transfer miles from one member's account to another's for a fee based on the number of miles transferred.

Extra miles? You can go on the Web site **Points.com** and exchange them for flowers or gift certificates at Barneys. Airlines don't sanction individuals auctioning off their miles, but people do it anyway, selling free-drink certificates and ticket vouchers on eBay. Or you can trade them with other fliers on Web sites like **Flyertalk.com.** Mileage brokers such as **Corpflyer.com** and **MrMileage .com** will pay per mile.

Another option is to donate miles to charity (though they aren't tax deductible) or to servicemen and women for flights home on leave (see **MileDonor.com**).

Do you have small lots of miles on a large number of carriers and find it impossible to keep up with it all? You can consolidate them using a third-party consolidator such as **Points.com,** though be aware that the exchange rate can be exorbitant (as of this writing, 5,000 Alaska Air miles would buy you 512 American Airlines miles).

If you want to hang on to all your miles but simply track them better, Web sites and software programs are the ticket. **Mile**

Tracker.com offers free and simple software that tracks all the major airline and hotel programs; MaxMiles Mileage Miner also tracks expiration dates.

THE RIGHT STUFF: LISTS AND LOWDOWNS ON THE AIRLINE CARRIERS

The friendly skies sometimes seem anything but. Carriers slashing consumer fares while business travelers pay through the nose. Carriers in and out of bankruptcy. Low-cost start-ups. Safety and security issues flaring up from time to time.

How is a harried consumer to know how to choose the right airline?

Well, for a lot of people it's easy: Business and other heavy-volume travelers tend to fly the airline on which they have racked up the most frequent-flier points; most other people look at price first. But there are many other factors—concerns as serious as safety and as peripheral as whether a certain airline serves Cosmopolitans on board or has in-seat satellite TV and game consoles for the kids—that matter.

For starters, there are tools for figuring out how airlines rate: You can get every airline's five-year average safety record, including statistics on accidents and near-air collisions on **airline-safety-records.com**; at **travel.simplyquick.com** you can compare airlines' business-class seats; and every year the University of Nebraska at Omaha's Aviation Institute puts out a report called "The Airline Quality Rating" (**ai .unomaha.edu**), which ranks the major carriers based on criteria like baggage handling, customer complaints, denied boardings and on-time arrivals. But with code shares and all kinds of other agreements, it can be hard to keep track of what you get where—or which airline you're even booked on. Here's our thumbnail rundown of the carriers:

AirTran Airways
Web site: airtran.com

800 #: 800-AIR-TRAN

Customer Service: 866-247-2428

Code: FL

Hubs: Hartsfield-Jackson Atlanta International, BWI

Frequent-Flier Program: A-Plus Rewards

Lounges: None

Partners: None

Flyspecks: Flies mostly to the Midwest, the East Coast and Denver, Las Vegas and Los Angeles, though also to the Bahamas; the fleet is dominated by Boeing-717s, which have quiet engines, lots of air circulation and more headroom than most aircraft. Upgrades are only $35 at the airport for most nonstop one-way flights. Special one-way fares as low as $49 aren't uncommon, with business class going for $149. XM Satellite Radio at every seat is being installed. No meals, even in business class.

Alaska Airlines

Web site: alaska-air.com

800 #: 800-426-0333

Customer Service: 800-654-5669

Code: AS

Hub: Seattle

Frequent-Flier Program: Alaska Airlines Mileage Plan

Lounges: Board Room Clubs. (Can use American Airlines, Delta, Continental, U.S. Airways, and Northwest Airlines clubs in some cities.)

Partners: 11 airlines, including American, Continental, Delta and Northwest.

Flyspecks: Based in the West, it has good deals to Canada and Mexico. Recently rolled out the movie- and music-playing digEplayer on some transcontinental flights, free in first class, and for rent in coach for $10. A small bottle of water awaits each passenger in first-class seats. No weekend-night stays required on its least-expensive fares.

America West

Web site: americawest.com

800 #: 800-235-9292

Customer Service: 480-693-6719

Code: HP

Hubs: Phoenix, Las Vegas

Frequent-Flier Program: FlightFund

Lounges: American West clubs with access to Northwest Airlines clubs

Partners: Northwest, British Airways, Hawaiian, BigSky and Virgin, plus others.

Flyspecks: Though it's one of the biggest carriers, it is considered basically a discount airline. Free meal service is only for first class.

American

Web site: aa.com

800 #: 1-800-433-7300

Customer Service: 817-967-2000

Code: AA

Hubs: Chicago, Miami, Dallas/Fort Worth

Frequent-Flier Program: AAdvantage

Lounges: Over two dozen in the United States alone

Partners: Oneworld Alliance (a consortium made up of American, Aer Lingus, Cathay Pacific, Finnair, Iberia, LAN, Qantas and British Airways).

Flyspecks: American offers bonus frequent-flier miles; has power ports on many planes. It has alignments with over 70 airlines, hotels, car-rental and credit-card programs.

American Trans Air

Web site: ata.com

800 #: 800-225-2995

Customer Service: 877-617-1139

Code: TZ

Hubs: Chicago Midway and Indianapolis

Frequent-Flier Program: None

Lounges: None

Partners: None

Flyspecks: ATA just added a business-class section and has indicated it will start flying to Europe soon.

Continental

Web site: continental.com

800 #: 800-525-0280

Customer Service: 800-932-2732

Code: CO

Hubs: Newark, Houston, Cleveland

Frequent-Flier Program: OnePass

Lounges: Presidents Club customers can use Northwest and Delta clubs when flying on those airlines

Partners: Alaska, American Eagle, Delta, Horizon, Northwest.

Flyspecks: Continental has begun giving full-fare passengers elite-level frequent-flier status for the day in domestic markets, including possible first-class upgrades and priority baggage tags for quick baggage service. The carrier also guarantees full-fare travelers an aisle or window seat, or it gives the customer 2,500 frequent-flier miles.

Delta

Web site: delta.com

800 #: 800-221-1212

Customer Service: 404-715-2600

Code: DL

Hubs: Atlanta, Cincinnati, Dallas/Fort Worth, Salt Lake City

Frequent-Flier Program: SkyMiles

Lounges: Crown Room Club Partners: Continental, Northwest

Partners: Continental and Northwest

Flyspecks: Complicated rules for the SkyMiles program, so check the Web site.

Frontier

Web site: flyfrontier.com

800 #: 800-432-1359

Customer Service: 800-265-5505

Code: F9

Hub: Denver International

Frequent-Flier Program: EarlyReturns

Lounges: None

Partners: Great Lakes, Horizon

Flyspecks: Second-largest carrier at Denver International. Offers TV on some planes for $5.

Horizon

Web site: horizonair.com

800 #: 800-547-9308

Customer Service: 206-431-3647

Code: QX

Hubs: Boise, Portland, Oregon, Seattle

Frequent-Flier Program: Alaska Airlines Mileage Plan

Lounges: Alaska Airlines Board Room

Partners: Alaska, Northwest, American, Continental, Hawaiian, Delta, KLM and Frontier

Flyspecks: Owned by Alaska Airlines, this carrier flies only in the West as Horizon Air and contracts with Frontier JetExpress for Frontier.

JetBlue

Web site: jetblue.com

800 #: 800-538-2583

Customer Service: N/A

Code: B6

Hubs: JFK, Long Beach, Washington Dulles

Frequent-Flier Program: TrueBlue

Lounges: None

Partners: None

Flyspecks: The carrier with free snacks but not meals and a TV at every seat says it will add XM Satellite Radio as well as News Corp.'s Fox TV programs and 20th Century Fox pay-per-view movies to its existing lineup of up to 36 channels of free DIRECTV programming.

Midwest

Web site: midwestairlines.com

800 #: 800-452-2022

Customer Service: N/A

Code: YX

Hub: Milwaukee

Frequent-Flier Program: Midwest Miles

Lounges: Best Care Club

Partners: American

Flyspecks: Flights to business destinations have all business-class service, with wide leather seats, chocolate chip cookies.

Northwest

Web site: nwa.com

800 #: 800-225-2525

Customer Service: 800-225-2525

Code: NW

Hubs: Detroit, Memphis, Minneapolis

Frequent-Flier Program: WorldPerks

Lounges: WorldClubs

Partners: Alaska, America West, American Eagle, Continental, Midwest, Delta and Horizon

Flyspecks: Known for a while as "Northworst" on a Web site devoted to complaining about it, but a recent upgrade of its fleet seems to have accompanied an upgrade in service. A good choice for travelers who fly internationally a lot. Northwest has a strong Asian network and its joint venture with KLM and membership in SkyTeam alliance, which includes Air France and Alitalia, have increased its presence in Europe.

Song

Web site: flysong.com

800 #: 800-359-7664

Customer Service: 800-359-7664

Code: DL

Hub: Crown Room Club

Frequent-Flier Program: Delta SkyMiles

Lounges: None

Partners: Owned by Delta

Flyspecks: This Delta creation serves food such as Pizzeria Uno pies and chocolates from Dylan's Candy Bar in Manhattan.

Southwest

Web site: iflyswa.com

800 #: 800-435-9792

Customer Service: 214-792-4223

Code: WN

Hubs: Phoenix, Las Vegas, Baltimore

Frequent-Flier Program: Rapid Rewards

Lounges: None

Partners: None

Flyspecks: Known as the friendly airline, Southwest has pilots and flight attendants who crack jokes and smile a lot, but it is a fierce competitor, entering new markets and offering bottom-barrel prices to compete. There's only economy class.

Spirit

Web site: spiritair.com

800 #: 800-772-7117

Customer Service: 954-772-7117

Code: NK

Hubs: Detroit, Ft. Lauderdale

Frequent-Flier Program: None

Lounges: None

Partners: None

Flyspecks: Preparing for a big expansion out of its Ft. Lauderdale, Florida, hub, the airline has ordered 35 Airbus aircraft to replace its current aging fleet of 32 MD-80s. Though its routes are mostly from the Midwest and the Northeast to Florida, 14-year-old Spirit also flies to San Juan, Nassau, Bahamas, Santa Domingo, Dominican Republic, Puerto Rico and Cancun, Mexico. It also added business class to its planes.

Ted

Web site: flyted.com

800 #: 800-CALL-TED

ANNUAL AIRLINE QUALITY RATINGS

JetBlue Airways was number one in quality among U.S. airlines in 2003, the first year that it carried enough passengers to be ranked, according to an annual university study based on Transportation Department statistics.

The budget carrier had the second-best on-time performance, arriving punctually 86 percent of the time. So few JetBlue passengers were bumped that they didn't register in the statistics used by researchers. JetBlue customers also filed fewer complaints—0.31 per 100,000—to the Transportation Department than all other airlines but Southwest Airlines.

The study's authors said the ratings show low-cost airlines are gaining market share because they perform well in ways that are important to their passengers. It "adds further evidence to the emerging performance gap" between the higher-cost carriers and the no-frills network carriers, said Brent Bowen, director of the University of Nebraska's aviation institute and a coauthor of the study.

The report rated the 14 U.S. airlines that carried at least 1 percent of the 587 million passengers who flew in 2003. Four low-cost carriers—AirTran, ATA, Atlantic Southeast and JetBlue—met that threshold for the first time in 2003.

Alaska Air Group's Alaska Airlines came in second. Southwest, which consistently generates the lowest complaint rate in the industry, was rated as the number three carrier in the report, with 0.14 complaints per 100,000 customers. America West came in fourth and US Airways, ranked number one last year when it was still in bankruptcy protection, was fifth.

Northwest Airlines, which came in sixth, was the most improved airline in 2003. It ranked ninth in 2002.

Below is the annual rating of U.S. airline quality, according to the University of Nebraska at Omaha Aviation Institute and W. Frank Barton School of Business at Wichita State University. The ranking is based on 15 elements important to consumers.

1. JetBlue Airways
2. Alaska Airlines
3. Southwest Airlines
4. America West
5. US Airways
6. Northwest Airlines
7. Continental Airlines
8. AirTran
9. United Airlines
10. ATA
11. American Airlines
12. Delta Air Lines
13. American Eagle
14. Atlantic Southeast

Source: Airline Quality Rating study, based on DOT data

Customer Service: 800-CALL-TED

Code: UA

Hubs: Denver, Chicago, San Francisco, Washington Dulles

Frequent-Flier Program: TedClub; United Airlines Mileage Plus

Lounges: Red Carpet Club

Partners: United Airlines owned-and-operated, it automatically became part of the Star Alliance, a worldwide partnership of 15 carriers, including Air New Zealand and Singapore Air

Flyspecks: United Airlines' riposte to Song, Ted geared up in 2004, serving 15 cities. It offers in-flight movies and games that you listen to through colorful headsets. It has a favorite beer, Foster's Lager, and passengers can buy souvenirs, including a stuffed bear named Ted.

United

Web site: ual.com

800 #: 800-241-6522

Customer Service: 877-228-1327

Code: UA

Hubs: Chicago O'Hare, Denver, Los Angeles, San Francisco, Washington Dulles

Frequent-Flier Program: Mileage Plus

Lounges: Red Carpet Club

Partners: Aloha, US Airways, plus others

Flyspecks: United offers two-way e-mail capability aboard all its flights within the United States, allowing users to check weather, news and stock listings; play games; and use the messaging services for $5.99 a flight.

US Airways

Web site: usairways.com

800 #: 800-428-4322

Customer Service: 866-523-5333

Code: US

Hubs: Charlotte, Philadelphia

Frequent-Flier Program: Dividend Miles

Lounges: US Airways Club

Partners: United, GoCaribbean

Flyspecks: This troubled airline has gone in and out of bankruptcy, and there's been speculation it will be acquired (United Airlines tried to buy it in 2000, but the Justice Department nixed the plan). One nice touch: The airline offers a deal where full-fare economy passengers can upgrade for free on some routes.

SECRETS OF THE SEATS: GETTING THE ONE YOU WANT

Exit rows and bulkheads are the twin saviors of economy class. Of course, airlines know that, and, though they rarely admit it, usually hold those spots for full-fare passengers and elite members of their frequent-flier programs—that's why they're always blocked out when you try to get a seat assignment online. But always ask for one when you check in, and if there aren't any open, leave your boarding pass at the gate with a request to be put in one if someone doesn't show.

Another trick: Check in with the curbside baggage services outside the terminal; you will have to pay a tip, but they can get you better seats while other people are still waiting in line. We've been told the bigger the tip, the better the seat.

In order to maximize your great-seat chances, knowing the type of aircraft is key, so ask before you book. If it's a so-called regional, or mini, jet (those with about 50 seats, most often Bombardier Canadair Regional Jet 400 or the Embraer ERJ 145), expect a noisy and cramped ride. Checking competing airlines' schedules may reveal that full-size jets fly those same routes, just at different times.

Our preference is to fly wide-body aircraft like a Boeing 767 or a Boeing 777 and avoid Boeing 737s and 757s, which tend to have narrower seats, less legroom and limited lavatories. If you have to take a narrow-body, pick the A320: The cabin is 8 inches wider than the Boeing 737 and that extra space means 1-inch-wider coach seats.

Seat configurations can make a difference, too: A typical plane with a 3-3-3 configuration must be 67 percent full before a middle seat must be assigned, but in that same aircraft with a 2-5-2 configuration, middle seats start at 44 percent full. Most airlines have seating maps for all their aircraft types online, where you can check which rows don't recline and which seats are next to or behind missing seats. The excellent Web site **seatguru.com** shows the best and worst spots to sit on most major carriers, though not for some of the smaller players.

There are all kinds of little things you can learn from **seatguru .com,** like if you want to use your laptop, fly American, Delta, United or US Airways and look at their seating charts to see where the power ports are; if you like movies, avoid Northwest, because they have no entertainment on most domestic flights; and for legroom, choose American, except for its Boeing 757s and Airbus 300s.

Scoring an upgrade is the best way out of this mess, and most of the people who sit smugly in their big seats while you're on your way to the back of the plane have done just that. You don't have to be an elite frequent flier to get there—you can use miles or buy upgrade certificates (fees range from $35 for a one-way nonstop flight on Air-Tran to $50 for a 500-mile segment on Delta). But it helps to be an elite flier— elites can upgrade on a discount ticket, while those lacking elite status can't.

Some airlines offer "fast track" programs to achieve elite status, where you have to fly a certain number of miles in a set time. There are other ways: You can buy upgrades from other people on eBay; American Express card members can buy points that can be transferred into upgrades; and you can subscribe to **firstclassflyer.com,** which constantly has new tricks and offers.

SEAT STRATEGIES: A SELECTIVE GUIDE TO THE BEST SEATS

American: Three-quarters of its fleet—including 737s and 767s— have extra legroom. Bulkhead rows are no prize on 757-200s because the doors let cold air seep in, there's no under-seat storage and the armrests are immovable. But there are some seats to covet on this airline: 17A, B, H or J (it can differ by plane) on the 767-200 are crew rest-seats, with more room and back support. You can't book them in advance but can sometimes get them at the airport if the crew isn't using them.

Alaska: If you fly Alaska, there's a good chance you will end up on a 737-400; they make up more than a third of its fleet. The only non–exit row seats with more room than usual are in the first row on the right. The next most common plane, the MD-80, has a wide disparity of pitch (you can examine it on the Web site, under "Alaska

Commitment Plan"). But what the Web site won't tell you is that the last three rows (31–33) are extra-noisy. Want an aisle or window? Odds are good. (The planes' 3-2 seat arrangement means fewer middle seats.) And you don't even have to sit in an exit row to get extra space—rows 17 to 19 and 27 to 30 have 33-inch pitches, an inch more than the norm.

America West: It's a budget carrier but it's still possible to find good seats. In general, avoid the last few rows, where there are narrower seats, and go for the exit rows, which is why we choose row 11 on the 737-300. But some of the carrier's aircraft have economy seats behind rows with missing seats, giving unlimited legroom—the case with 10A and 10F on the 737-200.

Continental: Take a deep breath. Some seats—the last two rows—on many of this carrier's 737s are only 16.2 inches wide, among the narrowest of the majors; legroom is on the lower end of the scale as well. But there is some relief: Most of these planes also have at least two economy-class seats with no seat in front. (The magic numbers: 14A and 14F on 737-300s and -700s; 10A and 10F on the -500.) Better still, aim for a 767, which has an inch more legroom on average and more storage space. And Continental is the most baby-friendly of the major carriers, with three of its aircraft types equipped with bassinets (the 767-400, 767-200 and 777-200).

Delta: With some of the most standardized seating plans in the business, Delta leaves less room to find wildcat seats. But there are some exit rows that are worth aiming for—row 34 on the 767-400, and row 18 on 737-800s. On the 767-400, 19B has a metal box under the seat. If possible, stay away from the 737s and 767s, some of which can have pitches as low as 30 inches and widths as narrow as 17 inches, and fewer lavatories—one toilet for every 66 passengers on the 737-800. There are some other tricks with this carrier: You don't have to be an elite frequent flier or pay a full-fare economy ticket to prebook an exit row—you just have to buy the ticket at one of the airline's ticketing offices (so they can see you are able-bodied). And there are some exit rows on some planes that are worth aiming for, such as row 34 on the 767-400 and row 18 on the 737-800. Delta's low-fare sibling, Song, has leather seats with pitches of 33 inches.

Northwest: The airline's planes have an average pitch of 30 to

32 inches, which is the space between one point on the seat and the same point on the seat in front. (The industry average is about 32 inches.) When you add in its thin seat widths of about 17 inches, it makes for tight quarters. Some strategies: In general, try to sit near the front. Most of the last rows have restricted recline—not to mention it'll take a long time to deplane from the back of a new, extra-long Boeing 757-300. Watch out for the DC-9s, where most seats have pitches of 30 inches. And then there's the middle seat that isn't. On some planes, there's a seat missing on exit rows for better emergency access (and more elbow room). The trick here: Nab the seat behind it, which is 15C on the DC-9-30.

Southwest: Every inch counts, so the plane to avoid is the 737-200, which has a seat pitch of only 31 inches, compared to 32 inches on the slightly longer 737-500 and 32.6 inches on the newer 737-700.

United: This carrier's "Economy Plus" section has up to five inches more legroom in most cases and ample legroom behind rows with missing seats. But to get there you have to pay a full economy fare or have elite-flier status. (Exception: When the plane's full, the carrier may stick regular fliers in the middle seats.) If you don't qualify, aim for the 767-300: The exit row (21) falls outside Economy Plus and reclines normally.

THE SAFETY ISSUE: MYTHS AND REALITIES

Let's just face the fact that most air travelers at least contemplate the possibility of a crash; some obsessively plot strategies on how to survive one. But when it comes to safety, there's surprisingly little agreement about the best place to sit. The conventional wisdom runs like this: Always sit in the back of the plane; always sit by an aisle; never wear high heels; count the rows between you and the nearest exit; be competitive; be cooperative; memorize the "brace" position. But aviation officials insist that crashes not only are exceedingly rare, but also have causes that vary far too much for any theory to work.

The only advice we can really offer: The FAA and the National Transportation Safety Board suggest counting the seats between you and the nearest exit; most experts advise picking nonstop flights and airports with long runways; and you can check out safety records by type of aircraft and by airline on **airsafe.com,** including descriptions of near-accidents and a list of airlines with no history of fatalities.

TAPPING THE INTERNET FOR AIR-SAFETY DATA

The most up-to-date source of information is the Internet. Here are some of the best sites:

1. faa.gov. The Web site of the U.S. Federal Aviation Administration is a good place to start, because it offers links to several other safety-related Internet sites. While this site tracks only accidents and incidents that occur to U.S. airlines or over U.S. airspace, the information has some relevance to foreign travelers as well.

2. airsafe.com. The FAA Web site is linked to this comprehensive site, which is run and maintained by Todd Curtis, a U.S. aviation consultant and former Boeing Co. engineer. (Boeing isn't affiliated with the site, according to Mr. Curtis.) This easy-to-navigate site allows users to view safety records of every international airline, categorized by region, airline name and aircraft model. It includes a plethora of informative lists, among them: accidents at major U.S. airports, which airlines have never suffered a fatal crash and fatal events by aircraft model. The site, in an "Advice" section, also deals with the safest-place-to-sit question by stating, *"The short answer is that there is no safest seat."*

3. airclaims.co.uk. While **airsafe.com**'s accident records are an unofficial tally, they are fairly consistent with compilations offered by the industry's official source: British Insurer Airclaims Ltd., which charges for access to similar information. Nevertheless, if you would prefer to see an official list of all airline accidents and mishaps, dating to the history of an airline, this is the place to turn. Airclaims' "Major Loss Record" categorizes accidents by airline and by region.

4. boeing.com. While much of this information is favorable to the airline industry, this Boeing site is still better than your average corporate site. It offers a section devoted to airline safety that addresses such issues as the safety of airline travel compared with other forms of transportation and what the riskiest portions of a flight are. It also gives consumers an audio primer on how modern commercial jets work—from avionics to propulsion systems.

5. aviationnow.com. *Aviation Week,* an industry trade publication, runs this site. It has data on recent international airline incidents and mishaps and also lets visitors search previous issues of the magazine for safety-related news.

THE HEALTHY TRAVELER

If you're concerned about your health, stay home.

Airplanes are a great way to give or catch a bug, or, even worse, the dreaded "Economy Class Syndrome"—deep vein thrombosis (DVT). The condition, in which blood clots form in the legs, can occur in healthy people who sit for long periods in cramped conditions, such as plane seats. If a clot breaks loose and travels to the lungs, the result can be fatal.

The good news: Death from a clot traveling to the lungs—known as a "pulmonary embolism"—is rare, and DVT itself isn't usually dangerous. The bad news: Hormone or oral contraceptive use, pregnancy, obesity, certain cancers and other conditions increase the risk of DVT, as does age.

Generally, a few simple precautions make DVT preventable. If you're on a long flight, try to stand, stretch and walk at least once an hour. Airplane air tends to be dry, so drink lots of water to avoid dehydration, which can abet clotting. (More about airplane drinking water below.) For the same reason, limit alcohol and caffeine, which can also lead to dehydration.

If you're still worried, or walking is a problem, you can look into any number of anti-DVT devices now on the market. Inflatable exercise cushions, which allow you to mimic walking from a seated position, are touted as a way to increase blood flow. They have names such as Lym-Gym, Airogym and Air Stepper and sell on the Internet. Some doctors, meanwhile, recommend compression stockings for their patients who might be considered high risk for DVT. You can buy prescription versions, which are custom-fitted, or get them over the counter at medical specialty stores. Make sure they are "graduated," meaning pressure is greatest at the bottom of the leg, forcing blood upward.

Now, about water on airplanes. While the airlines say they rarely serve tap water, many flight attendants say it isn't that uncommon: When the bottled water runs out, they turn to the tanks, which, under federal regulations, are supposed to provide drinkable water. Though the carriers say their galley and lavatory water is drinkable, some little-noticed studies from Japan to the Netherlands have turned up some unfriendly bacteria in the tank water, including E. coli and the germ that causes Legionnaire's disease.

The Wall Street Journal has even conducted airplane water tests, collecting water from the galley and lavatory taps, sealing them up and sending them to a lab for analysis. The results: a long list of microscopic life you don't want to drink, from Salmonella and Staphylococcus to tiny insect eggs. Worse, contamination was the rule, not the exception: Almost all of the bacteria levels were tens, sometimes hundreds, of times above U.S. government limits. And the Environmental Protection Agency recently followed with a test of its own, finding tap-water samples from 20 of 158 randomly selected commercial aircraft showed traces of coliform bacteria, and two of the planes tested positive for E. coli bacteria. Both are indicators that other disease-causing organisms may be present in the water, officials said, and could affect public health.

Bottom line: Bring your own bottled water when you fly.

JET LAG TIPS

Drinking water is also crucial to stopping jet lag, which is more than just loss of sleep, and not "curable" with a quick nap and a cup of coffee. In a nutshell, everything from sleep to digestion operates on an internal clock dictated by cues such as light, food, exercise and drugs. Crossing time zones changes the timing of those cues, hence throwing body functions out of sync.

Here are some suggestions for beating jet lag:

1. Light: When used correctly, it holds the greatest potential for helping travelers adjust to a new time zone; NASA occasionally quarantines astronauts prior to launch and douses them with light to help prepare their body clocks for space travel. Figuring out the precise time to use light is complex, but a general rule of thumb for U.S. travelers goes as follows: When headed east on an overnight flight, seek sun or artificial light in the mid to late morning at your destination, but wait until late afternoon and early evening when headed west.

2. Pills: As it turns out, just saying yes to drugs may be a good idea—at least for some long-distance journeyers. Check with your doctor but prescription sleeping pills got high marks from our experts, who suggest using them on the plane or when you're trying to get sleep in your time zone. The other popular popper, with both travelers and sleep experts, is melatonin, a sleep-inducing chemical produced naturally by the body. The theory: A dose of synthetic melatonin can boost drowsiness and help you sleep through a long flight. Again, check with your doctor, because it's not federally regulated and some doctors doubt its efficacy. For airsickness, some research shows that ginkgo biloba, an antioxidant, may help, as can Viagra, which blocks vasoconstriction. Doctors sometimes also prescribe Diamox (acetazolamide).

3. Food: Our experts were divided on the merits of munching as a jet-lag salve. While there's no firm scientific proof, anecdotal evidence suggests food might be one contributor to helping the body ease into a new time zone. One program available on the Internet, **StopJetLag.com,** provides fliers with a customized diet for the days leading up to departure.

LIFTING THE BURDEN OF BAGGAGE

Forget what's in your bag—the bag itself might be "illegal." While carriers have long restricted carry-on luggage, they have recently begun to enforce long-ignored rules that restrict the size of checked bags as well. Depending on the size and destination of the luggage, most major carriers charge up to $270—often more than the cost of the suitcase itself—for bags larger than 62 linear inches (defined as height, width and depth added together). The fees can be lower on domestic flights—usually $80—but they can quickly add up since the charges apply per bag per flight segment.

And we're not talking about unusual leviathan luggage. The suitcases in question often show up in the standard five-bag luggage sets sold by big manufacturers. Indeed, bags as small as 30 inches high (barely kneecap level) can violate the rules if they are stocky enough.

Travelers who fail to check size requirements before the flight have little recourse, because most airlines list the policies on their Web sites. Luggage sellers absolve themselves by warning customers to check with individual airlines for restrictions. And most luggage buyers don't give it a thought.

To add to the confusion, many retailers don't describe their luggage in terms of linear inches. Technically, all checked luggage, whether it's a hard-sided suitcase or soft-sided garment bag, must meet the size requirements or trigger extra fees. But consider the soft-sided duffel bag—its very elasticity simply makes it harder to measure.

BEATING THE GAME: SIZE

If you can't travel light, there are still tricks to beating costs. While many airlines charge for extra bags, those fees are sometimes lower than the ones on large bags.

BEATING THE GAME: LOCKS

To lock or not to lock: There is no definitive answer. The Transportation Security Administration and the luggage industry collaborated in 2003 to come up with special "Travel Sentry" locks—made and sold by various companies—that baggage inspectors would be able to open, solving the problem of locks being broken when a locked bag is chosen for hand inspection. Until these locks came online, TSA urged travelers *not* to lock checked luggage, so screeners would not have to break locks should they have to open bags for closer inspection. But there is still the danger that the screener, not recognizing the lock as a Travel Sentry kind, might cut through it anyway. Most Travel Sentry lock manufacturers and retailers will replace cut locks if passengers can provide a copy of the TSA's notification of inspection and the name of the airport where the incident occurred. Check **travelsentry.org** for where to buy the locks.

Of course, having a lock that screeners can open may be just as risky; a number of TSA employees have been charged with stealing things from checked baggage. Reimbursement is tough. For starters, it's usually impossible to prove when the theft occurred. Beyond that, while airlines will pay a passenger as much as $2,500 per claim, they exclude "valuables" like electronics, cash and jewelry. TSA, which encourages reporting of thefts through its 800 number, is working on a proposal for determining liability based on the time a bag spends under TSA control compared with the time it is with an airline. One tip: You can buy supplemental insurance for baggage through airlines and third-party insurance companies, but they won't cover checked valuables, either.

BEATING THE GAME:
THE SCOOP ON LOST LUGGAGE

Why do bags get lost?

The trouble can begin when a bag is checked to the wrong destination: SAN (San Diego), for instance, instead of SAT (San Antonio). Or another passenger's tag is put on your bag. Even the tag makes a difference; many simply come unglued. But flimsy bag handles are also a major problem. When a handle flies off, or is whacked by machinery, the destination tag and often the passenger's name tag are lost—often forever. Airlines open orphaned bags, searching for anything that might identify the owner. But if owners can't be located within three months, the luggage is auctioned off. About 30,000 bags met that fate in 2004.

Even if your luggage has been correctly coded for its actual destination and properly affixed to your sturdy bag handle, danger still lies ahead. Bags next go down a chute to a dark, noisy netherworld, called the "makeup room." Bar-code technology is used to sort bags on to their proper flights but it isn't 100 percent effective. When the scanner can't read the tag, bags have to be sorted the old-fashioned way—by a human. Your tag may say SAN but it could still be sent to SAT.

Arrival is even more perilous, particularly if you change planes. Here, baggage handling is strictly low-tech. Handlers read each tag to determine if the bag's next connection is within an hour. If the time is short, bags are driven from one plane to another. The system can break down quickly when storms or air-traffic delays mess up carefully synchronized flight schedules. There is some hope on the horizon: New security technology that should be widely used soon may reduce lost luggage and help find lost bags faster. Called "Radio Frequency Identification," it will be embedded in the luggage tag printed by ticket agents at the airport and read by new computer scanners as it travels between the point the bag is left by a passenger and the time it arrives on the plane.

TIPS FROM THE PROS

Here are some tips from industry insiders on how to improve survival chances for your luggage.

1. Put your name inside the bag. Tags can get torn or demolished. Airlines have to open bags, power up laptop computers, even check underwear for name tags.

2. Save receipts for items that will travel. With claim limits up to $2,500 per bag, some airlines now require receipts. It's a hassle, but it'll save you a big fight with the airline.

3. Don't put your name tag on the bag handle. If the handle comes off, so does your ID.

4. Buy sturdy luggage. Think of your bag as an object chronically under assault by uncaring metal machinery and indifferent bag handlers and choose accordingly.

5. Don't pack cameras and other valuables in checked luggage. You're asking for them to be stolen; you're asking for a fight with the airlines or your insurer; and as explained above, you may not be able to recover the full value of your losses.

6. Double-check your own tag before the bag goes down the chute. Agents make mistakes. We know people who refuse to leave the check-in counter until they actually see the agent put their correctly tagged bag on the conveyor belt.

7. Unzip garment bags when going through security. A folded-up garment bag can get you sent back to the ticket counter, having been declared too big to fit the baggage-sizing templates.

8. Don't overpack. But if you have overpacked, take items out of the bags so they'll fit through the security templates and the X-ray machines; usually security guards don't count bags. One trick: You can do this by using smaller plastic bags that can easily be restuffed in your rolling bag once through security. But remember, an overstuffed bag can still get you in trouble when you're trying to fit it in the overhead bin. You may have to remove some of the smaller bags and stuff them under your seat.

AIRPORTS: GETTING PAST THE HUBBUB

If you live in, or are flying to, New Orleans, your airport choice is easy unless you want to drive 75 miles to or from Baton Rouge, where you'll find fewer flights and carriers. But in many urban areas today, so-called "alternative airports" are no longer so alternative, sometimes offering access to start-up, low-cost carriers, less traffic and easier parking than the major hubs. So it pays to look at a map and figure out which airport is actually closest to where you want to end up. If it's Hollywood, fly into Burbank, not LAX; for downtown Manhattan, look at Newark instead of LaGuardia, and for the south side of Chicago, Midway is closer than O'Hare. Anyone who has battled traffic in San Francisco knows that travel to the East Bay is much easier via Oakland, where JetBlue flies directly from New York.

Next hassle is finding somewhere to park that's in the same state but won't cost as much as your mortgage. Parking fees, it turns out, are one of an airport's biggest sources of revenue. And, with income from landing fees and concessions down and security costs up, many airports have raised parking rates as much as 17 percent. Fees at some airport lots can now hit $30 a day.

Airport parking used to be an issue of short term or long term. Most airports have several different parking lots, with tiered pricing depending on how close you park to the terminal: Spots farther away can be between $6 a day (Dallas) and $16 (Boston), while those closer in can run from $17 (Pittsburgh) to $30 (Los Angeles). Rates charged by the off-airport lots are usually competitive with those at the airports' remote lots. But as parking fees climb steadily, a growing array of options are springing up.

Parking companies are now offering everything from bottled water to free car washes at lots just outside airports, while airports are responding with everything from

SHIPPING AHEAD

With airlines enforcing extra luggage fees more vigilantly, sometimes it costs about the same to ship your bags ahead. Here are some ship-ahead services, but keep in mind you should take enough in a carry-on to get you through a day, since ship-ahead carriers are subject to the same delays as airlines.

1. dhl-usa.com/home.asp
2. fedex.com
3. skycapinternational.com
4. sportsexpress.com
5. usxpluggageexpress.com
6. virtualbellhop.com

complimentary newspapers to changing the oil (for a fee). One way to find out about these deals is **Parksleepfly.com.** Another site, **airport parkingreservations.com,** lists off-airport parking lots by price and distance from the airport. Travelers can even book a space in advance.

And here's a novel approach to getting a cheap place to park at the airport: Rent a hotel room. Perhaps the most surprising new players in the parking game are hotels located near big airports. Some properties owned by Starwood Hotels, Resorts Worldwide's Sheraton and Hilton's Embassy Suites offer travelers parking for a price that sometimes beats the airport-lot rate—and it includes a night's stay.

Another idea: Don't drive to the airport. With almost everything about air travel getting more difficult, one improvement is better and faster trains to the planes. Chicago announced a $400 million plan for faster service between the downtown Loop and O'Hare International Airport and eventually to Midway. Minneapolis is starting a new express line to run straight from downtown, through the airport—and on to the Mall of America, while Denver is considering an ambitious project to connect Union Station directly to the Denver International Airport.

Other long-planned projects are nearing completion. San Francisco has opened an extension of its rail system out to the international airport there, and the AirTrain JFK to New York's John F. Kennedy Airport is already up and running. One of the most closely watched projects so far opened last fall at Newark International Airport near New York: The AirTrain—a monorail connecting with regional commuter lines that run directly into Manhattan. It's already seeing about 4,000 users a day, slightly exceeding expectations.

Still, it's important to make sure the money saved is worth the hassle; a handful of U.S. cities—including Chicago, Baltimore and St. Louis—already have rail links to their airports, but they tend to be slow and uncomfortable (think noisy subway cars moving at about 25 miles per hour, with no place for luggage). Chicago's new train, by contrast, will be an express that goes a third faster than the subway system and boasts a separate luggage

NAVIGATING THE AIRPORTS

There are dozens of Web sites that list and give links for all the airports in the country so travelers can find phone numbers, directions, information on flights, baggage and parking. Most important, they also list shops and restaurants and where in the airport to find them.

Here are a few of them:

1. quickaid.com/airports/
2. airwise.com/airports/
3. airnav.com/airports/
   www.independenttraveler.com/resources/

PLANES TO THE TRAIN

AIRPORT: **O'HARE (CHICAGO)**
RAIL LINKS: Current: the "L" to O'Hare; 45 minutes from downtown. In the Works: O'Hare Express, will take about 30 minutes

AIRPORT: **NEWARK (NEWARK, NEW JERSEY)**
RAIL LINKS: Current: AirTrain Newark; 30 minutes from Midtown Manhattan; 20 minutes from Hoboken's New Jersey Transit terminal

AIRPORT: **JOHN F. KENNEDY (NEW YORK)**
RAIL LINKS: AirTrain JFK; less than 45 minutes from midtown to airport, via Long Island Railroad and light rail

AIRPORT: **MINNEAPOLIS–ST. PAUL INTERNATIONAL**
RAIL LINKS: Brand new: Light-rail system; half hour from downtown to the airport

AIRPORT: **HARTSFIELD ATLANTA INTERNATIONAL**
RAIL LINKS: Current: Rapid transit train takes about 25 minutes to airport from downtown

AIRPORT: **SAN FRANCISCO INTERNATIONAL**
RAIL LINKS: Extension of BART to the airport will provide a 29-minute trip

AIRPORT: **REAGAN AND DULLES AIRPORTS (WASHINGTON, D.C.)**
RAIL LINKS: Current: Washington Metro takes 15 to 20 minutes from most downtown stations to Reagan. Proposed: Metro extension to Dulles; estimated 30 to 45 minutes

car. Check out the airport Web site (see Navigating the Airports box for how to find them) to find out how much time the train will take. Also on the airport Web sites: surprisingly thorough and clear details of their shopping, restaurants and other services.

GETTING THERE BY TRAIN

Trains long ago lost the race with cars and airplanes as the vehicle of choice for business and leisure travel. Still, with a certain scenic-minded, plane-phobic segment of the population, long-distance train travel still has its allure. Here are the most popular routes where trains still provide viable passenger service:

Train/Route: Coast Starlight/Los Angeles–Seattle

Features: The most popular long-distance train, features a 20-seat movie theater and a kids' play area, plus views of the Cascade Mountains and the Pacific, but plagued by late arrivals

Train/Route: Empire Builder/Chicago–Seattle and Portland

Features: Views of the Northern Rockies and the Cascade Mountains, offset by long stretches of flat, boring farmland

Train/Route: California Zephyr/Chicago–Emeryville, California

Features: Perhaps the most scenic route, with spectacular views of the Rocky and Sierra Nevada mountains, though often runs late; requires a bus transfer to San Francisco

Train/Route: Lake Shore Ltd./New York and Boston–Chicago

Features: Views of the Hudson River and the Berkshire Mountains of Massachusetts, but restricted to single-level cars; regularly delayed for connections at Chicago and Albany, New York

Train/Route: Silver Star, Silver Meteor/New York–Miami

Features: Serves popular Florida tourist destinations but suffers from dull scenery in the Carolinas

Train/Route: Southwest Chief/Chicago–Los Angeles

Features: Amtrak's fastest train between Chicago and the West Coast; serves Grand Canyon and Disneyland, but stops in the middle of the night in Kansas to drop off freight cars

Train/Route: Crescent/New York–New Orleans

Features: Convenient overnight Washington–Atlanta run, although not very scenic (think pine trees and kudzu); curvy Southern tracks slow down the train.

TRAIN RESOURCES:

1. Amtrak/amtrak.com/800-872-7245 (800-USA-RAIL). If you want to take a train to almost any U.S. destination, you'll need to board Amtrak. The nation's rail system serves 22,000 miles of tracks in 46 states.

Amtrak's Web site has an accommodations section that includes pictures of different sleeping cars and bedrooms, so users can determine whether the size will be appropriate for them and their travel companions. Tickets are easily purchased through the Web site, and visitors can peruse schedule options and price different trains.

2. Alaska Railroad (akrr.com/907-265-2300). One area of the United States not reached by Amtrak is Alaska, which has its own state-run railroad, covering more than 600 miles of tracks from such cities as Anchorage, Fairbanks and Seward. Alaska Railroad has teamed up with travel agencies to offer a number of special packages and tours, including a five-day, five-night trek to see Mount McKinley at Denali National Park, but riders can hop off at any point for a longer trip. Billing itself as the only full-service railroad in the United States, the carrier features cook-to-order food service on board, and local students travel on the train and act as tour guides. A first-class service will start in 2005.

3. VIA Rail/viarail.com/888-842-7245 (888-VIA-RAIL). The Canadian rails are favorites with many travelers who enjoy the change in topography from the cities in the East through the Midwestern plains and on into the Canadian Rockies. VIA Rail's Web site, like that of its U.S. counterpart, Amtrak, allows users to purchase tickets directly on the Internet. The site also includes dozens of links to rail-travel packages offered by a handful of travel agencies that specialize in Canadian train trips, whether you want to ride from Toronto to Vancouver or travel north from Winnipeg to look for polar bears on the Hudson Bay. A special section of the Web site is devoted to travel for older adults, with details about accommodations, services for those with special needs and meals for people with dietary restrictions. The reservation feature is easy to navigate and offers alternatives if a user's original choices aren't available. Make sure to book early; the trans-Canadian route is incredibly popular, and seats can be hard to come by.

4. Eurail/raileurope.com/us/877-257-2887. Savvy travelers are familiar with Europe's rails, which rank among the best in the world. Rail Europe provides an all-in-one site for European rail travel. The site offers a range of Eurail passes—from a country pass for travel in just one nation to a Selectpass that allows travel to a handful of countries—plus point-to-point tickets for any route in more than 35 European countries. The site also sells tickets for a variety of trains in Britain, as well as EuroStar service, for travel between London, Paris and Brussels through the Chunnel. Travelers who want to explore countries in more depth can purchase Rail 'n Drive packages that combine rail travel with a car rental.

Also, keep in mind:

5. E-Vacations.com, an affiliated Web site, offers built-to-order packages that may incorporate air travel, hotels and rental cars in addition to rail passes.

6. Elderhostel/elderhostel.org/877-426-8056. If you're a thinking person's train rider, Elderhostel offers nearly 60 "train trek" programs. The educational-travel organization for adults over age 55 uses the rails to take travelers farther into the field and teach them about a particular theme or subject. Some of the most popular and longest-standing trips include an eight-day journey through Mexico's Copper Canyon to study the area's natural history and geology, and a 31-day trek across Australia and New Zealand to learn about the countries' cultures and histories. The price of enrollment in one of Elderhostel's courses covers all meals, lectures, field trips, gratuities and medical or insurance coverage.

7. Rocky Mountaineer Vacations/rockymountaineer.com/877-460-3200. Rocky Mountaineer Railtours is known for its two-day, all-daylight rail trips. Vacationers travel between Vancouver, British Columbia, and either Jasper Banff or Calgary, Alberta, with an overnight stop in Kamloops, British Columbia. You can choose between the basic Red Leaf service, with meals at your seat, and Gold Leaf service, which includes access to dining rooms and a car with a glass dome for better views of those breathtaking mountains. One unique touch: Meals include local ingredients, so travelers are served Alberta beef or venison while traveling through that part of the country, and then receive wine from British Columbia's Okanagan Valley during the rest of the journey. You can't book your trip online, but you can check out the Web site for the regular-season schedule, which runs from mid-April to mid-October, in addition to a handful of winter rail trips offered during the holiday season.

8. Rail Travel Tours/railtraveltours.com/866-704-3528. Taking much the same approach as Elderhostel, this Winnipeg-based travel agency uses the Canadian rail system to teach travelers about the country's history, culture and geography. These aren't run-of-the-mill tours: A guided trip through Manitoba in October takes travelers into the heart of polar-bear country.

9. Maupintour/maupintour.com/800-255-4266. This Summerlin, Nevada, travel agency offers several guided or independent rail-travel packages throughout Europe, Africa, Australia, Asia and Canada. Take a 14-day escorted trip that zips you through the highlights of Europe, including Paris, Geneva, Switzerland and Rome, via first-class train, or set off on your own on the Orient Express to go from London to Venice in seven days. The agency will also work with travelers to create custom packages to suit their travel plans.

10. RailServe/railserve.com. Traversing Canada isn't exotic enough for you? Then maybe a trip on South Africa's Blue Train from Pretoria to Cape Town or a 4,000-mile journey across China's Taklamankan Desert will be more your speed. RailServe, an Internet clearinghouse for rail enthusiasts, has several sections where users can explore links to hundreds of rail systems and travel-package sites to create unique and off-the-beaten-path trips. More-adventurous travelers can use the links to generate ideas for trips, or book them directly through the participating rail system or travel agent.

11. Rail Travel Center/railtravelcenter.com/800-458-5394. This travel agency in Putney, Vermont, runs escorted train tours through the United States, Canada, Mexico and Europe. Travelers don't have as much flexibility because the tour dates are set, as are the itineraries, but escorted groups also remove the guesswork and stress of planning. Though the agency offers trips through such traditional destinations as the Canadian and U.S. Rockies, Rail Travel Center also takes groups on more unusual excursions to such countries as Russia, Greece and the Czech Republic.

CHAPTER TWO

CREATURE COMFORTS ON THE ROAD

The next time you see one of those breathless ads for a fabulous hotel touted as a bargain at $500 a night, here's our advice—don't go there.

HOTELS: NAVIGATING THE RED-CARPET JUNGLE

No, we don't mean boycott the hotel. We mean that if you're resourceful and patient enough, you probably *don't* have to plunk down $500 for the room, no matter what the ad says. We know plenty of ways to beat high hotel prices and snag bargains for both business and pleasure travel without resorting to Motel 6. On the other hand, there are times when the good ole Motel 6 makes perfect sense. The larger point is that America has become a nation where staying at the Four Seasons is no longer reserved for the very rich. So here's some help getting that Four Seasons experience without paying a Four Seasons price.

THE RATES AND RATINGS GAME

First thing to know: Going online will almost always get you the best price. The Internet travel agencies have increasingly adopted a "merchant model," in which the agencies negotiate prices with the hotels below retail rates, then mark them up to consumers for a profit. But we said "almost"—sometimes calling the property directly and negotiating can get rates down. That's why, just like with airfares, we suggest a step-by-step method that involves checking out a number of Internet sites.

1. **To get a sense of what's out there, get a copy of the Zagat Survey of U.S. Hotels, Resorts & Spas.** The most recent edition only lists upscale properties, but they're also often the same as those discounted on the Internet, and the Zagat gives a good snapshot of what each place is like.

2. **Then go online and check out Quickbook.com and Hotels.com;** though the two services usually overlap, there are sometimes deals on one that aren't on the other. They'll both provide a good overview of the properties, so you can narrow down your choice to a couple of places. You can book both online, which means middle-of-the-night planning is still an option.

3. Once you've done that, compare prices for those properties on Expedia.com, Travelocity.com, Orbitz.com and Travelweb.com (a more recent addition, which is controlled by the hotels rather than third parties).

4. Next, go directly to the Web sites of the hotels you are interested in; chains have had some success luring buyers back with tactics like "best-price guarantees"—assurances that travelers can book right on the hotel's site and know they're still getting the best rate. Some hotels even offer additional discounts if you manage to find the room for less somewhere else. But be careful: It can be hard to get refunds from the online agencies, so always keep printouts of the confirmation number and all transactions and know what the different policies are. For example, **Priceline.com** and **Hotwire.com** give no refunds, period; **Hotels.com** charges a fee for all cancellations, while **Quickbook** only charges if you miss the hotel's cancellation window.

5. Once you get all the Internet rates, call the hotels directly. Though there are flukes when the 800 number offers the best rate, you can't negotiate with the operators the way you can with a hotel manager on-site. Ask for all the special rates—AAA or AARP discounts, corporate rates (you never know), advance-purchase rates or specials for longer stays. Though we don't advocate cheating, some travelers make reservations for weeks longer than they'll actually stay to lock in a lower rate or to get a day that might be sold out and then cancel the extra time.

6. Still can't find a rate you're happy with? Gamble a bit and try booking through Priceline.com or Hotwire.com. Both sites let you state a desired neighborhood and type of property (a four-star hotel near North Michigan Avenue in Chicago, for example). At Priceline, you've also got to name the price you are willing to pay. If there's a match, it spits out a reservation—but you are obligated to pay for it, like it or not. Hotwire offers up a price, but won't tell you your hotel's name before requiring you to commit. There are now ways, however, to take some of the guesswork out of the process. Many travelers, for instance, consult **Biddingfortravel.com,** a site where people post their recent successful bids. One traveler claims that on Priceline he landed a room at the Beverly Hilton (home of the Golden Globe Awards) in mid-February for $86 a night.

BONUS TIPS FOR SAVING MONEY:

1. Ask about those extra charges. There's no point in spending all that time looking for a lower rate if you just eat up the savings with on-site charges. The biggest add-ons to a hotel bill are taxes, so inquire first to avoid surprises. Next is parking (that averages about $15 a night but can be as much as $50 in a place like New York); the best way to avoid that is to look for garages or parking options nearby before you go. Phone charges are another outrage: Never dial long-distance (use your cell), and try to negotiate a free local and 800 number calls rate; when even an 800 number costs $2, it's worth it to monopolize the pay phone in the lobby.

2. Beware the group grope. Even if you're traveling as part of a group—for a convention, wedding or other special event—don't always go for the group rate. Most people assume they're getting the best price that way, but increasingly that isn't the case. Official rates are often higher because event organizers need to make tradeoffs in order to reserve the big meeting rooms in the hotel. For example, a hotel may be happy to rent the space and not charge much for it—but only if the planners guarantee that attendees will fill a big block of rooms.

3. Go off-peak. It may sound obvious that going off-season is a way to save money on hotel rates, but most people can't get past the downsides, such as sweltering heat in the Caribbean summer or frostbite in Minneapolis in the winter. But there are some off-seasons that aren't so uncomfortable, where the benefits outweigh the negatives: Consider Scottsdale, Arizona, in July and August, for example, when ritzy resorts like the Phoenician and Boulders offer rooms at a third of what they usually go for and the swimming pools and golf courses aren't so crowded. Alaska in the winter may not sound like fun, but parts of the state can be surprisingly mild (Juno's temperature is often in the 40s) and there's lots to do: you can ski (Alyeska Resort, 40 miles south of Anchorage, is worth the trip), go to dogsled races, bathe in hot springs and watch the Northern Lights. Also think about going to a spa in the summer, which is considered off-season in the industry and can mean cut rates and free treatments at even the most expensive places.

THE DOPE ON THE MAJOR
U.S. HOTEL CHAINS

Whatever complaints people may lodge against the Wal-Martization of America and the generic spread of chains, one thing is true: The hotel business in the past two decades has undergone a makeover almost as striking as the airline industry, and the consumer is the winner. Business travelers now have a stunning array of well-located choices with increasingly techno-wired hotels that throw in perks like free breakfasts and actually useful health clubs. Meanwhile, frugal leisure travelers in most of the country no longer need to get stuck in the local No-Tell Motel, as Days Inns, Holiday Inn Expresses, Hampton Inns and the like proliferate. The era of the truly comfortable $49 a night hotel room has arrived. Here are thumbnail sketches of the major players in the U.S. hotel market:

Adam's Mark: 800-444-2326; about 16 hotels in the United States, mostly in the Southeast in places like Columbia, South Carolina, and Jacksonville, Florida, they are popular choices for meetings and conferences.

Best Western: 800-528-1234; with 4,000 hotels, more than half in the United States and the rest in about 80 other countries, these are a dependable standard for budget travelers. Most properties now have free high-speed Internet in public areas.

Days Inn: 800-325-2525; calling itself the "best value under the sun," Days Inn operates 1,900 properties worldwide under the Cendant corporate wingspan. The chain caters to frugal business travelers and budget tourists looking for more than a frugal room.

Doubletree: 800-222-8733; run by Hilton, there are about 160 hotels, typical with a full-service restaurant and lounge, room service, swimming pool and health club—plus signature chocolate chip cookies.

Embassy Suites Hotels: 800-362-2779; Hilton's 174 upscale all-suite hotels are mostly in the United States, Canada and Latin America. Suites are either one or two bedroom and come with kitchens, full breakfast and evening snacks, but no room service. Its largest hotel is the Niagara Falls–Fallsview: 512 rooms.

Fairmont: 800-257-7544; hotels owned by this luxury operator include such grand old dames as the Plaza in New York and the Copley Plaza in Boston. Also big resorts in Hawaii, Bermuda and Barbados.

Four Seasons: 800-332-3442; one of the top managers of luxury hotels and resorts, Four Seasons runs some 63 hotels in some 28 countries, primarily under the Four Seasons and Regent brands, though there can be surprises (the Ritz-Carlton in Chicago and the Pierre in New York, for example).

Hilton Hotels/Hampton Inn: 800-445-8667; there are about 200 Hiltons in the U.S., ranging from New York's Waldorf Astoria to the Hilton Waikoloa Village in Hawaii. Check out the Web site for Internet-only specials. Hilton also operates the value-priced Hampton Inn and Hampton Inn & Suites chains, with more than 1,200 locations, many in mid-sized towns.

Holiday Inn: 800-465-4329; Intercontinental's budget line, these 1,500 hotels, including Holiday Inn Expresses, are located around the world, usually with swimming pools and restaurants.

Hyatt: 888-591-1234; over 200 hotels and resorts, either under Hyatt Regency (often airport hotels), Grand Hyatt (large luxury hotels), Park Hyatt (smaller luxury hotels) or Hyatt International.

InterContinental Hotels: 800-327-0200; the flagship brand, there are about 140 hotels in some 75 countries, mostly in big cities, and they tend to be in older buildings and appeal to travelers looking for a feeling of grandeur.

Leading Hotels: 800-745-8883; if you're looking for a top-notch small property and aren't afraid to spend over $500 a night, try this network of 400 hotels around the world.

Loews Hotels: 800-235-6397; big, luxury hotels that try to be stylish but cater to a lot of conferences and business meetings. There are about 20 in North America.

Mandarin Oriental: 866-801-8880; best known for its Hong Kong and Bangkok properties as the high-end Asian chain, the company has made inroads in the United States with properties in places like New York, San Francisco and Washington. Locals rave about the spas.

Marriott: 800-228-9290; adored by business travelers for its frequent-guest perks and its consistent quality, Marriott rooms have large working spaces; there are about 400 properties with pools, fitness centers and restaurants.

Omni: 800-843-6664; known for its service, Omni focuses on "corporate business and upscale leisure" travelers, with 40 properties in North America. The typical Omni Hotel has 350 to 500 rooms, all with marbled bathrooms.

Ramada: 800-228-2828; a mostly budget-minded chain, with more than 1,000 hotels nationwide. Plain-old Ramadas often occupy inexpensive parts of cities and have no services; Ramada Inns often stand off busy freeways and have restaurants and room service; Ramada Plazas are usually located downtown—they are more upscale, catering to meetings and business travelers.

Residence Inn by Marriott: 800-331-3131; over 400 in North America, rooms have separate sleeping areas, kitchens and well-equipped work spaces. Free breakfasts and evening snacks, but no room service.

Ritz-Carlton: 800-241-3333; run by Marriott, the quality can vary by property, but overall the company has a reputation for luxury and elegance. Most of the 57 hotels worldwide (35 city hotels and 23 resorts) are in big cities or exclusive vacation spots, but sometimes one pops up in a place like Cleveland or Dearborn, Michigan.

Sheraton: 800-325-3535; this brand has become the plain-Jane sister of Starwood, which also owns W and St. Regis. If you're traveling in a big city overseas, chances are you'll find one of the 400 Sheratons, be it in Argentina or Zimbabwe.

Sofitel: 800-763-4835; the premium hotel brand of Accor (parent of Motel 6, among others), there are 180 hotels in 53 countries (10 in the United States, all big cities). Sofitel has its own loyalty program.

St. Regis: 888-625-5144; Starwood's high-end brand, the name comes from the grand St. Regis in New York, but not all of the properties live up to that legend of luxury.

W Hotels: 800-625-5144; the ultimate in corporate hip, these 17 or so high-end hotels are decked out in sleek designs, are located in the trendy parts of cities and have happening restaurants and bars. Part of Starwood's frequent-guest plan.

 Here's how the various hotel ratings systems are calculated:

Mobil: Professional inspectors visit hotels unannounced each year, rating them on thousands of criteria.

AAA: Sixty-five inspectors make announced and unannounced hotel visits. (Uses diamonds instead of stars.)

Priceline: Ratings are based on lists of amenities provided by hotels, and from recommendations of Priceline salespeople.

Expedia: One staffer speaks with hotel managers and Expedia sales staff, but doesn't visit the properties.

Hotwire: The site's sales reps rate hotels based on their sales visits and the hotels' own descriptions.

Hotels.com: Sales staff "inspect" most big-city properties. Hotels sometimes rate themselves.

Travelocity: Uses AAA ratings, customer reviews.

Westin: 800-228-3000; over 110 high-end properties aimed at business and leisure travelers, this brand is known for its "Heavenly Bed." Part of Starwood's frequent-guest plan.

JUDGING FREQUENT-STAY PROGRAMS

Generally, this is an uncomplicated issue. If you travel to cities that are Marriott-heavy, then join *that* program; if you like Kimpton boutique properties, choose them. But try to accumulate all your points in one group. If you're trying to decide between a couple different programs, the place to start is **webflyer.com**—this site will give you a comprehensive description of all the different hotel loyalty clubs, reviews, a list of blackout days and the success rates for getting upgrades. It also allows you to compare programs head-to-head.

Most chains, including Hilton Hotels, Marriott International and Starwood, will now let you convert hotel points into frequent-flier miles. But which is better? Given the dynamics in the travel industry right now—hotels are getting more generous just as frequent-flier programs are getting stingier—it turns out that it almost always makes more sense to go for hotel points. Then you can trade those points for a free night, which is often a better value than a free ticket. For example, 40,000 miles might get you, say, a $250 airplane ticket, but the equivalent in hotel points may get you several nights in a hotel, with a considerably higher value. In addition, booking frequent-flier seats is harder because most airlines have cut the number of flights they offer.

Here is a roundup of which programs are most suitable for travelers with particular goals:

Fastest Elite Status: Hilton makes it easiest to earn special perks. After four stays or a total of 10 nights in a year, a member can hit "silver" status, which entitles members to special treatment, such as better-room upgrades. In addition, Hilton's points become more valuable, too. For example, an elite member can trade in 100,000 points for a six-night stay in one of Hilton's Hawaiian properties. By comparison, nonelite members would have to cash in nearly double the points.

Quickest Free Room: Hyatt Hotels offers members perhaps the fastest route to a free stay. You can earn a free night after only two stays charged to a MasterCard. The downside, however, is that Hyatt has far fewer hotels than some other chains—in fact, fewer than a tenth of Marriott's nearly 2,300 hotels. Thus, Marriott provides more opportunities to rack up points for people who travel widely. In addition, Hyatt operates pricier full-service hotels, which may be a tough sell with the bean-counters as travel budgets shrink. The loyalty programs at Marriott, Hilton, Six Continents and Starwood all include the chains' lower-priced properties, such as Courtyard by Marriott, and Hampton Inn, Holiday Inn or Four Points by Sheraton.

Fewest Room Restrictions: Starwood puts the fewest restrictions on guests who want to redeem their points for free rooms—for instance, there are no blackout dates. In addition Starwood, which includes the Sheraton, W and other brands, doesn't limit the number of rooms available for redemptions, a common practice among other hotels (and, of course, among airline frequent-flier programs, too). The drawback is that you generally have to spend more money with Starwood to get the free rooms. A company spokesman says guests "have told us it's more important to have the ability to use their points where and when they want, even if we're more expensive."

Budget-Hotel Perks: For travelers who spend a lot of time at the other end of the spectrum, in the no-frills category, Choice and Cendant, which own and franchise brands such as Comfort Inn, Sleep Inn, Ramada Inn and Howard Johnson, give budget travelers a chance to earn free rooms and perks. However, your free room will be confined to their no-frills properties. Choice, however, offers other ways for members to redeem points, including gift certificates at retailers, and airline miles; Cendant plans to do the same.

Redemptions for Gifts: Six Continents touts the growing number of gifts and services that members in its Priority Club loyalty

HOW THEY STACK UP

 Hotel loyalty programs are becoming more flexible—for instance, all the chains listed here except Wyndham let you convert points to frequent-flier miles—but they still vary widely. A sampler:

HILTON—includes Hilton, Doubletree, Embassy Suites

> **Strengths:** Easy to attain VIP status; double-dip earning airline and hotel points
> **Weaknesses:** Hotels aren't as popular as Starwood or as widely spread as Marriott

MARRIOTT—includes Marriott, Courtyard, Residence Inn, Springhill Suites

> **Strengths:** Great geographic spread and plenty of budget-to-deluxe choices
> **Weaknesses:** No points at their Ritz-Carlton hotels; less generous than some

STARWOOD—includes Westin, W, Sheraton, St. Regis

> **Strengths:** No blackout dates or other limits; hotels have wide appeal
> **Weaknesses:** Most expensive program

SIX CONTINENTS—includes Intercontinental Crown Plaza and Holiday Inn

> **Strengths:** Good international reach
> **Weaknesses:** Lets you trade points for merchandise—but don't do it

WYNDHAM

> **Strengths:** Free phone calls; personalized amenities and services
> **Weaknesses:** No point program

program can purchase with their points. But it isn't much of a bargain: To get a set of 12 Titleist golf balls, for instance, you have to rack up $1,900 in hotel bills. (The golf balls cost 19,000 points, and you earn 10 points for every dollar spent.) You have to spend $22,500 just to get the 32-inch TV. The company notes that members can earn points in several ways, not just on their hotel bills.

To avoid complex points calculations entirely, there is Wyndham. The Dallas-based chain is one of a few (others include Ritz-Carlton) that have forgone points-based rewards altogether. Instead, Wyndham tracks guest preferences in order to personalize rooms with favorite perks such as wine or special pillows. Members also get free long-distance calls and high-speed Internet access—but no free rooms.

ROOMS: OF VIEWS AND VIEWPOINTS

Anyone who's ever spent a trip looking at a view of the parking lot knows the gray, hard truth: All hotel rooms are *not* created equal.

Behind those rows of look-alike doors lie dark mini-dungeons, hobbit holes where you'll bang your knee on the desk trying to get out of bed and, also, glorious gems with lots of light, space and inspiring views. The first rule of thumb for getting the best room you can is to *never accept the first room they show you* if it isn't up to par; ask for a better one immediately. Hotels usually try to get the worst spaces filled up first, and most front-desk clerks are used to moving people around. Don't worry—lots of people do it; you aren't being any more of a jerk than everyone else.

But how do you know which rooms will have that something extra? Scout the layout: The starting point for this kind of find is the hotel floor plan. Most properties will show this to you at check-in, and many will even fax it to you ahead of time on request. Unusually large shapes may mean bigger rooms in that wing; floor plans will usually tell you where the true corner rooms are.

1. **Learn the lingo:** The floor plan won't help if you don't speak the hotel's language, and it's getting harder to crack the code. Nationwide, U.S. hotels now classify 16 percent of their rooms as suites, double the percentage in 1994; the increase is even more striking at luxury hotels, where nearly one in every four rooms is now dubbed a "suite." If you can get a suite, you want it, because it almost always designates a larger room. But leave it to hotels to find more obscure ways of rating their own rooms: The W Chicago names its rooms "Wonderful" and "Spectacular"—both sound, well, wonderful, but in fact the latter has a better view. New York's SoHo House has "Playpens" and "Playrooms"—Playrooms are bigger. Hotels don't necessarily hide this information, but they don't publicize it either. The best bet: Get a reservation agent located at the hotel—not through a national chain's central number—and find out the class of the room you're booking, how the rooms in that class vary and what the other classes closest in price are like.

2. **Ask for amenities:** A treadmill in your room; a computer on the desk, hooked up for free; high-speed Internet access; a mini-kitchen—many hotels have these extras in some rooms, so ask ahead of time whether there are any special features to be aware of.

3. **Ask for two beds:** Even if you're traveling alone, rooms with two beds are usually bigger rooms.

And if you must smoke, head for Chicago: A study by PricewaterhouseCoopers shows the Windy City has the highest percentage of smoking rooms (20 percent of rooms allow smoking) in major urban hotel markets. About 15 percent of the hotel rooms in New York, Los Angeles and Miami are for smokers. "Those cities that have higher percentages of convention business" seem to be the most smoker-friendly, says lodging analyst Bjorn Hanson, of Pricewaterhouse, who did the research. Only 8 percent of rooms were for smokers in Dallas/Fort Worth, the metro area with the smallest number of smoking rooms.

GETTING THE UPGRADE

Frequent stay or loyalty programs, of course, are another way to get a room upgrade. Here's a roundup of the policies at some better-known hotel groups:

Program: Hyatt (Gold Passport)

Cost to upgrade: 3,000 points

The fine print: No minimum-night stay for Gold members, and the terms are pretty easy—you get five points for every dollar spent.

Program: Kimpton Group (In Touch)

Cost to upgrade: Forty-five nights as a paying guest

The fine print: Anyone can sign up to be an "In Touch" member, but "Inner Circle" folks (guests who stay 45 nights qualify) get automatic upgrades at check-in.

Program: Noble House Hotels (Returns)

Cost to upgrade: $50–$200

The fine print: You can pay for upgrades—but not at resorts in peak season. A new program launches in the spring.

Program: Starwood (Preferred Guest)

Cost to upgrade: 1,000 points

The fine print: Free sign-up, and you earn two points for every dollar spent. But it can cost more points to cash in at a St. Regis (up to 2,500) than at a Westin (1,000).

Program: Wyndham (By Request)

Cost to upgrade: Free

The fine print: The most generous program we checked out, with automatic upgrades and free domestic long distance. Must book through Wyndham.

THE BLISS OF SILENCE . . .

We went in search of hotels and resorts where you can spend a whole day at the pool without worrying you'll hear the "Theme from *Rocky*" ring tone. With two-thirds of Americans toting wireless phones—that's 160 million people, nine times as many as a decade ago—someone's bound to call you (or worse, the guy in the next beach chair). We found locations across the United States that offer the utter bliss and serenity of "no service"—the ultimate dead-zone destinations.

Resort: Cibolo Creek Ranch—Marfa, Texas

Atmosphere: Solitude by a five-star campfire

Where to get service: Second fort, 13 miles from main fort, sometimes has signal

Price Range: $450–650*

Comments: Resort features three adobe forts spread over 32,000 acres, with no-tech rooms (no TV or phones); communal meals prepared with local ingredients. A list of past guests that includes Julia Roberts, Mick Jagger and the Dixie Chicks. For the culture-starved, the media room has satellite TV and Internet access.

Resort: Deetjen's Big Sur Inn—Big Sur, California

Atmosphere: Hippie heaven

Where to get service: At nearby Post Ranch Inn

Price Range: $75–$195

Comment: National historic site is nestled deep in a canyon—that's why mobiles don't work—near fancy resorts like Post Ranch Inn. With bare rooms and lack of spa, it's not for the pampered set. Restaurant gets high marks, and it's famous for its alternative eggs Benedict, with avocado and fake sausage.

Resort: Garland's Oak Creek Lodge—Sedona, Arizona

Atmosphere: Readers and gourmands

Where to get service: Just about anywhere else: golf courses, resorts, parks

Price Range: $200–$235*

Comment: Five million visitors may come to Sedona annually, but Garland's keeps things quiet—in part because guests have to cross a creek, without a bridge, to get to this homey 16-cabin site. Eating's a big activity here, with homemade blueberry crumble at teatime and one-seating dinners included in the rate.

Resort: Lake Quinault Lodge—Quinault, Washington

Atmosphere: Like camping—without drawbacks

Where to get service: Lean over lake—or take out a kayak

Price Range: $70–$347

Comment: Grand 1926 lodge has tame rabbits on its manicured lawn, and it's surrounded by a national forest with mountains and giant fir trees. The lodge's one pay phone often has a line, and guests aren't told about the outlet for Internet access unless they ask. (Pssst: Try looking in the lobby.)

Resort: Mahakua–Hacienda de San Antonio—Colima, Mexico

Atmosphere: South-of-the-border lovers' getaway

Where to get service: About 5 miles up the road

Price Range: $800–$1,550*

Comment: Blame the volcano: Century-old hacienda, built as a coffee plantation and now run by Amanresorts, is by an active, reception-blocking volcano. (Need to find the spot on the road where coverage starts? Ask the resort's driver.) Low-tech vibe is popular with guests, who have included Courtney Love and Robert Redford.

Resort: Mayflower Inn—Washington, Connecticut

Atmosphere: Very New England

Where to get service: Certain spots along the road

Price Range: $420–$1,400

Comment: Located in a high-power, high-income area of Connecticut, this five-diamond inn gets its share of cell-phone addicts in withdrawal. House secret: One guest discovered his pager would work—but only if he went into the closet of the $1,400 Billington Suite, climbed up on a stool and placed it on the top of the window ledge.

Resort: Mountain Magnolia Inn—Hot Springs, North Carolina

Atmosphere: Night on Cold Mountain

Where to get service: Town's in a valley; drive outside of it

Price Range: $100–$250

Comment: This 1868 Victorian inn is set in a garden off the main strip in Hot Springs, a popular way station for Appalachian Trail hikers. Frank Abdoo, a counselor from Lexington, Kentucky, found his Treo 600 organizer worked fine here—but not as a cell phone. "When you first realize it doesn't work," he says, "you feel kind of alone."

Resort: Old Tavern at Grafton—Grafton, Vermont

Atmosphere: Lavish simplicity

Where to get service: Top of a hill, half mile away

Price Range: $135–$900

Comment: When Michael Eisner brings his Disney execs for a retreat, the inn's one fax is going all day and night, says the inn manager. Last March an in-house survey revealed an overwhelming desire for no in-room phones or TVs to appear, ever.

Resort: The Point—Saranac Lake, New York

Atmosphere: Ritz goes to summer camp

Where to get service: On croquet lawn . . . sometimes

Price Range: $1,650–$2,500*

Comment: You probably won't get cell reception—but the rate at this Adirondack lodge includes free calls anywhere in the world. (Catch: The outside line is in a room by the pub, and in-room phones call only the butler.) Also included: liquor from 24-hour bar.

Resort: Sandy Valley Ranch—Sandy Valley, Nevada

Atmosphere: Western kitsch

Where to get service: Spotty service around property

Price Range: $180*

Comment: First introduction to this ranch ("45 minutes and 100 years from Las Vegas") sets mood for some guests: Their bus is held up by "bandits" who confiscate phones. Guests stay in tents—or the resort's covered wagon with lace curtains and air-conditioning. It's popular with companies who come for team building, cowboy games.

Resort: Sorrel River Ranch Resort—Moab, Utah

Atmosphere: Family-friendly river retreat

Where to get service: Moab, about 17 miles away

Price Range: $149–$379

Comment: When we arrived, we found kids playing with a couple of leashed goats. But there's little roughing it at this roomy luxury complex on the Colorado River: Rooms have satellite TV and toiletries worth taking, and there's horseback riding, tennis and a spa offering "desert stone massage" for two.

Resort: Triple Creek Ranch—Darby, Montana

Atmosphere: Lavish dude ranch

Where to get service: On horseback, during cattle drive

Price Range: $510–$995*

Comment: This 550-acre dude ranch has meals and drinks included, and offers fly-fishing and horseback riding. Cattle drives are the big draw, though, and with 50 staffers for a maximum of 44 guests, dudes can always find someone to clean the cow pie from their dropped cell phone. "It makes me laugh to see people on their phones on horseback, surrounded by cows," says the general manager.

Resort: Twin Farms—Barnard, Vermont

Atmosphere: Luxury farmhouse

Where to get service: Top of ski mountain

Price Range: $950–$2,600*

Comment: Some guests figure they can make a call by hiking 15 minutes up the hill. What the hotel doesn't say: Sometimes there's also a signal in the employee parking lot. Resort is putting in a T1 line for faster Internet access. Rate also includes alcohol.

Resort: Wuksachi Lodge—Sequoia National Park, California

Atmosphere: Spare National Park lodge

Where to get service: Wolverton exit, 4 miles away

Price Range: $79–$219

Comment: Even the White House couldn't do anything about the lack of cell service: When President Bush visited this remote, modern park lodge a few years ago, the advance team ran 100 extra phone lines to the property. This minimalist lodge doesn't have loads of amenities; bring hiking boots and books.

*Rates include all meals (lunch not included at Sandy Valley Ranch, Garland's).

STAYING FIT ON THE ROAD

Some people pick a hotel for its beds; others, for its bar or for the location. And then there are those who know in every city hotel workout rooms with Precor EFXs and flat-screen TVs. While hotel companies churn out volumes of standards for things like room service and lobby décor—detailing everything down to fabric quality—most chains have no standards at all for their gyms. That's largely because gyms usually don't make money for hotels unless they farm them out to a separate operator, who sells memberships. So if you don't want to get stuck in a smelly little converted utility closet with outmoded equipment, you'll need to ask pertinent questions and perhaps shop around some. Is it a gym or merely an exercise room? Is the treadmill or weight apparatus a name you know? Are the hours flexible? Is there an extra fee?

If you have no choice in your hotel and you find its gym wanting, bypass it and head for a real health club. Chances are, your home health-club membership gets you into more gyms, both within the United States and overseas, than you think. A growing number of clubs—currently about 3,000—participate in the fitness industry's "Passport Program," which gives their members workout privileges at other participating clubs and discounts on guest-pass fees. Some clubs won't take walk-ins unless they're from another participating club.

Even if your club isn't a member, you may still be able to find a spinning class in Saigon or a steam room in Seattle. **Healthclubs.com** lets you search for gyms by activity or amenity. For yoga devotees, **Yogafinder.com** lists different classes in more than 60 countries, from Costa Rica to Switzerland. Expecting a long layover? **Airportgyms .com** lists places in or near airports to work up a sweat while waiting for your connecting flight. Another solution is to bring your own fitness equipment, be it a jump rope or a yoga video.

HOTELS FOR RUNNERS

Boston

Best Route: Charles River

Nearby Hotels: The Sheraton, Royal Sonesta Hotel, Hyatt Regency Cambridge

A pleasant city for running, but be cautious. On its jogging maps, the Sheraton Boston advises guests to run only during daylight hours, to be aware of hazards such as animals and traffic and to run with a companion. The Sheraton is in a prime running location, right next to our recommended path along the Charles River. The entire loop, which passes MIT, Harvard and Boston University, is 17.2 miles long, but you can use numerous bridges to carve out various distances. Stick to the path, as the drivers can be horrendous. If the Charles River runs gets too congested with bikers, try a wetlands preserve about half a mile from the Sheraton, called "the Fens," with water and bridges and gravel paths.

Dallas
Best Route: Turtle Creek and Lee Park

Nearby Hotels: The Mansion on Turtle Creek, Crescent Court, Hotel St. Germain

Dallas may be a shopper's paradise, but it's one of the nation's most unfriendly cities for joggers. It's hot, there are few paths with shade and there are no large parks or green areas downtown. Though hardly an inexpensive option, many runners recommend the Mansion on Turtle Creek, a luxury hotel in a residential area. The Mansion hands out maps of a recommended route along Turtle Creek and through Lee Park, a shady one- to three-mile jog. The hotel also provides transportation to a well-marked, nine-mile path around White Rock Lake. The Four Seasons in Las Colinas, which is about 30 minutes from downtown, has its own quarter-mile shaded running path and offers a map for a five-mile run in the surrounding neighborhood. But the concierge there warns of traffic. Travelers forced to stay downtown do have one good option: The YMCA, at 601 North Akard Street, arranges group jogs four times a day, each about seven miles long.

Los Angeles
Best Route: Santa Monica Pier

Nearby Hotels: Loews Santa Monica, Shutters, Hotel Casa Del Mar

Prime jogging occurs in Santa Monica, where hotels don't even have to offer running maps: They can just tell guests to point their running shoes toward the beach and a 22-mile-long, sand-bordered running trail. Everyone from Bill Clinton to Al Gore has used it. But it's not all perfect: Sparsely lined with tall palm trees, the trail has little shade and is often crowded with in-line skaters. To help out, beachside hotels such as Shutters offer joggers a towel and bottled water, while the Loews Santa Monica Beach Hotel rents jogging strollers for guests with kids. In downtown Los Angeles, meanwhile, some out-of-town joggers have discovered the Westin Bonaventure Hotel and Suites, which added a new indoor running track on the third level of the six-story atrium lobby last summer.

New York
Best Route: Central Park

Nearby Hotels: The Peninsula, the Plaza, the Wyndham, the Carlyle

For those who have to do business in the crowded, taxi-deluged city, the 843-acre park is a haven. The Road Runners Club has organized safety runs, open to all visitors, which leave twice daily from its headquarters on 90th Street at Fifth Avenue. There are lockers for suits and papers, as well as a shop that sells running gear—including New York City Marathon T-shirts. Runners recommend the Peninsula hotel on Fifth Avenue at 55th Street, which is just a few blocks from the park and has an especially good map of the park's paths. The hotel's fitness center will send a trainer with you for a fee. Upon returning to the hotel, you'll find lemon water, iced compresses and robes. Runners, however, have been sideswiped by taxis and even encountered gunmen.

New Orleans
Best Route: Audubon Park

Nearby Hotels: The Columns, Parkview Guest House, St. Charles Inn

Don't expect any marathon-length paths here. After all, it is the Big Easy. Athletic-shoe and clothing-sales executives favor the Columns Hotel, a bed-and-breakfast near our suggested 3.1-mile run in Audubon Park, with live oaks and a little lagoon. A good route is the 10- to 12-mile route along the Mississippi River Levee, which stretches all the way to Baton Rouge. Every other Wednesday night a group of runners meet at a bar called the Live Bait Bar & Grill at around 6 P.M., run the levee together and then drink the night away. There's no shade on the levee, but there's usually a breeze. Most downtown hotels, such as the Wyndham New Orleans, have maps that direct runners to the French Quarter.

San Francisco

Best Route: Embarcadero

Nearby Hotels: Hyatt Regency, Harbor Court Hotel, Hotel Griffon

At the Ritz-Carlton in San Francisco, there's a jogging station in the foyer every day from 6 A.M. to 8 A.M. stocked with maps, bottled water, apples and a Ritz-Carlton towel. But the problem with the Ritz-Carlton, some runners say, is it is on a steep hill—and what goes down must come up eventually. Sharp inclines are also a reason to avoid hotels on Nob Hill. Try the Embarcadero and run along the ocean toward Fisherman's Wharf and the Golden Gate Promenade. If you cross the Golden Gate Bridge, it's a 14-mile loop. You can also squeeze in a run when you have a layover at San Francisco's airport. Just south of the main terminal is a path along Old Bayshore Trail. It runs by many of the airport hotels, so it is just a shuttle-bus ride away, and there is airplane-watching and bird-watching.

Final tip: If your hotel can't tell you the best running route in town, have them phone the local running store for advice.

TIMESHARES, VACATION RENTALS AND HOME SWAPPING

TIMESHARES

Timeshares conjure up notions of Florida condos and pushy salespeople. But that's changed as more luxury hotels sell off floors of landmark properties everywhere from Manhattan to Aspen. The upscale properties come with extras like flat-screen TVs, high-end linens and the dedicated services of a hotel-style concierge. They use a simple sales pitch: Buy a lifetime worth of vacations at today's prices.

But the reputation of timeshares as money pits isn't totally unwarranted: They can mean unanticipated expenses for maintenance and upkeep—think leaky roofs and plumbing overhauls—as a property gets older, while the resale market is practically nonexistent. Interest rates are sky-high because mortgage brokers won't touch timeshares; after all, you're not buying property.

There are some bargains that can be found in the resale market. EBay lists a few hundred, and Timeshare Users Group, **tug2.net**, has about 2,000 listings as well as message boards where members rate resorts, air their beefs or solicit advice. It's also possible to test the time-share waters by renting.

If you are interested, first look at the terms of the plan. There are two ways to go: Deeded ownership means that you own a fractional interest of the timeshare unit—usually one week. You receive a deed, and can rent, sell, or leave the property to your heirs. Right-to-use ownership is also usually sold in one-week increments, but only guarantees the right to use the property for a certain number of years. As such, you do not actually own the timeshare real estate. You buy either a fixed or a floating plan: A fixed-week system means that you're committed to using the same week each year. This can make it easier to plan for your vacations, and guarantees that you'll get the week you want. A floating-week system gives you the right to occupy your unit during a specific window of time, but you must call your resort in advance to reserve the week you want. This gives you greater flexibility in your travel plans, but can be disappointing if another owner has already reserved the week you want.

Other factors to consider are your ownership rights, maintenance fees and how the timeshare is managed. At most timeshare resorts, some weeks are more popular than others; because of this, two of the largest timeshare exchange organizations, Resort Condominiums International (RCI) and Interval International (II), assign color codes to certain weeks based on popularity. When buying a timeshare, make sure you know what the color code is for your unit, and what that color represents with respect to seasonality.

Some questions to ask: Are there any special assessments pending against the resort? Can you "bank" a week if you can't use it during the assigned week? Is there a maintenance-fee cap? Also, add up everything before you make your decision—mortgage payments and expenses, maintenance fees, closing costs, broker commissions, and financial charges—and then compare that to what it would cost you to rent something in the area.

Which brings us to vacation rentals. Because of a general skittishness about vacationing too far from home, Americans are increasingly snapping up rental houses and condos at closer, safer-feeling destinations. Not only do they promise more space at lower prices than a resort, but they also offer conveniences such as washing machines and kitchens—no more raiding the mini-bar for the $5 snack packs. The pool of rental properties is also expanding rapidly right now, thanks to the rush in the 1990s to buy second, and even third, homes. Today, with the owners struggling to make the mortgage, those properties are popping up as rentals.

One result of all this activity is that it is getting nearly as easy to rent a house as a hotel room. But it's also getting easier to rent a lemon. Not only are there almost no national players in the market, there are no uniform standards, either. Unlike the hotel industry, which is dominated by big international companies and highly organized rating systems, vacation rentals are chaotic. An array of Web sites (listed farther on) and independent agents are scrambling for market share, spawning confusion. Many are simply listings of properties for rent, with no one but you to vet just how partial that "partial beach view" is.

Also unlike hotels or resorts, most rental houses require up-front payment or hefty deposits. That places much of the risk on the renter, who could have trouble getting a refund if things go wrong. The industry has no universal standards and ratings, though there have been some idiosyncratic attempts to fix that.

ResortQuest International, one of the few U.S. property managers with some national reach, ranks properties on **ResortQuest.com** in one of several categories, with names like "Quest" and "Bronze." Currently, it lists 20,000 condos and homes in 50 locations. But it won't guarantee a certain unit at a certain rating at some condos. Also, it charges the same price regardless of the rating. So it's conceivable that two families traveling together could stay in the same development, pay the same price, but get totally different surroundings.

While there may be cultural pitfalls to renting a place abroad, from foreign languages to foreign bathroom fixtures, some services can be quite detailed about the properties available. **Rentvillas.com,** for instance, rates each of its European units right down to how clean the bathroom is.

The best way to begin looking for a place in the U.S. is to simply do an Internet search for "vacation rental" and the name of your destination. That will almost certainly produce a lengthy list of options. City sites such as **Orlando.com,** as well as Web sites run by chambers of commerce or big ski resorts, also are increasingly listing vacation rentals. If nothing comes up that sparks your interest, call a local real-estate agent. Then the sleuthing begins.

For instance, **VRBO.com,** a listing site with relatively extensive national offerings (the name stands for "vacation rentals by owner"), puts you directly in touch with the owner of the house. Some owners on the site go to the effort of posting elaborate 360-degree photos online, as well as detailed descriptions, but others may be less forthcoming about their property's blemishes. Some good Web sites include VRBO rival **cyberrentals.com, Nomorehotels.com, Rentmyroom.com** and **Chicago-bed-breakfast.com** (both for Chicago) and **bnbphiladelphia .com** (Philadelphia).

Finally, you should feel free to negotiate on price. Some owners will readily give you a discount if you book for two weeks instead of one or if you're willing to rearrange your travel dates to snatch up a week they haven't been able to rent. And don't forget to check "comparables"—i.e., what similarly sized and situated properties are going for in that area. That's the only barometer you'll have of whether you're getting a bargain or paying too much.

Also, remember that failing to ask the right questions can leave you in a "fully equipped" home without bedsheets. Here's what to ask when grilling the rental agent or owner:

1. Ratings: Does the agent grade its properties? If not, ask: How does this one compare to the others they handle? What's its worst feature?

2. Appliances and extras: It pays to ask about things that you might consider routine: toasters, blenders and coffeemakers shouldn't be taken for granted, nor should getting an extra key. Does it have a barbecue grill and is it gas-operated or charcoal? In many cases, lakefront properties come with the use of canoes and kayaks, but in some states insurance concerns mean that owners require you to bring your own boat.

3. Food: Where is the nearest grocery store? The nearest restaurant?

4. Bedding: Is the "king-size bed" really king-size, or two twin beds shoved together? Are there linens and towels? If not, you'll need to know the size of beds in every room.

5. Furnishings: When was it last redecorated, and did that include the carpet?

6. Home entertainment: Does the "entertainment" consist of just a portable TV and boom box, or TVs in every room? If you care about cable, be sure to ask whether cable or satellite TV is part of the package.

7. Kitchen: Is it a full kitchen, with adequate cutlery, glassware and cookware, or a "kitchenette"? (Warning: That can mean a mini-fridge and a microwave.) If you're a wine lover, ask if there are actual wineglasses, and a wine opener. Otherwise, you'll know to bring your own.

8. Location: How is "beachfront" or "lakefront" defined? Is it truly on the water, or merely facing the water, separated by road or highway? If you want to be on a lake and value quiet and privacy, there are several things you need to know: How densely is the lakefront developed? How near is your nearest neighbor? Does the lake allow power boats and Jet Skis? Are there public launch facilities or beaches nearby that would draw crowds? Finally, is there construction nearby?

9. Is housekeeping provided? If something's amiss, is there a 24-hour contact?

10. Security: Are there known hazards (a busy highway you have to cross, for example) nearby?

JARGON: VACATION RENTAL GLOSSARY

Rustic: Beware! This can mean the mountain cabin of your dreams—or linoleum floors, tattered screens and a drippy faucet.

Close to Nightlife: Sounds fun, but if it's near bars and restaurants, it could be noisy.

Cozy: Small to minuscule. Plan to sleep there, but not much else.

Steps from the Beach: Agents tell us this can mean up to a quarter-mile.

Sleeps 12: That doesn't necessarily add up to six bedrooms—try pull-out sofa bed and a few foam mattresses.

Terrific Value: Brace for some sort of surprise when you arrive.

HOME SWAPPING

The least expensive vacation option is home swapping—but it's also the riskiest. An estimated 250,000 people participate in house swapping each year for weekends or week-long vacations that let them get out of their abode and into someone else's free of charge. Usually, people who are interested in home swapping post online or in a home-swapping catalog a description of their home, where it's located and what attractions are nearby. In the meantime, they peruse postings of others. When two groups have a mutual interest in visiting the other's home, they decide on a time to make the simultaneous switch. The prospect of letting strangers come live in your house sounds frightening to some people. Fans of the system, however, say the fact that you are living in their house while they are in yours fosters a mutual respect.

Typically, home-swapping organizations just provide a common place for postings; some have annual membership fees, but others are free. *The Home Exchange Guide: How to Find Your Free Home Away from Home* (Poyeen Publishing) helps find them. In some cases, you can exchange cars or even boats, though it is smart to make sure insurance covers the new driver. Intervac and Homelink are two of the oldest swapping networks, both started about 50 years ago. Homelink has more than 12,000 members and a $75 annual fee and is found at **homelink.org.** Intervac has about 10,000 members and is found at **intervaconline.com,** with a membership fee of $65.

CHAPTER THREE

GETTING PAMPERED, HAVING FUN AND ROUGHING IT

LEISURE AND ADVENTURE TRAVEL

It wasn't that long ago that traveling for fun was getting to be no fun at all. Airlines were jam-packed, flight delays inevitable, planes were overbooked, rental cars were sold out, hotel prices were ridiculous and Christmas reservations had to be made at least a year in advance. Then came the terrible events of September 11, and suddenly airports emptied and hotels drastically reduced rates. Since then, the travel industry has begun to recover, but it has faced such events as the Iraq conflict, SARS and an uneven economic recovery.

Hotels have started raising prices in many markets, but properties in most of the country are still recovering. Overall, there's been a shift in American travel patterns, with more last-minute booking, and a tendency to stay within the United States and closer to home. Here are segments of the industry that have benefited from these shifts and what you need to know about them:

A SPA FOR EVERY TASTE

People are busier and bigger than ever. So it's not surprising that one of the new national pastimes involves destressing and exercise. The number of Americans who went to a spa has doubled every two years for the past decade. It's become hard to find an upscale hotel without a "spa," but what exactly is the definition of a spa?

It seems it's everything from a fitness monastery in the middle of a desert to a glorified gym with a cramped locker room. There are books written on the subject of how to find the right spa for you, but we suggest just checking out the Web site **Spafinders.com,** which breaks them down by specialty and location. Because of the increased competition in recent years, most spas have started targeting niche markets (the bigger the spa, the more niches they're after). *The Wall Street Journal* has written about some, so here is a quick summary of what we've found:

EXECUTIVES

For execs, spas are pitching full-service visits, with room, meals and massages—plus extras for the rich and hurried. In Dallas, Cooper Aerobics' program teaches execs how to order healthy room-service food and get a good night's rest. And at Canyon Ranch, the Executive Health Program that targets what it calls the "O" market (CEOs, CFOs and COOs) gives hours of consultations with staff doctors, nutritionists, exercise physiologists and even a behaviorist.

TEENS

At SPAhhht, a teen spa at the San Antonio Hyatt Regency, there's nail art, brightly colored rooms with lava lamps and a disco soundtrack. The spa at Loews Coronado Bay Resort in San Diego offers temporary hair coloring and body jewelry, and it also does birthday parties. Nearby, the Hotel del Coronado has a "Lucky Chick" package for teen girls—including a massage, pedicure, facial and manicure—that has a lower price than the adult version of the package, but also shorter treatment times.

PET LOVERS

The Golden Door Spa at the Peaks in Telluride, Colorado; offers dogs a pick-me-up bath, followed up by an oatmeal shampoo, haircut, a 15-minute massage and a "pawdicure." W Hotels in New York is targeting pets as are others, including Loews Coronado Bay and California's Ojai Valley Inn & Spa, which is considering adding pet massages soon. And at Rosewood Hotel's Las Ventanas al Paraiso in Los Cabos, Mexico, dogs get in-room massages that last 50 minutes.

MEN

Some hotels and resorts are trying to lure the holdouts with rugged marketing pitches playing up "adventure," "survival" or "challenge" programs. Canyon Ranch now has a Golf Boot Camp; Miraval Spa in Catalina, California, is pitching its new "Conquering Your Inner Everest" program to men particularly, with a 7,700-foot mountain climb and lessons in starting fires with two sticks. And Red Mountain Spa in Utah offers a Slickrock Survival Massage.

MEDICAL

Dash in for a CAT scan between rounds of golf. The Ojai Valley Inn & Spa, Ojai, California, includes holistic treatments that come with its packages, while a one-day "express" package at the La Quinta Resort &

Club's WellMax Center involves eight hours of testing: ultrasounds, biofeedback and a bone-density scan. Canyon Ranch in Arizona offers a sleep wellness plan, which is aimed at people with sleep disorders.

ANTI-AGING

A number of spas and resorts are now offering anti-aging vacations. One option is "Optimal Aging" at Canyon Ranch Health Resort in Tucson, Arizona—a seven-night program with lectures, blood tests and a visit with a doctor. Bone and heart scans, genetic and other tests are available, but cost extra. At the Red Mountain Spa, in Utah, guests get daily guided hikes, fitness classes and lectures. Massages, facials, "real" age assessment, visits with a nutritionist and a chiropractor and medical tests are extra.

The Mountain of Youth Spa and Yoga Retreat, in Georgia, has a six-day program that includes 12 hours of lectures on diet, exercise and supplements, as well as white-water rafting, hiking and horseback riding. The Maui Wellness Institute at the Wailea Marriott Resort, Maui, has blood tests and consultation with a nutritionist, as well as advice on diet and exercise programs that are purported to boost levels of human growth hormone. Just a note about spa food: Remember when spa cuisine meant tiny portions on big plates? After years of counting calories and pushing health, spas are moving into comfort food in a huge way, with deli dishes, five-star desserts and all-you-can-eat pasta bars.

To find out what they're serving, *The Wall Street Journal* went on an eating tour of some of the country's top spas—and at a lab tested the meals for fat and calorie counts. Our biggest discovery: just how fattening a lot of the stuff was—and how wrong the menu calorie counts were. Of the 17 dishes we tested, the spas had undercounted the calories by more than 10 percent in more than half of the cases. Some had twice as many calories as advertised. So if it looks too good to be true, it probably is.

THEME PARKS

The problem: Your kids are crazy about theme parks, but your wallet isn't. The solution: These days, you can easily drop a couple hundred dollars just getting your family in the door. But there are a variety of ways to trim the bill, from half-off deals at some water parks after 4 P.M., to annual passes for frequent visitors. **CityPass.com** bundles admission to a handful of attractions in a particular region. (The Southern California pass, for example, which includes SeaWorld and the San Diego Zoo, costs $172, versus $248 if you buy the tickets separately.)

While Automobile Association of America cardholders automatically get 10 percent off at many theme parks, they can get fatter discounts by calling their AAA regional office. **MouseSavers .com** and **DisBoards.com**, both run by Disney aficionados, have trip-strategy message boards. (An example from MouseSavers: Disney vacation packages generally save you little, if any, money.) **ThemeParkInsider.com** has theme-park reviews and safety reports. Besides price, the other problem with amusement parks are long lines. About two dozen of America's 450 major parks have recently devised systems for shortening lines, including Disney's "Fastpass" and Universal's "Express" system, both of which let customers reserve ride times. Universal Studios Orlando has a "no line, no wait" policy for its resort guests, who need only flash their room keys to get to the front. Meanwhile, Six Flags Over Georgia is handing pagers to parkgoers, beeping them when it's their turn to board.

There are other ways to beat the system: Disney has VIP Tours, which for $125 an hour will get you special parade views, seats in private train cars, restaurant reservations and help navigating the system. The resort also hands out "special-assistance passes," some of which go to people with "hidden impairments," like endurance problems or bad eyesight; they also tend to wind up in the hands of the biggest whiners. You can stay on the special concierge floors of the Disney resorts, which, for a fee above the price of a standard Disney hotel room, gets you VIP seating at character breakfasts without calling ahead, and free breakfast, hors d'oeuvres, desserts and drinks on your floor. Occasionally, a concierge with the right contacts can get you back-door access to some attractions, or reservations at fully booked restaurants.

An alternative to traditional amusement parks are water parks, which are attracting about 50 million people a year. More elaborate ones keep popping up all across the country, like the $22 million park

ROLLER-COASTER RESOURCES

Site: ROLLER COASTER DATA BASE; RCDB.COM/

Description: Run by fans who have compiled a wealth of oddball facts about their objects of devotion

Ease of Use: Digital photos pop up quickly. To help plan road trips, the site calculates travel distances.

Comment: Top choice. Want to know a coaster's G-force? It's here. Also lists slowpokes, like Spacely's Sprocket Rockets, at 18 mph.

Site: ULTIMATE ROLLERCOASTER; ULTIMATEROLLERCOASTER.COM

Description: Forums where coaster fans can air gripes and sing praises

Ease of Use: Detailed list of coasters and specs. Even lists the most-visited. Top of the list: The Incredible Hulk.

Comment: Good flavor of the obsessive side. Latest feature: a funny forum on the best place to sit.

Site: AMERICAN COASTER ENTHUSIASTS; ACEONLINE.ORG

Description: Web site of the ACE, formed in 1978 after movie *Roller Coaster*, starring Henry Fonda

Ease of Use: Easy access to news about new openings and ride promotions, but not as speedy as other sites

Comment: Thorough reporting on new coasters, plus coaster memorabilia. A $50 membership gets discounts and entry into special events.

Site: ROLLER COASTER AND AMUSEMENT PARK INFORMATION; ROLLERCOASTERWORLD.COM

Description: Run by a loose-knit group of fanatics

Ease of Use: Handy map lets you click on a region to search for nearby rides.

Comment: Good photos—plus amateur video footage of some coasters. It's also one of the few sites with updates on coaster accidents.

Site: ROLLERCOASTERFANS.COM

Description: Fan-run site for people to describe their favorite thrills

Ease of Use: Fans write in a cutesy way, but it ends up reading a bit like "How I spent my summer vacation."

Comment: Not a wild ride. Photos are okay, but information is disorganized and the site lacks depth.

Source: Amusement Business

Dolly Parton built in Tennessee, and Splash Island, a Georgia attraction that lets folks battle with water cannons in a "rain fortress." The big draw in Traverse City, Michigan: a new year-round indoor park where children get soaked by a colossal bucket while Mom's at the Aveda spa next door. A few to check out: Lake Lanier Islands in Atlanta; Noah's Ark in Wisconsin Dells, Wisconsin; Blizzard Beach in Orlando, Florida; Schlitterbahn in New Braunfels, Texas; and Knott's Soak City in Buena Park, California.

CRUISES: SAILING NEW WATERS

Cruise travel was dramatically altered by the events of September 11; cruise lines took ships away from Europe and the Mediterranean and rerouted them to the Caribbean, Mexico, Hawaii and New England. Tapping into fears about straying too far from home, the companies added ships leaving from ports like New Orleans; Galveston, Texas; and Jacksonville, Florida. Though they're moving back toward Europe this year, the top summer destination is now Alaska—in theory, it couldn't get much safer than that.

Just like the hotel industry, the cruise industry is divided between luxury and moderate brands. The best single source of information on what's out there is at the Cruise Line International Association's Web site, **cruising.org**. Cruise aficionados always talk about the ship's "personality," and the importance of finding the one that suits you.

For those put off by the mainstream cruise lines, with their 3,000-passenger mega-ships and belly-flop contests in the swimming pool, the luxury lines offer a more exclusive environment. Typically the ships are much smaller—as few as 100 or so passengers in some cases—and routinely have a crew-to-passenger ratio of nearly one-to-one. (It's closer to three-to-one on mass-market ships.) And forget about stuffy, windowless cabins. Often the suites come equipped with features such as whirlpool tubs, complimentary minibars and 24-hour room service—even Bulgari toiletries in the bathrooms. While some mass-market cruises sound like a bargain by comparison, they often lure passengers with lead-in prices as low as $199, but then charge full price for everything from poolside piña coladas to soft drinks at lunch.

Prices at many luxury lines already include all that, as well as tips. Within the luxury segment there are differences in ship sizes, cabins and onboard activities. Seabourn, a luxury unit of cruise giant Carnival Corp., and Carnival-owned sister brand Windstar Cruises run 200-passenger and 300-passenger ships, with Windstar drawing more active vacationers who prefer to go kayaking or sailboating; Silversea's ships can slip into exotic ports such as tiny Portofino, in Italy.

There's been a glut of luxury ships that were ordered during the booming 90s, only to come into service in 2003 as travelers were staying away amid terrorism fears, shipboard virus outbreaks and the sluggish economy. Altogether, by January 2004 the luxury lines had added more than 4,000 berths—a nearly 50 percent jump in just over a year. That's put pressure on prices, and while they've been down and then up and then down (and then up), the net effect has been more access for people who couldn't have afforded them before.

To attract these folks, some luxury lines are doing a bit of a makeover to combat a snooty image and expand their appeal beyond their traditional base of well-to-do retirees. Seabourn is introducing more "adventure" shore excursions, including one that lets passengers climb to the top of the 1,650-foot-high Harbour Bridge in Sydney. (Participants are first required to pass a breath test for blood-alcohol level.) Crystal has relaxed its dinner-dress requirements, cutting back on formal nights that require gowns and tuxedos.

You may not want to cruise in winter, but that's the best time to start looking for deals; cruise operators try to jumpstart their bookings by offering discounts for the spring season. Most of the deals are on the most-traveled routes—these days, Alaska and the Caribbean. But before paying, be sure to ask what the added charges will be.

Should you book online of through a travel agent? It depends. It's always a good idea to check with one of the big cruising agencies (see a list on **cruising.org**) first, because they often hold reserved blocks of space at a reduced rate. And for people who have traveled with a particular line before, cruise lines sometimes will offer discounts or onboard credits to repeat travelers.

People who aren't certain what type of ship suits them best, or who want guidance on itineraries, might want to stick with a travel agent. But for travelers who aren't intimidated by doing their own research on ports-of-call and all the various cabin types, there's **Priceline.com, Travelocity.com, Expedia.com, cruise411.com, my cruisevalue.com** and **Icruise.com.**

Just like travel agents, the online agencies can negotiate rates with the individual cruise lines based on the volume of bookings they make; when you check prices and availability online, you are seeing real-time information direct from the cruise line for all of their available cruises. The attraction of the Web sites is their vastly improved booking tools, which now allow shoppers to see "live inventory," meaning they can see in real time which cabin they are booking. Travelocity allows shoppers to look on each deck to see which cabins are available and check to see if they are close to the gym or the buffet table, depending on priorities. For those who still want the hand-holding, check to make sure the online agents have call centers to handle questions—or to do the entire booking. There is a downside to trying to book online: If you make a mistake and run into problems, don't expect as much help from a Web site.

And don't expect much sympathy from us if you get sick. It's no secret that in recent years there have been a plethora of gastrointestinal viruses and other flulike outbreaks on the high seas. You can always check the results of health inspections for a particular ship by going to the Centers for Disease Control's Web site, **cdc.gov**, and looking under "Traveler's Health." The most common problem health inspectors find is improperly chlorinated drinking water, so if you must go, bring your own bottled water.

SCENES FROM THE CRUISE FRONTIER
by Raymond Sokolov

"I may vomit," I muttered to myself as I dug into my first meal on the Carnival Cruise Lines's *Fascination.*

Along with some 2,000 other passengers embarking in Miami for a four-day cruise to Key West and Cozumel, I had decided to entrust my gastrointestinal health to a ship that recently arrived in port with 200 cases of Norwalk-like virus. Those travelers and crew, along with similar sufferers on several other cruise vessels, spent two to three days with severe abdominal pains and explosive nausea.

I shoveled in the fried calamari slathered with sauce gribiche. Not crisp and way bland, but free. Well, there was no extra charge. And that is the big lure on board any cruise ship: Once you've got your ticket and passed through the security, which for my trip included a mandatory photo, you can eat all you want.

All day and all night.

"This sure isn't a Weight Watchers vacation," said a matron escaping the winter chill of Canton, Ohio.

Had she considered canceling her reservation because of the recent news?

"Oh, no," she said at the breakfast counter the first morning, while collecting her cooked-to-order omelet-with-everything (orange cheese shreds, mushrooms, onion). "I figure half of them were psychosomatic. But they sure did make the price right."

Like the preponderance of the guests, her body type could be described as "hefty." And the *Fascination* offered her and the rest of us many, many opportunities to stay that way. All afternoon, we wolfed down cheeseburgers, beef Stroganoff and roast turkey from steam-table service lines that reminded the college graduates among us of dormitory food. (Food, of course, isn't the only way Norwalk-like viruses can be transmitted, and for its part, Carnival says it has taken aggressive steps to disinfect the ship since the flare-up. "Everything is back to normal," it says.)

For the line-averse, there were tables of Technicolor cheesecakes and even buffets with less-fattening selections. But I never saw anyone go near one of them. On the other hand, the self-service ice-cream machine (pull a lever and vanilla, chocolate, or a mix of both pours into your cone) had plenty of takers. Like piglets at the teat, we learned to pull and get our food fix.

Coffee and hot chocolate were also available from machines out in the Coconut Grove Bar & Grill, a jungle of faux coconut palms with faux coconuts dangling under their faux fronds. For some reason, the coffee came out in an insipid stream for as long as you pushed the button, but signs warned you to push only once for the hot chocolate. Naturally, I tried both, before retiring for a nap in my lowest-deck, aftmost stateroom.

Speaking of drink, the *Fascination* didn't discourage the consumption of alcoholic beverages, unless you tried to bring your own aboard. Bottles purchased ashore were "held" for you until debarkation in Miami. (The exception: Passengers can bring along wine, but a $10 corkage fee applies.) But the sky was the limit at the seven bars throughout the public areas of the ship. Just hand the barkeep your Sign and Sail card and let the good times roll. Help Carnival Cruise Lines celebrate "30 Years of Fun" on this Fun Cruise, with a special Fun drink—fuchsia, fruity and complete with an umbrella and a special glass that you could keep.

Dinner takes place in two dining rooms, the Imagination and the Sensation. (Why does Carnival Cruise Lines choose names that sound like cheap perfume?) I am assigned to the early (5:45!) seating at table 210. Several empty seats separate me from a lively single woman stuffed into a decollete dress.

Across from me, watching the night fall over the ocean from the window at our elbows, was a retiree mourning the death of his girlfriend. We shared a bottle of excellent Spanish wine expertly served by our genial waiter, Junior. The menu was extensive and fun, if not grandiose, in a style popular during my long-ago youth.

Some of this fare tasted as if it had been prepared back then and resuscitated. Snails in garlic butter were tepid instead of sizzling. Then came the beef Wellington. Not since the heyday of Jack Paar had I put knife and fork to a slice of filet of beef coated with faux foie gras and baked in pastry.

Fascination's beef was tender, tasty and medium rare, as promised. The pastry was limp and tough, and the dark matter around the meat was an instant reminder of the Norwalk-like future we all risked. "Our food consistently gets very high reviews from our guests," says a Carnival spokesman, who also said that ending my trip early in Key West, as I had, didn't give me enough feel for the food.

As for my health: At one point I felt queasy, after passing through the various nightclubs and the casino glittering with neon, and finally reaching *Fascination*'s most extravagant space, the multistoried Grand Atrium. It was a mistake to look down this glittering space, this dizzying shaft of glass-fronted elevators and colored lights and a menacing sculpture of giant skewers leaning against each other and stretching from the floor far below almost all the way upward.

Was my tummy hip-hopping because of dinner or the atrial décor? Since nothing happened, and I was able to consume three slices of pizza at 11 P.M. from the 24-hour facility at the end of the aft bar on the Lido deck, I concluded that it was the gaudy lighting.

Back in my room, settling in, I suddenly remembered the afternoon's lifeboat drill and really felt ill. Between the closing of lunch service and dinnertime, they'd made us put on our international orange life jackets and assemble at various "muster" points, without benefit of elevators for the several-deck climb. The jackets included a whistle, which I blew, just to test it.

That was just before they warned us to keep the whistles out of our mouths because they might contain traces of hundreds of previous whistle-blowers. They didn't mention that one of those guests might have been a Norwalk carrier. And what if that victim had sweated into the jacket, just as I was? Pictures rushed to mind of a cruise-ship captain during the epidemic refusing to touch passengers. I took a shower as soon as the drill was over.

And then I went to dinner.

TRAVELING WITH KIDS
(AND WITHOUT THEM)

Kids. They can make or break a vacation.

But propelled by demand from the travel-happy baby-boom generation—in the midst of its own baby boomlet—segments of these industries that once merely tolerated traveling families are now bending over backward to make them feel welcome.

Business and luxury hotels are adding elaborate day-care programs. Pricey resorts in such places as San Diego and Hawaii are providing the equivalent of day camps to amuse Junior while parents spend the day golfing or snorkeling. And some cruise lines, once the preserve of honeymooners and swinging singles, have started to market themselves aggressively as a family-vacation alternative. One Web site, **thecruiseplanner.com,** devotes a section to up-to-date kids' programs that lines like Carnival Cruises now offer.

Club Med, whose specialty is fixed-price, all-inclusive vacations at its own resorts, began sniffing the winds of change in the early 1980s. Since then, it has essentially reshaped itself from a sort of free-spirited summer camp for singles to a leader in the family-vacation market. More than half of Club Med's clients these days are married couples. As of this writing, 14 of its worldwide destinations offer special programs—from Circus School to face painting—designed to entice parents by keeping their children busy. You can find them on the family travel link at **clubmed.com.**

We found three particularly useful Web sites that cover the gamut of family travel, from booking cruises to luxury hotels to safaris:

familytraveltimes.com, havechildrenwilltravel.com and **www.family travelnetwork.com.**

And finally, for families taking their kids to adventurous places, there's the federal Centers for Disease Control Web site at **cdc.gov/ travel/child_travel.htm.** It literally covers every country in the world that Americans can legally travel to and tells you, for example, what vaccinations you'll need if traveling to Kenya, or whether their have been any worrisome breakouts of contagious diseases in places like Zambia.

However . . .

If you want to avoid kids, there *are* a goodly number of adult-only resorts; most mean no kids under 21, though it's best to check. Some resorts, such as Sandals, with hotels throughout the Caribbean, allow "kids," 18 and older.

You can find scads of adults-only providers on the Internet. A few helpful Web sites: **lovetripper.com, signaturevacations.com** and, if you are feeling a little daring, **nudetravelguide.com.**

And then you can find hotels and resorts that don't ban kids but don't get very many of them. Your best bet is to look for places that stress "romantic" and "quiet" or cost an arm and a leg—in other words, go for a B&B, a small upscale inn or a five-star hotel where the rates generally mean a clientele of business executives or wealthy vacationers who've left Junior with the nanny. An increasing number of hotels and resorts also have adults-only pools and floors, so that's always an option.

ADVENTURE TRAVEL: WALKING ON THE WILD SIDE

Are you ready to be a "heli-hiker," dropped in a remote site by helicopter in the Bugaboo Mountains of British Columbia?

Ask your doctor. If he says okay, contact a travel-medicine clinic and the Centers for Disease Control and Prevention in Atlanta (**cdc.gov**) for current information on health situations where you're going. In many places in South America, for example, there's no malaria and you'd be wasting your money on malaria pills. But a doctor not associated with travel medicine may not know that. Adventure travelers are also advised to purchase travel insurance that covers trip cancellation and interruption as well as emergency medical evacuation.

It can be bought from the outfitter, a travel agent or directly from such companies as Access America, in Richmond, Virginia; TravelGuard, in Stevens Point, Wisconsin or Singapore-based International SOS.

Travel insurance also prevents you from losing a bundle on a Chilean rafting trip if your Santiago flight was cancelled because of a Miami thunderstorm or if you pull a muscle trying to get in shape for a trip and can't go. For travelers who haven't biked since they were kids or have never walked six or eight miles a day on successive days, conditioning is key. The pros advise starting a conditioning regimen two to three months before your trip and trying a weekend trip or two before plunging into, say, an intense two-week backpacking expedition.

It isn't easy choosing among the glossy brochures and fantastic Web sites of competing adventure-travel companies. There are blue-chip firms such as Mountain Travel–Sobek, Butterfield & Robinson, the Wayfarers and Backroads. And there are smaller companies such as Above the Clouds Trekking, Salmon River Outfitters, The Northwest Passage and Distant Journeys (see below for location and contact information).

Regardless of whom you choose, find out how long they've been in business, what their clients' average age is and what equipment they use. When a company like Backroads tells you that they replace their fleet of 1,500 Cannondale 21-speed hybrid bikes every two years, you can be reasonably sure that you won't get a clunker. Companies usually rate their trips from "easy" to "moderate" to "strenuous." But these terms are relative, since there are no industrywide standards. An outfit such as Backroads might have three daily distances on a "moderate" bike trip, pegged at 30, 40 and 50 miles, for example, in order to accommodate a wide range of participants. Ask the operator in detail what those ratings mean.

THE "SOFT-ADVENTURE" OPTION

Some operators who once specialized in white-knuckle white-water rafting trips are switching gears to lure families. A string quartet serenades floating travelers with Handel and Mozart during the eight-day "Classical Music River Journey" from Bill Dvorak's Kayak & Rafting Expeditions in Colorado. Several outfitters—including Dvorak, Class VI and Wilderness Tours in Foresters Falls, Ontario—are adding "activity guides" to play games and teach environmental awareness to children. Some others: Wilderness Tours family trips and Rocky Mountain

Adventures (carrier pigeons fly film from the river to a developer so pictures are ready when travelers come ashore).

Tip: Google "soft adventures" and the place or area you want to go and you're very likely to find some providers.

ADVENTURE TRAVEL COMPANIES

Above the Clouds

Specialty: Takes small groups to Nepal, Bhutan and other points in central Asia, but also ventures to such rural European backwaters as the Dios in France

Contact: Hinesburg, Vermont, 800-482-4848

Web site: abovetheclouds.com

Backroads

Specialty: "The World's #1 Active Travel Company," as it calls itself, has hundreds of well-planned biking, hiking and multisport trips worldwide

Contact: Berkeley, Calif., 800-462-2848

Web site: backroads.com

Butterfield & Robinson

Specialty: B&R conceived the idea of the yuppie bicycling and walking vacation more than 30 years ago and brings well-heeled travelers to places like Tuscany, Provence and Morocco

Contact: Toronto, Canada, 800-678-1147

Web site: butterfield.com

Ciclismo Classico

Specialty: Dedicated to cycling and hiking in Europe and parts of New England

Contact: Arlington, Massachusetts, 800-866-7314

Web site: ciclismoclassico.com

Distant Journeys

Specialty: You carry your own packs on their coast-to-coast walk in England and stay in rustic huts while hiking around Mont Blanc in France

Contact: Camden, Maine, 888-845-5781

Web site: distantjourneys.com

Geographic Expeditions

Specialty: Culturally savvy trips to Botswana, Sri Lanka and Patagonia, as well as expedition-style trips to islands like South Georgia

Contact: San Francisco, California, 800-777-8183

Web site: geoex.com

Mountain Travel–Sobek

Specialty: From Galapagos cruises to African safaris to trekking in Mongolia, Mountain Travel has been taking people hiking, climbing and rafting since 1969

Contact: El Cerrito, California, 888-687-6235

Web site: mtsobek.com

The Northwest Passage

Specialty: They go to Crete and Baffin Island but they also cover the oft overlooked Midwest, with sea kayaking in Lake Superior and hiking in the Porcupines of Michigan

Contact: Wilmette, Illinois, 800-732-7328

Web site: nwpassage.com

REI Adventures

Specialty: Aimed at fit but price-sensitive travelers, with a range of hiking and sea kayaking trips to the Rockies, Europe, Asia and South America

Contact: Sumner, Washington, 800-622-2236

Web site: rei.com/adventures/

Salmon River Outfitters

Specialty: They offer six-day, 80-mile trips along Idaho's Salmon River from June through September, featuring gourmet cooking and "Wilderness Wine Tasting"

Contact: Donnelly, Idaho, 800-346-6204

Web site: salmonriveroutfitters.com

Tauck Worldwide Discovery

Specialty: Soft adventure and cushy accommodations, featuring Canadian heli-hiking, African safaris and Galapagos cruises

Contact: Westport, Connecticut, 800-788-7885

Web site: tauck.com

Unicorn Expeditions

Specialty: White-water rafting, snowmobiling and cross-country ski vacations deep in the Maine woods

Contact: Lake Parlin, Maine, 800-864-2676

Web site: www.unicornexpeditions.com

The Wayfarers

Specialty: Synonymous with classic English walking trips to the Lake District, but they also go afield to Tuscany and New Zealand

Contact: Newport, Rhode Island, 800-249-4620

Web site: thewayfarers.com

CHAPTER FOUR

LOGISTICS

THE NUTS AND BOLTS OF TRAVEL

I f there's one thing insurance insures, it's confusion. But to clarify matters . . .

UNWINDING TRAVEL INSURANCE

When it comes to travel insurance there are two kinds: "travel medical" policies, which offer more medical coverage than basic policies—but usually no refunds if the trip is cancelled or interrupted—and "medical transport" policies, which offer emergency medical evacuation on a private plane. And since the September 11 attacks, insurers have added bells and whistles to many of these policies—for instance, beefed-up 24-hour emergency-assistance programs, once available only in a few policies, now are included in many of them.

The services extend beyond the basics they have always offered—helping travelers find a doctor, pharmacy or clinic, or arrange medical evacuation. They include pre-trip health advisories and, in response to growing concerns about terrorism, security warnings. One provider, Travel Guard Group, Inc., even offers to change flights and hotel reservations if you decide to leave at a moment's notice, and will track lost luggage through a hotline.

Yet as the options grow, the fine print is getting finer. While package policies are ideal for older adults because they include trip cancellation, they generally provide $50,000 or less in medical coverage. Travelers going on a trip of a month or more, or on several trips throughout the year, might want to supplement the package policy with a travel medical policy.

Hospitalization overseas can be hugely expensive, and these policies provide as much as $2 million in medical coverage for travel of up to a year in length. Most of the policies won't cover medical problems that have previously occurred within a specified time—usually one to five years—preceding the purchase of a policy. A few plans do offer as much as $2,500 of coverage for an "acute onset" of a continuing condition. The benefits under such plans also decline the older a traveler is: A plan offering coverage of up to $1 million for a traveler age 70 or under would drop to a maximum of $50,000 or $100,000 for those over 70, and then to as low as $10,000 for a traveler over 80.

Similar benefits and restrictions apply to multitrip medical policies, which offer medical coverage for multiple trips of as long as 15, 30 or 70 days throughout one year. Geared to travelers taking three or more trips a year, the plans offer as much as $1 million in coverage.

Benefits also decline with age. Because they don't include refunds for cancelled trips, they, too, work best as a supplement to a package policy.

For those who are headed to the jungle and really want to ensure they can be airlifted to safety, a medical transport or medical evacuation plan might be a good bet. Most package or travel medical policies already include some coverage for evacuation. But the evacuation is made at the doctor's and insurer's discretion, and is usually made by commercial jet.

Medical transport policies from companies like Medjet International Inc., based in Birmingham, Alabama, or International SOS Assistance, Inc., Singapore, offer patients a greater say in the timing, and most times transport is in a state-of-the-art, medically staffed jet. And in these uncertain times, an increasing number of package and medical policies are offering perks geared toward travelers feeling uneasy about staying abroad. One example is Travel Guard's "Livetravel," its 24-hour hotline for making emergency travel changes, like rebooking flights if you find yourself in need of a quick getaway because you're in a country that has suddenly turned into a hot spot.

Now there are also policies for protection against terrorist attacks—particularly a domestic terrorist attack. Basic plans typically let travelers cancel a trip and get their money back if there is a terrorist act in their departure city, their destination city or sometimes anywhere in the country they are traveling to. The cost of such coverage ranges from roughly 5 to 8 percent of a total trip's cost. These policies also typically pay medical expenses on the road, such as the cost of getting you home if you have a medical emergency. Lost luggage is also covered.

Policies vary widely, and there are sometimes details hidden in the fine print that could make the several-hundred-dollar investment pointless. Some, for instance, won't cover you if there is a gathering of more than 50,000 people (think the Olympics) in the city you are visiting. Others deny coverage if you're in the air or on the water—not exactly a comfort in a time of worries about stinger missiles and shoe bombs. In addition, no travel-insurance policy covers acts of war, only acts of terror.

For people who are passionate about hitting the road, travel coverage can make sense under some circumstances. The main question is whether your airline and hotel will let you change your plans in the event of a terror attack. Some hotels and resorts are dropping cancellation fees, too.

Buying travel insurance may also make sense for people whose health-care plans specify that they won't cover medical care overseas. The plans can be bought directly from an insurer's Web site, through a travel agent or through an online broker who compares a range of policies. The main variables are the age of the buyer and the price of the trip. It generally doesn't affect the price significantly if you buy the plans online rather than from a travel agent.

Some variables to watch out for:

1. Does the policy include domestic as well as international travel? Even if you are heading abroad, you might want domestic coverage if your itinerary includes layovers or flight changes at U.S. airports.

2. Look for policies with the most liberal cancellation terms. For instance, if terrorists strike, some policies will let you cancel only if you are departing within 10 days of the attack. But other policies will let you cancel a trip even after 30 days.

3. Check the policy to be sure it doesn't exclude your destinations on a technicality. Access America provides both international and domestic coverage for any terrorist event within 30 days before your departure. But it also has a clause that if you are going someplace that suffered an attack in the past six months you aren't covered.

Some policies also require you to buy the insurance within seven to fifteen days of making your first payment on the trip, in order to receive the terrorism coverage. Some insurers don't want customers to try to snap up policies at the last minute if global terrorism fears heat up.

Many insurers have also revised their coverage to protect you if your airline goes out of business—which can bring some peace of mind, considering the airline industry's financial woes. But check whether any airlines are excluded: Some insurers won't sell policies for people flying on carriers that are operating under Chapter 11 bankruptcy protection.

HEALTH: TRAVELING SAFELY ABROAD

To become a more prepared traveler, you can go to a host of Web sites and organizations for information about needed inoculations and

A RUNDOWN OF THE DIFFERENT TYPES OF TRAVEL INSURANCE

PACKAGE POLICIES
DESIGNED FOR TRAVELERS GOING ON A SINGLE TRIP

Pros: Offer a wide range of benefits, including trip cancellation, up to $50,000 in medical coverage, accidental-death coverage and emergency evacuation. Also include 24-hour traveler assistance and baggage-delay protection. Policies purchased within seven to fifteen days may also cover preexisting medical conditions.

Cons: Limit of $50,000 in medical coverage may not be enough for trips longer than one month.

MEDICAL TRANSPORT POLICIES
Medical evacuation—Supplement to package policy and/or travel medical policy

Pros: Medical evacuation to the hospital of your choice from virtually anywhere in the world, usually in a medically staffed jet

Cons: Insurance covers transport from hospital to hospital only. Medical coverage, or other trip coverage, not included.

TRAVEL MEDICAL POLICIES
MEDICAL COVERAGE FOR TRAVEL UP TO A YEAR IN LENGTH. GOOD SUPPLEMENT TO A PACKAGE POLICY, BUT DOESN'T COVER ALL TRAVEL NEEDS ALONE.

Pros: Lots of medical coverage: up to $2 million, depending on the policy. Some policies also include coverage for evacuation and accidental death. Most also offer 24-hour traveler assistance.

Cons: Trip cancellation not included. Most policies won't cover medical problems for which you've been treated in the past one to five years. Amount of medical coverage is determined by the age of the traveler, and amount declines sharply after age 70.

MULTITRIP MEDICAL POLICIES
ANNUAL MEDICAL COVERAGE FOR MULTIPLE TRIPS THROUGHOUT THE YEAR, WITH TRIPS RESTRICTED TO 15, 30 OR 70 DAYS. GOOD SUPPLEMENT TO A PACKAGE POLICY, BUT DOESN'T COVER ALL TRAVEL NEEDS ALONE.

Pros: Lots of medical coverage—up to $1 million, depending on the policy. Some policies also include coverage for evacuation and accidental death. Most also offer 24-hour traveler assistance.

Cons: Trip cancellation not included. Most policies won't cover existing medical problems. Amount of medical coverage is determined by the age of the traveler, and amount declines sharply after age 70.

PICKING A TERRORISM INSURANCE POLICY

 Companies are beefing up their terrorism coverage for travelers. Here are some major providers:

ACCESS AMERICA/ACCESSAMERICA.COM
Distinguishing Features: Policies have strict limits: They won't cover biological, chemical or nuclear attacks, and you're not covered if you go someplace where a big event like the Olympics is happening.

CSA TRAVEL PROTECTION/CSATRAVELPROTECTION.COM
Distinguishing Features: Some policies go so far as to pay off even if you are forced to cancel a trip because a nontraveling relative gets sick—even if it's due to a preexisting condition.

HTH WORLDWIDE/HTHTRAVELINSURANCE.COM
Distinguishing Features: Like many policies, it offers online access to security and health information. Also provides security alerts; security profiles by destination (including risk of crime and terrorism); emergency numbers for doctors and hospitals.

TRAVELEX INSURANCE SERVICES/TRAVELEXINSURANCE.COM
Distinguishing Features: Children under 16 get free coverage if dependent and accompanied with an adult who has purchased the travel insurance.

TRAVEL GUARD/TRAVELGUARD.COM
Distinguishing Features: Doesn't require the State Department to issue a travel warning before coverage of terrorist acts kicks in.

TRAVEL INSURED INTERNATIONAL/TRAVELINSURED.COM
Distinguishing Features: Covers terrorist events only that are included in State Department warnings. Therefore, this is only international coverage.

TRAVELSAFE INSURANCE/TRAVELSAFE.COM
Distinguishing Features: Has a broad policy to protect you if your airline goes out of business—and unlike other policies, even extends its coverage to carriers that are already operating under bankruptcy-law protection, such as USAirways and United.

health dangers around the world, as well as area hospitals, doctors and pharmacies. The first step is to find out what medical dangers, if any, there are and take measures to prevent them. Inoculations against an assortment of contagious diseases are a necessity if you are traveling in Latin America, Africa or Asia. Travelers also need to be aware of any outbreaks of disease (such as the SARS virus, which struck in Toronto and parts of Asia in 2003), food-borne illnesses, heat waves and floods, as well as the safety of the drinking water.

Web sites for the World Health Organization (**who.int**) and the federal Centers for Disease Control and Prevention (**cdc.gov/travel**) have data on disease outbreaks and epidemics around the world. The CDC also lists countries where travelers need inoculations or prophylactic medications, as well as advice for pregnant women, the disabled and breast-feeding mothers.

Taking precautions for existing illnesses also is key. If you have a medical problem, travel experts recommend that before starting your trip, you should find a doctor in the area where you will be staying. And you should take along medical records, or at least a list of illnesses and the medications.

The U.S. Department of State's Web site (**state.gov**) publishes lists of hospitals and doctors in dozens of countries and cities, including Austria, Botswana, Estonia and Ethiopia. U.S. consular offices where you're traveling can also prove helpful in finding doctors. Paying for any medical care when you find it, though, is your responsibility. So the Department of State, insurance-industry experts and AARP, an advocacy group for senior citizens, recommend purchasing special insurance policies that cover emergency medical care outside the United States or, at the very least, the cost of airlifting a patient to a U.S. hospital.

CUTTING TO THE (RENTAL CAR) CHASE

Nothing makes travel easier in America than the ubiquitous availability of rental cars at reasonable rates.

That said, no segment of the travel industry is more difficult to decode for the bargain-minded traveler. Avis will offer you a half-dozen insurance coverages and damage waivers. Hertz touts 14 different classes of cars and 16 specialty models. Competition may be fierce but there are no industry pricing standards, so companies can and do charge differently for the exact same cars. Meanwhile, add-on fees, which fund projects such as airport expansions and sports arenas, are multiplying even as rental companies roll out new options—in-car satellite radio, GPS navigation systems and cell phones—designed to tempt you into spending more money.

Here's our no-nonsense advice on navigating the system and saving money while you do:

1. Decline the insurance: The first way to save money is to decline the extra insurance. Check first to make sure you're already covered by your own insurance and whether it covers all areas of the country and all vehicles or only the same type/value as what you already drive; you may get additional protection from your homeowners policy (for items stolen from the rental car) or health insurance (for injuries, including hospitalization). Business travelers are often covered by their companies (indeed, Dow Jones, the parent company of *The Wall Street Journal,* specifically advises its employees to decline supplemental coverage).

If you do decide to pick up the additional coverage, make sure you know what you're getting. Most rental-car companies offer personal-effects insurance, which covers theft of personal items left in the car during the rental period but typically doesn't extend to such things as documents, stamps or pets. Likewise, collision and loss-damage policies are intended to pick up the tab if a rental car is damaged or stolen, but it doesn't apply if a renter causes an accident by speeding, driving on unpaved roads or driving while intoxicated. Liability insurance also has caveats: It is supposed to kick in if someone or something other than the renter or rental car is damaged in an accident. However, rental-car companies are required by law to provide only the minimum level of liability coverage required in a given state, which could be as little as $15,000. So they often offer additional coverage of up to $1 million, which isn't necessary if a driver already has liability coverage up to that amount.

2. Book early and often. We suggest four to six weeks out, which is when you get the best combination of price and choice. Unlike airlines and hotels, rental-car firms don't charge penalties for cancellations. As a result, a good way to lock in the best deal is make a reservation early, whenever you spot a good price. Then keep shopping around, and if you see a better one, book it and cancel the first one.

3. Play the date game. During most of the year, renting vans, pickup trucks and sport-utility vehicles during the week can save money, since demand for large vehicles is higher during the weekend. Conversely, renting luxury cars such as Lincolns during weekends is cheaper because demand for those cars is higher when road warriors travel on weekdays. And like airline tickets, renting a car with a Saturday night included can save money. Remember: Sometimes a weekly rate beats the daily rate. For example, a midsize car rented from Budget Rent A Car at Dallas/Fort Worth International Airport recently was $55.99, or $279.95 for five days. The weekly rate: $144.99.

4. Know what you want. Go online to the rental-car sites and look at their fleets. If you know exactly what model you want, you can price it across rental companies. Sometimes it boils down to location. Because many rental locations in business markets, such as Chicago and Dallas, don't have lots of small cars in their fleets, often they run out of smaller vehicles. Savvy travelers can take advantage of that by reserving a subcompact or compact car and then getting a free upgrade to a midsize or full-size car at the counter. Warning: This tactic is less likely to work in leisure markets such as Florida and Hawaii, where smaller cars are more abundant.

5. Get out of the airport. Renting at the airport is convenient for fliers but add-on fees can jack up a bill 12 percent or more. Because rates and taxes in New York City are so high, thrifty renters should almost always avoid renting in the city. An intermediate-sized car from Avis rents for $81.99 a day when picked up from a Midtown Manhattan location, but taking a train ride to suburban Scarsdale yields the same type of car for nearly $20 less per day. If there are several airports in the city you're flying to, check and see which is least expensive.

6. Think small. That's small companies, not small cars. Renting from smaller regional and local rental firms such as Advantage Rent-A-Car and Payless Car Rental can be cheaper than even the no-frills major companies such as Enterprise, Dollar and Alamo Rent A Car. The downside: Smaller players often don't offer the premium services the major companies do, such as express lines and frequent-renter clubs. And local firms often don't show up on major travel Web sites. That means more research is necessary, either by looking on airport Web sites or cracking open the phone book. **Orbitz.com** offers a comprehensive listing of smaller rental firms.

7. Start online. Travel sites usually offer the broadest sampling of rates, as well as estimates of taxes and fees. With that knowledge, call the rental companies to see if they will sweeten the pot. It's always worth pushing for a deal if you spot a better price at a rival: Most companies will match it, in keeping with an industrywide push to turn telephone inquiries into sales. As a general rule, traditional travel agencies won't offer the best prices on rental cars—with one notable exception: if it's part of a larger travel package. That's because rental companies sometimes offer travel agencies deep discounts as part of all-in-one packages.

8. Grab the extras. Frequent-renter programs are generally worth the time to sign up. They offer discounts and other incentives, including express lines, free upgrades and airline frequent-flyer miles. Sometimes you can get a membership for nothing: National Car Rental offers complimentary memberships to solve customer-service problems, or to people who simply ask for it. And sometimes they waive fees for authorizing an extra driver.

9. Choose unlimited mileage and prepay for the fuel. The difference between what the rental car company charges and the rate at the pump is pretty minimal, and with all the security you have to get through at airports now, worrying about stopping at a gas station isn't worth the extra stress. Also nice to know: Most companies won't charge you an extra day if you bring the car back an hour late—but check to make sure.

10. Don't lug child car seats. For a minimal fee, companies will provide nice new ones. But you'll often have to put them in yourself because of liability issues.

PASSPORTS

This should be the first thing you think about, not the last. But if you're due to leave the country in a few weeks, and you discover your passport is out of date, there are solutions. If you live in one of the 13 major cities with a passport agency, and can prove you're leaving within two weeks, you can make a walk-in appointment. Look under "Passport Information" on the State Department's site (**travel.state.gov**) for locations, forms and rules. Cost: $115–$145; the government promises to get your passport back before you leave.

You can also express-mail your application—the State Department site has details. Cost: $115–$145, plus express-mail fees both ways; turnaround is "approximately 10 days," according to the government.

If you are in a real pinch, you can hire a passport expediter, for between $60 and $150, on top of the $115–$145 government fee; turnaround is one to seven business days, and the more you are willing to pay, the sooner you'll have your passport. Type "passport" into a search engine for a list of companies in your city.

CHAPTER FIVE

AFTER HOURS

We have a pretty simple theory about having fun: You shouldn't have to think too hard about it or spend too much time planning it. So, here, we've compiled some tricks of the trade to speed your pursuit of pleasure—whether it's wining and dining, taking in shows and movies or steeping yourself in the joys of single-malt whisky—while saving you energy and money.

DINING OUT

Most of us spend a good chunk of our entertainment budget—not only in terms of money but also time and calories—on meals in restaurants. The good news about the upscale restaurant industry is that many things are changing that make it easier to land the table you want when you want it, become a VIP, and pay less for your meal. Another upside is that not everyone knows about these changes, so you can make them work for you without a lot of competition.

LANDING THE HOTTEST TABLE IN TOWN

It used to be that the only way to get into the hottest place in town was to get tight with the maître d', who held power via his little black book. But the advent of the Internet as well as innovations in the software that restaurants use to manage their businesses has whittled away somewhat at the exclusive power of the host. Restaurants have learned that they can use their plum seats as leverage in a variety of marketing initiatives, some tied to credit-card programs, others to Web sites and some to their own in-house public-relations efforts. The upshot is that there are now a number of ways to land a table at a crowded restaurant.

CREDIT-CARD CONCIERGES

If you have an Amex Platinum card or a Visa Signature card, you can get help getting into some bona fide hip restaurants. American Express Platinum Card holders are automatically qualified for Amex's Hot Plates and Fine Dining programs. The programs make deals with restaurants in New York, Los Angeles, San Francisco and Miami to reserve one table a night for members. The restaurant in the Hot Plates program are trendy, hip places, while Fine Dining includes more formal, classic restaurants. Call 1-800-345-2639 and ask them to make a reservation for you. The list of restaurants in Hot Plates includes 1220 at the Tides, one of the trendiest restaurants in Miami, as well as Drago in Los Angeles, Bix in San Francisco and rm in New York City, while fine dining includes Alain Ducasse in New York City and Fifth Floor in San Francisco. And, of course, new restaurants are likely to be added all the time.

Visa has a similar program for Visa Signature card holders. Call 1-866-346-3847 for information. While getting help making a reservation may not be a strong enough incentive to sign up for credit card programs that sometimes come with annual fees, the reservation help can be a nice bonus if you are already a card member.

ONLINE RESERVATIONS PROGRAMS

Another surprisingly effective way to get a table at a hard-to-get-into restaurant is to use one of the online reservation systems. These programs are relatively new—**Opentable.com,** the largest and best-known service, started in 1999 and now has over 2,100 restaurants in more than 30 markets. The reason for that growth: Restaurants have a strong financial incentive to use them. The average cost to a restaurant of taking reservations by phone is about $4 (when labor and phone-line costs are factored in); by contrast, Internet reservations cost the restaurants about $1 a person. Reserving online also saves you time—it's done in seconds, as opposed to lingering on hold, listening to Muzac on the phone.

Many of the nation's top restaurants use **Opentable.com,** including Masa in San Francisco and The French Laundry in California wine country, Lutece in Las Vegas and Bouley and Craft in Manhattan. One nice feature of the service is that you can write a note along with your reservation, asking, for example, for the restaurant to call you if an earlier table opens up. Just be careful to cancel any reservations you're not going to use—each user only gets four no-shows a year before privileges are cancelled.

Also, Opentable sweetens the deal by giving you frequent-diner points every time you reserve online, which can later be redeemed for discounts on meals. If you book your seat through **Opentable.com** and then follow through and eat at the restaurant, you receive 100 points. Once you reach 1,000 points, you get a $10-off certificate from Opentable for any meal you book. The service also offers a slate of restaurants that automatically reward you 1,000 points for booking a table—these tend to be less popular restaurants, or restaurants during off-peak hours, like 6:30 or 10 P.M. You can redeem your cash in $10 increments by calling **Opentable.com** and asking them to issue you a certificate. Then you can use the certificate as if it were cash to pay the bill or part of the bill at any Opentable restaurant.

There is a little-known way to rack up Opentable points even faster. An employee at **Opentable.com** told us that while the company doesn't advertise this trick, it doesn't mind if you do it this way: Sign up on the Web site as an "administrative assistant." This option was developed for secretaries who book tables for multiple executives, but you can use it to book tables for your friends or you and a friend can always log on to this account when you book. You currently get 300 points just for setting up an account. Then all of the points that come from tables booked through the administrative assistant accrue to one account, making it easier to rack up 10,000—that's $100 off your next meal.

If you can't get the table you want through **Opentable.com,** try **Savvydiner.com.** This is a somewhat less-convenient service because you don't find out immediately whether you got your table. **Savvydiner.com** takes your request online, then calls the restaurant, and then gets back to you—like an online concierge. But it may be able to get you a table that Opentable said wasn't available: Opentable allows restaurants to "black out" certain tables automatically. **Savvydiner.com** can negotiate with the restaurant to get you the table you need.

Another option is **iseatz.com.** The benefit of this site is that while the list of restaurants is small, they tend to be high-quality places. The site also allows you to reserve at a handful of restaurants in cities that don't usually have Internet reservation options, such as Nashville and Salt Lake City.

Most of the restaurants on this site just offer an opportunity for booking, but a handful of restaurants in each city also presell a meal at a discount. For example, you can prepay a three-course meal at Cuba Libre, a popular Philadelphia restaurant, for either $36 or $30.60, if you use a MasterCard. You then print a certificate on your home printer, book your table at the restaurant and present the restaurant with the certificate when you arrive.

Caveat: If you're using Iseatz, it pays to call the restaurant before pressing the "buy" button, because the deals may be loaded with catches. In the case of Cuba Libre, the restaurant only allows you to use the certificate at 5 P.M.—something the Web site doesn't tell you when you buy. At other restaurants, like the Four Seasons in New York, you can prebuy a four-course meal for $57.38 (using Mastercard), but the hitch is that you get no choice of menu options other than what is listed on the website (as of this writing, tuna carpaccio, asparagus soup, bison filet and a soufflé). Still, despite the hitches, restaurants say the program is very popular. On a recent Saturday night, the maître' d at Wolfgang Puck's Vert in Los Angeles said he had 13 tables booked for the **iseatz.com** discount meal.

THE OLD WALK-IN TRICK

Of course, the foolproof way to get the table you want is to book way in advance, or to be flexible—accept that you can't always get a last-minute table at 8 P.M. on Saturday at the hottest place in town. But failing those options, there's always the walk-in trick. Consider this: Twelve percent of all reservations are no-shows—it's the bane of the restaurant industry. The upside for consumers is that it means that sometimes simply showing up at 8 P.M. on Saturday will land you that coveted table.

One of our writers, Katy McLaughlin, put this theory to test on a recent visit to Philadelphia. Dying to get into a hot place called Morimoto (Chef Morimoto is a star of the *Iron Chef* television show), she attempted on Thursday to book a table for Saturday night. The pickings were slim: The sole reservation on Opentable was at 9:45 P.M. She had no intention of eating that late, so included a note in her Opentable e-mail asking the restaurant to please call if something opened up. Sure enough, the restaurant called and said it could move her up an hour. But not being satisfied, she walked in at 8:00. After a 15-minute wait at the bar, she got her table.

EATING WELL AND SPENDING LESS

THIRD-PARTY DISCOUNT PROGRAMS

"We don't do discounts."

It's the biggest fib you'll hear at a fancy restaurant these days, right up there with "This is low-fat" and "Our celebrity chef cooked it himself."

High-end eateries have long disdained coupons and discounts, which conjure up images of early-bird specials and all-you-can-eat buffets. But in recent years, one of the most significant innovations in the industry is the introduction of marketing programs that shave 10 to 20 percent off your total restaurant bill at some of the nation's top

SECRET NUMBERS

If all else fails, the following list may be of some help. Many cooler-than-thou restaurants maintain secret reservations phone numbers that they don't publish. The idea is that big shots can call and land tables at the very same time that mere mortals are being told, "Sorry, we're fully booked." Unfortunately, most restaurants know that just having the phone number doesn't quite make you Brad Pitt, but having the number can at least connect you to the person controlling tables, to whom you can make your case. Here's a list of several secret numbers, plus tips on how to get in if they don't bite:

METROPOLITAN GRILL, SEATTLE
VIP Trick: Call the VIP reservation line (206) 382-3555.
Internet Reservations: Savvydiner.com
Credit-Card Concierge: AMEX Platinum Fine Dining

BALTHAZAR AND PASTIS, MANHATTAN
VIP Trick: The unlisted reservation line for both places: (212) 625-8665.
Internet Reservations: No
Credit-Card Concierge: AMEX Platinum Hot Plates

DANIEL, NEW YORK
VIP Trick: Chef Daniel Boulud, says: Ask to speak with him. Hey, he said it, so it's worth a shot.
Internet Reservations: No
Credit-Card Concierge: AMEX Platinum; Fine Dining

restaurants. Furthermore, these programs are nicely designed to eliminate the humiliation inherent in handing over a coupon to your waiter (which inevitably makes you feel like a cheapskate for the rest of the night). Some of the programs are so subtle that nobody—not even the restaurant itself—knows that you're getting a discount.

The bargains come in a variety of flavors—some through credit cards, some through the Internet and some issued directly by restaurants. Particularly generous deals are available on **Dinnerbroker.com,** which lets you shave from 10 to 30 percent off the tab at places like Palio D'Asti, an upscale Italian restaurant in downtown San Francisco or Café des Artistes in New York City by booking online. In the past year, the number of participating restaurants has jumped 23 percent, the company says, and now about half the restaurants in its roster offer

SPAGO, BEVERLY HILLS, CALIFORNIA

VIP Trick: Ask to speak with Tracey Spillane, general manager. It also pays to ask if you can introduce yourself to celebrity chef Wolfgang Puck (he of frozen smoked-salmon pizza fame)—he works the room.

Internet Reservations: Opentable.com; dinnerbroker.com

Credit-Card Concierge: Visa Infinite, Visa Signature Concierge, and AMEX Platinum

CHEZ PANISSE, BERKELEY, CALIFORNIA

VIP Trick: Ask to speak with the general manager, Gilbert Pilgram. To reserve, call exactly 30 days before you want to dine (the place doesn't take reservations farther in advance)—and make the call at 9 A.M. (it'll book up fast).

Internet Reservations: No

Credit-Card Concierge: No

UNION SQUARE CAFE, NEW YORK

VIP Trick: Owner Danny Meyer says: Eat at the bar near the maître d' station and slip him your card. Mr. Meyer says his staff, and that of other restaurants, are trained to pamper people willing to eat at the bar, because it lets them make money without using up another table.

Internet Reservations: Opentable.com

Credit-Card Concierge: AMEX Platinum; Fine Dining

THE INN AT LITTLE WASHINGTON, WASHINGTON, VIRGINIA

VIP Trick: Guests of the hotel are guaranteed a reservation.

Internet Reservations: No

Credit-Card Concierge: No

the discount option. **Table1.com** is a similar service that just operates in New York City. Neither of the services charges users a fee.

RewardsNetwork.com, formerly known as **iDine.com,** is so discreet that the restaurant doesn't even know when you pay the bill that you are reaping a discount. Instead, a sizable refund simply appears on your card a few days after the meal. Membership costs $49 a year, worthwhile for people who dine out regularly, since the discounts can far outstrip the fee. While many of the restaurants enrolled are run-of-the-mill places, it sometimes has hip, new restaurants and even famous classic places. That's because of the program's unique business structure: Rewards Networks loans restaurants money and part of the loan package is an agreement that the restaurant will provide the discount to its members. If it seems odd that hot, trendy new

THIRD-PARTY DISCOUNT PROGRAMS AT A GLANCE

THE DEAL: **DINNERBROKER.COM**

How It Works: Book online at one of about 250 places. The restaurants take 10 to 30 percent off your check.

The Catch: Most good deals require booking at off-peak times, like before 7 P.M. or after 9:30.

THE DEAL: **RESTAURANT.COM**

How It Works: Buy a discount "gift certificate" (a $50 certificate costs you only $25) on **Restaurant.com**—or bid for it on **eBay.com**. After dinner, just slip the certificate in with payment.

The Catch: Some come with restrictions, so read the fine print online before buying it.

THE DEAL: **REWARDSNETWORK.COM**

How It Works: Buy a $49 annual membership at Rewards Network. Then eat at one of about 7,000 participating places. A few days after the meal, a 10–20 percent discount will show up on your credit card.

The Catch: Rewards Network can't be paired with other discounts—no double-dipping. Also, some places permit the deals only at off-peak times.

restaurants would do this, just consider the risky dynamics of the restaurant industry, in which ready accessibility to cash can make or break places.

Another way to save money is to buy a "gift certificate," which, truth be told, is really a kind of coupon, though the euphemistic name takes away some of the stigma. Gift certificates offered by **Restaurant.com** can be bought one of two ways: The Web site sells them for half price (so a $50 one costs you $25); or you try to get them for less by bidding for them on **eBay.com**—search for "gift certificate" or a restaurant name.

FREQUENT-DINER PROGRAMS

Good restaurants have always pampered their regulars, treating them to a free drink, free desert or giving them the table they want. But repeat diners are now the object of programs that resemble frequent-flier miles on airplanes—you get points for every dollar you spend in restaurants affiliated with the program. Some restaurants let big spenders graduate to "silver" and "gold" levels, where they earn points quicker.

The most common reward is money off your next meal, but some of the more elaborate programs let patrons redeem a mother lode of points for things like hot-air balloon rides and wine-country travel. Of course, it should come as no surprise that the programs are most popular with executives, who rack up points for personal use by spending on the company dime. The following box lists some of the oldest, most elaborate programs, but even smaller chains or restaurants also have programs. If you like a particular place and think you'll be a return customer, it pays to ask if they have any kind of frequent-diner plan. Sometimes restaurants are quite discreet about it and you wouldn't know until you ask.

THE DOUBLE DIP

When does stuffing your face in a fancy restaurant count as a competitive sport? When you're trying to see how many marketing programs you can pile on top of one another to shave down your bill. A "double play," for example, might involve using a promotional coupon plus a discount offered through an online-reservations system such as **Dinnerbroker.com**. Some serious type-A diners have even tried to score a "triple play," using three discounts at once, though that is extremely difficult to do because many promotions have restrictions attached. Here are two double plays a couple of well-fed *Wall Street Journal* reporters enjoyed while investigating restaurant discount programs:

The restaurant: Night Monkey; San Francisco

The deal: We paired a **Dinnerbroker.com** booking with a free-dessert offer from **Forfoodies .com** and racked up a 28 percent discount.

The catch: We had to book an early evening table to pull off the deal.

The restaurant: Provence; New York City

The deal: We knocked almost 40 percent off the tab by pairing discounts from **Restaurant.com** and **Dinnerbroker.com**. We even got a break on the booze.

The catch: We got greedy and tried to apply an iDine discount, too. But iDine won't work with other offers.

FREQUENT-DINER PROGRAMS AT A GLANCE

COMPANY/RESTAURANTS:
LETTUCE ENTERTAIN YOU ENTERPRISES, INC.,
70 RESTAURANTS IN CHICAGO AREA

How it works: Costs $25 to enroll, though that is refunded if you dine three times that year; one point per dollar spent

Sample reward: For 21,000 points, a chef from one of the restaurants cooks a four-course meal for 10 in member's home.

COMPANY/RESTAURANTS:
UNIQUE RESTAURANT CORPORATION,
13 RESTAURANTS AND SEVEN CATERING COMPANIES IN MICHIGAN

How it works: Costs $19.95 to enroll; one point for every dollar spent. Free bottle of champagne on member's anniversary

Sample reward: For 15,000 points, a limousine takes a party of six to one restaurant for appetizers and champagne, to another for a meal with wine, and a third for dessert and after-dinner drinks.

COMPANY/RESTAURANTS:
GASTRONOMY, INC.,
9 RESTAURANTS IN SALT LAKE CITY

How it works: $15 fee to join, which earns you 15 points; then one point for every dollar spent

Sample reward: For 350 points, you receive a $25 certificate that can be used at any restaurant, as well as at a bakery or fish market.

THE SAVVY DINER: DECODING
FOOD COSTS

So once you get into the restaurant of your choice, the next question is: What should you order?

The dollop of Kobe beef carpaccio for $49.99 or the flake of yuzu-marinated yellow tail for $36.80? The numbers to the right of the menu items can seem like comedy prices. A little insight into how food is priced and marketed in restaurants may help you make decisions that will satisfy both your appetite and your sense of justice.

Restaurants' food costs—the amount the owners spend on the raw ingredients that go into a dish—average about 30 percent of the price of the meal. Of course, some items cost the restaurant more—prime aged beef, for example, is usually a low profit–margin item for restaurateurs, which is why they so often sell it à la carte. Then they try to make up the loss in profit with high markup side items such as the sides of creamed spinach and baked potato you order with it, or high-markup entrees.

You'll know these dishes, because they are usually listed up high on the menu or featured as specials that the waiter describes in mouthwatering detail.

Mussels are a prime example. Restaurants love to feature them because they're cheap to buy wholesale and can be marked up as much as 650 percent and still seem reasonably priced on the menu. If you are a vegetarian, the price multiples on your entrees are so high that you basically are subsidizing the carnivores around you. Chicken, pasta and salad are notorious cheapo ingredients that restaurants love to sell and, lucky for them, the average American restaurant patron loves to order. But the biggest sticker shock of all may be on a big pink fish. Farm-raised salmon—referred to in the trade as "the chicken of the sea"—could well be the food industry's best-kept secret. It costs just around $3 a pound wholesale and is often priced at a whopping 900 percent markup or more.

So why don't restaurants simply charge more for high-cost dishes and less for cheaper ones? After all, shoppers who buy a Brand X blouse at a department store don't subsidize society dames who buy designer wear, and compact-car owners don't pay more so the dealer can cut deals for luxury-sedan customers.

The answer is partly marketing and partly psychology. Straying outside a certain price range can be risky for a restaurant. A $3 soup on a menu where most appetizers are in the $8 to $12 range will either cause a run on the soup or scare people away because they think something is wrong with it. Likewise, a dish might not find takers if it is priced too high.

Oddly enough, the least-expensive item on a menu occasionally is put there as a matter of reverse psychology. Restaurants know that some people simply won't order the cheapest thing on the menu because they don't want to look stingy; they then make sure that the next two or three least-expensive menu items are high markup dishes that have the greatest profit margin.

Of course, some chefs have such a magical touch with even the cheapest of ingredients that you would be hard-pressed to imitate the meal at home—and some dishes with humble ingredients are so labor intensive that they cost the restaurant plenty to serve. Bottom line: Order whatever you want but be aware that restaurants love to serve the following dishes because they rack up big profits:

Cheapie: Farmed salmon

Average wholesale cost: About $3 a pound

Markup: Up to 800 percent

Cheapie: Mussels

Average wholesale cost: About $1.80 a pound

Markup: Up to 650 percent

Cheapie: French fries

Average wholesale cost: About 65 cents a portion

Markup: Up to 1,000 percent

Cheapie: Salad

Average wholesale cost: As little as 24 cents an ounce

Markup: That $8 green salad with vinaigrette could represent a 1,500 percent markup

AND NOW FOR SOME LOW-MARGIN
MENU ITEMS . . .

Ironically, some of the most expensive items on the restaurant menu are the ones that are least profitable. That's because the restaurant pays steep wholesale prices but can't mark up the retail cost too high, or no one would order the dish. These can be good values in restaurants. A few classic examples:

Item: Prime aged beef

Typical Markup: 100 percent

Comment: Prime aged beef is so expensive because the aging process causes the meat to lose moisture and thus up to 20 percent of its weight. This concentrates flavor but requires the restaurant to compensate on what it charges. Restaurants, however, try to keep the markup low, making it up by charging high markups on side dishes.

Item: Foie Gras

Typical Markup: 200 percent

Comment: Foie gras costs restaurants around $25 to $35 a pound, which means that even an appetizer-sized two-ounce portion can cost the restaurant over $4 to serve. It is often paired with other pricey ingredients, like Sauterne wine sauce or currants, which jack up the raw material costs some more. Foie gras is also hard to find outside of a restaurant, and you have to pay through the nose to get it—Dean & Deluca charges $160 for a 1.8 lb. "lobe." So while it can be one of the pricier items on a restaurant menu, it's usually a pretty good deal.

Item: Wild-caught seafood

Typical Markup: Varies

Comment: We live in funny fish times. Restaurant menus are chock full of traditionally luxurious items, like shrimp and salmon, at all-time low prices. Yet fish—bluefish or mackerel, for example—that we used to consider low-class or cheap, is becoming harder to find and more expensive. What's going on can basically be explained in one word: aquaculture. Fish farming, largely of shrimp and salmon, has changed the economics of seafood by making varieties that are farmed—even on the other side of the world—far cheaper than the fish that swim wild nearby. Thus, restaurants pay a premium to get their hands on fresh, wild-caught fish, and markups are often lower than on the farmed stuff.

MORE THOUGHTS ON ORDERING FOR VALUE . . .

Restaurants are also a great place to try things that you can't easily find in your local supermarket—think of it as paying a premium for access. Examples: vegetables like cardoons, salsify, fennel and celeriac (also known as celery root); a wide variety of mushrooms, including bluefoot, hen of the woods and, of course, truffles; game meats such as pheasant, squab or venison; and unusual flavorings like everything from bee pollen and yuzu, an Asian citrus fruit, to microgreens, which are tiny, intensely flavorful sprouts.

Another way to get value is to order foods you don't know how to cook yourself. These days chefs are enamored of all kinds of organ meats, from sweetbreads to tripe, and other lowly but tasty cuts, like pork belly and short ribs, that can intimidate home cooks either because they're unusual or time-consuming. Using your restaurant outing to expose yourself to these items can make it worth the price of admission.

THE MONEY-SAVING PRIX FIXE

The best way to get a square deal on your meal is to simply order the "prix fixe," if one is offered. This the most common form of restaurant discounting, though restaurateurs try to obscure that fact by using a fancy French term meaning "fixed price." The prix-fixe concept has caught on big-time across the country in recent years because of a downturn in business spending that accompanied the economic downturn of 2001 through 2003. The only downside, culinarily speaking, is that you are limited to a few usually rather conservative choices.

Nonetheless, many prix fixes are superb and often feature the very same items on the à la carte menu. If you want to eat in a particular restaurant but are worried you'll have to take out a second mortgage on your house, call up and ask if they have a prix fixe. We found it easy enough to Google up some prix fixes in a number of major cities. City online restaurant guides, as well as the dining-and-leisure sections of major newspapers, are also good sources. Some examples:

THE JOYS OF RESTAURANT WEEK

Restaurant Week is another recent innovation that lets restaurateurs offer cut-rate prices and generate publicity without appearing to be desperate. The concept started in New York City in 1992 as a promotion during the Democratic Convention. Back then, restaurants offered three-course meals for $19.92. In 2004, three-course lunches cost $20.04 and dinners $30.04—that price will go up by a penny in 2005. The city usually schedules the event for one week at the end of January or the beginning of February, and then again at the end of June or the beginning of July. However, many restaurants choose to extend

RESTAURANT: COMPASS, NEW YORK CITY

Regular cost-per-diner: $48.50 average

Prix fixe: $35 for three courses (or alternately, a $38 low-carb-dish option)

RESTAURANT: ASIA DE CUBA, SAN FRANCISCO

Regular cost-per-diner: Family-style portioned appetizers run about $20; entrées $30 to $50.

Prix fixe: Lunch $25; $19.95 during special promotions

RESTAURANT: ROY'S RESTAURANTS,

IN 21 U.S. CITIES, INCLUDING ATLANTA, BALTIMORE AND PHOENIX

Regular cost-per-diner: About $45 à la carte

Prix fixe: $33 three-course meal includes an appetizer sampler, choice of meat or fish main course and choice between two desserts.

RESTAURANT: LUCQUES, LOS ANGELES

Regular cost-per-diner: Three-course dinner, about $46

Prix fixe: On Sundays, the restaurant serves a "Sunday Supper" 3-course meal for $35.

RESTAURANT: NACIONAL 27, CHICAGO

Regular cost-per-diner: Five-course dinner with wine pairings for each course costs $68.

Prix-fixe: On Wednesdays, the restaurant offers the five-course meal with wine pairings for $44—still something of a splurge, but a good value.

the restaurant "week" offerings for many months—especially throughout the summer and dead of winter, which are traditionally slow times for them.

New York's promotion was so successful that many other cities have jumped on board. There are now restaurant weeks in Washington, D.C.; Philadelphia; Chicago; Boston; Atlanta; Miami (actually Miami's is "restaurant month") and other cities. And not all cities charge New York prices—the Dine-Around-Seattle promotion features 25 high-end restaurants that charge $25 for a three-course dinner and $12.50 for lunch. **Opentable.com** is a good place to find out about restaurant week—the site usually highlights which restaurants are participating.

Here's a list of websites for individual city promotions:

New York City: **nycvisit.com;** search for "restaurant week"

Washington, D.C.: **washington.org/restaurantwk**

Atlanta: **atlantadowntown.com;** go to "having fun" and then "downtown Atlanta Restaurant Week"

Boston: **bostonusa.com;** search for "Restaurant Week"

Philadelphia: **centercityphila.org;** search for "Restaurant Week"

Chicago: **chicagodineout.com**

Miami: **miamirestaurantmonth.com**

San Francisco: **dineabouttown.com**

Toronto: **toronto.ca;** in the "Search" area, type in "Winterlicious" for the winter promotion, and "Summerlicious" for the summer promotion

GETTING THE BEST OUT OF RESTAURANT WEEK

1. **The most desirable restaurants fill up fast, so book early.** If you can't book a table, try walking in. One of the reasons restaurants participate in this promotion is that it is hard for them to fill all their tables during the summer, though they might not want to admit that over the phone.

2. **Stay away from second-tier places.** As the promotions have expanded, more restaurants have jumped on board, but not all of them are expensive enough to make the Restaurant Week prices a good deal.

3. **Note that some restaurants charge an arm and a leg for items not on the prix-fixe menu,** like bottled water, wine and coffee. If you're watching your budget, ask the price when they offer you that fizzy water or ply you with espresso.

4. **Beware snarling waiters.** Restaurant Week fills typically expensive, exclusive restaurants with hordes of bargain-hunters, and waiters

sometimes get testy about it. It's probably not the best time to take out that special date or sensitive business contact. (**Note:** This observation was made after going to lunch during restaurant week at a few places in New York City, where a snarling waiter is never too hard to find.)

LIBATIONS: THE COCKTAIL RENAISSANCE

Next time you belly up to the bar in the nearest watering hole, remember this: You're living in the golden age of the cocktail. That's what liquor marketers are calling it anyway, and for good reason. Fifty-three new cordials and liqueurs were introduced in 2002, up from 18 in 2001 and 17 in 2000, according to the Distilled Spirits Council in Washington.

Four times the number of flavored vodkas and rums were introduced in 2002 as in 1999, and more have hit the market in the past two years. The cocktail trend is being fueled by factors including generous liquor-marketing budgets—hard alcohol companies started advertising on television again in 1996, after a 50-year self-imposed ban. Low-carb dieting and a more positive outlook on eating red meat have caused a return to steak-house dining, a traditional bastion of cocktail drinking. In the tradition of the celebrity chef, there are even celebrity bartenders now, known as "bar chefs."

Restaurants, hotels and bars are delighted to embrace the cocktail trend, particularly because the raw ingredients of the average cocktail account for only about a fifth of its retail price, a markup significantly higher than that for restaurant food. The upside for consumers is that many barkeeps are now making authentic classic cocktails, like Manhattans made with rye, not bourbon, or margaritas mixed with fresh juice rather than packaged drink mix. The downside: The $10 cocktail is now ubiquitous, while some bars have the gall to charge $16 or more for one drink. Even more outrageous: Expect others to try to match the $69 margarita at Suenos in New York City. (It's made with a kind of tequila that costs nearly $40 a shot, expensive Grand Marnier, and the juice of blood oranges—a ruby red, sweet-tart kind of orange.)

Fortunately, there are ways to enjoy the cocktail renaissance without getting ripped off. David Wondrich, a cocktail consultant to bars and restaurants and author of books on cocktails, says the most common way people waste money on booze is by asking for super-high-end vodkas when ordering a mixed drink. "You never need it for a mixed drink," says Mr. Wondrich, explaining that the subtle qualities of ultra-premium vodka get washed out by fruity mixers like cranberry or grapefruit juice. Premium brands like Absolut and Stolichnaya are fine for mixed drinks; save the superexpensive French handmade vodka for a martini or drink it straight-up.

By contrast, the average consumer acts like a cheapskate when it comes to ordering tequila—yet spending extra money on a premium brand can make all the difference in a margarita. Ask your bartender if they have a range of tequilas. Tequila imports are up 17 percent since last year and companies are rolling out more ultra-premium tequilas made with 100 percent blue agave, a succulent plant indigenous to Mexico. (The paint-remover type of tequilas most Americans are familiar with are made with 51 percent blue agave, blended with other sugars.)

But there are a few things to keep in mind when you order fancy tequila. Lola in Denver says the bar looked on in shock when the first customer to order a $90 snifter of the best tequila tossed it back like a shot. **A tip:** It's supposed to be sipped and savored for its subtle notes of vanilla, wood and pepper. Also, don't embarrass yourself by asking to shoot the worm—that's only in Mezcal, which is a different drink.

Mr. Wondrich also says that if you're a bourbon lover, there's no shame in ordering relatively inexpensive, oldie-but-goodie brands like Wild Turkey. That's because bourbon is one of the spirits that is so strictly regulated in terms of what it can be made with and how the distilling process works that producers just don't have room to cheapen it much. Therefore the cheap stuff is pretty close to the expensive stuff and is a good value—especially if you're mixing it. If you're drinking straight up, you might want to experiment with some of the new, micro-distilled bourbons—small lots of handmade whisky being produced by boutique distillers and even microbrewers—coming onto the market.

SPOTTING THE NEW TRENDY DRINK

Vodka has had a great run throughout the 90s, with the huge popularity of things like vodka martinis, Cosmopolitans, and even Red Bull and vodka (don't worry if you've never heard of it—it's a cocktail, made with the Red Bull energy drink, favored by the twentysome-thing set). But spirits-industry experts are predicting the next decade will herald the return of "brown goods," as they are known in the trade—darker liquors like bourbon whisky and rye (go ahead, sing it if you must). Single-malt scotch is also reaching a wider audience, and Americans now have access to artisanal sakes that can be exquisite if you know how to approach them. Here are three spirits categories that have seen recent innovations that can boost your reputation as a drinks connoisseur.

RYE

Rye was the ubiquitous American whisky until Prohibition nearly stamped it out, but bartenders are now reviving rye with cocktails popular 80 years ago, like Sazeracs and real Manhattans. (Rye differs from bourbon in that rye must be made with at least 51 percent rye grain, while bourbon must be made with at least 51 percent corn. Scotch, meanwhile, is made with barley.) Ironically, rye is being redis-covered and appreciated more in England than in its homeland. At the bar Hush in London, a pour of Old Portrero Rye, a microdistillery brand that bartenders love, costs $28.

How to drink it: straight up is preferred, or with just a splash of water; it's great in Manhattans and Sazeracs.

SAKE

For years, a sushi meal wasn't complete without a cheap thimbleful of hot, medicinal-tasting sake. Turns out we've been drinking rot-gut. So say a growing brigade of premium-sake marketers, who are trying to make up for a drastic drop-off in Japanese sake consumption by bring-ing the good stuff, which can cost as much as $180 a bottle, to the United States. While most bad sake tastes the same—like a hot cold remedy—there is as much variety among good sakes as there is among wines. Some are lightly effervescent, others have a slightly creamy texture, and there are lots of light, almost fruity sakes. Sake brewers, aficionados and crazed sake fans have begun to promote sake in a big way on the Internet. One good site is **sake-world.com**, written by John Gauntner, an American who writes about sake for the Japanese press.

A growing number of restaurants (even non-Japanese ones) are stocking high-quality sakes. There's no shame in asking the waiter or sommelier at these places to help you select a sake or two to taste. In 2003, True Sake, a sake-only retailer, opened in San Francisco, and high-end restaurants started throwing sake-pairing dinners. Benihana restaurant founder Rocky Aoki recently even started a sake-of-the-month club. Rice wine and sake imports from Japan were up 7 percent in 2003 over the year before.

How to drink it: Forget the warm stuff—most premium sake is served and sipped chilled, much like white wine.

SINGLE-MALT SCOTCH WHISKY

Single malts represent a small slice of the overall scotch market—about only 5 percent of the bottles shipped worldwide last year. But they're the industry's fastest-growing segment, according to the Scotch Whisky Association. To be called scotch, whisky has to be made in Scotland and be at least three years old. It's called malt whisky because, like beer, it begins with barley, a grain that is "malted," i.e., soaked in water until it germinates, creating starch that, when yeast and water are added, is turned into alcohol. Part two of malting is to roast or dry the barley; with scotch, this is usually done over slow-burning fires of peat, a dense, mossy fuel harvested from Scottish bogs. Peat smoke often plays an important role in a scotch's flavor. Some people like the peaty flavor and others don't. The Scottish Malt Whisky Society (**smws.com**) and the Scotch Whisky Association (**scotch.whisky.org.uk**) offer tips on how to choose a good single-malt.

How to drink it: First, nose the whisky. One of the great joys of single-malt scotch is the aroma, with its floral, spicy, fruity, peaty overtones; these are often the portal to a whisky's taste. Second: It's a sin to mix good single-malt whisky with soda. And *don't* serve it over ice. Take a sip of the scotch neat. Then, add a wee splash of water and taste again. The water can have the effect of "loosening up" the scotch, giving you a more flavorful, rather than diluted, experience.

Bonus: Some single-malt whisky-makers also bottle the spring water used at the distillery. Use that water (stores with good selections of single malt often sell it), or some other soft, noncarbonated bottled spring water.

A LITTLE ADVICE ON WINE

Scores and scores of books have been written about wine, wine-making, wine regions, how to choose wine, etc., etc. In this guide, we're sticking to giving you some practical advice as a companion to your dining-out experiences.

Here's an amazing fact: About 8 percent of all wine on the market is bad—as in, undrinkable, stinky and "off." And yet, consumers regularly taste this bad wine in restaurants, flash a smile at the sommelier or waiter and urge them to pour it for the whole table. Sommeliers have told *The Wall Street Journal* that they can sometimes smell the rotten wine from their position at tableside—but patrons insist that it's delicious anyway.

Wine imperfections are usually not the fault of the restaurant, nor the winemaker, but rather of the primitive technology of bottling wine with corks, which is why the wine industry is desperately trying to get consumers to accept things like plastic corks or screw-top bottles. One way wine consumers can help in the battle against bad wine is to stop being snobby about real corks. Plastic corks or even screw caps are not signs of inferior wine at all, but rather examples of wineries trying to modernize and make the product more consistent. Meanwhile, you can protect yourself against musty, vinegary or otherwise nasty wine by learning to recognize "off" wine.

Here are four easy steps:

1. **First, the waiter presents the unopened bottle for you to look at.** All you're looking for here is to verify that the bottle you're about to drink is the one you ordered. Just make sure the name and year match up with what you saw on the menu—nod or say "fine" if they do, complain if they don't. Look for signs of imperfections—broken seals or leakage.

2. **Next, the waiter or sommelier uncorks the bottle and pours a bit for you to taste.** This is to make sure the wine is not "off"—that's all. It's not a taste test to see if you want to renege on what you originally ordered, and you're not expected to rattle off some spontaneous wine comment, like "It's a bit cantankerous, but fruity." If it's corked, it will have a musty, moldy aroma and taste. If you smell or taste any notes of wet

cardboard, chances are that some bacteria infected the cork and caused the wine to go bad. If it tastes like acid or vinegar, the wine is spoiled.

3. Give the wine a quick swirl before tasting it. This will let a little air into the wine, which will help release the aroma—good or bad—in the wine. If you're still not sure whether you're getting a good bottle, it's perfectly acceptable to ask the sommelier or waiter to take a whiff or a taste to help you figure it out.

4. If you sense that your wine might be corked, all you need to do is tell the restaurant. The restaurant must provide you with another bottle, which you should also taste to make sure it is not corked. If the wine tastes fine to you, all you have to say is, "This is fine," or even just nod at your server to signal that the wine is fine to pour for the table.

THE NO-BRAINER WAY TO ORDER WINE IN A RESTAURANT

Great wine surprises await you at every good restaurant. Too many people go to restaurants and order the same wine they drink at home, at double the price. That's screwy. Truth is, many of the world's better wineries try to place their wines at good restaurants, which means you can have special wine experiences at restaurants that you could never have at home. Having a new wine should be part of the fun of eating out. The next time you're looking at a restaurant's wine list, find something that you've never seen before.

Order it—and enjoy the roller-coaster ride.

1. Take your time. When the waiter asks for your selection, say, "You have such an interesting list. I'll need a few minutes."

2. Decide red or white, thus cutting the list in half.

3. See what country or region most of the wines on the list come from. If most are, say, Italian, that's where the restaurant's heart is. Go with it.

4. Nix the "showcase" wines, like the exorbitant "first growths" from Bordeaux and the wildly expensive Gaja wines from Italy. They're often there just for show or for people on expense accounts.

5. Decide what you're willing to spend—be flexible here—and ignore everything above that amount.

6. Eliminate everything you're already familiar with. It's scary moving into uncharted waters, but grit your teeth and do it. (Ignore this advice when it's important to go with a sure thing, such as if this is a make-or-break business meal or you're about to propose marriage.)

7. Of the limited number of wines left, pick two or three and say to the waiter, "What can you tell me about these wines?" Chances are these will be interesting enough that the waiter will figure you know what you're talking about, and then will call over someone who really does.

8. Watch the waiter's eyes. When they light up as he or she is discussing a specific wine, order it.

9. Enjoy it. Maybe you'll really like it; maybe you won't. But it will surely be something new and different. And you chose it.

10. If you like it, don't be shy about asking to take the bottle, or at least the label, home with you. How many times have you said to yourself later, "I wish I could remember what the wine was"?

—JOHN BREECHER AND DOROTHY J. GAITER

BARLEY MATTERS: THE NEW NEW BEER

Beer is one of life's simple pleasures, but in recent years, it's gotten a lot less simple and yet a lot more pleasurable. The story of beer's modern evolution begins in the early 1980s, when America's beer industry, which numbered about 700 breweries prior to World War II, had consolidated into three huge companies, Anheuser-Busch Cos., Miller Brewing Co. (a unit of SABMiller PLC) and Adolph Coors Co. and about 40 regional holdouts. They largely make mass-produced lagers—the clear, golden brew, usually at 3.2 percent to 5.25 percent alcohol, of which Bud Light is the best-selling example.

The pioneer microbrewers (so-called because they make relatively small lots of beer) felt that the big beer-makers were paring down and homogenizing beer to appeal to lowest-common-denominator tastes and had given up on beer's more complex possibilities. They set about to change that. The results: Today, the U.S. supports more than 400 breweries and 1,000 brewpubs. Collectively, the newcomers who prefer the term craftbrewers over microbrewers have put at least 10,000 individual new beers on the market. The upshot for consumers is that there is now a great justification for making a hobby of beer drinking. In fact, Jim Koch, founder of the Boston Beer Co. and the Sam Adams label, told us that "America at the moment is the best *ever* in the world to drink beer."

So what's the fuss about? Here's one example:

CONFESSIONS AND ADVICE OF A HOPHEAD

About a year ago, after wandering the American beerscape with conflicted preferences, I came out of the closet. As a Hophead.

Hopheadism has no cure, save one: to find and drink nicely hopped beers—that is, beers whose signature is the floral aroma and sometimes mouth-puckering bitterness imparted by the cones of the hops plant. And if you love nicely hopped beers, there's a good chance you'll become a fan of perhaps the hottest beer style in brewing: India Pale Ale, or IPA for short.

IPA wasn't invented or originally made in India. It descends from seasonal "March" or "October" beers brewed on 18th-century British estates when Britain was the world's unrivaled brewing power. India entered the nomenclature in 1767, when entrepreneur George Hodgson cut a deal with the East India Company to start providing beer to the British civil-service and merchant classes manning its colonies there. The Brits had long known that hops, besides imparting flavor, also act as a preservative (as do high alcohol levels). So Hodgson made his beer strong and hopped it at double the usual rate, and—blimey!—the beer not only survived the long, hot sea voyage to the subcontinent but aged extremely well. It caused an instant stir.

IPAs splashed onto the American scene about two decades ago with the advent of the craft-brew revolution. From perhaps a score of IPAs at the end of the 1980s, the style has gained so many adherents in the past decade that Greg Kitsock, editor of *Mid-Atlantic Brewing News,* an Arlington, Virginia, beer publication, estimates that well more than half of America's 1,500 brewpubs and craft brewers are making some variation of the style.

Beer is made with four things: water, malt, yeast and hops. Malt—

a grain, usually barley, that has been sprouted and kiln-dried—is the soul of beer, determining body and color (the darker the malt, the darker the beer). Yeast is the mojo, fermenting malt sugars and turning them into alcohol while also producing carbon dioxide, which provides beer's foamy head. Hops give beer its sex appeal, adding the perfume, the spice, the heat. (Hops, as a first cousin to the marijuana plant, also are a mild soporific.)

I gathered up 11 IPA brands at a local liquor store and put together a tasting with a panel of family and friends. We followed a few of the rituals I'd picked up at beer tastings I'd attended (yes, Virginia, there are beer tastings): water to rinse glasses between brands, a swill bucket to dump the leftovers and crackers to cleanse the palate between samplings. We also tried to see how the beers matched up to the description of a classic IPA offered by a home-brewers' outfit called the Beer Judge Certification Program: An IPA should exhibit "a prominent hops aroma of floral, grassy or fruit characteristic . . . with assertive hop bitterness."

The best IPAs are balanced by "sufficient malt flavor and body"—that is, it isn't just a matter of dumping tons of hops into a beer and calling it a great IPA.

—KEN WELLS

Below are our top two recommendations, which also happen to be reasonably widely distributed throughout the country. But to learn more about IPAs, craft beer and beer-making in general, below we've also laid out a few extremely helpful websites.

BEER GEEK SPEAK

Let's say you're a Budweiser drinker. That's great with us. There's nothing better than a cold lager on a hot day at the beach or at the ballpark. However, we're also going to assume, if you've bought this book, that you may have an interest in getting up to speed

---

TWO IPAS WE LOVED AND WHY WE LOVED THEM

DOGFISH 60 MINUTE IPA; DOGFISH HEAD CRAFT BREWERY, MILTON, DELAWARE

Our opinion: The best balanced of all the IPAs we sampled; one taster practically swooned over it. Hop flavors and aroma were robust. And Dogfish makes several other IPA varieties—including one called "120-Minute IPA" that comes in at a shattering 22.5 percent alcohol-by-volume.

VICTORY HOPDEVIL IPA; VICTORY BREWING CO., DOWNINGTON, PENNSYLVANIA

Our opinion: Blessedly hoppy. But this beer, for all its hop taste and aromas, had an extremely smooth, slow and creamy finish. Beyond that, it was a beautiful color. We wanted more.

on the conversation about America's micro-brew revolution. While craft brew represents only about 3.4 percent of U.S. beer sales, it is unquestionably at the creative heart of contemporary American brewing. By boning up just a little on beer's chemistry and learning a little jargon, you won't become an instant Beer Geek (which, by the way, isn't a pejorative but an honorific bestowed on those of unusual beer knowledge and enthusiasm). But you can begin to talk intelligently about the New Beer on the Block.

First thing to know: America's River of Beer divides into two distinct styles:

Ale. The world's oldest beer style, loved by pharaoh and Pilgrim alike; the beer of Shakespeare and the British pub; the beer that arrived here on the Mayflower in 1620 but was largely chased from the American beerscape two centuries later by the beer juggernaut known as lager. Derisive (and ignorant) American drinkers often put down ale as "that warm British beer," but ale—meant to be served at cellar temperatures—has undergone a makeover, notably at the hands of American craft brewers, who will even serve it to you slightly chilled. Technically, ale is brewed from top-fermenting yeast that work best at warm temperatures; it is characterized by an earthy, fruity flavor and a wide color spectrum. Well-known modern examples: Sierra Nevada Pale Ale and Bass Ale.

SOME GREAT BEER WEB SITES

The Association of Brewers at beertown.org. A craft brew and homebrew association site with great information on brewing, craft-beer history, plus a good source of brewing books

Beeradvocate.com, a great beer enthusiast's site, where you can find (and post) ratings on hundreds of beer brands

Beerhunter.com, a site operated by the internationally famous beer writer Michael Jackson; a terrific place to learn about beer styles, beer history and to get the lowdown on hundreds of specific beers

BeerServesAmerica.com, a site put up by the Beer Institute and the National Beer Wholesalers Association. It's a good place to pick up on arcane but interesting matters of beer history and beer's contribution to the U.S. economy.

Brewer's Association of America at beeradvocate.org. It features comprehensive stats on the microbrew industry, with links to beer events and a plethora of other useful beer sites.

Realbeer.com, a first-rate consumer site with great beer-education links, not to mention links to breweries and brewpubs around the nation

Lager. The clear, golden beer that, thanks mostly to the Czechs and Germans, conquered the world and nowadays accounts for 95 percent of all beer consumption worldwide; the beer in America synonymous with the beach, the ballpark and the frat party. Lager is brewed cold from yeast that ferments near the bottom of fermentation tanks; it gobbles up more fermentable sugars than does ale yeast, producing a taste that most palates discern as crisper, cleaner and drier than ale's. Pilsner Urquell was the world's first clear, golden lager. Well-known modern examples: Budweiser, Corona and Miller Lite.

Then, let's say you're at a party and you encounter a real Beer Geek. Here's the most intelligent question you can ask to break into the conversation: **Do you like hops or do you like malt?**

In the gist of this question lies another beer subdivide. Hop lovers tend to drink hoppy beers, which tend to be ambers or lighter-colored ales or lagers. Malt lovers tend to drink stouts—these are dark-colored ales, like Guinness, where the predominant taste profile comes from the malt, not the hops. For example: The darker you roast the malt, the darker the beer and the heavier and roastier it is likely to taste.

And then there's the Extreme Beer movement. And just what is Extreme Beer? It isn't so much a technical term as it is a catchword that has sprung up to identify breweries dabbling in beer styles (aged beer, ultra-strong beer, beer made with exotic ingredients) that are far from the everyday lagers like Budweiser, Miller and Coors.

Here are a couple of examples:

Boston Beer Co. for the past few years has annually been putting out a limited brewing of stouts called "Utopias." The last one, in 2004, came in at about 25 percent alcohol-by-volume. Given that most lager is about 5 percent, that's extreme. If you want to sample some, watch the company's website (**bostonbeer.com**) or bid for some on eBay.

Dogfish Head Craft Brewery (whose IPA we admired above) makes a wildly interesting ale called "Midas Touch Magic Elixir." What makes it unusual? It's brewed from a 2,700-year-old recipe reverse-engineered from beer dregs found at the bottom of a royal tomb unearthed by archaeologists in the 1950s. So many gold artifacts were recovered that researchers think the king for whom it was built was the model for the legend of King Midas. Dogfish Head (**dogfish.com**) has a Web site link that tells you how to find their beer in your area.

To find more Extreme brews: Nearly all major cities have one or more bars that specialize in craft or microbrews and would very likely have a bartender up to speed on the Extreme Beer movement. Go in and ask for one and see what they say. **BeerAdvocate.com** also features pieces from time to time on Extreme Beer and you can also get information on an annual Extreme Beer festival that has been held annually in Boston since 2002.

YOUR TICKET TO TICKETS ON BROADWAY AND AT THE MOVIES

What do commercial airlines and Broadway theaters have in common, beyond cramped seats, negligible legroom, ill-mannered neighbors and sometimes iffy entertainment? In both cases, that woman on the aisle or that couple seated in front of you may have paid substantially less for their tickets than you did for yours.

Several Web sites provide copious information on theater around the country, with an emphasis on New York's Broadway, and frequently they also offer ticket discounts with absolutely no service charge. A good one is **BroadwayBox.com,** which lists advance-purchase discount offers for Broadway and Off-Broadway shows. Look for discount information posted by readers and follow the instructions for each show, or sign up for "discount alerts." The site is pretty bare-bones, but you can land discounts of 25 to 50 percent off.

Other top picks in the theatergoer's cyber arsenal include **TheaterMania.com** and **Playbill.com.** Each offers a free online membership that allows access to special services. Both offer e-mail updates alerting members to special ticket offers. **Broadway.com** offers a range of convenient theater-hotel packages.

And every good theatergoer should know about Telecharge (**telecharge.com**) and Ticketmaster (**ticketmaster.com**). They offer on-line ticketing access to nearly every theatrical event in New York—and while they don't offer direct ways to save money, they are still a useful tool for the bargain hunter. After logging on to Telecharge or Ticketmaster, check the location of the available tickets. This should tell you whether the performance you want to see is close to selling out. A similar approach involves checking the weekly sales figures for a given show. At **Playbill.com,** look at the column to the left, and click on "Broadway Grosses" under "Features."

If you are in Manhattan and you know that a show isn't selling out consistently, you can try getting tickets through the Theatre Development Fund TKTS booths, which offer discounts of 50 percent or

25 percent (there is a small fee). One location is in Times Square; it sells tickets on the day of performance only. The other is in South Street Seaport. It offers evening tickets on the day of performance and matinee tickets that must be purchased the day before. All purchases require cash or traveler's checks and a wait in line, and there is no guarantee that the show you wish to see will be available.

Another tip: You can also log on to **tdf.org** to see what shows were offered at TKTS the previous week. This serves as a tip as to which tickets will be available at steep discount.

If all else fails, there is always the traditional way of getting a discount: Buy a cheap seat. You will not find yourself dealing with bleacher bums on nickel beer night; this is Broadway, and even the last row is closer than you think. In fact, many civic centers around the country are two to three times the size of the average Broadway theater. If you are used to peering over 4,000 heads to see the stage, looking past 1,000 or even 1,500 will seem like nothing. Fair warning . . . as with any bargain, the cheap seats often go quickly.

ROAD SHOWS . . .

For information about national tours of Broadway shows, go to **livebroadway.com.** The "Shows on Tour" section gives you descriptions of the shows. From there you can link to the websites of each show, where you can read schedules, and buy tickets.

MOVIE TICKETS

Buying a movie ticket used to mean nothing more than just getting in line and then handing over cash to the ticket-taker. But all that has changed in the Internet age. These days a whole crop of companies, from **Cinemark.com** to **Moviefone.com,** let you buy tickets online instead, and most even promise a way to print tickets on your home printer.

There's also another new buying method: Those ATM-like machines that are popping up in theater lobbies. Known as ABOs (automated box office), they let you swipe a credit card and punch up the movie you want. Then they print a ticket.

Moviegoers seem to like the new options. Online sales have tripled during the past couple of years, according to Jupiter Media

The Internet can be a big help both for picking which show to see and plotting your plan of action for landing tickets.

Site: **BroadwayStars.com**

Description: Digest of theater news, with links to Broadway-related media, chat rooms, databases and awards shows

Ease of Use: Frugally formatted for simple scrolling. Click on links above the news listing to read (or add) star biographies, find ticket discounts and submit gossip.

Comment: Users should link to performers' home page where provided, as fan-submitted information is only spottily updated.

Site: **Playbill.com**

Description: Leading news resource for Broadway, updated around-the-clock

Ease of Use: Provides news and features, show schedules and statistics.

Comment: "Playbill on Opening Night" feature, amply illustrated with on-the-spot snapshots, takes you behind the scenes of Broadway premieres, with commentary from a veteran theater critic.

Site: **TheaterMania.com**

Description: Comprehensive site covering New York and regional theater

Ease of Use: Find detailed reviews at the bottom right of the home page. On the left, the TheaterMania Restaurant Guide tells which Broadway bistros offer deals.

Comment: "Ticket Discounts" tab atop the page helps users save as much as 50 percent on some shows, including those on Broadway, off-Broadway and off-off-Broadway.

Site: **TalkinBroadway.com**

Description: Chat site for Broadway gossip and information

Ease of Use: Click on "All That Chat" and get ready to dish. Or just lurk. Members comment on daily performances, critiquing the fine points of a show, seemingly minutes after the curtain falls.

Comment: "Broadway 101" gives the origins and history of Broadway in text and pictures. The nickname "The Great White Way" came from the illumination of electric signage along Broadway and Times Square.

A list of services and how they work:

SERVICE: **FANDANGO.COM**
How it Works: Pick a movie, date, theater and showtime, then follow instructions. There is a surcharge from $.75 to $1.50 (it varies depending on location). Though this site is known for the print-at-home feature, it's only available for use with limited theaters.

SERVICE: **CINEMARK.COM**
How it Works: Make your choice of movie and time, type credit-card info in, and click "Print." You don't actually get a "ticket," you get a code that gets scanned at the box office or you plug it in yourself at a Cinemark kiosk, which spits out your tickets. Fees: about 75 cents to a dollar, though it's free in some parts of the country.

SERVICE: **MOVIEFONE.COM**
How it Works: Select movie and showtime; pay with plastic; print a confirmation. There is a surcharge per ticket, usually $1. Bring your credit card to the theater to claim the tickets. You can't use this option for all movies, however; in some cases you are required to phone in your order.

SERVICE: **AUTOMATED BOX OFFICES (ATMs FOR TICKETS)**
How it Works: Swipe your credit card, select a movie on the little screen—and voilà, tickets print out. Some have no fee and others charge $1 on top of the ticket price. These things typically stand in the theater lobby, and since they're still relatively unknown, it's sometimes a good way to bypass all those people standing in line. But don't be tardy—sometimes the machines will try to sell you a ticket for the next showing even though you're just a few minutes late for the current one.

Metrix, and now hover around the $400 million mark.

But be warned: There are glitches. **Fandango.com**'s print-at-home feature, for example, works in 40 or so cities—but the site doesn't tell you whether it works at the theater you've picked until you've already bought the ticket. Some sites charge up to a $1.50 premium over the ticket cost. And some sites deliver the tickets directly to your theater of choice—and now and then they don't show up on time.

AND BEAR IN MIND . . .

Another good place to look for tickets, for theater, concerts and sporting events, is on **Craigslist.com,** a community board for a wide range of cities. It's also a good place to unload tickets you can't use. There's no fee to either post or answer advertisements, and you don't have to register. Just go to the city of your choice and click on "Tickets." You contact the poster of the ad directly and make a deal.

CHAPTER SIX

GADGETS

LEARNING TO SPEAK GEEK

I t's both the great promise and the great annoyance of the world of electronics that nearly everything about it will have changed by the time you finish reading this sentence.

Okay, that's a mild exaggeration, but who hasn't bought a computer or cell phone or digital camera that endowed bragging rights to being state-of-the-art for all of a week or two—before being eclipsed by model 2.0 that not only did a lot more, but was also smaller, faster and cheaper? Not only are electronics products themselves morphing all the time, but entire product *categories* are, too. *All you have is a cell phone/camera/music player? You mean it doesn't take seismic readings, too?*

This state of endless flux makes dispensing advice about electronics a somewhat perilous business. Recommending specific models is a nonstarter, since they are likely to be off the shelves a few months after they are put on them. Even mentioning manufacturers can get you in trouble, as companies reinvent themselves all the time.

As a result, the approach we're taking in this chapter is to acquaint you with some of the basic themes and trends in computers and consumer electronics generally, and then, for a number of specific product categories, to give you the basic education you need to be able to walk into a store (or visit a Web site) and begin asking intelligent questions. You're still going to do some work yourself; we hope to make that as painless as possible.

THE BIG PICTURE: BIG IDEAS SWEEPING THE TECH WORLD

Before getting to the basic product categories, here are some big ideas to keep in mind:

1. Globalization: That word is shorthand for the massive changes under way in the manner computers and electronics are being designed, manufactured and sold. By now, most people appreciate that Asian companies make most of the living-room gadgets that Americans buy. The same, though, is true for computers—even when a U.S. company has its name on the case. Not only are Asian companies manufacturing these products, in a growing number of cases they are designing them, too. In laptop computers, for instance, a few Taiwanese suppliers design and make nearly all of the laptops sold by the big American computer companies.

The moral: When evaluating two similar products from competing companies, don't sweat the details. Odds are good they have more similarities than differences; they may have even been made in the same place. This rule is most applicable to Windows PCs—it's very likely that the same Taiwanese company, perhaps with actual manufacturing operations on Mainland China, is behind the "competing" models you are looking at. It's not just computers, though. In televisions, for instance, big-name brands often get their key components from other big-name competitors.

2. Quality: If there were a motto for this sector of the economy, it would be "Buyer, relax." Consumers can take solace in the fact that most computers and electronic products are remarkably well made. (We're talking hardware manufacturing here; software engineering is another matter, and many of these devices are harder to use than they ought to be. In the case of computers, software reliability problems are epidemic.) Partly because of the globalization trend mentioned above, the difference between the best-made and worst-made piece of gear in any particular product area is probably smaller in electronics than it is in just about any other part of the economy.

Think about the difference between, say, a really lousy sofa and a really good one: You're not likely to find the same sort of quality differential among TVs or camcorders or computers—assuming you stick with a top-flight brand.

Of course, this is not to say that you might not be happier buying one model over another. Some models will have more features than others—or fewer, if that suits you—or simply be better in other ways. But in general, you're much less likely to encounter a lemon in electronics than you are just about anywhere else.

The major exception is telephones—not portable cell phones, most of which are top-flight, but the traditional sort that you use in your home. The quality variations in phones are wide and unpredictable. It seems manufacturers, even of top brands, have contented themselves with adding features to their phone models with little regard for basic quality issues. They also seem to use the least-expensive components they can get their hands on, which is one reason that the handsets on many house phones sound like bad transistor radios from the 1950s. We don't discuss phones in this guide, either cell phones or landline phones. Cell phones are not really a hardware purchase; most people these days get their phone in connection with a service agreement, and those have more variations to them than a Bach fugue. As for landline phones, the best advice is to ask as many people you know as possible what they use, and what they like and don't like about it.

3. Convergence: One of the added challenges of buying electronics these days is that product categories are blurring. This is most clearly happening in cell phones, which are rapidly adding the features of Palm Pilot–style organizers, cameras, MP3 music players and more. Camcorders and cameras are another example: These days, camcorders can take still pictures, and "still" cameras are able to record primitive videos. Electronics manufacturers do this because they can. Most of these products use silicon chips of one kind or another, and the factories that make these chips are able, with each passing year, to cram more functions onto ever-smaller wafers of silicon.

There are, however, downsides to this convergence. It's hard, for instance, to buy a plain vanilla phone or camera anymore. And as a result, learning to use your new gadget can take longer than many people have the patience for. What's more, as product categories come together, it's sometimes hard to know what you need to buy. "If I get a cell phone that takes pictures, do I still need a digital camera?"

The best way to deal with this is to remember that a hyphenated product will always be best at the first term in its name, which is the thing it started life as. A cell phone–MP3 player, for instance, will probably be a great phone, but just so-so at playing music.

Keep in mind, though, that the technical progress in this world is unrelenting, meaning these combination devices will keep getting better in everything they do. While a cell phone–MP3 player won't ever hold as much music as a stand-alone music device, it will soon be able to store and play enough to keep all but the most demanding MP3 buffs happy.

4. Price/Performance Bands: Manufacturers in nearly every single category of electronics are always looking over their shoulders at their competitors. What's more, all of them usually have the same technological building blocks to work with in making their products. The result is that in any given product category—digital cameras, for instance— you'll typically find products grouped together in three or so discrete price/performance bands. Usually, these correspond to entry-level, mid-tier and advanced. Prices change all the time, but an entry-level camera, for instance, might cost $150 or so, while an advanced one will run $500 or $600. (We aren't talking about professional models here; they can be many thousands of dollars.)

Making a purchase decision, then, means first figuring out what sort of consumer you are, and what your expectations for the product will be. In cameras, for instance, if you only want to take the occasional snapshot, an entry-level model will work just fine, and more than likely, all of the ones you see available will have similar features. If, however, you want to indulge your inner Ansel Adams, you'll probably want to get a higher-end model.

In electronics, like in everything else, you need to bring a certain amount of self-knowledge to the process. Are you thrilled by gadgetry, or bored by it? Is "good enough" good enough for you? Do you enjoy reading manuals and mastering new products, or is doing so a kind of torture? If you know the answers to those questions, many of the rest of the decisions you have to make will be a breeze.

HOW TO SIZE UP AND BUY THE LATEST DIGI-GADGETS

THE JOYS AND PITFALLS OF MALLS AND STORES . . .

For most big purchases, a trip to the electronics store will at some point be essential, as you can look at what you are thinking about buying in the flesh and kick the tires. But there are a number of potential problems with stores. Many of them limit the number of brands they carry to a few preferred suppliers. Sales staff, especially minimum-wage workers at big chains, often barely know what they are talking about. What's more, it's common for manufacturers to offer special incentives to floor salespeople to "push" certain models at certain times. This isn't to say you should never trust what any salesperson tells you; it's just that "buyer beware" should very much be the operative phrase.

The Internet, of course, has revolutionized electronics shopping, certainly for products like cameras that can easily be shipped. Few people these days make a big purchase without doing research online. But there are caveats here, too. With some Web sites offering product advice, you can't be sure of what role vendors had in influencing the recommendations, perhaps through advertising.

USING THE INTERNET SMARTLY
TO RESEARCH CONSUMER PRODUCTS

Searching the Internet for information about a new gadget can feel like a plunge down the rabbit hole. Web sites are chockablock with product data, but how can you be sure the information isn't out of date? Reviews are easy to find, but who's writing them? Is there any substitute for a hands-on inspection? And how on earth do you start?

The same way you'd sort out a confusing situation in the real world: Have a little patience and apply some old-fashioned horse sense. Given those two things, the Internet will yield its secrets, connecting you with people who have already done their homework, letting you compare prices and raising red flags. And even if you don't feel comfortable buying online, you should be able to go shopping in the real world with confidence—and a short list of candidates.

STEP 1: GETTING YOUR FEET WET

Whether you're buying a boom box or a flat-screen monitor, you want to be comfortable with your decision. To get to that point, you'll need to figure out what features you want in a product, read a range of reviews and find out what you can expect to pay.

When researching on the Internet, it's best to remember that finding a person knowledgeable about a given category of products is a more reliable method than searching for information piecemeal. You may want to know, for instance, how many MP3s an Apple iPod will hold, but what you really need to find is someone who not only knows the correct answer, but also can put that answer in the context that makes sense to your needs.

Fortunately, those people are out there—Andrew Gershoff, associate professor of marketing at Columbia Business School, calls them "highly involved consumers." They're the kind of people who not only love stereo gear, for example, but also like to evangelize about the best components.

How do you find them? Don't overlook the simple answer: Go to one of the Internet search engines and type in the product you're looking for ("boom box" or "flat-panel monitor") and the words "buying guide." Or find a couple of different brand names and models—don't worry if you're not sure they're exactly right for you—and enter both into a search engine. Poke around the list of sites returned by your search. With a little luck, high on the list you'll find an overview of products put together by the kind of knowledgeable person you need.

For example, someone interested in MP3 players might search for "ipod," "nomad" and "lyra," all of which are models of MP3 players. Although the first page of results returned by that search on Google has shopping sites that are light on basic information, it also includes links to overviews of MP3 players by *The Wall Street Journal*'s Walter S. Mossberg, the *Men's Journal* magazine and a CNET Reviews site dedicated to portable audio. All are good starting points, and the CNET site has a wealth of helpful links about MP3 basics. Don't just stick to Google, though, when searching; **teoma.com,** another search engine, breaks down the results of your search into subcategories, showing, for example, links involving "iPod Batteries," "iPod Reviews" and more in connection with an "iPod" search.

STEP 2: OTHER PEOPLE'S HOMEWORK

Not every enthusiast has turned his or her insights into a Web site, but many people have written reviews of products they have purchased. Their experiences can be different from those of expert reviewers: The pros get hand-holding from companies and often don't use a product long enough to see its quirks emerge.

Christopher Kelley, an analyst at the Cambridge, Massachusetts, market-research firm Forrester Research Inc., suggests looking for both expert and user reviews, a combination that lets you benefit from the experts' broader perspective about a product category and users' real-life experiences.

Where do you find user reviews? Try price-comparison sites, retailers' sites and sites dedicated to products and/or product news. In practice, retailers' sites are the best bet, with **Amazon.com** and its many overseas divisions the best example.

But how can you tell if a reviewer is a shill for a company or has an ax to grind?

You probably can't—but that doesn't mean reviews are useless. Many sites let users comment on other reviews, offering corrections or alternate views. And trust your own judgment: If you were chatting with a reviewer in the real world about Product X, would you find her comments insightful?

While ratings offer valuable at-a-glance information, Professor Gershoff warns that it's important to look at the reasons for a rating: If you want a pair of speakers ideal for reproducing classical music, a five-star rave that Model X speakers won't catch fire while blasting heavy metal isn't helpful.

Finally, don't miss the forest for the trees: A single review's conclusion may be suspect, but if multiple reviews reach the same conclusion, that's significant.

STEP 3: THE PRICE IS RIGHT

Price-comparison sites and tools abound on the Internet, and they can be valuable, particularly when they sit alongside customers' ratings of retailers. But price-comparison sites aren't the best place to start an online shopping expedition: Too often their product features and user reviews are skimpy or buried.

If price isn't crucial to you, start researching without worrying about it—you may learn more by getting familiar with product features than by zeroing in on a few models too early. Besides, your price range may be too low for the features you want, or too high for something that will meet your needs. Both are good to know.

Once you're down to a few models, by all means use the Internet to compare prices. Just make sure to perform some due diligence if you decide to order from an online retailer you've never heard of.

Finally, Professor Gershoff warns that online shoppers who have an unsubstantiated preference for a specific product can trick themselves by looking only for information that supports that product and underweighing evidence that argues against it. So while a few dissenting voices shouldn't worry you, you should keep an open mind.

STEP 4: KICK THE TIRES

No matter how much online research you've done, you may not feel comfortable making a purchase sight unseen. Fair enough—go kick the tires. Prepare yourself with product specs and price information about the models you're considering, as well as the questions you want answered, and head to a local retailer who has display models. (Print the data out—you think you'll remember what you really care about, but you won't.)

Once in the store, don't be shy. Interested in boom boxes? Bring along a favorite CD and let 'er rip. Need a monitor? Play with the settings and type a letter.

THE RENT-A-GEEK OPTION

The fact that modern electronics are well made doesn't mean they are easy to use. Many of them aren't, even for experts, and there is no shame in admitting to being perplexed by things.

If you don't have a tech-savvy spouse, child, friend or neighbor, then shelling out $50 or $100 to have someone spend an hour or two setting up a wireless network or a home theater could be the best money you ever spent. A good online source for this sort of hired help is **craigslist.com;** community newspapers or your local computer store are another. Make sure that your expert not only gets things working for you, but also teaches you how to use everything yourself.

COMPUTER HARDWARE

MAC OR WINDOWS?

When first entering the computer market, or coming back for a refill, the average person has to decide: Windows or Macintosh? Folks who write about computers know that making a recommendation here is a bit like recommending one religion over another; you're going to get into trouble no matter what you say.

Windows machines are used everywhere, typically cost less and, of course, are available from a number of different companies. While they aren't as hard to use as biased Mac owners claim they are, Windows machines, it's true, don't have the integrated elegance that you see in much Macintosh software. *The Journal's* office, with some exceptions for high-end graphics uses, operates in a Windows environment, and thus most of us have Windows machines at home (simply because it makes it easier to transfer work-at-home files back and forth). But for a home user, we would never try to argue someone out of buying a Macintosh. There is no right or wrong here; if it feels good, do it.

WHAT SORT OF SYSTEM TO BUY?

In many ways, the computer industry solves this problem for you. Computers are so powerful that an entry-level system sold by a big-label manufacturer is going to do just about anything that the average person would want to do. The exception is video-editing, such as assembling camcorder footage into a personal documentary. This takes a lot of computer power, and if you plan on spending much time playing with computer video, be sure to get a fast microprocessor and lots of memory and a capacious hard drive. As of this writing, a $500 entry-level Windows computer from the Dell website was equipped with a 2.4 gigahertz Intel Celeron microprocessor, which is the baby brother of the Pentium; 512 megabytes of memory; a 40 gigabyte hard drive and an optical drive that will read CDs. For another $300, you can get a full-blown Pentium; double the memory and hard drive and an optical drive that will both read and write CDs as well as DVDs. You'll definitely want the beefier model if you're going down the path of video-editing.

The one option that home users overlook involves getting a notebook PC, and then using it as their main desktop machine, while also being able to take it on the road. Nearly all notebooks let you plug a monitor into them as well as an extra keyboard and mouse. (Most people find using a regular desktop mouse much easier than anything built into a notebook.) While notebooks are always more expensive than desktop systems—and get even more expensive when you go the route of buying an extra monitor—their space-saving profiles and portability may be worth it for you.

Flat and light LCD display screens have gotten so inexpensive that they are rapidly replacing traditional CRT tubes as the main display device for computers. With good reason; they take up less space and produce less heat. These monitors keep getting bigger; 19 inches (measured diagonally) is now the norm, and 21-inchers are becoming more common. Get as big a screen as you can afford: You can never have too much screen real estate.

OF INK-JETS, LASERS AND FAX MACHINES

Printers

We can remember paying $500 back in the 1980s for one of the first HP inkjet printers—a blocky-looking behemoth that spit out about a page a minute, black-and-white only. These days, $500 will buy you a high-speed monochrome small-office laser from HP that will churn out your manuscript at 20 pages a minute (or a pretty good color home-laser).

Suffice it to say that printers have undergone the same kind of price and technological revolution as have PCs. Indeed, when you can march down to the local Best Buy and snag a compact, reasonably high-resolution color ink-jet for $49 on sale, the era of the disposable printer is perhaps at hand. So, before you buy that printer, you should ask the salesman what the replacement cartridges will cost you. (**Hint:** Many cost about the same as the printer, though we're not actually recommending tossing out the old printer and spending $49 on a new one each time.)

Like PCs, we're going to avoid recommending brands. Hewlett-Packard is still among the leaders, but there are lots of competitors offering lots of machines with lots of competitive prices and features. Instead, we'll give you our tips for choosing the right printer for you.

1. Know what you need. If you're a work-at-home mom whose job it is to edit manuscripts, you probably don't need a color printer. Instead, take advantage of the new generation of home-office lasers that start at $199 or monochrome ink-jets for half that much. You'll get speedy printing and save a ton on color ink-jet cartridges. If you're a serious digital photographer wanting to do high-quality prints at home, don't bother with some $99 run-of-the-mill ink-jet that will give you run-of-the-mill 8×10s. For $400 to $500 now, you can get state-of-the-art ink-jets capable of producing studio-quality large-format prints. If you're buying a printer for your kid at school, you don't have to spend more than $80 for a color ink-jet perfectly fine for rendering science reports with colored charts and the like. Just make sure Junior's not printing out every page he downloads from the Internet in four colors. Otherwise, you'll be paying a fortune to regularly replace those color cartridges.

2. Don't buy just on price alone. One tip the PC store salesman is sometimes reluctant to give you: Certain higher-priced ink-jet printers end up saving you money because they have demonstrably lower per-page ink costs than the cheapies. So over time they may be the real bargain. And even with our caveat that global manufacturing is falling into fewer and fewer hands, there indeed may be quality issues among printer brands. Most PC magazines have ratings features online, as do consumer sites like **shopping.Yahoo** and **shopping.CNET.com.**

3. Give the printer a good visual once-over before you take it home (and if it's hooked up, give it a spin). Will it really work for you or does it have features that will drive you crazy? Examples: Some printers are exceptionally noisy. Others claim to have the standard 50-sheet page-feeder but if you actually load them up with 50 sheets, you'll get constant paper jams. Does it matter whether the paper loads from above or below? It could, depending on your desk space and configuration. A friend, meanwhile, bought one of those nifty all-in-ones—scanner, printer and personal copier—only to find that the scanner and copy functions were a hassle to use in the enclosed space he had for the printer.

4. To save money on ink-jet printing, use "draft mode." Ink-jet printers let you print out at several different quality levels. The lowest is often called something akin to "Draft" mode, and while it doesn't look as good as the high-quality level you would use for a photograph, it's perfectly fine for some driving directions or a recipe you will only look at once. It also uses substantially less ink. You choose the output mode at the time you print something; it's usually listed in the "Preferences" section of the program's print menu. An even better step is to set the Draft mode of your ink-jet as the printer's "default" mode, meaning that it will always print that way, unless you tell it otherwise. (To do this on a Windows XP machine, go to the Windows Start button, then Settings, then Printers and faxes; right click on the printer, then go to Properties. Somewhere there will be a setting for print quality; change it to the level you want.) Obviously, if Draft is your default, you'll need to set it back to a higher quality when printing those baby pictures you want to pass around at work.

Fax Machines

Our advice on printers pretty much applies here, too. These days, you can get a perfectly workable plain-paper fax and copy machine for as little as $70. For well under $500 you can equip your home office with a plain-paper fax-copier with a 500-page paper tray and as many features as are found on the fax machine in the high-rise office where you work. If you have a busy fax life—let's say you sell real estate from your home office—go for the high-end, high-capacity version. But if you're simply going to use your fax now and then to send recipes to your mother or fax the kids' report cards to the grandparents, you can easily live with the bargain-basement models.

There isn't much to setting up modern fax machines. The only real issue is whether you want to have a separate, dedicated line. If you don't or can't afford it, there are lots of devices now, among them Catch-A-Call, that let you receive faxes while you're on the phone.

And don't forget the old computer-fax option—software programs that mimic fax functions by capturing incoming faxes via modem to your hard drive. Many people don't like them because they tend to be a little hard to set up—but they do have the virtue of taking up zero space on your desk. Winfax Pro ($119 retail) is probably still the gold standard, but you can find a dozen other providers on the Internet.

GETTING A HANDLE ON BROADBAND

"Broadband" is a generic, somewhat imprecise, word for any fast Internet connection. How fast? Well, at the very least, faster than the speeds you'd get from an old-fashioned dial-up modem, the sort that used a regular phone line and made all those shrill hissing noises.

The two most common methods of broadband are DSL, which stands for digital subscriber link, and cable modems. Each of them piggybacks an Internet signal on top of an existing wire: your phone wire, in the case of DSL, and your cable TV cable, in the case of cable modems. Adding either DSL or cable-modem service won't disrupt either your telephone service or your cable TV reception, since each of them operates on frequencies that aren't being used. In the case of DSL, for instance, you can make and receive telephone calls as usual, even if someone happens to be on the Internet at the same time.

Neither system is inherently better than the other; the quality of your service (meaning its speed and reliability) depends on your local phone company, in the case of DSL, or your cable provider, for cable modems. One neighborhood's DSL might be better than another's cable modem, and vice versa.

As happens with cell-phone plans, there is usually a nonstop price war among broadband providers, especially as cable and phone companies compete to be the one-stop supplier for the "converged" digital home. The plethora of offerings makes a decision tough to come by;

then again, potential customers can take satisfaction in knowing that it's a buyer's market.

Most of the first generation of broadband services are in the neighborhood of 500 kilobits a second, which is roughly 10 times what you'd get with dial-up. The technical details of how fast that is don't really matter; the important point is that 500 kilobits is fast enough to surf the Internet without encountering significant delays when big pictures and other graphics are being loaded. It's also fast enough to download music files, from a provenance either legal or illegal, without appreciable delays. But the Internet is changing, and one of the biggest changes involves the slow but steady introduction of services like telephony video.

But you'll need fast-as-possible Internet connections to make all this happen. If you *can* buy faster broadband speeds than the entry-level offerings, the extra money may well be worth it. Of course, there will still be other Internet bottlenecks you'll have to worry about; the fastest Internet connection in the world won't do you any good if the machine at the other end, the one transmitting the data, is too slow to keep up.

Take the case of Voice over IP, or VoIP. Think of this as Internet telephone service—the "IP" stands for "Internet protocol," and it's the way messages are passed back and forth. Traditional phone service—at least, the landline variety—uses its own network of copper cable (plus some behind-the-scenes fiber) to transmit voice signals as analog data. In VoIP, though, a special box hooks up to your broadband connection; you then plug a regular phone into that box. You still have a regular phone number, and you can use your phone just as you always did. But in a way that is invisible to you, your voice is digitized and then transmitted over the Internet to the person at the other end of the line.

The chief advantage of VoIP is that it is very cheap; you can get basic service for as little as $15 a month, with long-distance calls costing pennies a minute. (It helps that VoIP service isn't taxed, at least not yet.) VoIP started out as an offering from a new breed of Internet companies; Vonage is the best known of them. Since VoIP is cutting into their profit margins, established phone companies are being forced to offer it themselves.

In VoIP systems, you can be on the phone while someone else is on the computer. But because the two devices are sharing the same data "pipe," you may notice a lower quality in your telephone signal when someone is online. That's another reason to get a fast broadband connection, as the problem will be mitigated.

A last word on broadband: If you've ever ordered and tried to install broadband service, you know it can be a trying experience. Many large broadband providers such as Verizon push consumers to install software and modems themselves, while offering to send out real-life installers for a fee. Again, the rule of thumb is: If you're not a tech enthusiast or, worse, if technology scares you, spring for the installation fee. Also, remember that we're still in the early days of the Internet, and it often takes two or more visits from an installer to get broadband working right. Stick with it; lots of other people have the same sort of horror stories.

GOING WIRELESS

If you buy a notebook computer, it will almost certainly come equipped with some sort of wireless, aka "Wi-Fi," connection. That means you can sit with it in a coffee shop or airport lounge, should you want to, and read your e-mail or surf the Net.

You can use the same Wi-Fi technology in your home to connect two (or more) computers without running cables between them. For example, if you have a computer in the front of the house that has a broadband connection, you can share that connection with another computer upstairs in the bedroom. This means, of course, extra gadgets, but their prices have fallen faster than in just about any product category in electronics. A wireless connection for a desktop computer, for instance, will run you $15 or less; the "access point," which is like a transmitter that sends out data signals, now is as low as $50.

Planning a Wi-Fi network in your home can be a tricky business; depending on your existing setup, for instance, you may or may not want to add some sort of "router" to your access point, to control who can come onto your network. This is one area where you are best served by heading over to a computer store and simply telling the salesperson what you want to do. There is some combination of two or (maybe) three products you are going to need, and any salesperson working in the networking department for more than a few days will know what to tell you.

HOME NETWORKS: THE OLD IS NEW

Introducing the hot new trend in computer networking: copper wire.

But there are many situations where wireless computing doesn't work: for example, when the walls of a home or office are too thick for Wi-Fi signals to pass through. Or when the distance between two computers is too great. Or when appliances like refrigerators or microwave ovens or cell phones interfere with transmissions.

Until recently, the only way to get around these problems was to set up a network the old-fashioned way, by stringing a thick Ethernet cable wherever the networked computers needed to be. But now a relatively new networking system called "Powerline" lets you forget those cables, and instead rely on a somewhat surprising connection source: the existing copper electrical wiring inside your house.

It sounds like it won't work, but it does, very nicely, delivering speeds of 14 megabits a second—in other words, fast enough to keep up with even the fastest broadband networking connections. What's more, Powerline doesn't interfere with existing electrical appliances. And even faster versions of the technology are expected in another year or two.

Powerline was developed in 2000 as an industry standard by a group of computer and electronics companies. Most of the big home-networking companies, like Belkin Corp., the Linksys unit of Cisco Systems, Inc., and NetGear Inc. now sell products that implement the Powerline standard. Just as with 802.11 Wi-Fi, all of the products are designed to the same specifications, meaning products from one company work with products from another. All the Powerline suppliers have product and pricing information on their Web sites; in addition, Powerline products are available at most major online gadget retailers. For more information, the consortium that developed Powerline has its own webpage, **Homeplug.org.**

Powerline officials don't try to argue that their system is better than Wi-Fi, which tends to be cheaper and faster. Indeed, Powerline shipments are but a fraction of those for 802.11-based Wi-Fi systems. The officials instead are targeting Powerline for places where Wi-Fi isn't available.

Powerline's current speeds are fast enough for nearly all customers of today's broadband systems: DSL and cable modems. But Powerline officials are working on a new generation of the technology that will be up to 10 times faster than the current Powerline. That will be fast enough to allow users, for example, to transmit TV signals from a PC to a living-room set. The new Powerline won't be ready for another year or so; Wi-Fi developers have a similar speed increase planned for future versions of their system.

There are cases where Powerline won't work, like in the small minority of houses, apartments and offices that are served by two separate power grids that have no physical connection to each other. What's more, there are some electrical appliances that are especially "noisy," or run electrical interference, such as drills, hair dryers and halogen lightbulbs. These will affect network performance by slowing down data-transmission rates.

If Powerline can't work for you, you might want to consider Phoneline, a similar technology that uses telephone wiring to make its connections. There are fewer Phoneline suppliers than there are Powerline ones, but you can find them on the Internet.

THE SOUND OF MUSIC: PORTABLE MP3 PLAYERS

First off, the phrase "MP3 player" is somewhat misleading; MP3s are just one of several forms of digital music files. The Apple iPod, for instance, which is the best-known product in this category, plays MP3s as well as AAC, or Advanced Audio Codec, an entirely different way of compressing music in a digital file.

MP3 players come in two varieties. Some, like the iPods, contain a thumbnail-sized version of the hard-disk drive you have in your computer. Others use "flash memory"—computer chips that can store data, even with the power off. MP3 players based on disk drives will always have greater storage capacity than those based on flash memory; however, the latter can be made smaller and more rugged, since they have no moving parts. In terms of price per gigabyte of music storage capacity, flash devices will always be more expensive.

Much of the attraction to specific models of MP3 players involves fad and fashion, rather than the technical strengths of the devices. If you did a blind hearing test among the leading players, you'd be hard-pressed to tell the difference among them—certainly using the low-end earplugs with which most of them come equipped. The iPod wins points for cool, but just about any of its competitors will play music just as well. As a result, as long as an MP3 feels right to you when you handle it in the store, and as long as the interface to it seems easy to use, you might as well buy the one that gives you the most music storage for the least money.

SEEING IS BELIEVING: HDTV, HOME THEATER AND DVRs

In many ways, the most exciting part of the electronics world is video. That's because home television is in the middle of a revolution, one that is bringing an experience much like the cinema into everyone's living room. The most obvious sign of this is the remarkably vivid, awesomely large TV displays you can see at any electronics store. And if you've ever seen a movie at the house of a friend with a home-theater setup, you know it's hard to watch TV any other way afterward.

The less-than-fortunate aspect of home video is that this is one area of consumer electronics where prices still are sharply above the $300 median that is common elsewhere. High-definition televisions, to be sure, are coming down in price, but you can still expect to pay several thousand dollars for the wide-screen varieties. Add multiple hundreds more for the audio, and you have a big hunk of change. Nonetheless, millions of Americans have taken the plunge, and most of them wouldn't dream of going back.

TVs

Let's start this discussion with the picture.

What makes a TV an HDTV? Two things: the shape of the screen and the resolution of the picture.

For shape, traditional television sets have the dimensions, or "aspect ratio," of 4×3, meaning sets are built in multiples of 4 wide and 3 high. (A 16-inch-wide set would be 12 inches high, giving it a diagonal of 20 inches.) An HDTV set is much wider, more like a movie screen; its aspect ratio is 16×9. That's why HD sets look much more cinematic. That's also why when a high-definition picture is being shown on a standard set, you'll see dark, empty bands on the top and bottom of the screen. As happens with a "letterbox" movie, the picture doesn't fit properly, because it's a different shape. (The bands are on the sides of the screen when a standard picture is being shown on an HD set.)

The second major difference between TV and HDTV involves the quality of the picture—the heart of the matter in terms of "high definition." There are, inevitably, a lot of numbers involved in this part of the discussion. Just remember that for all the technical talk, the differences here are very dramatic and immediately apparent to anyone. Think, for instance, of a low-quality, smudgy color picture in some weekly shopper newspaper, and then imagine what the same picture would look like in an expensive and elegantly printed coffee-table book. That, in effect, is the difference between current TV and the best of high definition.

Standard broadcast television is the sort that's been around for decades. In the United States, this can be thought of as a grid that is, roughly, 480×500, or 240,000 "pixels" of information. There are a number of different specs associated with HDTV, but all of them involve putting substantially more pixels on the screen. (With pixels, more is always better.) They range from $720 \times 1,280$, or 920,000 pixels, all the way up to $1,920 \times 1,028$, or two million pixels. (Sets that can show that highest standard are only now being introduced; they will be considerably more expensive, at least for now.)

To show a high-definition television picture, you need a high-definition signal; alas, this is another area where HD shopping gets complicated.

If you simply plugged, for example, your existing cable TV cable into an HD set, you would still only have a standard-quality picture. It might even look worse, as the higher quality of the screen could show off flaws in the image that weren't noticeable on a standard set. In the early days of HD, there weren't many high-definition sources out there, and the added resolution they offered could only be noticed when playing a DVD movie. That situation, though, is changing, though not fast enough for many owners of big new TVs.

In major metropolitan areas, for instance, the major networks are broadcasting a standard as well as an HD signal; assuming you are in line of sight of the broadcast tower, you can pick up the HD signals for free using a conventional antenna.

Of course, most people get their TV signals these days from either a cable or a satellite company. The big cable and satellite companies are adding more and more HD channels to their lineup all the time;

check with your local provider to see what they have, and whether or not you'll be charged extra to get them.

Yet one more twist to HD shopping: When you buy a set, be sure to find out what else you might need to receive an HD signal. Some HDTV manufacturers build the HD tuner right into the set—meaning, just like with standard TV, you hook up an antenna and you are in business. But many other models require an external tuner, which is typically a set-top box-style device costing several hundred dollars. And be aware that these tuners will usually only pick up HD signals broadcast freely over the air; to get high-definition programming from your cable or satellite company, you'll probably require a new set-top box from them.

Now that you know a little about what HD is, you can move on to what are essentially hardware-related questions about the alternative ways of watching it.

Many people know the term "plasma," and use it as a kind of generic term for any of the big sets you see in an electronics store. Plasma, though, is just a particular technology used to make TVs. You can also get an HD set as an LCD, the "liquid crystal display" system used in laptop computer screens. Another up-and-coming system is called DLP, for "digital light processing," which is a kind of projection system that can be housed in a relatively thin (about 18-inch) set. There are other technologies on their way, too; a veritable alphabet soup of technologies and acronyms.

Note that you can also get an HD version of a cathode-ray tube-style television, which is the technology of traditional living-room TVs. However, for all practical purposes, it's physically impossible to make a CRT TV in the 40-inch and 50-inch size that consumers have come to associate with high definition. As a result, most people think that CRT TVs will slowly go the way of slide rules.

When buying an HD set, you'll have to choose one of these technologies. This, sadly, is probably the hardest decision to make in all of consumer electronics.

Plasma screens were the first to enter the big-screen market. They are bright, thin, lightweight and have good resolution. Their downside, say video buffs, is that they don't show the darker colors as well as other systems. They also suffer from "burn in," the ghostlike reside of an unchanging video image, such as a network logo in the bottom-right corner of the screen. (Most plasma sets, though, have methods of controlling burn-in.)

When big-screen TVs first came out, plasma sets were the only ones with the brightness needed for regular home viewing. (In fact, some videophiles think plasma sets are too bright for viewing in a darkened room, as many people do in home theater setups.) In the last few years, though, the other systems like LCD and DLP have been greatly improved. LCD systems, for instance, were at first too "slow" to show high-quality video; a moving image would leave visible trails on the screen. That problem and others have been largely resolved; every single display technology has one or more big electronics companies standing behind it, pouring hundreds of millions of dollars into R&D to make it better. LCD and the alternatives retain their biggest advantage over plasma: They cost less.

Picking which sort of system to buy is still not, well, a black-and-white issue. If it's any consolation, even the experts sigh in despair when asked how exactly consumers should make a decision about an HD set when wandering the aisles of an electronics store.

At best, they offer the most general sort of advice. Robert Hartley, author of *Home Theater for Everyone,* says don't just buy the brightest set; instead, go for the one with the most natural colors. Look at flesh tones, he says, or expanses of grass as indicators of color naturalness. Mister Hartley also notes that most displays are shipped from the factory at their brightest, visually "loudest" settings, in order to stand out on the showroom floor. He suggests changing the setting to the built-in one for playing movies, to give a better sense of what the display can do.

THE WAR FOR YOUR REMOTE: SATELLITE GAINS ON CABLE

The tide is turning for television addicts.

Cable companies have long dominated satellite TV in the battle for the remote controls of America's couch potatoes.

Now satellite, which has for years been associated with rural areas where cable was out of reach and with sports fanatics who want access to games in other cities, is catching up. By finally finding a way to include local channels in their packages—and by offering lower prices—satellite companies are starting to convert a sizeable number of cable subscribers. Last year, satellite companies signed up 2.3 million new subscribers, while cable started losing customers for the first time.

Cable has been fighting back with beefed-up features such as video on demand and is managing to hang on to its biggest-spending customers.

But one of the main reasons for satellite's recent gains is that cable companies, which still have three times more subscribers than satellite, have lost what has long been one of their most compelling competitive advantages: the ability to offer local channels. That includes the local affiliates of networks such as CBS and Fox, and popular shows such as the local news. In recent years, the two major satellite providers, DirecTV and EchoStar, have added enough satellite capacity to accommodate these extra channels in most major markets. EchoStar offers them to more than 92 percent of U.S. households.

Satellite providers also recently have recruited a critical ally: local telephone companies. Most major regional phone companies—including Verizon Communications Inc. and SBC Communications Inc.—have struck alliances with satellite operators to offer phone, TV and high-speed Internet services at a single discounted price. Those packages have been a hit thus far. Already, more than 200,000 households have signed up for satellite service through their phone companies, according to industry estimates. (Cable companies don't have such alliances because they compete with the phone companies.)

For consumers, the question of whether to choose satellite or cable involves a number of factors. Satellite generally offers cheaper packages. Both generally provide the same basic channels, such as ESPN and MTV, as well as premium channels such as HBO and Showtime.

But while satellite companies usually trump cable on price, cable has its selling points. Cable offers features that satellite can't, such as video on demand (the exception being DirecTV), which lets users order from a list of movies and programs anytime they want. It also offers local channels on high-definition TV, something satellite can't do. And cable isn't vulnerable to signal interruptions during thunderstorms.

Satellite traditionally has been the first to offer innovations such as high-definition TV and digital video recorders, which let you tape and pause live TV. But cable in recent years has been able to match many of those features. Cable, for instance, came out with its digital cable service in response to satellite's all-digital offering.

To lure customers, satellite companies recently have begun dropping the price on their equipment. DirecTV recently began offering its TiVo digital video recorders to new customers for $49, down from $99 earlier this year. EchoStar used to charge extra fees to hook up additional TVs. But recently, it started offering to connect up to four TVs at no additional charge.

Cable companies, meanwhile, are trying to leverage their edge in video on demand. Comcast Corp., the country's largest cable operator, with more than 21 million subscribers, has begun offering free on-demand highlights of National Football League games a day after they're played. Comcast subscribers who pay for premium channels such as HBO can watch back episodes of programs like *The Sopranos* and *Curb Your Enthusiasm* whenever they want.

Satellite companies can't offer video on demand because their subscribers communicate with the central office through a telephone line rather than a wide cable that allows much better two-way interaction.

All this is just the latest phase of more than a decade of cutthroat competition between cable and satellite. About 73 million households subscribe to cable compared with just more than 23 million for satellite. Cable companies offer both analog and digital services—the latter is more expensive but boasts better picture quality. Satellite, by contrast, offers only digital service.

Digital subscribers tend to be more loyal to cable because they get features like video on demand and more premium channels for the same price. They are also more likely to order additional services from the cable company, such as high-speed Internet.

But increasingly, satellite companies are winning over customers who have been paying for analog service from a cable provider and are looking to upgrade to digital. These new customers are drawn in part by the prospect of getting more channels for the dollar. Last year, the average satellite subscriber paid 38 cents per channel, according to a Carmel Group survey. Analog cable costs an average of 64 cents a channel, while digital cable cost 43 cents.

While satellite's price advantage is narrowing in most markets (both cable and satellite face the same increasing programming costs), it is still big enough to appeal to economy-minded households. In San Diego, Cox Communications Inc. charges $39.95 for a standard analog package of 72 channels. By comparison, EchoStar charges $29.99 a month for some 60 channels.

Consumers also continue to rank satellite much higher than cable on customer satisfaction. In a survey released in August of 2004 by

CABLE VS. SATELLITE:
COMPARING THE OPTIONS

 Some sample cable and satellite packages

SATELLITE

ECHOSTAR

Price: Least-expensive package is $29.99 per month for 60 channels. Each extra TV receiver costs $5 per month.

HDTV Channels: Five for an additional $9.99 per month

DVR: $4.98 per month; no additional installation fee

Unique features: Subscribers get more than 20 channels of games, news, weather and sports scores.

DIRECTV

Price: Least-expensive package is $36.99 per month for more than 125 channels. Each additional TV receiver is $4.99.

HDTV Channels: Five channels for $10.99 a month

DVR: $49 upfront cost for a TiVo; plus $4.99 a month

Unique features: NFL Sunday Ticket and Mega March Madness sports packages.

CABLE

COMCAST, ATLANTA

Price: Standard analog package is $42.50 for 73 channels. Digital subscribers pay an additional $15.49 for 71 more channels.

HDTV Channels: Nine for an additional $5 a month equipment charge

DVR: $9.95 per month, but only available to digital subscribers

Unique features: About 2,000 video-on-demand programs. Two-thirds of it is free, including college football and basketball games.

TIME WARNER CABLE, HOUSTON

Price: Standard analog package is $38.99 for 86 channels. Digital subscribers pay $52.99 for over 200 channels.

HDTV Channels: Seven channels for free

DVR: $6.95 per month

Unique features: More than 300 hours of movies on demand for a fee, and more than 250 hours of free programming on demand

CHARTER, ST. LOUIS

Price: Standard 81-channel analog package is $47.99 per month. Digital subscribers pay $52.99 extra for 226 channels.

HDTV Channels: Six

DVR: $9.99 per month

Unique features: About 1,043 video-on-demand programs, most of them for a fee

Note: HDTV channels do not include premium channels like HBO.

market-research firm JD Power and Associates, satellite operators got an overall customer-satisfaction score of 723 out of 1,000, compared with 659 for digital cable and 621 for analog cable.

Both sides are busily developing more sophisticated interactive services, like the ability to play games, vote on game shows, and even place bets on horse races with a remote control. They're also working on improvements to program guides and ways to get shows, movies and other content off the Internet.

SOUND DECISIONS: HOME THEATER SOUND SYSTEMS

The other advantage of HDTV is that nearly all high-definition signals are accompanied by surround-sound audio. (DVD players come equipped with surround sound, too.) If you're spending the money on a new HDTV set, you might as well bite the bullet and get a home-theater sound system at the same time. In fact, the improvement in the overall experience you'll get from surround sound may be more dramatic than the one you get from adding a big screen.

You'll see in discussions of home-theater systems many references to "5.1" sound systems. Just like a traditional living-room stereo system has two channels—right and left—a 5.1 system has five of them. There are right, center and left channels for the front, and then right and left in the rear. The front channels handle most of the audio in a TV show or movie, including dialogue; the back two are for atmospherics—the "surround" in surround sound. The ".1" in "5.1" refers to the subwoofer, which sends out deep bass signals, and which can be placed anywhere in the room. There is also a 6.1 system, which adds a center speaker in the rear.

To have home-theater audio, you'll need a new receiver that can handle 5.1 or 6.1 channels. (Your old stereo receiver won't do.) You plug your video source, like a DVD player, into the home-theater receiver, and then run cables to your speakers. There is nothing special about the speakers used in a home-theater setup; except for the subwoofer, they are just like the speakers you might have now in your living room. What's more, all five (or six) of them are identical to each other, and can be placed interchangeably. You shouldn't, though, cobble together a home-audio system using different sets of speakers from your earlier stereo systems, since the sounds they produce probably won't be balanced or in synch.

Note that two brands you see a lot of in the home-audio world—Dolby and DTS—have nothing to do with the number of channels of sound you get. Dolby and DTS are competing technologies for encoding sound, and while you can have a Dolby 5.1 or a DTS 6.1 system, the number of channels and the encoding method used to pump the sound over each channel are entirely unrelated issues.

Home-theater audio systems start at as little as $350, including speakers, and go up from there. (And up and up and up, if you move into audiophile territory.) If you think there are a lot of choices in TVs, wait till you get to audio. The number of available models increases exponentially, on account of the innumerable manufacturers of medium- and high-end audio equipment. Do your homework, talk to people, then finally, listen to what your ears are trying to tell you.

THE DIGITAL RECORDING REVOLUTION: DVRs

Digital video recorders are the other must-have item for a sophisticated home-theater setup. These devices—TiVo is a brand name for the best-known of them—are like mega-capacity VCRs on steroids; they transform virtually everything about the experience of watching television.

A DVR is, in effect, a computer with a very high-capacity hard-disk drive built in, though it looks and works nothing like the PC on your desk. Instead, it sits on top of your TV; you control it with a remote control, just like you do your television.

The biggest advantage of a DVR is that it allows you to determine in advance what shows you want to record for later viewing. It's easy to tell the machine to record the nightly news, or your favorite series, or the big game. You can also, every few days, look to see what movies will be coming up, and click to record those, too. The amount of programming you can store on a DVR depends on the size of its hard drive; newer DVRs have pushed the total past several hundred hours.

Once a show has been recorded, you can watch it whenever you want to. You can tell DVR owners at a party because they are the ones who aren't rushing home to catch something on TV. And in viewing your recorded shows, you have all the pause–rewind–fast-forward options that you have with a DVD player. In fact, since the DVR is always working in the background to record what is on the TV, you can pause and replay even "live" TV, to run to the kitchen or to review something you've just seen.

If you decide to go the DVR route, you'll need to contact your cable or satellite provider, since many of them provide their own DVRs that are compatible with their programming. You may be charged extra for the device, though cable and satellite companies are increasingly including them in their basic offerings.

Note that high-definition TV complicates the DVR situation. The first crop of DVRs only work with standard television signals. Lately, though, companies have been bringing out new HD-compatible DVRs. Because there is so much extra information in an HD picture, a DVR that could store 100 hours of standard television programs will only be able to hold about 20 hours of HD. The good news here is that disk drives are getting bigger all the time, and it won't be long before DVRs can be loaded up with hundreds of hours of high-definition signals, too.

CAPTURING LIFE: DIGITAL CAMERAS AND CAMCORDERS

Think of the ascent of digital cameras and camcorders as a victory of convenience over charm. In the old days of film, you'd get back from a vacation and wait for the pictures to come back from the drugstore; everyone would then huddle around while the snapshots were inspected—or, even more dramatically, sit in a dark room and watch movies of the adventure. In the brave new digital world, though, you can take a picture on a camera and then see it right away, and e-mail it around the world in seconds. And in the case of camcorders, you can watch the movie on the camcorder's LCD screen even while it's being taken. Those with extra patience can edit the movie on their PC, and then mail off DVD copies of their cinematic life and times.

As noted earlier, cameras and camcorders are one of the many areas in electronics where product categories are converging. In a few years, it may be possible that all you'll need is a single camera-camcorder that will handle all of your filming and photography needs. For the time being, though, you'll want a digital camera if you mainly want to take still pictures, and a camcorder if you mostly want to take movies. If you haven't checked lately, you'll be pleasantly surprised at the prices: Entry-level models for cameras and camcorders can be had for $125 and $250, respectively.

How to shop for them? Let's take still cameras first.

A PRIMER ON BUYING A DIGITAL STILL CAMERA

Like all high-tech products, digital cameras are described by a dense jargon of techno-babble, designed in part to confuse civilians and separate them from their money. As the cameras have soared in popularity, this terminology problem has actually grown worse.

So here's our buyer's guide to digital cameras. It's a quick road map to the most important features to look for when buying a digital camera, and to the terminology salespeople and "experts" are likely to hurl at you.

This guide is meant for average, casual photographers. If you are a photo hobbyist or enthusiast, you will likely want to consider many more features than these, and you may want to focus more on such traditional photographic issues as lenses and optics. This guide mainly focuses on the cameras' basic digital characteristics.

Camera Categories

Digital cameras for consumers can generally be grouped into three categories, unrelated to price: pocket cameras; point-and-shoot cameras; and models that resemble old film cameras, with lots of manual overrides. Pocket cameras are my favorites. These are usually under an inch thick, but often still include zoom lenses, LCD screens and the capability to take high-quality photographs. Point-and-shoot models are geared to be comfortable in your hand, without being too small. Higher-end models tend to be larger and heavier, with more dials and buttons and menus, and a greater emphasis on optics.

Megapixels

A camera's megapixel number—3.2, 4, 5 and so on—is used as a general indicator of picture quality, but it's a crude measure that doesn't always reliably predict how you'll feel about the output of a given camera. It actually measures the maximum resolution of an image taken by the camera at its top-quality settings. But in reality, many other factors contribute to photo quality—lenses, sensors, flash systems, various technical settings. And you may not want to shoot at the camera's top settings, which produce huge images that can quickly max out your memory card.

Not only that, but more megapixels can actually mean a worse image in some cases. That's because to get more megapixels out of a camera, the manufacturers often shrink the size of each pixel, reducing the amount of color information each can hold. As a rule of thumb, an average family photographer can do very well with a 3.2 or 4.0 megapixel camera, even if she is making large 8 × 10–inch prints from the images. You might want more megapixels, however, if you do a ton of cropping and editing and still want large prints. That's because cropping and editing throws away pixels.

Bear in mind, though, that most digital pictures are never edited or printed at all. They remain on a computer and are mainly viewed on a screen, or e-mailed around. And most of those that are printed become relatively small snapshots.

Optical vs. Digital Zoom

The optical-zoom feature on a digital camera works just like the zoom feature on a film camera—the lens actually extends to make distant objects seem larger and closer. (On some cameras, this lens extension is invisible, because the lens body is mounted inside the camera, for compactness.)

But the camera companies try to confuse digital-camera buyers with something called "digital zoom." This is nothing but a computer trick that blows up a portion of the picture. And this gimmick has a price: It lowers resolution, and in many cases, it can make for a grainier photo. If a camera boasts only digital zoom, it doesn't have a real zoom capability at all. If it says it has a combined 12× zoom, but only 3× of that is optical, then it really has a 3× zoom. I don't recommend relying on digital zoom, but I do recommend a 3× optical zoom for family photographers.

LCD Screen, Optical Viewfinders

When digital cameras first appeared, people were so excited to be able to review photographs on the camera's screen that they didn't mind that the screen was tiny. Now a few companies have designed liquid crystal display (LCD) screens that are much larger, measuring two inches or more diagonally. But make sure the image on these larger screens remains sharp and crisp.

These screens make reviewing photos much easier, and they can also be used to frame the shot and aim the camera. But I don't consider them an adequate replacement for an optical viewfinder. If you aim with only the LCD, your arms will be extended and you'll be more prone to shake the camera than if you use the optical viewfinder, with the camera held closer to your body. Some cameras omit the viewfinder and force you to rely solely on the screen, but I don't recommend these. The best combination for viewing subject matter is a large LCD screen and an optical viewfinder.

Also, if you do a lot of outdoors shooting, look for a camera that stresses that its LCD screen can be seen well in daylight. Many can't.

Start-up Time

Like a computer, a digital camera needs time to start up. But if a camera takes too long to start up, you can miss capturing baby's first steps. With that in mind, most camera-makers are striving to reduce start-up times. Look for a camera that's ready to shoot in a second or less.

Shot-to-Shot Time

This is the time it takes after the completion of one shot for the camera to be ready to take another. Many factors contribute to this lag time, including the need to save the image on your camera's memory card, and the need to recharge the flash. Like a slow start-up time, this shot-to-shot delay can rob you of valuable photographic opportunities. Unfortunately, many camera-makers don't even publish specs on shot-to-shot time.

Continuous Shooting

To partially compensate for the shot-to-shot lag, many models have a special setting called "burst" or "continuous" mode. In this mode, the camera can take a limited number of shots without pausing. The shots are usually held in a memory buffer and then processed and saved all at once. This mode might come in handy for hobby enthusiasts at sporting events or with family action shots. But continuous mode doesn't really work well if the flash is being used, or if you need to refocus between shots.

Battery Life

Make sure the camera you buy matches your style of shooting. A good rule of thumb is that a camera should be able to get a day's worth of shooting out of a single battery charge. Depending on how you use your camera, this could mean 20, 50, 100 or 200 shots. Battery life varies, depending on the size and quality of the images, how much of the time you use flash and whether you keep the LCD screen on all the time or use it sparingly.

Many cameras use expensive, proprietary batteries. Some allow you to pop in drugstore alkaline batteries in a pinch. It's a good idea to carry a spare, so check on the cost of batteries. Also, note how the battery can be recharged. Some cameras require you to charge the battery either inside the camera or in a separate charger. Others give you a choice. Some have a charger that can handle two batteries at once.

Memory Cards, Cradles

Various types of memory cards can be used in digital cameras, including Secure Digital (SD), Multimedia, Compact Flash and Smart Media. Sony cameras are able to use only Memory Stick cards, which look like a stick of chewing gum. The Kyocera high-speed models require a new kind of high-speed SD card, which can save images more quickly than standard cards.

This isn't something that should worry the average consumer. There is no need for you to worry about whether the memory card in your new camera is compatible with the one in, say, your MP3 player. For starters, it is unlikely that you will ever need to exchange information directly between the devices.

More important, all of the devices can hook up to your PC, which becomes the common ground translator for all of them. Virtually all camcorders, cameras and the like come equipped with a high speed cable, usually either USB or 1394 "Firewire" that connects to a computer.

There are other methods for making this data transfer. Some computers, for instance, have built-in readers that accept certain kinds of memory cards. And some device manufacturers are starting to sell "cradles" that not only handle the data from your device, but keep it charged as well. In general, though, the high-speed cable that comes with your new gadget is all you will need to keep it hooked up to your computer, and thus to everything else you own.

Bonus Tip: Printers You Can Live Without

Many camera and printer companies try to sell you printers that hook up directly to the camera. We consider these products a naked conspiracy to sell "consumables"—paper and ink. Most families these days are perfectly happy sharing photographs online, or by way of Internet services like Imagestation, Shutterfly, Ofoto or Snapfish. These sites— many of which are free—let you upload your pictures to a central server. You then send a weblink to friends and family; it's much faster than e-mailing the pictures themselves.

Those rare cases are easily handled on a PC and a regular ink-jet printer. Those printers start at less than $100; if you don't have one, the photo-sharing sites will also sell you film-style prints of your digital photos. The point is that most people enjoy the new-fashioned world of digital photography without ever needing old-fashioned prints of the pictures they take. And when you do need prints, use your computer just to make the prints you want, as opposed to outputting everything in your camera, as in the old days.

—WALTER J. MOSSBERG

CAMCORDERS: THE CHANGING FACE OF HOME MOVIES

First, a brief history of home movies.

In the beginning was film: 8mm and Super8 movies that came in three-minute rolls. You shot a roll or two, took them to be developed and then watched them on a projector when you got them back. In the 1980s, the VCR revolution began to enter the home; video cameras let you record onto videotape, although you had to run a cable from the camera to the TV to see what you had filmed. Then came camcorders, with their built-in screens. By today's standards, they were bricks, weighing as much as 10 pounds.

They got smaller in the 1990s, when the cartridges used to record the image shrank from the size of a VHS tape to about the size of a box of matches. The video, though, was still analog video, meaning it had the quality of a VCR.

The next big leap in camcorders came in the late 1990s, when the mini-DV camcorder was born. While these machines still used a tape to record video and audio, they stored their data digitally. That means they had a sharper image—in the same way the DVD offered an improved picture over a VCR. Being digital also meant you could hook up your camcorder to your comcuter, and import your video files for viewing or editing.

In the last few years, new models of camcorders have dispensed with the tape altogether, and substituted a small version of a DVD disk as the recording medium. This makes your movies easier to view; you can simply pop out the disk from the camcorder and pop it into any DVD player. (With tape-based camcorders, you need to connect the camera to a TV via a cable, and then play the taped movie.)

When buying a camcorder, the tape-vs.-disk decision is the first one you will need to make. Tape-based camcorders can record up to 80 minutes per tape, compared to only 30 minutes for the newer disk-based machines. They also record in a higher resolution; images put on disks are compressed much more than those stored on tape. However, even the compressed image of a disk will be perfectly acceptable to most people, especially when considering the convenience of having an easily portable disk.

The other issue in buying a camcorder involves the extent you want it to be a still camera. Increasingly, the price difference between low- and medium-grade camcorders is explained by features involving traditional photography, such as having a two-megapixel camera with accompanying storage built in. Obviously, you'll want to pay more for that only if the idea of a dual-purpose gadget is attractive to you. Just remember the general rule here, which is that something that does two things isn't going to do them as well as two specialized devices.

When shopping for camcorders, you'll find the usual price bands, with entry-level models under $300 and high-end ones triple that amount. Among the other features that separate more expensive models from cheaper ones are the quality of the lens, the ratio of its optical zoom, the size of the built-in display screen, the life span of the battery, the presence of some sort of built-in light source and the general level of miniaturization in the camcorder's design.

Manufacturers add features to camcorders at breathtaking rates, so you're going to need to do a little bit of homework before making a decision on one. For example, camcorders of late have included the option of shooting images in a 16-×-9 aspect ratio, for display on wide-screen TVs. Note that the aspect ratio is the only thing about these camcorders that is "HD"; the actual videos they take are at lower resolutions than what you'd get in a true high-definition broadcast. True HD camcorders are available, but remain very expensive, costing thousands of dollars. This is one product where the best advice is simply to bide your time.

WHEN GOOD GADGETS GO BAD: THE REPAIR CONUNDRUM IN A THROWAWAY SOCIETY

Ron Mason's apartment is a junkyard of broken gadgets: a busted cell phone, television and videocassette recorder, along with a computer monitor and printer. It's all headed for the trash. Get things fixed?

"What's the point?" asks the New York computer consultant. "For a few dollars more, I can just replace it with something brand-new."

If you've tried to get something repaired lately, you know it's frustrating—but you might not realize just how bad things are. The number of repair shops across the U.S. has dropped by half during the past decade, to about 9,000, even as consumers snap up a record $95 billion worth of gadgets a year. Much of the blame goes to the falling price of electronics, which has made it tempting for people to throw broken items away and prompted makers to pare back on service. Now, with the sluggish economy making people think "repair" instead of "replace," finding help can seem impossible.

We should know. We spent the past few months trying to get 14 items repaired, from a scanner that wouldn't scan to a printer that wouldn't print. Depending on what the makers told us, we sent about half of the items to the companies, and half to local repair shops. A couple of items we even sent to both places, waiting patiently on 800 numbers and punching in choices on phone trees. Along the way, we had moments of euphoria (one local shop fixed our printer—free of charge) and frustration (we had to e-mail one maker three times to get a phone number).

In the end, we found that it's still possible to get many things fixed—seven of our items came back working—but the chances vary widely, mostly according to the gadget. Surprisingly, price has little to do with it: No one would touch our $149 scanner, but our cheaper portable CD player was replaced for free. As a rule, local shops did better, although we did track down a far-flung hospital for TiVos (hint: Mount Rushmore). While dealing with the makers could be a hassle, some companies actually let us trade in the busted goods for new items—at almost a third off.

It's clear, though, that these days some people are looking closer at the repair option. Sony, for example, says demand for repair support from customers is up 15 percent this year, while Philips Electronics says calls are running 5 percent higher. (In contrast, over the last decade nearly a quarter of the almost 60 million households with broken items opted to ditch them, according to a survey by eBrain Market Research.)

But in order to defray costs, many companies, including Sony, Epson, Hewlett-Packard and Handspring, now charge a fee—ranging from $9.95 to as much as $25—just to talk to a technician on the phone. In some cases, they're taking planned obsolescence to new heights, making gadgets that can't be repaired—with backs sealed shut or batteries that can't be replaced. At the same time, local fix-it shops, squeezed by low reimbursements for in-warranty repairs and the low prices of replacements, are raising prices—or going out of business.

If you're seriously considering the repair option, here are some tips:

1. The best time to consider repairs is when you buy a gadget. If you end up at Best Buy or Comp USA to buy a laptop, ask about their repair policies—could they fix your PC on-site? Do they ship it back to the manufacturer? What are average turnaround times? (These are also good questions to ask Internet-based vendors.)

2. Consider repair or replacement insurance options. All electronic stores will offer them to you. Some will seem expensive—for example, a three-year extended warranty on a 17-inch LCD monitor may cost $100. On the other hand, to replace the least expensive component on such a monitor will probably cost that much—not counting labor. Some such policies also have the added advantage of instant replacement—that is, if your gadget is dead, they'll give you a new one on the spot, often with no questions asked. We recently had a dodgy, 18-month-old MP3 player replaced under just such a policy.

3. Finally, if you don't have a repair policy or your appliance is out of warranty and you think it makes financial sense to fix it, start with the gadget-maker's website. Many have a list of local repair affiliates or provide an address to which you can send the item for repair.

CHAPTER SEVEN

THE GREAT
GAME

BUYING, FINANCING AND KEEPING
A CAR IN SHAPE

Buying a car has long been an irritating game of cat-and-mouse—
but now the cat is better equipped.

THE CHANGED WORLD OF BUYING

Thanks to the Internet, no longer can dealers closely guard the actual costs of vehicles and reap big profits from uninformed shoppers. Now buyers are better prepared than ever for negotiations, armed not only with dealers' actual costs but also with competing prices and a raft of details about cars' specifications and features.

The Internet is loaded with information about vehicles. In a matter of minutes you can learn about a car's dimensions, color choices, upgrade packages and price, and compare it with other models—free of the sales pressure of a showroom. Some dealers put their entire inventory online, allowing you to search in your area for an exact model in a specific color. You can even have them e-mail you their best offer. Of course, even when you use the Internet, you'll still most likely end up going to a local dealer. But you'll be going more prepared.

So what's the best way to buy a car on the Internet?

Auto-industry analyst Chris Denove, a partner at JD Power, breaks the process into three steps.

1. **Begin the search by doing research online** at sites such as **Edmunds .com,** an auto-information service based in Santa Monica, California, and Consumer Reports Online, to see which cars meet your needs. People can also arm themselves with invoice prices from such sites, useful figures in any negotiation.

2. **Go for a test drive.** The Internet, no matter how sophisticated it becomes, will never adequately replicate the emotional and physical experience of driving a car. At this point, consumers should go into a dealership and kick the tires of a few cars.

3. **Seek multiple offers.** Mr. Denove suggests that once car shoppers are 100 percent sure which vehicle they want, they submit online purchase requests from at least two Web sites: a site run by the car manufacturer, most of whom operate referral services for dealerships that sell their cars, and an independent car-referral site such as Carpoint or Autobytel. Those requests should generate responses from several dealerships with price quotes for a car. The quotes can be negotiated, though many dealers will give rock-bottom prices up front, Mr. Denove says.

Here are the most useful Internet sites:

1. Autobytel.com: This site lets you compare a dozen or more vehicles in a side-by-side chart that lists their price, features, horsepower, mileage, legroom, options and other data. You can read multiple reviews for most models and even take a 360-degree photo tour of car interiors. Then you can request prices from a retailer in your area. A handy calculator tells you how much your monthly payment will be if you buy a car on credit. But beware: Because its business is to help sell cars, the site has a strong marketing flavor. Its reviews tend to be gushy, and light on listing shortcomings.

2. Consumerguide.com: This site is packed with specs, prices, shopping tips, a list of "best buys" and advice on issues such as leasing versus buying and types of financing available. Its reviews are thoughtful and comprehensive, rating such things as a vehicle's acceleration, quietness and value within its car class. It gives a numerical score to each car so you can readily compare the lot. The reviews also give a history of each vehicle, describe upcoming models (useful if you can wait to get a car) and discuss the competition.

3. KKB.com: Established in 1926 by car buff Les Kelley, the Kelley Blue Book has research tools and up-to-date pricing on thousands of new and used vehicles, including the company's New Car Blue Book Value, which reveals the price dealers pay for new models.

4. Consumerreports.org: The online version of the respected, nonprofit magazine provides a bunch of information free of charge, including tips on how to narrow your choices, negotiate prices and save money on leases. If you pay to subscribe to the site you'll get much more, including extensive test-drive reviews, the magazine's unique reliability predictions based on readers' experiences, safety ratings and feature stories on cars. But the best stuff will cost you. And its prim, nononsense reviews give you little feel for a car's aesthetic qualities.

5. Edmunds.com: Along with specs, links to local dealers and the pricing data that are this guidebook company's foundation, the full-featured site includes snappy reviews written chiefly by Edmunds's own staff. Like some car magazines, Edmunds acquires cars for long-term testing and periodically reports on how they are faring. Its advice section includes a very useful "10 Steps to Buying a New Car." One unusual feature: a "town hall" message board in which consumers banter about the pros and cons of various vehicles, gossip about expected model changes and offer advice—and arguments. The site also offers driving and maintenance tips. Car freaks could spend hours here.

6. Autos.msn.com: Microsoft's MSN Autos, formerly Carpoint, gives you a capsule description and history of each model. You can quickly compare two models based on more than 60 criteria. Click on the features you want and up pops the sticker price. You can then get price quotes from local dealers. The site also has reviews from its own contributors for most models, as well as financing and insurance tips.

7. Autos.yahoo.com: The Yahoo Autos site lets you compare a car against three other models and do side-by-side comparisons of the different trim levels within a model, allowing you see, for example, what the Taurus Premium offers over the Taurus Standard. As with Autobytel, you can get a 360-degree view of a car's interior. You also can get a price quote from dealers.

8. eBay.com: According to eBay, an SUV sells on the site every 21 minutes. Most vehicles automatically come with protections such as purchasing insurance at no extra cost. There's usually buyer feedback, so you feel more comfortable making such a large purchase online. Try to find a car auction where there's no minimum bid.

Finally, check out the Web sites of car magazines, including *Car and Driver* (**caranddriver.com**), *Motor Trend* (**motortrend.com**) and *Road & Track* (**roadandtrack.com**), which offer reviews, industry news and buying advice. And, of course, the Web sites of each carmaker give lots of information—along with hefty doses of hype.

WHEEL LIFE: WE GO SHOPPING ONLINE

To gauge how easy it is to look for wheels online without being taken for a ride, we decided to price an Acura TL—we were hoping for satin silver metallic, with "ebony leather" seats—using five different tools ranging from **autos.yahoo.com** to **Car.com**. We priced our dream wheels in Los Angeles. Our goal was a decent price, of course, along with the least amount of hassle.

The first thing we learned was, you can run but you can't hide from your local car dealer. Turns out that most of the national services we tried weren't dealers themselves. Rather, they either negotiated with local dealerships on our behalf—or sent us directly to a dealer they have a business relationship with. Yahoo's service sent us to another third-party Web site, which ultimately put us in touch with a dealership.

Essentially, the services are useful for people who want to save time and avoid the on-the-lot haggling. Industry observers also say dealers generally consider online shoppers to be better informed—and less patient—than walk-ins. As a result, the price they shoot back is likely to be closer to reality, eliminating some of the haggling you'd have to do on the lot. But if you're a good on-the-lot bargainer, it may make more sense to hit the dealership in person and cut out the middleman.

We started with **CarsDirect.com,** which bills itself as a no-haggle service. Of the five methods we tried, it was one of the most user-friendly. It also was one of the quickest: We had all our information within about an hour.

You type in what you want, and it spits out a price. Then you get a phone call from a "specialist" to discuss the details. Our guy quoted us $32,345, a number that is slightly less than the manufacturer's suggested retail price. We pushed for a better price—but we got nowhere. "If you were looking for a Civic, I'd have you below invoice," he said. CarsDirect says it has prenegotiated prices with car dealers.

At **Autobytel.com,** we put in our request and the site immediately told us the name of a dealer that would be contacting us. We heard back the same day from the dealership, in an e-mail. They did have our color, but not the interior we were hoping for. When we phoned the salesman to discuss the price—$31,500, the best one we got—he said no to negotiation. **AutoNation.com** is the only one of the services we used that is an actual dealership itself, though it also has some partnerships with other local dealers. It gives you a list of available cars, and the option to click on the one you are most interested in. After that, the dealer for that particular car is supposed to get in touch with you. We clicked on our silver Acura over the weekend, but never got a response, though when we tried again on Monday, we did hear back from a dealer. AutoNation says our initial weekend request didn't show up in its system.

COMPANY: **CARSDIRECT.COM**

The Pitch: Promises no-haggle prices and minimal contact with dealerships.

Best Feature: A customer rep, "Don," phoned us in less than an hour to talk turkey.

Comment: Easiest and quickest of the services we tried. We had all our info in under an hour.

COMPANY: **CAR.COM**

The Pitch: "Quick, free quotes from **Car.com**'s *Best Dealers* in your area."

Best Feature: The site is well laid out and simple to use, but . . .

Comment: The service couldn't find our car in the two cities where we shopped—Atlanta and Los Angeles.

COMPANY: **AUTOS.YAHOO.COM**

The Pitch: Bills itself as a comprehensive mix of services for researching and pricing vehicles.

Best Feature: Lets you search prices on up to three other national car-shopping sites at once.

Comment: Confusing layout and seemingly endless resources mean it's not always clear how to find what you want.

COMPANY: **AUTOBYTEL.COM**

The Pitch: "The best place to research, buy and sell"

Best Feature: Compiles a helpful snapshot of actual sale prices for the model you're interested in.

Comment: It returned the lowest price—$31,500—of the services we tried.

COMPANY: **AUTONATION.COM**

The Pitch: Says it keeps over 100,000 vehicles in stock.

Best Feature: It's the only actual car dealer (as opposed to middleman) of the five online services we tried.

Comment: Company says typical response time is usually less than 30 minutes.

Yahoo acts as a clearinghouse of other pricing services. It has partnerships with 15 other services, including companies such as **Autoweb .com** and AutoNation: You tell it what you want, and it goes out and searches them for options. In our case, it steered us to **Autoweb.com**, which is owned by Autobytel. At **OnCar.com**, owned by StoneAge Corp., we were told there were no participating dealerships in our area—we tried once in Atlanta, and then in Los Angeles. A spokesman said the company negotiates with individual dealerships to be listed in its service and is in the process of recruiting more to participate.

BEWARE THE ADD-ONS

So, let's say you've successfully navigated the Internet, found the car you want at a dealer near you. Your next hurdle is to avoid getting stuck with expensive dealer add-ons. Here are the most common add-ons and the questions you should ask to see if they make sense for you:

Loans

Smart questions: What is the interest rate they are offering versus what you can get from your bank or credit union? What are they charging you to help you get the loan? (That figure is usually tacked on to the interest rate without you knowing it.)

Extended Warranty

Smart questions: All new cars, and some used cars, come with a manufacturer warranty. What does the additional coverage offer beyond that? If you miss an oil change or other routine service, does that invalidate the extended warranty?

Prepaid Maintenance Plans

Smart questions: What does this plan cover, besides routine oil changes and lubrication? Does the math work in your favor?

Theft Etch

Smart questions: A dealership etches a number in a window as a theft deterrent; if the car is stolen, the owner gets $2,500 to $5,000, depending on coverage. Is this really a deterrent against theft? (Many experts say no.) Will it help me get my car back? (Many experts say it very well could serve as an identifier even if the thieves have attempted to eradicate things like your engine number.)

Total-Loss Protection or Gap Insurance

Smart questions: If the car is stolen or totaled, the policy pays the difference between the car's current value and the loan balance. Does such a policy make sense if I've bought a car with little down payment? (Probably not.) Does it make sense for lease vehicles? (Generally, yes, since a lease car's residual—i.e., the value the dealer has assigned it at the end of your lease—might exceed what your private insurance company is willing to pay.)

Chemical Protections

Smart questions: Dealers often want to sell you things like seat protectants, paint sealants, undercoatings and even sound-proofing materials. Since many cars come factory-equipped with these things anyway, what real level of protection are you getting for your money?

IF YOU FALL IN LOVE, BE PREPARED TO PAY FOR IT

The big story of the auto industry of late has been massive discounting—an average of $3,000 is knocked off the sticker price of every new car sold these days. But there is another side to this story. In an effort to create more buzz around their new models, automakers are producing smaller batches of cars. Those smaller production runs also help carmakers avoid getting stuck with lots of unsold cars. For consumers, the result is that demand is outstripping supply on an increasing number of popular new cars, creating a run on some unlikely vehicles.

This is giving dealers some new powers. Instead of being at the mercy of hard-bargaining customers, they can now pad the sticker price on a surprising array of cars. Another by-product: Waiting lists, once reserved for limited-edition cars like Ferraris, are becoming more common for mass-market models, including Acura SUVs and Honda minivans. The dealer markups on popular vehicles come in several different forms. In addition to the "market adjustment," some dealers now charge "finders' fees" for hot models. Others offer customers the chance to jump up the waiting list for a particular car—if they pay the dealer extra. (Line-jumping fees range from a few hundred dollars to as much as $2,000.) Meanwhile, more customers are buying cars loaded with options they don't really want, such as alarm systems and compact-disk changers, because those are the only models available at the showroom.

While carmakers discourage dealers from charging more than the advertised sticker price—they fear it will tarnish the carmaker's reputation among consumers—there are no rules against it. For their part, dealers say they are simply responding to market cues. Most of the cars hit with these premiums are rated at the top or near the top of their class. In a way, this is the dealers' revenge for what the Internet has done to their margins. While customers can now easily find out exactly how much a dealer paid for a particular car, dealers, too, have some useful bargaining intelligence: They know which cars in any given segment are selling the fastest nationwide, and thus which models customers will pay extra for.

For people who aren't in a hurry to get their favorite model, one answer is to wait. The sluggish economy and large number of new models has hot cars cooling off quickly.

WARRANTY WARS: A BOON TO CONSUMERS

Most new cars come with two warranties. The common one, from the dealership, is known as an "adjustment warranty." That means that if your car has a rattle, a squeaky windshield wiper, or a dodgy power window, they'll fix it for free. The second is the manufacturer's warranty, which covers most bumper-to-bumper items; the power train (the hardest working part of your car, including parts of the engine, transmission and drive axle); rust and corrosion and your car's emission equipment. To fuel car sales, manufacturers are lengthening these warranties and wrapping in new services, to boot. Chrysler, for example, has recently extended what it calls its "basic limited warranty" to three years

THE MUSTS OF RESALE VALUE

The time to consider a car's resale value is when you buy it. Dealers will tell you that some features that you may pay extra for up front are worth it when it comes time to trade in or sell. The big ones:

1. **Bigger engines are usually better.** Go for the six-cylinder, not the four-banger.

2. **Silver is a classic car color.** So are black and white.

3. **Power is good.** In these days when people are accustomed to powered appliances, make sure your car has power locks operated with a remote, keyless entry; power windows and cruise control. Power seats aren't a bad idea, either.

4. **Tinny FM radios won't do.** Go for the CD player (or on newer models, MP3 players).

5. **Spring for the cowhide.** Buyers love the smell of leather interiors, and they hold up better than cloth.

6. **Shiny is best.** Alloy wheels are popular; they help to keep your car looking sharp.

or 36,000 miles, but it also gives a seven-year or 70,000-mile warranty on its power train. And it throws in free towing service for the full seven years. Lexus, meanwhile, has a four-year, 50,000-miles basic warranty and six years or 70,000 miles on the power train. And it also includes free roadside assistance.

Warranties do vary greatly from automaker to automaker and it pays to read the fine print before you buy. And remember: Warranties don't cover routine maintenance such as oil changes, lube jobs or ordinary tune-ups. Warranties also require you to pay attention, lest you risk invalidating them and getting stuck with hefty repair bills.

Here's how to get the most out of your car warranty:

Basics:

1. Keep up with recommended maintenance, especially oil changes. Fill out the service log and save receipts.

2. Avoid repairs and upgrades that might void the warranty, like installing parts that don't meet the manufacturer's quality criteria.

When You Have a Repair Problem:

1. Find out if other drivers have had the same problem. The Center for Auto Safety at **autosafety.org** tracks common problems with each make. The National Highway Traffic Safety Administration also posts defect bulletins at **www.nhtsa.dot.gov** under their "Service Bulletins Database" link.

2. Appeal to the manufacturer if the dealer won't fix your problem under the warranty.

3. If both the dealer and the manufacturer turn you down, the Center for Auto Safety, **autosafety.org,** offers legal advice for car owners.

After the Warranty Expires:

1. Ask your dealer if there are any "policy adjustments." Manufacturers regularly authorize repairs beyond the terms of the warranty if something is a common defect, but they don't usually notify consumers about the free fix. If your maintenance records show that the problem started under warranty, then you have a better chance of getting it fixed free.

USED CAN BE A THING OF BEAUTY (AND ECONOMY)

Many people want the smell and tightness of a new car—who wants to spend thousands of dollars on something someone else has spilled coffee on? But if you can get past that emotional hurdle, it makes sense to go for an older model. Auto-market analysts and Web sites say the minute you drive a new car off the lot, the chances are it will have lost anywhere between 10 percent and 25 percent of its value. A well-kept used car, however, will lose only about 10 percent of its value a

HOW RELIABLE IS YOUR CAR?

The most reliable cars in the U.S. are Toyota Motor Corp.'s Lexus models, and the least reliable are Ford Motor Co.'s Land Rover sport-utility vehicles, according to a study released in June 2004 by JD Power & Associates. Here's how others stacked up:

RANKING THE BRAND: PROBLEMS PER 100 VEHICLES

TEN BEST		FIVE WORST	
Lexus	162	Volkswagen	386
Buick	187	Isuzu	393
Infiniti	189	Daewoo	411
Lincoln	194	Kia	432
Cadillac	196	Land Rover	472
Honda	209		
Acura	212	Industry average:	269
Toyota	216		
Mercury	224		
Porsche	240		

year—even less if you can negotiate a good price and/or buy a car with collectible potential.

Indeed, checking several Internet sources, we found that the average price of a new car in 2004 was about $27,000, while the average used car sold for about half of that. And the disparity in prices in the luxury-car market can be exponentially greater, because well-heeled consumers are less likely to buy used cars that may be more prone to breakdowns. What's with the "budget" gap? Aggressive dealer incentives and 0 percent financing deals on new cars have combined with a growing glut of used-car inventories to hammer the market for used cars. After a disastrous 2002 for the used-car market, industry-watchers had predicted that used-car prices would rebound. But as of this writing, the recovery hasn't materialized.

But know the risks: A report by the National Highway Traffic Safety Administration suggests there are more than 450,000 cases of "odometer fraud"—the crime of rolling back a vehicle's odometer to make it appear to have lower mileage than it does—in the United States each year. Consumers who buy such rolled-back cars pay an estimated $2,336 more than they should, the report says. That totals more than $1 billion in losses for U.S. consumers every year.

To prevent odometer scams, officials suggest having a vehicle checked by a mechanic to ensure its "wear and tear" is comparable with its mileage. For a fee of $5 to $15, buyers can obtain title histories through the Department of Motor Vehicles or Internet record-search sites, though the data isn't foolproof. The main perpetrators of odometer fraud, a felony under federal law, are usually the wholesalers who sell the vehicles to automobile dealerships, not the dealerships themselves, Mr. Morse says.

A tip: For a fee, **Carfax.com** can determine, using the vehicle's identification number, where the car has been, its accurate mileage and whether it has been damaged in a crash or flood.

BEGINNING THE HUNT

Many car-shoppers start off looking for a specific make or model. But the hunt for a good deal in a used car should begin with comparison shopping. Why? If you fall in love with a make or model too quickly, there's a better chance you'll end up paying more than you should because you've failed to consider your options.

Jeremy Anwyl, president of **Edmunds.com,** suggests focusing on a specific category of vehicle that you find attractive—say, a convertible, minivan or sport-utility vehicle—and then comparison-shopping among automakers with models in that category. "If you're flexible, you're going to get better deals," he says.

FINDING A GOOD VALUE

Which category stands out as a bargain-hunter's paradise? We chatted with the folks at Automotive Lease Guide and they told us sports-utility vehicles were ripe for plucking good bargains, especially in contrast to three years ago when it was a seller's market. That said, don't expect to find much wiggle room to negotiate the so-called crossover SUVs, such as the BMW X5 and the Lexus RX300. As of this writing, they were red-hot.

Getting a low price doesn't necessarily mean you're getting a great value, however. If you'll likely sell the car in a few years—and why not if you're buying nearly new—you want to buy something that will be worth selling a few years down the road. Which preowned cars best retain their value?

"Two words: 'Toyota' and 'Honda,' " says Erica Eversmam, general counsel with auto-industry data provider Vehicle Information Services, in Bath, Ohio.

AND IF YOU'RE REALLY ADVENTUROUS . . .

If you're shopping luxury, and you're willing to purchase a car that's made its way through an auto-body shop, the prices of used luxury cars are sometimes comparable to mid-priced cars, says Eversmam. The rule of thumb is that the more expensive the vehicle, the greater the negative impact when it has an adverse history. For example, if a brand-new $64,000 Jaguar was broadsided and experienced $20,000 in damage, the car's value would probably drop by about $20,000, even if it was repaired. That said, a car that has experienced major structural damage may well cost a whole lot more down the road, which is why many used-car buyers—particularly those purchasing luxury models—choose to stick with automakers' "certified" pre-owned vehicle programs.

"Certified" means just that—that it is still covered under the original warranty or has been found fit enough by the dealership to be covered by an extended warranty. Such warranties provide buyers with a measure of peace of mind. The key for buyers of certified cars is to make sure the warranty is transferable at resale time.

SELL YOUR CAR ON EBAY!

One corner of the auto industry is showing some extra zip: used-car sales on the Internet. After hitting a rough patch during the dot-com collapse two years ago, business is picking up speed again. Online listings of used cars were up 15 percent in February of 2004, to 1.6 million, compared with a year earlier, according to CNW Marketing Research of Bandon, Oregon.

Another sign of the vibrancy of the market: Dealerships, which account for a large share of the online postings, are starting to assign salespeople to work exclusively with their Internet customers. For buyers, this means some personal attention without being hounded on the car lot.

To see whether things are as attractive on the selling end, we listed our 1996 Toyota Camry XLE on five sites, ranging from paid venues like **Autobytel.com** to free ones like **iMotors.com**—we even posted on eBay. We were curious about service, ease of use and, of course, how quickly we could find buyers in our price range.

The first roadblock we hit was uneven advice on how to price the car, which has 108,000 miles on it and a V-6 engine. We initially went by the online pricing guide Black Book, which said our model in "average" condition might be worth $6,725. But competing guides give different guidance. The *Kelley Blue Book,* for instance, suggested that the same car would actually be worth $6,275, almost $500 less.

Another pothole was the popular tool CarFax, a $19.99 service that does background checks on particular cars. The reports are a popular way to get alerted to any potential problems with the vehicle. Our report, though, made no mention of the fact that the Camry had been stolen once (and later recovered), even though we had filed a police report on the incident. Officials of CarFax say the state of California, where we live, doesn't share its stolen-vehicle records. We also got a lesson in trendiness. Our Camry is green—a color that is apparently no longer in vogue. "Green was peaking when you bought your car," says Charlie Vogelheim, editor of the *Kelley Blue Book.*

We began our sales quest in early February, optimistic that a model like ours with a high reputation for quality would go fast. Our first asking price was $6,995—a smidgen higher than what the *Black Book* recommended—to give us some haggling room, we figured. When we didn't get the nibbles we wanted, we gradually lowered the price on each of the sites to $5,500.

Our best experience was with **Cars.com.** It yielded the most sales leads—about 40, more than triple the next best. (The best offers, though, were all under $5,000.) We also liked a link on the site that took us directly to a used-car pricing guide. **Cars.com** wasn't perfect, though. After we had spent 15 minutes inputting data for our ad, all the text suddenly disappeared. Autobytel didn't provide us enough digital space to post a picture of our car, so we had to run a stock photo of a newer 1998 Camry. Officials of Autobytel say they hadn't received many complaints about photo size; the site, following our query, expanded the space allotment.

Part of the problem we ran into in trying to sell our car is that Internet shoppers are particularly sensitive on price. What's more, any car over 100,000 miles is exceedingly difficult to sell—even on the Internet. Adding to the challenge for us, the market is awash in old Camrys, according to industry experts. Dealers with volume—and time— tend to fare better on these used-car sites than individual sellers, experts say.

The low point of our test was iMotors. Our e-mail to their help desk was kicked back as "Invalid final delivery." A technician promised he would research one of our concerns and call right back. He never did. We later discovered that our iMotors ad was never even seen by the general public because the site allowed access to ads only for post-1997 models. This, despite iMotors sending us this notice after we posted our ad: "Your advertisement is now live and can be accessed by millions of car buyers." The founder of the company behind the site says it has been undergoing an overhaul.

EBay may be the marketplace to the world, but it didn't help us. Our seven-day eBay auction (cost: $47) produced not a single bidder, despite going with a start price of $5,700. An eBay rep did send us a nice e-mail, though. ("Don't give up," it said.) In the end, we had to lower our asking price so far—to $5,500—that we decided to just keep the car. At least our six-year-old, Jimmy, is happy. It was the car he rode home in from the baby nursery, and he's grown attached to it.

THE MONEY GAME: FINANCING YOUR NEW LOVE

You've found that great new car. Now how to pay for it?

Luxury automakers have been loosening the purse strings, offering incentives and other financing deals on used cars to clear out backed-up inventories. For example, at some dealerships around the country, you can now finance certain certified pre-owned Lexuses at a 1.9 percent interest rate for up to 48 months. A survey by **Cars.com** found that 18 automakers—11 of them luxury-car makers—were offering subsidized financing rates for their certified used vehicles. Recent rising interest rates still haven't damped such offerings.

Still, don't jump on dealership financing offers until you shop car-loan rates in your area. Be sure to ask about any fees or penalties you may incur with the loan. The Online Journal's Money Toolbox includes an auto calculator from **Edmunds.com** that will compare average car-loan rates and fees in your area. You may want to consider your home as another alternative to auto financing. The mortgage-refinancing and home-equity credit boom has enabled many consumers to avoid car loans altogether. Indeed, many consumers used the windfall in low-interest-rate mortgage refinancing to pay off higher-rate automobile loans.

Beyond that, you'll have to ask yourself a really basic question: Lease or buy?

Many personal-finance experts say that leasing is almost always more expensive than buying—even buying with a loan. The main reason, of course, is you're merely renting the car. You have to finance typically about half the car's purchase price, and you also have to pay a variety of fees, including origination and disposition charges. And at the end of the lease, you end up with nothing—except the need to find another vehicle. Another potential big hit: charges for excessive wear and tear on the vehicle or driving more than the allotted number of miles, typically between 12,000 and 15,000 annually.

Leasing advocates say such thinking is shortsighted, and doesn't factor in a return on the money a leasee isn't spending on a car loan's higher monthly payments—as well as the lease's lower down-payment requirements. Leasing, they say, keeps your monthly payments lower and traditionally requires a smaller down payment than buying; and you don't have to deal with a trade-in or carry the risk that the vehicle loses its value.

Other advantages: Monthly payments for a leased car are tax deductible if the car is used for business purposes; for a car you finance, you have to stretch out the depreciation over a long period of time. Thus, for many car-dependent occupations such as real-estate brokers, leasing makes good financial sense. Another advantage: In most states, leasees pay sales tax on their monthly payments, not on the total value of the vehicle. (A few states, however, tax the entire purchase price of the vehicle. The culprits: Illinois, Maryland, Oklahoma, Texas and Virginia.)

Cash or Loan?   Since a car is a depreciating asset, most financial planners suggest clients pay cash. It's usually easier to negotiate a better price when you are paying cash and then the buyer could earn more money by investing elsewhere, such as a risk-free investment like high-quality municipal bonds. On the other hand, when low interest rates are offered by automakers, including the much bally-hooed 0 percent deals, the scales tip toward financing. However, financing at 0 percent is almost always offered as an alternative to a large rebate, say some advisers. So whichever is worth more—the rebate or the total interest you could earn if you turn around and invest the 0 percent loan—that's the deal you should take.

Home-Equity Loan?   The experts are split on the wisdom of using a home-equity loan to purchase a vehicle. Some say that if you must finance, it makes sense to try to make the financing deductible. A home-equity loan is probably the best way of doing that. But others think the assets of a home are best left alone and warn of the dangers of spreading the home-equity loan over too long a time. The worst-case scenario, some say, is to be paying for a vehicle that you no longer have.

KNOW YOUR OWN CREDIT REPORT

No matter what, before you go to a dealer, check your credit report. Dealers and lenders will use your credit report and score to determine the terms you'll receive on an auto loan or lease. You'll qualify for a lower interest rate the higher your credit score, since you're seen as less of a credit risk. Most lenders use the FICO score, from the rating system developed by Fair Isaac Corp., which ranges from 300 to 850. Someone with a credit score of 720 or more will typically qualify for an interest rate of 6 percent or lower on a new car, while a person with a score below 650 may be socked with rates as high as 19 percent. Raising your score by 100 points can save you thousands of dollars in interest. (We delve more into FICO below.)

That's why it's a good idea to shop for a loan before you start shopping for a car. In addition to getting a FICO score at **myfico.com**, consumers should examine copies of their credit reports from each of the three major credit bureaus, Equifax, Experian and TransUnion. Since you don't know which reporting agency the dealership or bank will be pulling their reports from, you'll want to make sure that the reports from all three bureaus are error-free. In June of 2004, U.S. PIRG, the Washington lobbying office for state Public Interest Research Groups, released a survey showing that about 80 percent of credit reports had mistakes; one in four had errors serious enough that credit could be denied.

What's more, if you request the reports directly from the agency instead of having the lenders pull them, you'll limit the amount of credit inquiries—another factor that can weigh down your score. The good news is that if you're shopping around for a car loan or a mortgage, multiple inquiries within a set period will only count as one inquiry for each loan type when generating your credit score.

In general, better terms are available for loans through a bank or a credit union than from a dealership. But if you do decide to finance your purchase through a dealership, bring copies of your credit report with you and ask what terms the dealer thinks you might qualify for. To be sure, financing a car purchase has the potential to significantly affect your credit rating, since the amount you've borrowed and your payment history on your loans will typically account for about two-thirds of your FICO score. Other factors include the length of your credit history, the number of times you have applied for credit and the type of credit you have.

INSIDE FICO

Do you know your FICO score? Do you know what a FICO score is? Before you finance a car at a dealership, it might be a good idea to find out.

The auto-retailing trade has gotten plenty of bad press in recent months over allegations of deceptive and discriminatory lending. Some state regulators, such as New York State activist Attorney General Eliot Spitzer, are cracking down on car dealers' financing practices and demanding more complete disclosure of auto-loan pricing. The auto-finance arms of General Motors Corp. (GM) and Nissan Motor Corp. (NSANY) have settled lawsuits charging they enabled car dealers to charge minority consumers disproportionately higher rates for loans than white shoppers. GM and Nissan denied discriminatory behavior, but agreed to menus of reforms, such as caps on the amount dealers can increase a loan's interest rate from the rate offered to the dealer by the finance company. The actions are all designed to give consumers more protection, without altogether cutting off the dealer's profit potential.

Now some dealers are trying to get out in front of the critics and litigators. One tactic is to tell consumers in stores or in advertisements just what kind of credit rating they need to qualify for a certain loan rate. An advertisement from a Long Island Dodge dealership, pointed out by a colleague in New York, trumpets low monthly payment deals on about a half-dozen models, and in the fine print at the bottom of the ad, it states that the advertised specials are available to consumers "with approved 750 FICO score."

FICO scores are front and center in the finance process at the nation's largest Toyota dealership, Longo Toyota in El Monte, California, near Los Angeles. Longo posts its loan rates on placards that are set on the desks and tables in the showrooms, like the daily-specials menus at a neighborhood restaurant.

In Longo's Scion showroom area, computer screens deliver the day's lending rates keyed to FICO scores. All Scion dealers operate this way, under new agreements Toyota crafted to make the Scion brand appealing to younger buyers, who tend to have more concerns about their credit scores and are likely to have researched online the best available financing deals.

FICO scores appeal to car dealers as a yardstick for pricing loans, in part because the rating methodology invented by Fair Isaac Corp. (FIC) of Minneapolis doesn't factor in race. "One of the reasons FICO scores are being more and more used is that they are color-blind," says company spokesman Ryan Sjoblad. "For a lot of lenders it takes the weight off their backs."

Sjoblad says income is not a factor in developing a FICO score, either. I could, in theory, have a better FICO score than Bill Gates, if I have religiously paid all my debts on time and Gates somehow let his Visa bills fall under the couch. Other factors include how long you have been borrowing money (longer is better, if you pay on time), and what mix of credit you have. A mix of a mortgage, some credit cards and a car loan looks good; no assets and 25 credit cards looks bad.

The median FICO score for Americans is 720 on a scale that goes from 300 to 850, Sjoblad says.

About four years ago Fair Isaac began making scores available to

---

TO FINANCE OR LEASE: HOW THE EXPERTS SEE IT

FINANCING

Pros: You'll own the vehicle at the end of your loan.

Cons: Could require a substantial down payment. If you don't get a good deal, you'll end up paying more than the vehicle's worth. And you'll have limited tax benefits.

LEASING

Pros: You can often drive away in a very expensive car for little money down and affordable monthly payments. And there are tax benefits if you use a leased car in your business.

Cons: You don't own the car at the end of your lease (though you have an option to buy it). You'll never get rid of your car payments. And you could get hit with substantial end-of-lease penalties if you overdrive the annual mileage allotment of your lease or have substantial wear and tear.

BOTTOM LINE: For most consumers, buying is ultimately the better deal.

individuals. To learn your FICO score, grab a credit card and go to **myfico.com,** where Fair Isaac will charge you from $12.95 to $38.85 to learn how your credit stands with the three major credit bureaus. If it irks you to pay a corporation to give you information about yourself that was developed using data about your personal life and spending habits, you can always wait until you need credit. The lender will almost certainly ask a credit agency for your FICO score.

Most savvy consumers didn't need to hear from the press or Eliot Spitzer that financing a new car at a dealership can be an unpleasant, confrontational process. The steps the industry is taking to demystify the auto-lending process are good news. But consumers need to remember that unless they plan to pay cash, negotiating dealers down from sticker price is just half the deal.

The program is currently available in only a few states, though State Farm says it will roll it out more broadly over the next year. All-

PUTTING THE BRAKES ON TEEN CAR EXPENSES

Teen drivers, start your engines. But check your wallet first.

Owning a car is getting more expensive, due in part to rising rates for auto insurance. Thankfully, there are things teens and their parents can do to keep those rates low.

1. **Get on your parents' insurance policy.** In most cases, being on your parents' plan is cheaper than taking out your own insurance.

2. **Stay away from muscle cars.** If you or your parents are buying your first car, don't go for the coolest set of wheels. Certain models cost more to operate than others. A high-performance sports car will cost you an arm and a leg in insurance, and if you can't afford the insurance, you can't afford the car. Insurance agents are more than willing to sit down with you and discuss rates before you buy your car.

3. **Check into discount programs insurers have for teen drivers.** Many, though not all, insurers offer rate reductions of 5 to 25 percent for young drivers who maintain a B average or above in school. To receive the discount, you'll have to provide the insurance agent with a copy of your report card or transcript.

There are also discounts that don't depend on grades. Most companies, for instance, provide a rate reduction for taking driver's-education courses. State Farm has a program called Steer Clear, in which young drivers maintain a logbook of their driving experiences. After 20 to 30 trips through different types of conditions, such as night driving and highway driving, State Farm cuts the insurance rate by around 15 percent.

state has its own teen discount program, called "Teen Smart." It gives a 10 percent discount after teens take a computer-based driver's-education course the company offers.

With both programs, if you get in an accident or receive a traffic ticket, you lose the discount.

Another way to keep your rates low is to not get into trouble financially. That's because insurers use credit-reporting scores to determine driver's insurance rates. If you haven't paid a cell-phone or credit-card bill, that can affect your rates or eligibility for coverage, even as a teenager. On the non-insurance front, think about piggybacking on your parents' auto-club membership. AAA says most of its local clubs offer a discount for additional memberships within the same household.

—JOSEPH B. WHITE

BUYING INSURANCE

While the formula for calculating insurance premiums is complex, several sites can get you started. On **Edmunds.com** (click on "True Ownership Costs"), you can type in a make and model (going back to the year 2000) and find out the average insurance premium in your state. For slightly older cars, **HwySafety.org** (click on "Vehicle Rating") can provide some insight. It has safety scores, a big factor in determining insurance premiums, for cars such as a 1997 BMW 540i. Of course, a whole range of personal details can also affect your insurance costs, from how many miles you drive to where you live. On the Web sites of some insurers, including State Farm and Progressive, you can type in these details and get instant price quotes.

Overall, auto-insurance rates are on the decline after four years of sometimes-sharp increases. State Farm Automobile Insurance Co., Allstate Corp., Farmers Insurance Group and USAA are just a few of the insurance companies that recently have cut rates. But that doesn't mean all consumers will get a break. Some insurers are using sophisticated pricing tools to decide which buyers get the best rates, so shopping around may be more important than ever. In the past, insurers used just a few factors to figure out what to charge. The most typical: broad age categories and driving records. Now, some insurers split the age categories more finely, assess credit histories and even look at the amount of insurance coverage you carried on your previous policy. The change has been driven by, among others, Progressive Corp., which now uses thousands of variables to determine its rates. Why would an insurer care how much insurance you bought under the policy you are replacing? Progressive thinks that a driver who chose a state-required minimum is a riskier driver. Another refinement: A car that is considered a good risk in some neighborhoods is now given more scrutiny in others.

BECOMING SERIOUS ABOUT CAR SAFETY

Safety Statistics: The National Highway Traffic Safety Administration releases rollover rankings (available at **safecar.gov**) every year that include a ranking system of one to five stars for cars and trucks, with five being the best; it is based on a driving test that measures a vehicle's chance of tipping and each vehicle's percentage chance of rolling over in a single-vehicle crash. That's just one of the tools car buyers can take to the dealership. Consumers Union (**ConsumerReports.org**) and the Insurance Institute for Highway Safety (**iihs.org**) also conduct various kinds of safety tests and provide vehicle ratings.

You should also understand your car's vulnerability points and safety features. Here are the major ones:

Tires: Keeping tires safe requires vigilance. Any checklist should start with an old-fashioned tire gauge. Underinflated tires wear unevenly and ultimately fail. Don't trust your eyes: A tire can shed up to half its pressure and not "look" flat. The correct pressure is listed in your car's manual; it may also be printed on a sticker found on the door post, door edge, glove-box door or possibly on the fuel door. And some tires have suggested pressures stamped into the sidewalls.

It's best to check when tires are cool, since they heat up as they roll down the road and that increases the pressure. Watch for trouble signs, like gouges or bulges in the sidewalls. Also check the treads. Tires need to be replaced when the tread is worn down to $\frac{1}{16}$ of an inch. One way to check is to stick a penny into the groove of a tread. If any part of Lincoln's head is covered by the tread, you still have enough rubber left. If you can see his whole head, time to get a new tire. You should be sure your car is properly aligned and that you rotate your tires. A good rule of thumb for tire rotation is once every 6,000 miles.

You should also be cautious when loading your vehicle. Consult the owner's manual or the tire-information sticker on the car to be sure you're not overloading it. Too much weight is another enemy of tires that can cause them to fail.

When buying new tires, it's important to stick with the specified size for the vehicle. Also, the same size tire comes in various load and speed ratings. It's important always to buy the same- or higher-rated tires. Beyond that, you should look for tires that suit the kind of driving you do and the climate where you'll mostly operate the vehicle. For instance, if you live in a rainy region like the Pacific Northwest, you should get tires that have good wet-weather traction. And always check when buying a used car to make sure the tires on the vehicle are the correct size.

Air Bags: Head-protecting air bags are the great new hope in car safety, with research suggesting they can sharply cut death rates in crashes. But they're rarely provided as standard equipment, and can run as high as $7,000 and add weeks of wait time to get a vehicle. Or consumers must buy a pricier "luxury" edition of vehicles that includes the head air-bags. One thing to look for is side-curtain air bags; they deploy from the ceiling and inflate next to a vehicle's side windows and are different than side air bags—often called "combination bags"—which typically deploy from the side of the seat and protect the thorax and in some cases the head. When a vehicle is hit from the side, side curtains reduce the chance of fatality by 45 percent, according to the Insurance Institute for Highway Safety. Following the 50 percent-by-2007 target, all vehicles are supposed to have them for the 2010 model year.

Maintenance: Many people don't automatically equate maintenance with auto safety, but they are most definitely linked. Poorly maintained cars are more accident-prone—and not just from, say, a blowout or having a car that overheats and catches fire. Every year motorists are killed when they break down on busy, high-speed freeways and get out to seek help or make repairs.

But finding a good auto mechanic has become harder in recent years as the ranks of auto-repair specialists have plummeted. There were 88,000 fewer auto-care workers in 2001 than five years earlier, a 10 percent decline, according to the U.S. Bureau of Labor Statistics. Many workers who have the computer skills needed to fix today's cars have been lured away to higher-paying jobs. At the same time, American roads are more jammed than ever. Making things worse, garages aren't expanding to handle the new wheels. So unless fixing cars becomes very popular, very fast, consumers will have to work even harder to find a good repair shop. What can you do to help yourself? Try these tactics:

1. **Seek advice.** Ask friends and neighbors for a shop with a reputation for fair service. Try a part of town where real estate is cheaper. Check with your local consumer agency to weed out mechanics with a history of problems. In some places, the state attorney general's office or the department of consumer affairs has complaint records on file. Or call the local Better Business Bureau.

2. **Don't wait for a breakdown.** "Find a quality repair facility before you need one," says John Nielsen, director of auto repair at AAA, the national automobile service and lobbying group. "When your car breaks down, you don't have the luxury of shopping around." Grease the wheels. The AAA's Mr. Nielsen suggests taking your vehicle to the same shop for routine items, such as oil changes and tune-ups, to build a sense of familiarity and loyalty. "You get to know them, they get to know the car," he says.

3. **Don't be afraid to go independent.** "Independent repair shops tend to have more satisfied customers than dealers do," says Robert Krughoff, president of the Center for the Study of Services, a consumer research group in Washington, D.C. His group publishes the *Consumers' Checkbook* magazine, which evaluates local businesses in service areas such as car repair, health care and banking.

4. **Don't mistake price for quality.** A *Consumers' Checkbook* study of car mechanics in the Washington, D.C., area found that not only were consumers less satisfied with the workmanship of dealer shops, but they also tended to pay more for the same work than at nondealer shops. One component of cost—the average hourly labor rate—was $72 at dealers, $61 at nondealers.

5. Check for certification. Some car owners look for professional certification. The National Institute of Automotive Service Excellence, or ASE, is the largest such program, with more than 431,000 certified mechanics. Mechanics must pass a test and have two years' experience to be considered certified in a specific field of auto mechanics, such as brakes or engine work. AAA recommends looking for mechanics with the ASE symbol. Although, while ASE certification may prove a mechanic is capable, it doesn't mean he or she will do a good job.

6. See if there's an AAA sign. AAA has its own garage-assessment program with around 7,600 shops in the United States and Canada. Each "approved" shop is monitored by AAA and has to abide by certain procedures, such as offering a year warranty on most services and parts. And AAA members can use the program's arbitration mechanism to resolve complaints with AAA garages.

7. Communicate like crazy. AAA says lots of car-repair conflicts—78 percent in one study—arise from poor communications. Be sure your car's problem is clearly stated on the service order. If your auto won't back up, say so, and make sure the counter attendant writes that down. Learn enough about cars to understand the terminology; some local AAA clubs, community colleges and adult-education programs teach basic car-repair knowledge.

TECHNOLOGY: THE CAR GADGETS YOU CAN HAVE NOW

Sooner or later they're coming: cars that drive themselves. Meanwhile, computer technology is already beginning to change the car in dramatic ways, offering drivers new ways to listen to music, communicate with the outside world, track their locations with onboard GPS locators and even have remote mechanics diagnose engine problems in real time through wireless computer links.

Been to a mechanic's shop lately? There's a good chance your friendly local grease monkey is wearing a computer around his neck as he checks your engine, which is already laded with lots of hidden microprocessors, which control everything from fuel flow to your air-conditioning system.

For the purposes of this book, however, we're going to take a look at stuff you can get now or in the very near future.

THE FUTURE IS NOW IN CAR AUDIO

by Joseph B. White

Detroit—I've heard the opening riff of Deep Purple's classic rock hit "Smoke on the Water" about 5,000 times. But never quite like this: I'm sitting in the driver's seat of a Hummer H2 with a blasting six-channel DVD audio system that reproduces the music with such clarity you can almost hear the tubes melting in Ritchie Blackmore's cranked amp.

This demonstration was a glimpse of what the post-compact-disk world could sound like. It's a world the auto industry finally wants to enter.

What's in the center of your dashboard "is changing more in the next five years than it has in the last 30," says Mark Weston, product-marketing manager for audio and multimedia systems at Visteon, the big Dearborn, Michigan, supplier of vehicle audio systems.

Within the next five years, Weston says, the CD/AM/FM formula will give way to a variety of new technologies, including DVD audio, MP3 players, Super Audio CD players and High Definition Radio that receives digital radio signals and can translate them into a surround-sound experience. That's not counting satellite radio, pay-for-subscription services that are already a small but growing niche in the mobile-audio business—with two major competitors, Sirius (**sirius.com**) and XM Radio (**xmradio.com**). And it doesn't count features not directly related to music playback, such as voice-activated controls and navigation systems.

This will happen not just because millions of consumers are bored by CDs and conventional radio, but because the auto and audio industries are highly motivated to develop something new that people will be excited about buying. What's one more luxury sedan with a six-CD changer? How about a luxury car with whomping surround-sound DVD audio?

Right now, DVD audio seems to be the big noise in mobile audio circles, although backers of a rival enhanced-music format, Super Audio CD, or SACD, would beg to differ.

Both formats can produce a surround-sound experience like a home-theater system, and both cater to the business aspirations of the consumer-electronics and entertainment industry. To experience DVD Audio or SACD, you need to buy new hardware and lots of new "software" in the form of disks.

Which one will win in the mobile marketplace isn't clear. So far, there are more SACD titles on the market, industry officials say. But the companies backing DVD Audio say they will catch up soon.

But DVD Audio has an advantage in the auto business simply because DVD is something most people know about—which appeals to carmakers' conservative instincts. Moreover, carmakers already are putting DVD players in vehicles to handle rear-seat entertainment and navigation systems, notes Tom Dunn, marketing director of Panasonic's Automotive Systems Company unit.

General Motors Corp. (GM) Vice Chairman Robert Lutz was so impressed by a demonstration of DVD Audio that he spread the word through the number-one automaker's product-development organization, where DVD Audio was already under consideration. Honda Motor Co. Ltd.'s (HMC) Acura luxury division already includes DVD Audio in its redesigned Acura TL sedan. The technology will be pricey for the next couple of years, but by 2007 it will no longer be limited to luxury nameplates.

Millions of consumers scorn standard CDs—their music collections, whether nicked from sites like KaZaa or purchased legitimately—are stored as MP3 files on computer hard-drives. It has taken a remarkably long time for the mobile audio and auto industries to respond to the MP3 revolution.

As of the 2003 model year, only 2 to 3 percent of vehicles were offered with audio systems capable of playing back compressed-music-files MP3s. But that number is expected to jump radically by 2005. One bottleneck: Factory-installed MP3 players will mostly require customers to burn their compressed music onto CDs, since there isn't yet an industry standard for other devices—flash memory cards, for example—that allow transfer.

Which means the compact disc will live on—at least for a while.

TECHNOLOGY TO THE RESCUE

Meanwhile, thanks to technology, there's no reason any longer to be stranded on a dark, lonely road, your cell phone dead, wondering how you'll ever get rescued. So-called emergency-alert systems are widely available on many car models, though there are still nagging questions about their reliability. Most depend on analog cellular networks, which have gaps in service, and the systems can be damaged in severe crashes. Here are the options:

ONSTAR: Available on most GM vehicles, and some Acura, Lexus, Volkswagen, Audi, Subaru and Isuzu models; more than 2 million subscribers
> **Cost:** Standard or part of package on many models; $695 as option (includes one year of service); $199 a year for basic emergency service
> **Other features:** Roadside assistance, automatic door unlocking, stolen-vehicle tracking; for extra cost: hands-free phone, voice-activated Internet, routing assistance, concierge service

TELE-AIDE: Available on all Mercedes vehicles; about 400,000 subscribers
> **Cost:** Standard on most models; $775 as option (includes one year of service); $240 a year for emergency service and routing assistance
> **Other features:** Roadside assistance, automatic door unlocking, stolen-vehicle tracking; for extra cost: concierge service

THE LIGHTER SIDE

Technology doesn't just want to rescue you. It wants you to be seen better; it wants to see for you and it wants you to feel very, very cool. Here are some other tech-inspired gadgets that are now showing up on new cars:

LED Taillights

Does the world need a better brake light?

LEDs—the same kind of technology associated with computer and cell-phone screens—are showing up in taillights. Not only do LED lights last longer than conventional bulbs; they blink on in a fraction of a second faster. That can make a big difference when you've got a multitasking driver behind you, drinking coffee and talking on a cell phone. Indeed, by one estimate, stopping distances at 60 miles an hour can be improved by 25 feet.

Cars That Have Them: Mostly luxury vehicles, including the Infiniti Q45, Cadillac STS, Mercedes-Benz S-Class and BMW 6 Series.

The Downside: If you do end up getting rear-ended, repairing or replacing LED lights can cost up to 20 percent more than conventional bulbs, according to Carstar, a collision-repair chain based in Overland Park, Kansas.

Backup Cameras

Common for a while in some commercial vehicles, such as rental-car shuttles, these are cameras mounted on the back of a vehicle to help drivers make sure they don't plow into someone, or something, when backing up. When the vehicle is in reverse, the camera sends a wide-angle view of the area behind the vehicle to a video monitor near the driver.

Cars That Have Them: Infiniti FX, Toyota Land Cruiser, Lexus RX 330. They mostly show up on SUVs, minivans and pickup trucks (which tend to have bigger blind spots back there), but Lexus is now offering one on a sedan, the 2005 LS 430.

The Downside: The camera lens is tough to keep clean, giving you blurry or gritty pictures. They're also expensive. Backup-camera systems are typically sold as part of a package of extras—including high-tech gear such as navigation systems—that can cost up to $6,800.

Xenon Headlights

If you've had Xenon bright beams flashed in your eyes by an oncoming car, you don't forget them. Named for the Xenon gas inside, they are super-bright lamps with the blue tinge. They shine brighter and last at least three times as long as conventional halogen bulbs, and offer wider, uniform illumination of the road.

Cars That Have Them: Most high-end cars such as BMW, Mercedes-Benz and Porsche, and now some lower-priced models, such as the Volkswagen New Beetle and Mini Cooper.

The Downside: They're a hot commodity for thieves, and replacing them can cost thousands of dollars. The National Highway Traffic Safety Administration also is looking into numerous complaints about the lights' blinding glare.

Cool Seats

If heated seats don't offer enough pampering, there's a new option: high-tech seats that keep you cool. There are two dueling technologies: One uses special refrigeration circuitry imbedded in the seat; the other recirculates cool air through the upholstery. That means you no longer have to adjust the air-conditioning vents or fight with your passenger over the controls.

Cars That Have Them: Luxury vehicles such as the Infiniti M45 sports sedan; Lexus ES sedan; BMW 7 Series; Cadillac STS and the Lincoln Navigator

The Downside: Both technologies take a few minutes to get cranked up, so you're still on the hot seat for a while. And they're not the cheap seats: Typically sold as an add-on with heated-seat capabilities, this option can add anywhere from $600 to $3,500 to the cost of a car.

And finally:

SMART CARS CAN KILL TRAFFIC

You're trying to get away for a summer weekend, but instead you're sitting and fuming in stop-and-go traffic. Drivers are hitting their brakes for no apparent reason, causing everyone behind them to do the same. Soon what had been a smoothly if lethargically flowing stream of traffic looks like a bunched-up caterpillar. You also see drivers changing lanes erratically, causing the same ripple effect. You're sure the highway could handle this volume if only the other drivers weren't idiots.

Guess what? You're right.

L. Craig Davis is too polite to put it that way, preferring to couch his findings in more positive terms. But in a study published in the June 2004 issue of the journal *Physical Review E,* the physicist at University of Michigan, Ann Arbor, concludes that many traffic jams could be prevented if a mere one in five vehicles on the road used the new technology of adaptive cruise control rather than being piloted by their human driver alone. In other words, flesh-and-blood drivers make avoidable traffic-jam-causing moves that a computer does not.

"It's a very interesting result," says civil engineer Hani Mahmassani of University of Maryland, College Park. "With ACC, by eliminating the spacing you need because of driver reaction time, you can get four times more volume on a road by letting vehicles follow each other closely at high speed."

Professor Davis is the latest physicist to weigh in on a subject that has long been dominated by traffic engineers and "operations research" scientists. A little more than a decade ago, scientists realized that vehicles behave like molecules in a gas. In the most notorious similarity, cars ahead of you that stop or merely slow down can cause a compression wave—a patch where the cars are jam-packed—to propagate backward until it reaches you. The wave can persist for hours after the initial bunch of cars hit their brakes, with the result that drivers who never saw that deceleration are totally clueless about why they aren't moving. An estimated 75 percent of traffic jams are like this, having no visible cause.

In both traffic and gases, tiny perturbations can have effects out of all proportion to their size. In this state, called "synchronized flow," traffic is moving, sometimes at a good clip, but it's so dense that the vehicles are in sync, like cars in a train. Synchronized flow is, in physics-speak, in unstable equilibrium: The slightest change, such as a driver changing lanes and forcing others to brake, tips the system into a new state. The result is stop-and-go traffic, a true jam.

Physicists are exploring whether adaptive cruise control can prevent this. In ACC, a radar sensor gauges the distance between cars, automatically adjusting speed to maintain a safe distance. Because ACC, which has become standard on some luxury vehicles, can adapt instantly if the lead car brakes (humans take about 0.75 second to react), cars can tailgate safely. ACC can therefore pack more cars into a mile of highway, increasing a road's de facto capacity.

But it can do more, Professor Davis finds. Packed cars are a traffic jam waiting to happen. "When you have dense traffic at highway speeds," he says, "if someone brakes, the flow can break down. That doesn't happen with ACC," because the ACC vehicle never actually stops unless a car in front comes to a complete halt. "Perturbations due to changes in the lead vehicle's velocity do not cause jams," he says. Instead, by refraining from excessive braking, an ACC car simply gets closer to the car in front of it. The dreaded compression wave never forms.

It isn't even necessary for all vehicles to be driven by these smart systems. On single-lane roads with high-speed traffic, if a mere 20 percent of vehicles used adaptive cruise control, traffic jams could be eliminated altogether, Professor Davis concludes from his computer simulation. Put another way, even if fully 80 percent of vehicles had an idiot at the wheel, there would still be no traffic jams. The fact that jams still exist means that not even 20 percent of drivers are minimally competent. But you already suspected that, didn't you?

Human drivers have a tendency to brake harder than the car in front of them did, erring on the side of safety. That can make a bad situation worse, says Professor Davis. But "ACC eliminates the tendency to overbrake. It smoothes out the overreactions, correcting for bad drivers."

A little of that goes a long way. Remember the last time you were zipping along a highway in light traffic, approaching an on-ramp and thinking that the highway could easily handle the merging traffic? Yet the flow seized up, or at best tipped into the dreaded synchronized flow. "Braking at merges can create those shock waves," says Professor Mahmassani.

But if half the cars in the lane receiving the mergers are driven by ACC, the average velocity at the merge drops but traffic keeps moving, Professor Davis finds. "When half the vehicles in the receiving lane have ACC, there is a region of reduced speed, but no jam," he says.

A single additional vehicle driven by adaptive cruise control could spell the difference between moving traffic and a traffic jam. Put another way, in some situations it's possible to prevent a traffic jam if only a single driver refrains from dumb moves. You know who you are.

CHAPTER EIGHT

REAL ESTATE

BUYING, SELLING AND UPGRADING YOUR HOME

Ever since the stock-market crash in 2000, there have been predictions that the real-estate market is bound to follow.

HOME-PRICE INFLATION: THE PARTY CONTINUES (FOR NOW)

By now, almost everyone knows someone who postponed buying a house "until prices cooled off"—and most of those buyers are still waiting (unless they've given up and bought, before they get completely priced out of the market).

It's been a bizarre recession, with the real-estate market one of the few areas of the American economy emerging not just seemingly unscathed, but truly energized. Economists are quick to credit interest rates that got as low as they've been since the Eisenhower Administration. Indeed, the low interest rates have enabled lots of home-buyers to get more house for their money, or to lower their costs substantially by refinancing once they've already bought. Another force driving the real-estate market: affluent buyers who feel real estate is a better investment than stocks.

But even during some of the biggest boom years for residential real estate ever, there have been signs that inventory is building up at the high end of some markets (e.g., certain areas of Los Angeles County). Now that interest rates are headed upward, a lot of homeowners are wondering if this could be the start of a flattening out or even a downward spiral for home prices. Suddenly there's a lot of anxiety for buyers and sellers. Is it the right time to buy, or is it better to rent and wait for a more favorable buyer's market? If you're located in a market like Los Angeles or New York, where prices have risen in double-digit percentages for the past few years, should you cash out of your home, rent for a while, and wait till prices drop before buying again? What if prices don't go down?

These are points that have been debated on and off for the last few years, and with interest rates rising, the pundits are buzzing again. On the one hand, real-estate bears point to home values that have risen much faster than median incomes in some areas. They note that the availability of cheap money, which has kept the market artificially strong, won't last forever. When it gets more expensive to borrow, they predict inventory will build up and prices could drop 10 percent or more. That in turn could spell bad news for homeowners who are too leveraged, where a 10 percent drop could mean the loss of all the equity in their homes.

Real-estate bulls, on the other hand, say that prices will continue to go up, albeit perhaps at a slower rate. Why? For one thing, they always have, at least for the nearly four decades since prices have been tracked. And in much of the country, they point out, values have historically risen at a moderate pace, maybe one or two percentage points ahead of inflation. With the exception of a few mostly urban markets, that overall moderate trend hasn't changed much, even during the most recent run-up in prices. Homes in Cuyahoga County (the nicer suburbs of Cleveland) haven't tripled in value since 2000. So if the market gets softer, they argue, it's not like there's far for prices to fall.

Taking a view somewhere between these two poles would translate to a yellow light: That is, exercise caution. Here are some ways to do so:

BUYERS

1. Be careful not to stretch too far by buying a bigger house than you really need. That could leave you vulnerable to a big drop in prices (and it may get harder to unload those bigger homes).

2. Shop assiduously for a mortgage—and be sure you really understand which one is best for your particular needs. An adjustable-rate mortgage (ARM), for example, can look tempting with an initial rate that can be in the low 4 percent range. But this type of mortgage can cost you more in the long run, especially if you hang on to your property longer than expected and rates go up substantially. Also, don't be afraid to haggle. As rates start to tick up, lenders are going to get more competitive, not less, in order to win or keep your business.

3. Get a home inspection. Surprisingly, 25 percent of buyers still don't undertake this one measure that can save them huge hassles and expenses down the road.

4. Investigate your real-estate agent. While the majority of agents are capable and honest, we've heard enough horror stories to make this one of our mantras. Bear in mind that real-estate exams aren't necessarily taxing—and in a few states not even necessary. If your agent really seems clueless, chances are he or she *is* clueless—not a good thing when hundreds of thousands of dollars could be on the line.

5. Use the Internet. Real estate Web sites have gotten better in the last few years, with better images, and virtual tours that let you get a pretty good idea in advance whether it's worth your time to see a property or not. Also, there are lots of sites that can help you find out more about, say, the sales history of a town's properties or even statistics (crime, school ratings, etc.) about a given neighborhood. Many of these sites are free—take advantage of them.

SELLERS

1. Be realistic up front about your asking price. Look at the most recent comparable sales in your area, and find out what the discount was off the asking price. Get an appraisal if you think the comparables are shortchanging your home's value.

2. Looks count. Take a long hard look at the way your house shows, then fix it up. Cut the clutter. Move the high-school hockey trophies to the attic. If you've painted in bright colors, repaint in monotones. If necessary, hire a professional "fluffer" to make your house look as appealing as possible to potential buyers.

3. Knowledge is power. Be prepared for buyers to know more about your house than you do. With prices as high as they are and interest rates rising, buyers are likely to be doing a lot more research than ever before. This can make for tougher negotiations than sellers may be expecting.

4. Think outside the box. If your house is really unusual for its area and/or hard to price, consider putting it up for auction. Auctions aren't just a measure of last resort anymore—they're increasingly being used by owners of multimillion-dollar properties who want to know for sure they're going to sell on a given date.

LOCATION MATTERS: CAUTION ZONES

Below are 15 metropolitan areas that have had the biggest run-ups in median single-family home prices during the past three years. That could make them more vulnerable to stagnant or even declining prices.

AREA	3Q 2003	Change from three years ago (in thousands)
West Palm Beach–Boca Raton, FL	$245.73	76.9%
Providence–Warwick–Pawtucket, RI	234.97	73.5
Nassau–Suffolk, NY	370.73	72.9
Sacramento, CA	248.04	68.7
Monmouth-Ocean, NJ	291.64	68.7
Bakersfield, CA	186.31	64.5
Riverside–San Bernardino, CA	226.90	64.5
Los Angeles–Long Beach, CA	361.54	64.3
Redding, CA	292.99	63.7
Fresno, CA	214.00	62.7
Miami, FL	232.77	61.0
San Diego, CA	428.70	60.0
Fort Myers–Cape Coral, FL	152.49	60.0
Merced, CA	220.45	58.7
Orange County, CA	499.35	58.0

Source: Fidelity National Financial Inc.

THE ABCs OF BUYING

How much house do you really need?

Keep in mind that the bigger the home, the more you're paying in mortgage interest, maintenance costs and property taxes. A quick look at maintenance costs alone can tell you what you need to know: Assuming annual costs of 2 percent of a home's value, that's already $8,000 a year for a $400,000 house, and a sobering $16,000 a year for an $800,000 house.

On top of that, if you're considering trading up from a smaller home to a bigger home, there are costs involved in the transactions— broker's fees, mortgage-application costs and moving costs—that can eat up 10 percent or more of your old home's value. Of course, if you have a growing family and need the extra space, by all means buy bigger. But remember that as an investment, given the costs above, there's no guarantee that a bigger house will automatically lead to bigger profits when you sell.

And then there are possible lost-opportunity costs. Income you put into your house can't go into your 401(k). If your home, like most, appreciates at a rate just one or two percentage points ahead of inflation, it may make more sense to go for a smaller house and put the money toward retirement. And as for the bigger tax deduction you get with a larger house, that's generally one for the plus column. But remember that, depending on your income level, mortgage-interest-rate deductions may be capped, while your 401(k) contributions are 100 percent tax deductible.

THE SPACE CHASE

Shopping for real estate, given the financial stakes and emotions involved, can be maddening. These days there's an unprecedented amount of accessible information available but how to sort through it all. And what if the home you want isn't listed? Here are ways to cut to the chase:

1. **Start with the Internet**—for background and to get an overview of the market in a given area, it's an unparalleled tool. A national Web site like **Realtor.com** will have most of what you'd find in the local Multiple Listing Service, if there is an MLS where you're looking (some areas, like New York City, don't have one, and then you're limited to whatever information is available from big firms, newspapers and word-of-mouth). Remember to check Web sites of area real-estate agencies.

2. **Badger the listing agent.** Find out if they have other listings or know of other properties for sale that aren't in the MLS yet. You'd be surprised—it takes a little while for listings to get posted. And not everything for sale ends up on the MLS. Some sellers, especially owners of more expensive properties, simply don't want their properties advertised. Also ask the agent about open-house tours for brokers—how many there are in the next week or two and if it would be possible for you to tag along. If so, this is a good way for you to see a lot of properties in a short space of time. Second: The number of broker open-house tours can tell you something about the market—a lot of them could mean a buyer's market.

3. **Pound the pavement.** This approach isn't for everyone, but going directly to homeowners in a neighborhood is the best way to find out

REVEALING INTERNET SOURCES

DOMANIA; DOMANIA.COM

What's On It: Home-price database of past sales—27 million of them

Usefulness: To get details on comparable sales you have to register; even so, some 25 percent of results lack info like number of bedrooms or square footage.

NEIGHBORHOOD SCOUT; NEIGHBORHOODSCOUT.COM

What's On It: Neighborhood census data (crime rates, school scores, home prices)

Usefulness: Launched in 2002, the site lets users browse by location, or put in attributes they want and find a town that matches.

PITKIN COUNTY ASSESSOR'S OFFICE; PITKINASSESSOR.ORG

What's On It: Sales data for Aspen, Colorado, with addresses, publicly recorded name on deed and basic property info

Usefulness: See what your neighbor paid for his house. Prior sales prices will be available online soon; meanwhile, you can get them by calling.

PALM BEACH COUNTY PROPERTY APPRAISER; PBCGOV.COM/PAPA

What's On It: Property records searchable by owner, address or record number

Usefulness: Site lets you look up last recorded sale date, assessed value and whose name is on the deed. To get sales history, contact the county clerk.

HONOLULU PROPERTY TAX SITE; HONOLULUPROPERTYTAX.COM

What's On It: Search past sales by address and parcel ID; also has assessed values

Usefulness: Speedy, easy to use—but the site doesn't allow searches by owner. (Hawaii and Oahu county sites do, though.)

NEW YORK CITY REAL-ESTATE RECORDS; NYC.GOV/HTML/DOF/HOME.HTML

What's On It: Everything from liens to mortgages to power-of-attorney documents

Usefulness: Unlike other locales, New York has scanned in actual documents. But the site is confusing and hard to use—though there is a tutorial.

who's willing to sell—even if their home isn't officially on the market. You can leave notes at homes you're interested in, saying you're a potential buyer and asking if the owner would consider selling to you. Writing letters works, too, and so does e-mail if you can get an e-mail address.

DOING RESEARCH: THE INFORMED BUYER

The Internet is a great tool for real-estate shoppers. Of course, there are the virtual tours and MLS listings you can find on sites like **Realtor.com** and individual real-estate firms' websites. But well beyond those basics, there are places to find out how much a seller paid for the property (and when), how large a mortgage there is on the property and statistics about the neighborhood, from crime rates to how good the schools are.

While you can't find out all of that in every single area (some states, like Texas, don't report sales prices of residential real estate publicly, for instance), you'd be surprised how much data is now online. Below are some of the larger national and metro-area sites. **Tip:** Try Google to see if your county or municipality has sites like those operated by Aspen, Colorado, and Palm Beach County, Florida.

SHOW ME THE MONEY: SHOPPING FOR A MORTGAGE

Once you've figured out how much house you want (and where), it makes sense to go shopping for a mortgage before even looking at properties. Sellers are much more likely to deal with buyers who are preapproved for a mortgage—it shows the buyers are serious (and that the deal probably won't fall apart due to lack of financing). Right now, the array of choices for mortgage shoppers is kind of dizzying. In the past few years, online lending sites have mushroomed, and there's been a push to come up with creative types of mortgages to keep housing affordable for as many as possible. (In today's home-price environment, that is a serious concern—as of October 2004 fewer than one in four California households can afford the median-price house using a conventional 30-year fixed-rate mortgage, according to the California Association of Realtors.)

The first step: Check your credit. Many buyers don't realize it, but errors in credit re-

CONTACT INFORMATION FOR THE THREE MAJOR CREDIT BUREAUS

Equifax Information Service, 800-685-1111, **equifax.com;** P.O. Box 105851, Atlanta, GA, 30348

Experian, 888-397-3742, **experian.com,** P.O. Box 2104 Allen, TX, 75013

TransUnion, 800-916-8800, **transunion.com,** Consumer Disclosure Center, P.O. Box 1000, Chester, PA, 19022

ports that can affect your score—and your ability to get a loan—are pretty common. These can be fixed by contacting the credit bureaus, but the process has been known to take months. It's worth it to make sure everything is cleared up before you present your finances to a bank, especially because not only can a bad credit score prevent you from getting a loan, a good credit score can get you better terms and a better rate.

LOAN LIMBO: GETTING THE BEST RATES

Should you use a mortgage broker?

Get a quote directly from a lender?

Shop online?

Probably all of the above. Start by going online and checking rates advertised by big lenders on their websites—**Countrywide.com, LendingTree.com, E-loan.com,** and **WashingtonMutual.com,** to name a few. These sites all post rates for a 30-year-fixed loan and a 15-year-fixed loan, as well as for some adjustable loan rates. By all means check with your own bank—there may be special offers for existing customers. If you belong to a union or other professional association, check with them—they may have worked out a deal with a lender that's better than what you'd find in the open market (you can also ask your local bank).

While shopping, make sure you've been quoted all the relevant costs for each loan—including closing costs, points (if any) and private mortgage insurance (you typically only pay that when your down payment is less than 20 percent). Once you've seen what's out there, you have a choice—you can go directly to a lender and apply for a loan, either by calling and getting an application or directly from the lender's Web site.

Alternately, you can call up a mortgage broker and see if you can get a better rate that way. Even if the mortgage broker can only match the best offer you've seen, it may be worthwhile to go this route, simply because a good mortgage broker will make the paperwork a lot less of a hassle. And in most cases, it won't cost any more to go through a broker than to go to the bank directly—the broker is paid by the lender, but the lender is also saving money and time that it would otherwise spend on paperwork. It also makes sense to deal with a human being (this can be a mortgage broker or a loan officer at a bank) if you have less-than-perfect credit—the automated underwriting technology used by lenders' online sites won't be as flexible in complicated cases.

There are a few caveats when dealing with mortgage brokers, however. It's really important to make sure the broker has relationships with no fewer than around 10 to 15 lenders. The smallest mortgage brokers—particularly those who have just a handful of lenders they deal with—probably don't have a wide-enough base to ensure the best deal. Also, your mortgage broker should be willing to come to your home or office to help with the tedious paperwork. The National Association of Mortgage Brokers has a list of certified brokers on its site, at **namb.org/consumers/consumers_home.html**. Laws regulating the process vary from state to state, so chances are there's also a local association of mortgage brokers wherever you're buying.

WHAT TYPE OF MORTGAGE?

While trying to find the best rates, you'll also be looking at a dizzying array of loan types. There are the standard fixed-rate loans—30 year and 15 year, which can seem attractive while interest rates are still relatively low (a 15-year term, while requiring bigger payments, will be much cheaper in the long run). But what if you know you're likely to move in, say, five years? A hybrid adjustable-rate mortgage (ARM) with a five-year fixed rate may be the way to go.

The rule of thumb: Take a time frame you're comfortable with, then add two years—for example, if you think you'll be in a location for five years, consider a hybrid ARM that's fixed for seven years.

Then there are a raft of newer types of mortgages, from "interest-only" mortgages to "piggyback" loans that combine a standard first mortgage with a home-equity line of credit. There are even loans that allow some borrowers to skip as many as 10 payments over the life of the loan.

Rising home prices are encouraging lenders to get creative, as it's getting tougher—even with low interest rates—for many buyers to afford the house they want. In 2004, median existing home prices rose 8.3 percent—the biggest increase in more than two decades, according to the National Association of Realtors. With prices as high as they are, many buyers are opting to purchase less-expensive homes that need work—prompting some lenders to promote "purchase-and-renovate" loans. The loans, based on the value of the home post-improvements, allow a buyer to finance the cost of the home as well as the renovation expenses.

But all this flexibility can get expensive. If you skip payments on an interest-only loan, for example, those payments get tacked onto the back end of the loan—meaning you pay more in interest overall. Since the loans are interest-only, borrowers don't build up any equity—and can owe more than the value of their home if home prices fall. Purchase-and-renovate loans tend to be an eighth to a quarter percent higher than conventional mortgages, since they're riskier. As for piggy-back loans, borrowers with lines of credit risk paying more when interest rates start to climb. Here's the skinny on some of these creations:

1. Fixer-upper mortgages. The loan is based on the value of the home after renovations. It includes money to be used for home improvements.

2. Miss-a-payment mortgages. Lets borrowers skip up to two mortgage payments a year and up to 10 payments over the life of the loan without ruining their credit rating.

3. Interest-only mortgages. Borrowers pay interest but no principal in the early years of the loan.

4. Payment option mortgages. Borrowers have four payment options each month. Borrowers who elect to make the minimum payment could actually see their loan balance rise rather than fall.

5. Piggyback mortgages. Loans that combine a standard first mortgage with a home-equity loan or line of credit to avoid private mortgage insurance or the higher interest rates on jumbo loans.

HOMEOWNER'S INSURANCE

For years, homeowner's insurance was a loss leader for insurance companies, who made their money on the more profitable auto insurance. But with claims for homeowner's policies ballooning (and auto claims going up, too), insurers are cracking down. Many have pulled out of states like Texas, thanks to huge numbers of mold-related claims. In the areas where they do write policies, premiums have gone up, and coverage has gone down. Guaranteed-replacement coverage, for example, is now a rarity; many of the biggest insurers—State Farm, Allstate—don't include it in a typical homeowner's policy. Instead, they'll pay up to about 120 percent of your home's value (with the extra cash meant to cover building-cost overruns and such unforeseen expenses).

So it's important to make sure you and the insurer agree on what your home is worth. If you think the insurer's numbers are off, by all means double-check, either by getting an appraisal or asking a contractor to give you an estimate of what it would cost to rebuild your home.

Once you've already bought, you still need to keep tabs on what's going on with home values in your area, and get reappraisals as necessary. If you make improvements to your home, those will add to the value as well, and you should let the insurance company know about them.

A high assessment value doesn't necessarily mean a huge premium—there are ways to adjust other variables, such as paying a higher deductible, in order to keep yearly costs down. Shopping around helps, and sometimes getting auto insurance and homeowner's insurance from one company will get you a discount. Bottom line: While being overinsured isn't good, this is an area where you really don't want to cut corners, either.

HOW MUCH IS ENOUGH?

Here's a checklist for making sure you have adequate coverage on your home.

If you answer yes to any of the three questions, you should reappraise.

1. **Has it been more than a year since your insurer last appraised your home?**

2. **Have you made any big improvements (e.g., new kitchen) recently?**

3. **Have home values—or building costs—risen or fallen dramatically in recent months?**

If you're considering increasing your coverage, here is guidance to help you pick the right policy:

1. **Are your homeowner's and auto policies with the same insurer? If not, you might be able to switch to a single carrier and get a discount.**

2. Do you have a home that would be considered historic or unique in some way? If so, consider one of the few insurers that still offers full replacement value.

3. Does your homeowner's coverage include the value of the land under your house? If yes, you may be overinsured; land value shouldn't be included.

Now, some questions to ask your insurance agent to get a good price:

1. Is your homeowner's deductible lower than $1,000? If yes, ask how much you could save by raising the deductible.

2. Do you have any discounts based on age? Some companies offer cheaper rates for retired policyholders older than 55.

3. Do you offer discounts for smoke detectors, burglar alarms, dead-bolt locks and similar items?

WHAT IF YOUR HOUSE IS UNINSURABLE?

Here's another nasty surprise for many would-be buyers: Even if you personally have no history of filing homeowner's claims, the house you want to buy may have a past. And in some cases, insurers are refusing to write policies for homes that have a troubled insurance history.

The source of all the trouble: an obscure insurance-industry database known as CLUE (for Comprehensive Loss Underwriting Exchange). CLUE contains about 90 percent of the insurance claims made in the United States. And while for years insurers used CLUE to assess the risk of individuals, the big change is that insurers are now also doing background checks on individual homes.

Owners have a right to request a CLUE report on their property, but buyers don't have any legal right to view the report before closing on the house. That doesn't stop a buyer from requesting that the seller provide them with a CLUE report as a condition of purchase, however. It's not a common

HOUSES WITH CHECKERED PASTS

 Here are three red flags that might prevent an insurer from covering your home:

1. Water claims
2. Wind/hail damage
3. Burglaries

To request a CLUE report, call 1-800-456-6004. The cost is just $9, but it can take several weeks.

ChoicePoint has reports available online for $9 to $20 (**choicetrust.com**). Only the home's owner can request a report.

ASSOCIATIONS OF INSPECTORS

American Society of Home Inspectors (ASHI), **ashi.org,** 1-800-743-ASHI (2744)

National Association of Home Inspectors (NAHI), **nahi.org,** 800-448-3942

American Association of Home Inspectors (AAHI), **aahi.com,** 806-794-1190

practice yet, but it's likely to happen more in years to come. Anyway, it can't hurt to ask.

HOME INSPECTIONS

The home inspection is probably the most important research you can do when you're considering buying a home. Do one, even if the seller is only willing to sell you the property "as is"—you still need to know what you're getting into. Right now, roughly 77 percent of all buyers do home inspections, according to the American Society of Home Inspectors. That means that around one in five still does not. That's their problem.

That said, buyer beware: just over half the 50 states specifically regulate the home-inspection industry, and the stringency of the regulations vary widely (for more information on this, go to **ashi.org.**). In many states pretty much anyone can hang out a shingle and declare him- or herself a home inspector. So check with accrediting organizations to see if a home inspector you're considering is a member. (In addition to ASHI, there is NAHI, the National Association of Home Inspectors, and AAHI, the American Association of Home Inspectors.) Ask for a couple of references, and check with the local Better Business Bureau to make sure no complaints have been filed against the inspector's company.

Sellers, too, should get an inspection done before even putting a house on the market. The buyer will do one anyway, so you might as well get there first, and make any necessary repairs in advance. It also is a good idea in terms of knowing what (if anything) needs to be disclosed to potential buyers.

THE ABCs OF SELLING

CHOOSING A BROKER

If you don't have the time or inclination to deal with showings, open houses and advertising on your own (not to mention the intricacies of a contract), you'll probably end up listing your home with a real-estate agent. But when auditioning prospective candidates, be aware that—as is often the case when the job market slows—there are a lot of newly minted Realtors out there. In fact, becoming a real-estate agent doesn't take much in most states—usually somewhere between 40 to 100 hours of classes and a passing grade on a standard exam.

Some states, like Maine, don't absolutely require you to take classes to get a real-estate salesperson's license—you can just take the test, and you only need a 75 to pass. What's more, most new Realtors don't last more than about a year in the business—it takes a while to earn any money, and the rising competition isn't making things easier.

Obviously, getting friends or neighbors to recommend an agent is preferable. But even if you do have a referral, there are a few common-sense question you can ask.

1. **How many sales has the agent closed in the past**?

2. **Does he or she come prepared with a list of comparable sales in the surrounding area**?

3. **What's their take on the nature of the local real-estate market, including home-price appreciation (or not), crime, schools, new developments? Does the agent seem up to speed**?

4. **Does he or she have knowledge of issues specific to the area you are in, such as water rights**?

5. **What are the agent's concrete plans for marketing the property**?

If your candidate seems unable to answer any of these questions or seems to lack good answers, you'll probably want to keep searching. You can also find out if the agent is a salesperson (the entry level for real-estate agents) or has a broker's license (which takes more training to get and which a Realtor must have before opening an agency). Not having a broker's license doesn't make an agent unqualified, of course, but more training doesn't hurt, either.

Remember, too, that states regulate the real-estate profession and, beyond setting licensing requirements, post consumer-useful information on their Web sites. At **nj.gov/dobi/remnu.shtml,** for example, the New Jersey licensing authorities Web site, you can not only find out whether your agent is in fact licensed but you can also file complaints. **Tip:** On Google, type in your state ("California," for example) plus "real estate licensing," and you should quickly find the state agency you're looking for. We tried it and it worked every time.

CUTTING THE COMMISSION

 Six to seven percent may seem like a lot to pay at a time when houses are virtually selling themselves. Here are a few ways to save while making sure the deal gets done right:

1. **List with a discount broker.** Some companies, such as Wall Street Properties in Bend, Oregon, will list your house in the local multiple-listing service for a set fee. Commissions are typically around 2 to 4 percent and there may be an additional listing fee in the $2,000 to $3,000 range.

2. **Negotiate a lower commission with a regular broker.** Most brokers would rather take a reduced commission than be shut out. If you have some leverage—several interested buyers that you found on your own, for example—but don't want to negotiate or do the paperwork, this may be an option.

3. **Negotiate a flat fee with a broker.** Some brokers are willing to handle a specific part of a sale for a set fee, such as preparing a package for the board if the property being sold is a co-op.

4. **Shop around for a real-estate lawyer.** In some states, buyers and sellers routinely hire lawyers to put oral agreements in writing and make sure the closing goes smoothly. Closing fees range from about $1,000 to $2,000.

5. **Sell it yourself.** The Internet is now full of sites that let owners list and sell their own homes. Two prominent ones: **forsalebyowner.com** and **homesbyowner.com.** A search of Amazon will also net you about 20 how-to titles. **Tip:** Many experts recommend self-sellers engage a real-estate lawyer to handle contract and closing issues. Most charge a set fee that works out to be far less than a broker's commission.

STAGING

Beyond doing a home inspection and making some repairs, there's an important presale step that involves taking a good long look at your interior design. If it's what agents gently refer to as "overpersonalized," that could mean a lower resale value. And lately there's a growing school of thought that the best way to fix the problem is to remove every trace of your personality from the home. Sad as it is to box up the Indonesian statuettes and 1970s bead curtains, there's actual research showing that such "staged" homes sell faster, and for more money, than homes that aren't.

Specifically, Los Altos, California, agent Joy Valentine published a study in 2000 showing that "staged" homes went for 6 percent over list price and sold in just under 14 days, half the area's usual time on the market. Naturally, agents and interior designers have figured out there's money to be made here by offering professional staging services, and it's become a growing niche business within the real-estate industry. Some call it "staging" and others "fluffing," though lately the insider's term for it seems to be "blanding," which perhaps most accurately describes the process. It's not cheap—it starts at about $100 an hour and can go up to $100,000 for a complete makeover of an entire house.

Is it worth your while to spend that kind of money on advice—remove clutter, paint the walls beige—that can seem pretty basic? It depends how design-challenged you think you are. Also, whether you're willing to take a risk that you may not get back all—or any—of what you spend on the professional when the house sells. Finally, keep in mind that while bland seems to be winning the hearts and minds of professional stagers right now, there is a competing school of decorators who insist that adding color (and homey touches like family photos) is the best way to sell a house.

AUCTIONS

If your home is so "overpersonalized" that no amount of staging will help, or if it's just unusual for its area—say, a 15,000 square-foot house surrounded by 2,000 square-foot homes—or even if it's just ahead of its time architecturally, selling the traditional way through an agent may take a long, long time. Another option: selling the home at auction.

Residential real-estate auctions used to be an act of desperation on the part of developers who couldn't unload spec homes in their subdivisions. That's what happened, at least,

 If you want to go bland, here are a sampling of companies that do it:

ARTFUL ARRANGEMENT, DALLAS
Price: $125 an hour
Recent job: Convinced a client to remove 20-foot Confederate flag from foyer, paint over blue-and-gray walls

DESIGN WITH STYLE MOVE WITH STYLE, MILLWOOD, NEW YORK
Price: $150 an hour
Recent job: Chucking out a seller's heavy black living-room furniture and replacing it with airy rental stuff

DESIGNED TO MOVE, LOS ANGELES
Price: $10,000 to $100,000
Recent job: This company specializes in a complete furniture makeover, tossing out the old and bringing in the new. The seller can get a rebate if the buyers choose to keep the look.

REAL ENHANCEMENTS, WESTLAKE VILLAGE, CALIFORNIA
Price: $125 an hour
Recent service: A bare-bones approach, with minimum two-hour consulting appointments that tell sellers how to rearrange or pare down existing furniture for maximum effect

STAGEDHOMES.COM, SAN FRANCISCO
Price: $150 an hour
Recent jobs: 1,500 stagings later, the company goes for complete makeovers to achieve maximum effect. It also offers staging videos and training courses for would-be stagers.

during the real-estate recession of the late 1980s. But in the last five years, many individual owners of unusual and high-end homes have been turning to real-estate auction companies.

There are some definite advantages to choosing this route—rather than waiting around for a buyer to show up, sellers can pick the date they want to close on the sale of their homes. Even if the sale price is lower than what the sellers were asking—it usually is—there's money saved on taxes and upkeep of a house that would normally take months or years to sell the traditional way. And the companies that organize the auctions typically offer national marketing campaigns to reach as wide an audience as possible. Finally, just the threat of an auction can sometimes inspire existing potential buyers to move faster, and maybe even buy the home preemptively before the auction takes place.

On the other hand, there's a risk that the bids will be low, forcing the seller either to sell the home on the cheap or reject the bids and face starting from scratch. Country singer Barbara Mandrell got just $2.1 million for her Nashville estate (she'd been asking $7 million). Michael Egan, founder of Alamo Rent-a-Car, sold a house in Florida for $5.2 million (he'd been asking $12 million). And buyers are typically buying a house at auction "as is," so they have to get their own inspections before bidding—or risk some expensive surprises. Still, the possibility of picking up a trophy home on the cheap is hard to resist, so the auctions will probably remain popular.

MAKING THE MOVE

With low interest rates driving a lot of buying and selling, there's a whole lot of moving going on, too. And moving is often the worst part of selling your house. The good news is that moving companies, squeezed by tighter corporate relocation budgets, have started to offer white-glove service in an effort to counter their image as china-breaking, price-gouging goons. The extras range from the practical (hooking up your Internet service) to the New Agey (one company will bring in a feng shui expert to help you figure out the best place to put the couch).

Is it worth it? It can be—but getting an estimate is just as important with pricey movers as it is with the cheaper kind. And sometimes the basics—taking care of the furniture—get neglected by companies willing to fold your clothes for you and sign your kids up for ballet classes at the new location.

Below is a recent test of three high-end moving companies.

A REALLY MOVING EXPERIENCE

For our test, we did two short moves plus a longer one, paying for the extras for our test-case families. We picked movers and consultants who promote special services, but also tracked the basics, like how close they came to their estimates and how careful they were with our valuables. Below are the highlights of our truly moving experience, with total prices for the move, along with per-mile charges to help you compare.

Low End

The Mover: Pack Rat Relocation

Price: $1,272, Orlando, Florida, to Tampa, Florida ($15 a mile)

The Pitch: We're small, but we'll do it all.

Nicest Touch: Designed three different layouts for our living room

When we heard that even the U-Haul people were offering "concierge" services, we were intrigued. So we went to the company's **Emove.com** Web site, where folks who are moving can hire a variety of services, such as landscaping help and a driver for that rental truck, eBay-style. After punching in the location of our move and what we wanted (packing help, maid service and personal-shopping errands), we got a list of moving specialists, with estimates ranging from $500 to $1,400, including our U-Haul rental. We settled on Pack Rat, which had testimonials from two dozen happy customers.

Considering the low-end price, we were pretty impressed with Pack Rat's can-do attitude. Our request to pick up a prescription and sweep the back porch clean for the new owners didn't faze the team of three men and one woman, and they promised to fold our T-shirts. One surprise: They offered to design a furniture layout in our new home, which ended up making our living room look even bigger. "We'll do right by you," said Ivy Moore, Pack Rat's manager. Indeed, by the time they were done mowing the lawn, we had a yard to make the neighbors jealous.

Still, it's clear the bargain approach has a long way to go. The move had its share of bumps, literally (the hidden shock detectors went off in two of our boxes, and both a dining table and a filing cabinet were damaged in transit). Two of the movers were new, and it showed. They spent 10 minutes trying to squeeze our couch through the door until someone came up with a solution: Unscrew the feet.

Middle

The Mover: What's Organized?

Price: $2,403, Palatine, Illinois, to Lake Zurich, Illinois ($343 a mile)

The Pitch: Consultant handles what the movers won't

Nicest Touch: A closet layout that makes it look like we have fewer shoes

One of the newer twists on the moving scene is the professional organizer, with more than 600 nationwide now specializing in relocations—up 50 percent from just five years ago. They promise to make the whole ordeal painless by dealing with the movers for you—while doing all kinds of extra work around the house, like alphabetizing your CD collection or stocking your pantry with groceries. Indeed, consultants across the country say business is booming, from Move-In Made Easy in Oceanside, California (triple the staff since 2002) to New York's Cross It Off Your List, where sales are up 20 percent from a year ago.

For this category, we called an outfit called What's Organized? which promised it could handle anything from straightening out closets to setting up kids' homework schedules. In our case, they got busy right away, calling in one of several "subcontractors," who got to work on the wrapping. Eight hours later, he was done.

At the new home, the move leader roamed around with clipboard in hand, posting numbered signs in each room to indicate where all of our boxes should go. That didn't impress the movers, including one who told her he'd "never seen this system before." (Her response: "It works—trust me.") Things only got worse from there: By the end of the day in our new house, with the meter running at $45 an hour, she still hadn't unpacked a box and had misplaced our "open me first" box with basic necessities. Our move was done on unusually short notice, she says.

As much as we loved finding our toiletries organized by type (hair ties, cosmetics), we couldn't believe the bill. To move a four-bedroom home just seven miles, she charged $1,600—fully twice what we paid the movers themselves.

High End

The Mover: White Glove Transportation Services

Price: $3,125, New York City to Cambridge, Massachusetts ($14.50 a mile)

The Pitch: Full service from a national hauler

Nicest Touch: Dropped off our unwanted clothes at Goodwill

By this point, we were ready for a truly hassle-free move, and White Glove, a local affiliate of moving giant Bekins Van Lines, said they could deliver on our special requests—for a price. The estimate for our 200-mile move to Boston came to a whopping $4,600 at first, though our estimator immediately offered a 30 percent discount. A little more haggling, and it was a further $230 off, making us wonder if we should have pushed for more.

The company is relatively new to the "concierge" business, but they arrived like veterans in the upscale-move wars, wearing "White Glove" shirts and driving a freshly washed truck. The four-man team took their places immediately, mopping the floors, spackling painting holes, and wiping dust off furniture before packing it. A fellow named Edwin even repacked a box of china after noticing we'd done a bad job ourselves. They wouldn't prearrange our phone service, but told us they were looking out for us (protecting our privacy). "Don't forget to fax my boss to tell them how great I was," one mover said.

Without all these extras, the relocation might have cost us about half as much. But compared with our two other movers, White Glove actually charged the least when you factored in the distance—about $14.50 a mile. More important, though, the team left our house in pretty good shape—and invited us over for dinner anytime we want. Our clothes were folded, our shoes were lined up and the carpets were all vacuumed. And even though it was 90 degrees, thanks to the air conditioner our movers installed, we were sitting cool.

SELL STOCKS AND BUY REAL ESTATE?

Does it make sense to take your money out of stocks and invest in a residence? The short answer is most likely yes, if it's a first residence, and most likely no if it's a vacation home.

While your primary residence may not outperform stocks—it probably won't, considering that home prices typically outpace inflation by about one or two percentage points a year—it is a form of forced savings. Rent payments don't build wealth, and there are mortgage deductions when you own a house. In addition, since 1997 the capital-gains tax exemptions have become extremely generous. The 1997 law allows homeowners to exclude as much as $250,000 of home-sale profit (or $500,000 if you're married and filing a joint tax return), provided you meet certain conditions. One of the main conditions is that the home has to have been your primary residence for at least two of the five years prior to the sale. And there are even circumstances in which homeowners who have owned for under two years qualify for the exemption.

Vacation homes, by definition, don't qualify for the capital-gains tax exemption. In addition, you'll have to pay maintenance and insurance costs on the second home. Should you need to sell it quickly, you may not be able to (whereas stocks can be sold in minutes). If you're counting on renting it for the summer to cover the mortgage, proceed with caution—vacation rental markets have been spotty in the past few years. And it doesn't hurt to ask yourself—are you really cut out to be a landlord?

Naturally, there are exceptions—if you choose a good location, in an area where the housing supply is relatively fixed, and you rent it out year-round, there's a chance you can beat the stock market. But then, of course you don't get to use the place yourself. And that is one feature of residential real estate that beats the stock market without question—you get to live in it.

YOUR HOME AS AN INVESTMENT AND ATM

THE HOME AS ATM

One of the reasons this latest recession hasn't followed a pattern seen in previous recessions—the jobless recovery, the continued robust consumer spending—is that homeowners have been able to get so much cash out of their homes. Imagine the home as an oversize ATM machine—that's how it's been viewed in the past few years by a lot of Americans. In 2004, homeowners took out $99.3 billion in cash when they refinanced their mortgages, according to research firm **Economy.com,** in West Chester, Pennsylvania. On top of that, they borrowed $431 billion using home-equity loans and lines of credit in 2004, according to SMR Research Corp. in Hackettstown, New Jersey.

One popular way to get cash out of the house is a cash-out refinancing, which is basically taking out a new, bigger mortgage at a lower interest rate and keeping whatever cash is left over once the old mortgage is repaid. But this option is less attractive with interest rates starting to rise. And in any case, even if the monthly costs aren't that much higher, it does mean extending the amount of time it takes to pay off the mortgage (and in some cases increasing total interest costs).

There are home-equity lines of credit, variable-rate loans that allow a borrower to withdraw a certain fixed maximum amount over time and pay interest only on the part withdrawn. And unlike unsecured credit-card debt, the interest on the first $100,000 is usually tax deductible. The downside here, again, is the potential for rising interest rates.

Though some lenders cap the rate at six percentage points above today's rates, that can still be a huge difference in monthly payment, and a problem for a borrower whose finances are already tight. Finally, there are home-equity loans, which are more like mortgages—a borrower takes out a fixed amount and pays a set loan payment monthly. These have been less popular, since the rate is typically one to two percentage points higher than on a traditional 30-year fixed-rate mortgage.

Aside from rising interest rates, another risk in borrowing against your home is that if home prices drop, you can end up owing more than your home is worth.

THE ART (AND SCIENCE) OF REMODELING AND DESIGN

BUILDING TRENDS: THE DYSFUNCTIONAL FAMILY HOME

One of the biggest changes in home-building in the past few years has been a shift away from the open floor plan that was so popular in the 80s and 90s—the home with the huge great room/kitchen/living area, the home that let everyone be together as much as possible. The new blueprint for domestic tranquillity seems to involve walling people off from each other, with builders pushing single-person "Internet alcoves," "away rooms" (with doors that lock) and twin home offices (on opposite ends of the house). At the International Builders Show in Las Vegas in early 2004, Pardee Homes of Los Angeles built a model home, billed as "The Ultimate Family Home," that barely had a family room. (The space was divided into a media center and separate "home management center" that was itself divided by a countertop.) Even the family dog had a separate room under a staircase.

In some houses, the separation translates into "his and hers" everything—bathrooms, closets, home offices, sections of the living room and even garages.

Builders say one of the reasons there's more demand for this new separation is it seems to help keep marriages intact—especially with lots of blended families around, including older kids from previous marriages and younger kids from the current one. And it's not a problem to build new houses this way—if you have the space and enough money. It's a little harder to do in existing homes—and in terms of re-sale value, when space is limited, it's worth thinking about which resells better locally, two closets in the master bedroom or a bigger kitchen? (Many developers will say a bigger kitchen—even in urban areas where few people cook at home all that often.)

BUILDING FOR RETIREMENT

With America's 76 million baby boomers edging toward retirement, design for "aging in place" is catching on. Even homeowners in their 30s are sometimes thinking ahead to retirement when they build their homes, installing features like extra-wide doorways (easier to get a wheelchair through) and space for a future elevator.

So-called universal design has been around since the early 1990s, when the Americans with Disabilities Act required public spaces to be handicapped accessible. The early universal-design products were unattractive and obvious, though. The products have since evolved to be more discreet, and are finally starting to catch on with homeowners and builders. Some of the products have an industrial look that fits in with the industrial urban-loft aesthetic, like motion-detector faucets and sinks that can be raised or lowered electronically. There are elevator cabs that can be hidden in a closet, and handhold recesses in shower walls make an unobtrusive substitute for grab bars.

The improvements are coming none too soon, especially given that in some places (Florida; Pima County, Arizona) builders are required to put in some elder-friendly features. But the additions can be pricey—an elevator can run as high as $30,000. And it can take some adjustments for younger homeowners to learn how to live with universal-design elements—doors with levers instead of knobs may be easier for the elderly to open, but toddlers have an easier time opening them, too. The same goes for lower shelves and light switches. Still, given the aging of the population, it's probably worth at least taking universal design into consideration when building a new home.

PREFAB

Yes, prefabricated homes are making a comeback. If the term "prefab" brings to mind a too dark, Swiss chalet–style kit home from the 1970s . . . it couldn't be further from what a handful of name-brand architects are touting today. The new prefab homes are all about looking cool and cutting-edge, with clean lines, geometric shapes and lots of steel and glass. They're called "modular homes"—the term "prefab" does have some stigma to it still—and the upscale designs are about 10 percent of the $6.5 billion modular-home market (five times the share a decade ago, according to Fred Hallahan, a modular-home consultant in Baltimore). Some sell for north of $1 million.

The advantages: Homes in a box—even the high-design ones—tend to go up faster, and cost less than their custom counterparts. And the new crop of designs aren't all literally the same—thanks to

GOING FOR THE OLD

With baby boomers creeping up on retirement age, there's a growing market for elderly friendly products. Here are some of the latest:

Approach sink, ad-as.com; a motorized kitchen sink that can be raised to standard height or lowered for wheelchair-users at the touch of a button. Idaho universal design company's sales have quadrupled, to $1 million, over the past two years.

True Touch dimmer, leviton.com; one of a series of senior-friendly products from a lighting-controls company, it's designed for people with limited range of motion.

Delta e-Flow faucet, deltafaucet.com; it turns on and off electronically with a wave of the hand. Good for those with arthritis—but kids can have a little too much fun.

Duet washer and dryer, duet.whirlpool.com; a high-end front-loading washer and dryer with an optional pedestal drawer that eases loading and unloading.

Brass Leaf lever, door-hardware.net; an arthritis-friendly door lever, shaped like a leaf, that makes opening a door easier and has a patented latch that can't be locked accidentally.

THE FABULOUS PREFAB

 A sampling of architects across the country who have begun offering prefabricated homes:

**RESOLUTION: 4 ARCHITECTURE;
NEW YORK; RE4A.COM**
Features: Floor-to-ceiling glass, rooms that merge into open-air decks. At $250,000 to $500,000 for a 2,000-square-foot home, these are some of the pricier prefabs. It takes two days to assemble one, but three months before it's move-in ready.

**JENNIFER SIEGAL; OFFICE OF MOBILE
DESIGN; VENICE, CALIFORNIA;
DESIGNMOBILE.COM**
Features: Use of "plyboo" environmentally friendly bamboo flooring. Ms. Siegal's work is on display at the Smithsonian's Cooper-Hewitt, National Design Museum in New York. Her 720-square-foot "Portable House" arrives fully assembled.

**ROCIO ROMERO; PERRYVILLE, MISSOURI;
ROCIOROMERO.COM**
Features: Rectangular-box shape; this 32-year-old architect built her first prefab home in Chile for her parents. One project: "Fish Camp," a $20,000 back-to-nature retreat.

**WILLIAM MASSIE; TROY, NEW YORK;
MASSIEARCHITECTURE.COM**
Features: Curving lines, building on or around rocks, mountains; one project: a "challenging," 3,000-square-foot home to be built within the rim of a canyon in Wyoming.

LOT-EK; NEW YORK; LOT-EK.COM
Features: Use of large-scale industrial objects such as water tanks. Talk about a tight fit. The "mobile dwelling unit" is a 550-square-foot house made out of a shipping container. (It does include windows.)

**CUTLER ANDERSON ARCHITECTS;
BAINBRIDGE ISLAND, WASHINGTON;
CUTLERANDERSON.COM**
Features: Lots of glass; energy efficient; James Cutler, known for his work on Bill Gates's home, insists that prefab manufacturers guarantee architects can customize each site. Assembly time is expected to take between five and nine months.

**ANDERSON ANDERSON; SEATTLE; SAN
FRANCISCO; ANDERSONANDERSON.COM**
Features: Striped, modular designs; rectangular shapes; architects started doing prefabs in Japan a decade ago.

computer-aided design, they can be varied somewhat to meet the needs of individual homeowners.

On the minus side, the high-end architects designing these homes tend to have fairly avant-garde tastes, so it takes an adventurous buyer. And there is a certain lack of flexibility in buying a mass-produced home.

BRIGHT LIGHTS, BIG SYSTEMS

PRODUCT: GRAFIK EYE; LUTRON ELECTRONICS; LUTRON.COM
What it Does: One-room system with multiple lighting scenes

PRODUCT: TOSCANA CONTROLLER; LEVITON MANUFACTURING; LEVITON.COM
What it Does: System recognizes the time of day and automatically adjusts lights to preset levels. You can also hook up your appliances, like your coffeemaker, to this device, too.

PRODUCT: COMPOSE PLC; LIGHTOLIER CONTROLS; LOLCONTROLS.COM
What it Does: A whole-house system doesn't require additional wiring; it allows you to preset up to 13 lighting scenes; fade rate can be set as slow as one hour.

PRODUCT: SMALL REMOTE CONTROL; VANTAGE CONTROLS; VANTAGECONTROLS.COM
What it Does: Allows remote control of up to eight lighting scenes in each room

PRODUCT: HOMETOUCH; LITETOUCH; HOME-TOUCH.COM
What it Does: Keypads replace existing switches and dimmers; can be used on one floor or the entire house. The company sells custom-engraved buttons, like "pool," "BBQ" and "driveway"; timer module has a vacation mode.

PRODUCT: WEB-LINK II; HOME AUTOMATION; HOMEAUTO.COM
What it Does: System dims, brightens and controls lights using a PDA or any computer with Internet access. User-friendly icons make this system easy to use online, but it works only with the maker's systems.

THE HIGH-TECH HOME

As homes have gone increasingly high-tech, the headaches accompanying the new technology seem to have grown in direct proportion. Architect Grant Kirkpatrick of KAA Design Group in Manhattan Beach, California, says one of his biggest bugaboos is the high-tech lighting system. "Nobody has the time to figure out how to work them," he says. "Have you seen the manuals that come with those things?"

They're not cheap, naturally—the average American spends about $4,000 on lighting controls, and that doesn't include the cost of a lighting designer, and a programmer to create various lighting settings, such as "welcome home," "entertaining" and "homework time." (Or return visits from the electrician if something goes wrong.) The instructions can run to 40 pages, and an engineering degree—or at least a teenager—is sometimes necessary to decipher them. Some homeowners need special tutorials from their lighting designers before they feel in control of the switches. But the systems are hard to resist for gadget-loving homeowners—and the lighting industry is still coming out with new ones. Here are some examples:

WI-FI STRESS

Then there's Wi-Fi stress. Wireless technology can be addictive—it is fun to roam around with your laptop. But there's a hitch—Wi-Fi systems can have the same dead spots that drive cell-phone users to distraction. The wireless systems themselves have gone mainstream, and aren't too expensive—a basic Wi-Fi setup runs about $120. It's after they're installed that the problems arise, including everything from baby-monitor interference to water molecules in large houseplants that block signals (really). Even building materials (brick, thicker woods) can be a problem. In ranch-style homes, signals can fade from one side to the other (solution: Put the base station in the middle of the house, in a high spot). Two-story homes face another problem—getting the signal to reach all the way up (try putting the base station on the first floor).

To combat the Wi-Fi dead spots, some companies are selling antennas that boost the wireless base station's signal (the range of the antennas is limited, though). Then there are more expensive "range extenders" and "repeaters" that pick up fading signals and rebroadcast them at full strength to areas of weak reception. But put too many repeaters in the same vicinity and they'll fight for the airwaves and knock you offline. And, yes, there are even consultants you can hire to help figure it all out (figure on spending several hundred dollars).

INTERIOR DESIGN: HIRING AN INTERIOR DESIGNER

Americans are doing a lot of interior decorating—over $100 billion worth annually, according to U.S. Commerce Department figures. And more are getting professional help when they decorate—even

Home Depot employs interior designers who make home visits. But the experience can be intimidating—not to mention expensive. In a *Wall Street Journal* test of interior-design services on the low, medium and high end, some rules of thumb emerged.

1. **Low-ball the budget up front by at least 20 percent, because no matter what figure you pick, your decorator will most likely exceed it.**

2. **If you want to keep most of your possessions, steer clear of commission-based consultants—they have a built-in incentive to get you to buy all new belongings.**

3. **If there's nothing you want to keep, getting furniture through a designer isn't necessarily a bad deal—they can get professional discounts of as much as 40 percent off retail, and they'll typically pass along maybe half that savings to you.**

4. **Be prepared to have someone else's taste imposed on you, at least to some degree.**

THE THREE-DECORATOR EXPERIENCE

by Asra Q. Nomani

The Budget Person

"This is great. I love it," says Carol Safier, stepping into the apartment. We should have stopped there.

Ms. Safier, of CS Interiors, New York, has stopped by for a 40-minute consultation—something design experts recommend before signing up. Hers is free. We tell her we want to spend up to $10,000.

"Lighten up the room. It's too dark," she says from the living-room sofa. She eyes the wall that separates the living room from the smaller,

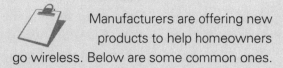

BLANKET COVERAGE

Manufacturers are offering new products to help homeowners go wireless. Below are some common ones.

AIRPORT EXTREME BASE STATION; APPLE.COM

What It Is: Wireless router; this device from Apple gives you the option of attaching an external antenna to increase range.

OUTDOOR ANTENNA; HAWKINGTECH.COM

What It Is: Antenna that mounts outside; you still need a wire to connect this antenna to the router indoors. Words to decode: "directional" (beam it at a specific destination) or "omni-directional" (blanket a backyard).

POWER LINE ADAPTER; NETGEAR.COM

What It Is: Wall-plugged Ethernet to send an Internet signal through power lines; you can place routers in different parts of the house without using wires. With its limited speed, it's best only to surf the Internet.

ROUTER/REPEATER KIT; BUFFALOTECH.COM

What It Is: Router (base station) sends wireless signal; repeater picks it up and sends it farther. After strong sales of its repeater, Buffalo Technology started packaging the router and repeater. But this repeater won't work with routers made by other companies.

second bedroom. "This is so stupid. Take the wall down. My guys could rip it up in 15 minutes." She spots the Ikea floor lamp. "Get rid of the lamp shade," she snaps. "It's ugly."

Four dark-wood Ikea bookcases line one wall in the living room. "I don't know why these are here," she says. The lighting fixtures in the foyer must go: "A chandelier. It needs a chandelier." A paint job is indicated. "This white is awful," Ms. Safier says.

In the bedroom, two rough-hewn window frames that contain mirrors rather than glass hang over the bed. (We bought them at a neighborhood sale for $18, thinking how popular this look had become at retailers such as Pottery Barn.) "Enough already with the windows," Ms. Safier says.

"Some of the little knickknacks would have to go," she mutters, looking in the direction of the fireplace mantel, where a purple hippo Beanie Baby reclines. Above it rises a five-foot-wide mirror that extends to the ceiling. "It looks awful. I'd frame the sides," she declares. Hmmm, that doesn't sound so attractive. "It'll look great," she vows. Ms. Safier spots something she likes. Finally. A dark-finished china cabinet picked up for $75 in Chicago. Whew, a winner.

The fee she quotes us—$2,000 up front, no commission, "no hidden costs"—places her at the lower end of the designer-fee spectrum. Still, Ms. Safier drops addresses of ritzier clients: Manhattan's Trump Tower, where a family is spending half a million dollars; Central Park West. "You're going to have to buy a lot of stuff," she warns. For $10,000, "you'd have a palace," she predicts, as she trails off to field a call on her cell phone. "Your bathroom? It's beeeeautiful," she coos to a client.

No hidden costs, but we ring someone else anyway: Steve Lyons, owner of No Big Deal Interior Decorating. His fee: $150 for a consultation and $50 an hour after that. "Lowest in the city," he says, promising a plan if we sign up. "It's not a floor plan. It's a plan of action."

Five days later, a half hour late, Mr. Lyons, a 20-year-veteran, trudges up the stairs, a bulging black briefcase in hand, looking like the used-car salesman of interior design. "Let's talk," he says, stepping straight through the foyer into the living room, without comment. The previously stated fees aren't all he charges. For furniture purchases, we pay him the equivalent of half of the 40 percent discount he gets off retail prices. So for a $3,000 sofa, he gets a $1,200 discount and buys it for us for $1,800. We buy it from him for $2,400. "We share the discount," he explains, as we do the math and calculate that he makes a 30 percent commission on the deal.

He scans the room. What about the wall in the living room? "It ruins the original design," he says. "Do you use the extra room?" Uh, yes, we say, not knowing what the right answer would be. "Yes? Keep it, then. It's practical." Relief floods us. Briefly. The sofa, bought at a suburban Chicago furniture store: "Ditch it." Arms too big. Dominates the room. Takes up the sitting space of at least one person. "An L-shaped couch. I'd recommend a sectional."

Then it's all new stuff to buy: an easy-chair with an ottoman, an entertainment unit or armoire, a cocktail table, a dining table, an area rug. To the bedroom. "You want a new bed, an armoire with drawers and two bachelor-chest nightstands. They have three drawers in them," he says. He eyes the bare wooden floors. "I'd like to wall-to-wall," he says.

We set a shopping date for the Design Center in Midtown Manhattan, 16 floors of showrooms where only design professionals can buy—at wholesale. "I don't do my trip," he says. "I do your trip." He trudges out with his $150 check.

Armed with a floor plan, Mr. Lyons takes his shoppers to the Nicoletti showroom, where a saleswoman greets him happily, "Stevie!" Over about two hours, he coaxes and guides us to spend $21,152— almost twice our budget—on a three-piece sectional couch covered in velvety fabric with leopard spots (or polka dots, depending on how closely we look), cocktail tables, an entertainment unit, a dining set, a bedroom set and a leather recliner. All of this while sitting at the dining table, where he flips through catalogs, rising only occasionally to rhapsodize "Isn't this fabulous!" about something on the showroom floor.

For his efforts, Mr. Lyons would get his $400 in fees, plus another $4,000 in commissions that come from the $21,152 we would spend on furniture. We beg off buying on the spot. Good thing: We were swept away by his enthusiasm, but a week later, we realize leopard-skin and leather just aren't us.

Mid-Price Designer

You can't get any more mainstream than Macy's or Bloomingdale's, both units of Federated Department Stores Inc. Macy's has a cheaper $250 retainer, which gets deducted from the bill when you buy $1,500 in furniture, but their designers don't do home visits and just work from photos and floor plans. At Bloomie's, it's a $750 retainer, of which $500 is refundable after $10,000 in purchases.

Taking notes, congenial interior designer Carla Bloom Katzen peppers us with questions as she guides us through Bloomingdale's furniture department. "What do you think of metals? Rattan?" Our budget: $15,000, but we might go higher. "I live vicariously through other people's lives," Ms. Katzen pronounces.

She discovers for us that we like rattan. She also gets us excited about the Tradewinds line designed by the retired head of her department. A $3,700 refectory gaming table with leaves to seat eight is perfect for New York apartments, she declares. She guides us to a leather armchair. "Like it?" Actually, yes. She lifts the $1,465 price tag and says, "Believe me, I wouldn't let you buy anything for full price. We'd get it on sale." Later, she'll get the dining table down to $2,960 on sale. Ms. Katzen doesn't get paid by commission but rather by salary, though bonuses are pegged to how much business she rings up.

It's like *The Price Is Right* without Bob Barker. Ms. Katzen recommends a $1,200 wooden armchair, although it doesn't look that comfy. Skip one Ralph Lauren bedroom set. "It's dark, clubby. It's a look," she advises, leading us to a massive bed frame that will do great for $3,500, even though we'd prefer a bed with a canopy. She summons us to look at a sleeper sofa priced at $1,865. "Really, it's great!" she says. An hour later, we've got just about everything we need. The folder Ms. Katzen gave us at the outset includes something special: a credit-card application.

Armed with a 25-foot measuring tape, Ms. Katzen diligently arrives the next day to measure the apartment: "If somebody says, 'I don't do measurements,' don't listen to them." She is merciful. The china cabinet: "It's good for now." The bookcases: "They're harmless." The window-pane mirrors: "We can use them for something"—take that, Cheap Decorator Number One. That vexatious living-room wall? "We can keep it if you want." We decide guests will be happier even if Cheap Decorator Number One isn't. We keep it.

Ms. Katzen won't even discuss the details of the new apartment she envisions until she presents her design, eight days later. With a bundle of swatches and a floor plan, she says she prefers now to tear down the wall. Her scheme is gorgeous for $37,898.75—more than double our initial budget. It doesn't include a silver-framed double dresser mirror she hasn't yet found, not to mention the dreamy canopy she plans to have her window-treatment man create for the Tradewinds queen four-poster bed. Yeah, she listened, about the style if not the costs. But on second thought, looking over the estimate, do we really want the $106.50-per-yard zebra fabric for the black-painted wooden armchair?

High-Brow Designer

Prospective clients ask interior designer John Saladino's assistant, Jane Seamon, whether he is scary. She assures them he isn't. Oh, but he is. A 30-year-veteran, he runs a sprawling design shop on the top floor of the Design Center, and cuts an imposing fire-hydrant-like figure. Designer to the superrich, Mr. Saladino, 59, sits at the conference table where clients come to interview him. But really, he says, "I interview them." It costs $35,000 just to get a design plan. Then the firm bills by the hour for shopping, installing, remodeling. Mr. Saladino's time goes for $500 an hour, the rate we pay him for two hours of consultation.

He's picky about clients. One profession he bars: trial attorneys. "They're not visual. They're insecure in this field." So there. He recoils if called a "decorator." "Women in between marriages become decorators." He prefers to be called a "designer." The biggest problem with the profession: "Women will buy a Judith Lieber handbag for $6,000 and never discuss it with their husband. But they have to discuss a $6,000 sofa with their husband, and they have to sleep on it. They have to show it to their friends. The sofa has to go to the grave with you."

The son of a Kansas City doctor, he remembers every detail of the childhood home he helped decorate at 16. When he enters our humble abode, he is kind—at first: "It's gracious." But then, in the foyer: "You set the tone with the entrance. The lighting here is ghastly. Get rid of the fixture." The replacement: a chandelier lantern. Win one for Cheap Decorator Number One.

Out go the French curio tables that display the childhood bangles and the Presidential Physical Fitness Award. "They're Bombay Company," he scoffs, a dig at the midprice retailer. He prefers another furniture line: his own. Picking only items from the Saladino line, he suggests a pair of $1,746 "Tube Floor Lamps" on both ends of new bookcases that would replace the Ikea stalwarts. Next to the bookcases, two "Sleigh Chairs" for $1,500 each.

In the bedroom, he dictates a French white-on-white carpet. "Almost wall-to-wall, with a foot on the sides." Score one for Cheap

Decorator Number Two. He calls for a fruitwood sleigh bed facing the opposite way everyone else pointed the bed. And he sees more colors, more clearly. "Let's say we did the bed in different shades of pink, red and fuchsia. You'll match well with it." Thanks. We think.

Stepping into the living room, his reaction is instant: "Tear down this wall." It "absolutely violates the integrity of the room. It's ghastly. The original intent of the architect has been ruined." Ms. Cheap Decorator Number One, also a wall-basher, scores major points. The room, he says, was meant to be a 19th-century parlor. To restore the octagon shape he wants to put a cupboard in two corners. Inside, "you have to buy beautiful porcelains for $700 each." The mirror above the mantel "is a poor attempt to open up the room. It's Joan Crawford 1954," he says. It's far too frightening to even contemplate asking what he means.

The current dining table with its carved legs goes, but "the dining zone" stays where it is, with its view of a church. The table must be replaced with the "Balustrade Dining Table," for about $5,000, draped to the floor in fabric. We take solace in knowing that at least we picked an acceptable "dining zone."

By now, we're a little insecure about our white walls. That's confirmed. "A real pale pink," he says dreamily. The sofa: "It's ugly," he says, not that we really care anymore. Much. It would be replaced with the "Landau Sofa," about $8,000 for a custom-made velvet piece with a sleeper sofa (now that the guest room is gone). "In the winter, I'm going to do this in a deep duck-pond linen velvet," he says, looking into space. "In the summer, the slipcover would be a pale-pink cotton." Oh, the sofa ottoman gets to stay, disguised with a slipcover.

Mr. Saladino accepts something else. The Ikea floor lamp. "I can use the lamp—with a new shade." We can almost hear the echo of Ms. Cheap Decorator Number One. A final dagger comes when he spots the china cabinet, accepted by even Middle-of-the-Road Bloomie's Designer. "Out!" he declares. "It reminds me of a struggling family where the poor wife kept the few pieces of porcelain that she used once a year." And we've only got one paltry piece of terra-cotta in there.

The price tag for this extravaganza: about $65,000, just for the furnishings. That's $72 a square foot—or about double the cost of renting space at the Empire State Building. Tack on his designer fee and hourly rates, and the total soars into six figures.

Mr. Saladino must be feeling a little guilty. On the windowsill in the little room with no integrity, he eyes seashells saved from beach vacations. We forgot to hide them. "I like the seashells," he declares. And two lively accessories, eclectic and playful, get to stay: Billie and Billuh, the apartment's cats. "Puddy cat, puddy cat," he mews to Billie, sitting on the rejected dining table, next to the rejected sofa, next to the rejected bookcases, next to the integrity-violating wall. "I like you."

INTERIOR DESIGN TRENDS

Interior design is, in a sense, fashion for your home—there are looks that go in and out of style, some fairly rapidly. It's fine to look up-to-the-minute, but most architects and designers caution that there are certain design elements that can instantly date your house, and that's generally not a good thing. Remember shag rugs, paisley-print curtains, beanbag chairs? Having a style so clearly associated with a specific point in time (in that last case, the 1970s) can hurt resale value. On the other hand, there are always more practical innovations. Below is a look at some of the major interior-design trends of the new millennium.

Low Furniture

In the 21st century, a look that's gotten popular is low, modern furniture. It's evolved partly as a minimalist reaction to the overstuffed, hulking sofas of the 1990s, and partly as a way to make ceilings look higher (from the retailers' point of view, it doesn't hurt that the short, modern pieces tend to look better in matched sets, tempting buyers to purchase more than one piece).

But it's not the most practical of looks—getting up off a low couch can be a humbling experience, especially for aging boomers. And tall people may find themselves with their knees up to their chins.

Weird Sinks

Another design feature that's just everywhere in all the shelter magazines: weird sinks, including everything from those abovecounter "bowl" sinks to glass sinks that resemble fish tanks to sinks inspired by horse troughs. In general, architects say, if you're going to install a sink that doubles as artwork, it might be best to limit it to a half bath, where it's just used for hand-washing. (This is especially true for abovecounter sinks and glass or bronze sinks, which are tricky to keep clean.) Also, make sure you're thinking about counter height, which will need to be adjusted down if your sink is above the counter. And be aware that you may need to get special faucets to accommodate your offbeat sink, too.

Contemporary Kids' Furniture

It used to be that parents whose taste in furniture ran contemporary didn't have many options. Custom furniture is beyond many buyers' budgets, so for a long time IKEA and a handful of small retailers were the only places to go to furnish a nursery with furniture that matched the rest of a modern house. But that's started to change in the last few years, with some of the most original furniture designs turning up in the kids' section. And part of the appeal of the new pieces is that they're nice enough to recycle as adult furniture (or at least a piece of art) somewhere else in the house once the kids are done with them. Jerry and Jessica Seinfeld bought a $2,280 crib-and-changing-table from a New York designer that converts into a storage unit for adult use. A Philadelphia toy and furniture company sells inflatable plastic chairs shaped like sea urchins that can support up to 300 pounds. And a round table with a chalkboard surface and a cylinder in the middle for storing art supplies has been pressed into service by some buyers as a cocktail table (the cylinder is also a perfect wine chiller).

High-End Fakes

With the economy as muted as it's been, homeowners have tended to rein in decorating budgets somewhat. But it doesn't necessarily show in the décor. That's because faux furniture—along with faux every-thing, including handbag knockoffs—have improved steadily in quality over the last decade. In a test that involved building a living room and a kitchen using fakes (and mixing in some upscale stuff), then bringing in a panel of experts to see if they could tell the real from the faux, the fakes did surprisingly well. A $20 magazine rack from Target fooled most of the panel (the competition was a $400 designer magazine rack). A machine-made oriental rug ($700) beat out a handmade one that cost twice as much. A $1,400 sofa fared better than a leather sofa that cost nearly $8,000. But no one was fooled by the knockoff version of a commercial stove next to the real item, or the Formica laminate counter next to the granite countertop.

DRESSING YOUR HOME

Redecorating and remodeling are extensive processes; homeowners spend tens of thousands even on small projects and there are shelves of books that you could read before choosing each appliance. Given that, we've decided to give a broad overview of the various components, providing tips and general guidelines.

1. The Kitchen. Keep a number of things in mind when shopping for appliances. First, make sure to ask for discounts if you're buying a whole set of appliances rather than just one. It takes some haggling (try the tried-and-true technique of holding brochures from competing retailers while talking to a salesperson). Don't take the first offer and don't forget to ask about other fees that might be added later, like a charge for actually carrying your fridge up the stairs. Also, remember that there are a lot of extra costs when purchasing appliances, including possibly having to upgrade gas and electric lines, as well as making sure your plumbing is up to snuff.

2. Refrigerators. All kinds of gizmos here. Do you want side-by-side doors, built-in ice dispensers, or Internet access? A freezer on the bottom? One new trend is glass-faced refrigerators, but you have to have confidence about sharing what's inside.

3. Stoves. At the high end, price differences aren't as stark in this area, especially as compared with refrigerators. One thing to keep in mind when pricing stoves is the need for a hood, duct cover and riser (which sits on the back of a slide-in stove to protect the wall).

4. Cabinets. Cabinetry is one area where homeowners shouldn't try to cut corners. While there's no structural advantage to custom-made if your standard cabinets are made well, the difference between a well-made and a poorly made cabinet is night and day. Over time, low-quality cabinets will warp; shelving will become uneven; the finish will start to wear off. Cheap hardware will eventually mean doors or drawers that don't close properly. In major metropolitan areas with lots of competition, price will be a good barometer of quality. Your best bet for making a good choice is to ask people you know who bought the same make and model you're considering how well the finish, shelves and hinges are wearing.

5. Flooring. Since water is the enemy to a lot of building materials in kitchens and bathrooms, homeowners often replace vinyl or linoleum flooring with harder surfaces, such as ceramic tile, slate or granite. The harder a tile floor is, the better it will hold up over time. More durable tiles are more expensive to make and ship. But in flooring, price and durability don't necessarily correspond. You can find strong tiles for under $10 that will withstand miles of foot traffic and dozens of dropped pots and myriad spills. If you're concerned about a pricey tile's quality, ask the salesperson why it's expensive. If it's because it was hand-painted or handcrafted, and it seems you'd be paying more only for the labor/artisanship, ask how durable your selection is compared with other tiles. Save fragile hand-painted tiles for a decorative area in front of your fireplace or a little-used guest bathroom.

FURNITURE

Furniture makers are getting more experimental. After years of safe, boxy sofa systems and understated side tables, many makers are trying to be different, edgy and unique. You want see-through tables, ottomans in animal-skin fabric, couches made from totally recycled materials? All that's possible these days. But here are some no-nonsense guidelines about buying furniture that transcends trends and style:

1. Pay the smallest deposit acceptable. That way, less of your money is at risk if the store should go out of business. Paying the deposit by credit card also gives you some protection.

2. Check out the return policy. Under what circumstances are refunds given, and is the total amount refunded? Some refunds mean store credit only. Furniture stores often charge a "restocking fee" (which can be as much as 20 to 25 percent of the item's price) for items that are returned due to the consumer's change of heart. Also, many stores don't take returns of custom-made furniture, as when you order a sofa in a special fabric—so be sure you can live with your choice.

3. Think about financing offers carefully. "Zero percent financing/no payments for a year" offers are only a good deal if you are certain you will be able to pay off the total amount before the year is up. If you don't, you are usually charged interest retroactively from the day of the purchase.

4. Get an estimated delivery date in writing. If it doesn't come on time, you might (depending on your state) have the right to cancel the sale and receive a full refund or a credit equal to your deposit, negotiate a new delivery date or choose something else to purchase instead of the original item.

5. When arranging for delivery, ask if there are extra charges for flights of stairs, and if the delivery team will assemble or set up the furniture for you.

6. Don't sign for acceptance of the delivery until you have made sure that all the items are there and you have inspected them. If an item is defective or damaged, you can refuse to accept delivery or accept it, but note the damage on the delivery form. Either way, contact the store and ask for a replacement or repair.

7. Floor models and closeout items are often sold on an "as is, all sales final" basis. That means you are accepting the visible condition and any disclosed defects. However, hidden defects are still covered by an implied warranty.

THE ELEMENTS OF STYLE

When it comes to style, it's not as easy to give advice. But keep in mind there are five major categories: casual (overstuffed sofas; earthy colors; oak, pine, ash and maple woods); contemporary (bold colors, sharp lines, metal and glass); country (soft cushions, floral prints, distressed and painted wood); traditional (antiques and antique styles, wingback chairs, damask and chintz, cherry and mahogany woods); and eclectic (ethnic or artisan pieces, a mix of compatible styles and periods, highly individual).

The type of material used for upholstering is also important and should be matched to your lifestyle—what kind of wear and use your furniture will receive. Basically, there are two types of fabrics; naturals (cotton, linen, silk and wool) and synthetics (acetate, acrylic, nylon, rayon and polypropylene); often fabrics are a blend of natural and synthetic. Generally, fabrics with tighter weaves and durable fibers such as polypropylene or nylon stand up better to the hard use. One exception: leather, which holds up well.

Wood furniture: All woods used for making furniture fall into two categories: hardwoods and softwoods, but the designation doesn't really have anything to do with how hard or how soft the wood is. "Hardwood" identifies the trees that lose their leaves seasonally and "softwood" refers to those that keep their foliage all year. Among the hardwoods frequently used in making furniture are ash, cherry, maple, oak, pecan, teak, rosewood, walnut, mahogany and poplar. In the softwood category are cedar, fir and pine.

According to the National Home Furnishings Association, more-expensive furniture is generally made of fine hardwoods such as maple, cherry or oak, or of "selected" softwoods such as pine. Medium-priced furniture may have a combination of different woods on exposed surfaces. Because trees don't grow in the shapes and sizes required for making furniture, pieces of wood are bonded together in different ways to achieve the necessary sizes and shapes. Four types of bonding are often used:

1. Wide boards are often cut into long narrower planks and bonded back together. In solid wood furniture, strips are carefully glued together to form the tops, sides and door panels. The interior may be of another wood.

2. Shaping is achieved by gluing blocks of wood together. These blocks can be machined for a deep carved pattern or turned and shaped into a leg, pedestal or post.

3. Combination-wood panels are made by mixing wood particles, chips or flakes with resins and binding agents. These sheets are formed under extreme heat and tremendous pressure, making them exceptionally strong, stable and resistant to warping. Called "chipboard," "particleboard," "fiberboard" or "engineered wood," this material is frequently used on the backs of cabinets and doors or as cores for tops and panels.

 Here's the National Home Furnishings Association's checklist for buying wood furniture:

- Doors and drawers fit well
- Drawers have glides and stops
- Drawers glide easily when pulled
- Drawers have dust panels
- Drawer corners are joined securely
- Insides of drawers are smooth and snag-free
- Long shelves have center supports
- Doors swing open easily without squeaking or rubbing
- Long doors are attached with sturdy hinges
- Hardware is secure and strong
- No rough edges on hardware
- Interior lights operate easily
- Entertainment units have a hole for electric cord
- Heavy balanced feeling when table is rocked
- Table leaves fit properly
- Finish feels smooth to the touch (except distressed)
- Distressed finish has randomly spaced dark marks

4. Ply-construction is achieved by adding layers, placed at cross-grain, to a solid wood or particleboard core. Adhesives are placed on each layer and this "sandwich" is permanently bonded under high pressure. Modern glues and manufacturing techniques have made ply-construction very strong and resistant to warping.

FINDING GREAT ART FOR YOUR HOME

Let's say you've decided to invest $5,000 in art to decorate your home (or just to invest in the art market). Where should you go?

Across the country, there are dozens of art dealers, auctioneers and cyberspace sellers eager to school, or snare, new collectors—but each method of buying has its pluses and pitfalls.

Auctions

Auction houses, in general, are a good place to find art under $5,000, simply because of the large volume of works they carry. Giants like Sotheby's and Christie's turn over several hundred thousand items a year, but there's a greater selection in this price range at regional auctioneers like Skinner Auctioneers in Boston, Leslie Hindman in Chicago, Bonhams & Butterfields in San Francisco and about two dozen others nationwide. And while auction houses are generally thought of as the places to buy million-dollar masterpieces, they often sell off the entire contents of one or more houses in order to land a couple of major artworks, hence the phrase "house auction." The house should be able to provide basics like a biography of the artist, the history of the piece, a written report on its condition and a price list of what similar items have sold for at auction. They'll even help you learn the basic rules of bidding. Much of your auction-house buying, including the actual bidding, can be done over the phone, but it's chancy to bid on art you haven't seen in person.

Auctions have their drawbacks, principal among them "auction fever," which can kick in if you don't set a bidding limit, and a 15 to 20 percent buyer's commission. You should also familiarize yourself with arcane auction code: Tiny symbols like check marks or triangles next to the title of an artwork in a catalog, for example, flag that the auction house is actually the owner of the property, or has loaned money against it, which makes the auction expert's advice suspect.

A PASSPORT TO DESIGN

 A look at some major cities that are considered design centers:

LONDON: The British favor classic designs with a twist, such as Terence Woodgate's softer interpretation of the leather Chesterfield sofa. Also, color is king in Britain—Tim Power's asymmetrical coffee table is turquoise.

MILAN: At the Milan Design Week in April 2004 (an annual event that is open to the public on certain days), designers pushed styles that were still minimalist but with more decorative touches than in the past.

NEW YORK: Since its start 16 years ago, the International Contemporary Furniture Fair has grown into an important design event.

STOCKHOLM: Think beyond Ikea when it comes to Swedish design. The traditional look is muted, but contemporary design is youthful—designer Anna von Schween's "Hug" and "Big Hug" chairs have arms that open up.

TOKYO: Tokyo Design Week each October attracts local and international designers. The smaller Tokyo Designers Block Show, held the same month, features upstart designers.

Galleries

Art dealers often can get you the best deal, since they get pieces privately placed by sellers who don't want the notoriety of an auction or fair, or works done at the beginning of an artist's career, before prices take off. But galleries have their drawbacks: They carry a fixed roster of artists or artworks, not necessarily the ideal venue for a first-time buyer. It's important to check a dealer's track record. Ask to see the résumés for artists a dealer represents (generally kept in a book behind the front desk). They should show artists increasingly featured in exhibitions and museum shows in other cities. If the artist has only had shows in resort towns, like Honolulu; Laguna Beach, California; and Nantucket, Massachusetts, that's a clue to move on. In general, art dealers who target a tourist trade may not have an established resale market for the works they sell.

If the art gallery stocks works by well-known artists, ask to see the catalog raisonné, a reference book documenting an artist's body of work. Savvy collectors refer to these books to make sure their potential purchase is listed and is considered a good example of the artist's work. (Doing a little homework before buying—in the form of museum visits, reading up or dropping by auction-house previews—will also help you get the most for your money.) Don't be afraid to bargain. A 10 percent cut off the asking price is standard; 20 percent for cash isn't unheard of. Make sure to ask for a written description of the artwork, including its condition, and of the dealer's return policy. If you later tire of an artwork, many dealers will agree to a partial refund or a credit toward the purchase of an artwork of equal or greater value.

Art Fairs

These are another excellent source of affordable investment-quality art. But don't show up on opening night, when the dealer is generally schmoozing big-ticket clients. Instead, visit in mid-afternoon, when dealers have more time to talk—and then come back right before the fair closes, when dealers cut prices rather than ship pieces home. Look for a fair featuring more than local artists and galleries, and one that's "vetted." Vetting committees are made up of dealers who review each piece in a show, and often weed out some that are considered low quality. Before buying, find dealers selling similar wares and ask them about your pick at their competitor's booth.

Unfortunately, while antiques fairs abound across the country, most art fairs are held in New York. A handful of notable exceptions that feature some works for $5,000 or less include the huge Art Basel Miami, held every December in Florida, and the Art Chicago contemporary art fair held in that city every May.

The Internet

Nearly four-dozen Web sites sprang up to sell art and antiques during the 1990s boom. But collectors proved resistant to spending thousands of dollars sight unseen, and some highly publicized incidents of online fraud cooled the market further. After pouring more than $40 million into its own online sales venture, for example, auctioneer Sotheby's quit the online art market. Today, only a handful of online art-sales sites remain, but some are thriving.

Guild.com, a Madison, Wisconsin-based online seller of artist's crafts and prints, has seen double-digit sales growth every year since it launched in 1999, with particular demand for its prints by American artist Jamie Wyeth. British-based **Eyestorm.com,** in business five years, sells limited-edition artworks by artists like Damien Hirst and Helmut Newton. Dealers and auction houses primarily use **Artnet.com,** which offers an online database of art-auction prices throughout the world and features highlights from the inventories of 1,300 dealers. There's a monthly fee to access the price database, but window-shopping the galleries is free. However, Web sites can skimp on crucial information—for example, listing photographs without saying whether the artist developed the negative. And buying from a faceless seller can raise the issue of authenticity and legal title.

HOW TO FINANCE HOME RENOVATIONS

Cash, or a cash-out refinance?

Homeowners have an array of options when deciding how to

finance a home-remodeling project. Rising home prices and low interest rates make borrowing an attractive choice, even for homeowners who haven't built up any equity. Here's a look at the advantages and disadvantages of various forms of home-renovation financing:

Source: Cash

Definition: Money from your personal savings

Pros: No interest charges or fees; no debt

Cons: Depletes personal savings; no tax advantages

Source: Cash-out refinancing

Definition: A refinance where you borrow more than the amount of your current mortgage

Pros: Current interest rates are low; tax deduction on interest payments

Cons: May require private mortgage insurance; fees and rates are higher on large loans

Source: Home-equity loan

Definition: A lump-sum loan secured by the equity in your home

Pros: Current interest rates are low even for this type of loan; cheap fees; you get a tax deduction

Cons: You carry both mortgage and home-equity debt; no flexibility in how you borrow; may be a limit on tax deduction

Source: Home-equity line of credit

Definition: Funds are secured by equity in your home, but you can borrow in increments

Pros: Current interest rates are low; cheap fees; tax deduction; flexibility in how you borrow

Cons: You carry both mortgage and home-equity debt; may be a limit on tax deduction

Source: 203(k) loan

Definition: Government-backed remodeling loan for homeowners with little or no equity; essentially combines a construction loan and a mortgage in one package

Pros: Loan is government-insured, which encourages banks to lend; requires no home equity; home is appraised at post-renovation value

Cons: Rates are higher to pay for insurance; the lender assumes a role in the remodeling project.

Source: Fannie Mae Homestyle loans

Definition: Similar to the 203(k) loan, but it's not government-backed

Pros: Requires no home equity; home is appraised at post-renovation value

Cons: Not insured by the government or Fannie Mae; the lender assumes a role in the remodeling project

WHAT'S WORTH DOING?

Renovations

It's long been known that when it comes to renovating your home, it isn't how much you spend—it's how you spend it. Bathrooms and swimming pools have always added value, but some other home improvements are more susceptible to fading in and out of fashion.

A study sponsored by the National Association of Realtors analyzed the effect of various housing characteristics on residential property values these days, shedding light on what renovations have integral value and what kind of housing styles are gaining or losing popularity.

What homeowners are currently willing to pay more for:
- central air-conditioning and fireplaces
- eat-in kitchens
- utility rooms
- in-ground swimming pools

What they aren't:
- dining rooms
- dens or studies
- intercom systems
- kitchen pantries
- aboveground swimming pools
- home offices
- in-law suites

MORE THINGS WORTH DOING

As reliable as the daffodils, each spring the housing industry encourages owners to renovate their homes to enhance resale value. Remodelers talk about investing in new bathtubs or windows, while real-estate agents tout the value of new carpeting and countertops. It makes sense, at least on the surface. But experts say that unless an upgrade is to correct something functionally obsolete—say, to add a second bathroom in a four-bedroom house—most remodeling projects return only a fraction of their cost. Studies by organizations ranging from consumer groups to trade magazines show that, on average, improvements made in the year before a home's sale return only about 70 or 80 cents on the dollar.

There are exceptions, of course. Studies have shown that larger, upscale remodelings in hot housing markets like Washington, New York or San Francisco can even turn a profit for the homeowner. But whether your house is in a sizzling market or one that is stagnant, you have to be smart about the kind of improvements you undertake.

The trick is to bring your home up to neighborhood standards, but no higher. But how do you know the difference between an improvement that's excessive and one that will help sell your house—and maybe pay for itself? *The Wall Street Journal* asked a number of experts which modest upgrades would bring the best returns in today's market, and which are a waste of money. Since remodeling for resale value is a dicey proposition, we limited our inquiry to projects or products that cost less than $10,000.

Worth Doing:

1. Granite countertops: Price: $3,600 for 90 square feet. At $40 a square foot or more installed, granite is about 40 times as expensive as plastic laminate. But upscale-home buyers have come to expect it. Although honed, light-colored granite is trendy, stick with polished black stone—it's elegant-looking, and more durable.

2. Carpets: Price: $6,375 for 2,500 square feet with a 10-year wear warranty. Yes, how boring, but next to a paint job, nothing makes a house look fresher. Though the Federal Housing Administration demands a minimum of $3/8$-inch pad and 23-ounce density carpet, choose a half-inch pad and a 27-ounce density. And don't stray from earth tones.

3. Pull-out kitchen faucet: Price: $300 for a European-style chrome faucet. Faucets occupy center stage in a kitchen, so they attract buyers' attention. Trendy finishes like brass and nickel cycle in and out of style, so stick to standard polished chrome. Gooseneck styles high enough to put a pot under are currently popular, but pull-out styles with a hose are the most versatile. Forget redoing bathroom faucets, though. They're more a matter of personal taste, and a buyer may just junk yours.

4. Melamine closet systems: Price: $1,600 for a walk-in closet with three rods, six shelves and five drawers. Coated-wire systems are okay for mid-range homes, but upscale buyers shun them. On the other hand, furniture-finished wood is overkill if you're remodeling for re-sale. Spring for shelves made of melamine-surfaced particleboard or medium-density fiberboard. Melamine is a plastic laminate available in different finishes, but consider a wood-look finish.

5. Synthetic entry doors: Price: $1,730 for a fiberglass door with beveled glass inserts and two sidelights. Front doors are the first things a buyer sees up close, so they shouldn't look dumpy. Five years ago, most synthetics looked fake, but improved veneers and finishes have made fiberglass and steel doors resemble the real thing. And though fiberglass dents and steel rusts, both provide better security with less maintenance than solid wood, especially if the door faces the sun.

6. Laminate wood floors: Price: $1,630 for a 15-×-15-foot room. Made of either thin-wood veneers encased in plastic, or photographs of wood on a plastic base, laminates have also become more realistic-looking in the past couple of years. Because you can wet-mop it, laminate has become more popular than real wood for areas subject to spills, like kitchens and basements. It can't be refinished three or four times like real wood can, but if you're moving soon, who cares?

7. Body-spray showerheads: Price: $2,383 for shower tower with two telescoping overhead sprays, four moveable body sprays and a handheld spray. Multiple-showerhead systems do everything from misting to massage. They're still rare enough to get a buyer's heart beating faster.

8. Garage storage systems: Price: $220 for hanging storage-wall starter kit with 11 hooks, a wire basket and a shelf. A recent survey by real-estate brokerage Century 21 found that the garage is the most important amenity to buyers, outranking a large kitchen, formal dining room or big backyard. And what they prize most about the garage is its storage capacity. But you don't need to add pricey cabinets, which can easily push the bill for a storage wall into the thousands. Just give buyers the idea of how they can personalize, while you get your hoes and rakes off the floor.

AND . . . MORE THINGS TO SKIP

1. Wet bars: Save the $1,875 average price. Novel in the 80s, wet bars have become clichés. Unless you plan to turn a corner of your basement into a wine cellar, they're losers.

2. Concrete countertops. At around $9,000 for an average installation, they're hot and trendy—but Realtors report far too many buyers hate them. Plus, they need resealing twice a year and are prone to cracking. Moreover, they tend to bring out the inner artist in homeowners—we've seen owners incorporate everything from computer chips to toy plastic people into designs. Remember: Another person's art may be hard to live with.

3. Chandeliers. Save the $4,000 for the Italian crystal gold-leaf model. Like concrete countertops, they alienate too many buyers in a world in which chic recessed lighting is increasingly popular.

4. Structured wiring. It seemed a good idea five years ago to spend $5,000 to hardwire your home for broadband PC networks and stereo speakers. But wireless has come and changed all that.

5. Saunas. Spend the four grand if you like them, but like wet bars, they're yesterday's ideas.

6. Indoor swim spas. The $5,000 you spend on one of these 14-foot-long tanks that lets you swim against the current will attract a certain kind of fitness-inclined buyer, but too many others will worry about maintenance, leaks, humidity and mildew.

SOME BASICS TO REMEMBER

1. **You're in for the long haul.** The National Association of Home-builders says to count on a major home remodeling taking as much as twice as long as you'd planned.

2. **Expect the unexpected.** The National Association of the Remodeling Industry recommends setting aside as much as 20 percent of your budget for contingencies.

3. **Relationships with contractors are everything.** One common mistake—many people don't complain at the beginning, then blow up at the end. Communicate all the way through.

4. **Details, details.** Count on as much as a fourth of your budget being taken up by finish-work, which includes everything from light switches to the kitchen sink.

5. **Don't pay too quickly.** If you do, you won't have leverage if something goes wrong. Experts recommend holding back 10 percent of fees.

CHAPTER NINE

HEALTH AND FITNESS

TAKING CONTROL OF YOURSELF

Good health doesn't just happen to you. Your health is a direct result of the innumerable small choices and lifestyle decisions you make every day. What food do you eat? Do you sit down to a family meal? Do you eat in front of the television? Do you kiss your spouse good-bye in the morning? Do you wear your seat belt? Do you enjoy your job? How do you spend your evenings and weekends? It all counts.

To be sure, genetics and luck obviously play a role. But that's why it's so important to take charge of the health issues over which you really do have control. All of the major health risks we face in our lifetimes—heart attacks, cancer, strokes and diabetes—are influenced by the daily decisions we make. "We need to get over the notion that diseases are just caused by some force outside of us," says Graham Colditz, director of the Harvard Center for Cancer Prevention at the Harvard School for Public Health. "There are things we can do that will change our risk."

And taking control of your health is more than just living a healthy lifestyle. It's about seeking out the best medical advice, availing yourself of the latest medical tests and technology, finding the most-skilled doctors, searching out the best hospitals and learning how to navigate the medical system. Most important, it requires a dramatic shift in thinking for most of us. Modern health care is predominantly based on disease *management.* If you get sick, you go to a doctor, who then prescribes a treatment plan. But good health should be centered around disease *prevention*—tapping into all the expertise, technological advances and resources of the health-care system to stop illness before it starts.

CHOOSING A DOCTOR

One of the most important steps is to find the right doctor, yet most people put more effort into finding their car or house. Sadly, patients often choose doctors based on proximity to the doctor's office from home or work. But the decision is far too important to base solely on geography. Ideally, you should build a long-term relationship with a primary-care or internal-medicine physician—someone who knows you well enough to catch potentially serious health problems early and help you find the best specialists when the situation warrants.

The first step in choosing a doctor is a practical one. Find out how much flexibility and choice your insurance company gives you. Some plans offer indemnity insurance, which gives patients freedom in choosing doctors and hospitals, but holds them responsible for a portion of the bill. People in preferred-provider organizations, or PPOs, have the option to see doctors outside the participating network. But they are then typically responsible for 20 to 30 percent of their bills. About 70 percent of the nation's insured population is in one of these two types of plans. But even patients who are limited in their choices by a managed health plan can still shop around for the best care within their plan if they follow some basic advice.

1. Ask a health-care professional. Most workers know who the top performers are in their office, and the same is true with doctors and nurses. Nurses know better than anyone which doctors take good care of their patients and which don't. If you don't know a nurse, you can also ask other physicians for leads. Note that doctors are sometimes obligated to refer patients to someone in their own medical or insurance group. To make sure you're getting the best advice, ask a doctor or nurse where he or she would send a family member. If you don't know a doctor or nurse, you can refer to local rankings of top doctors or try **bestdoctors.com.** For a fee, the site will refer you to a local doctor, based on a database of doctors rated by their peers as top experts in their field. Finally, seek a recommendation from somebody who has been sick. Sick people don't lie about which doctors give good service.

2. Schedule interviews. Once you've picked potential candidates, schedule an appointment to interview each one. Insurance won't cover the cost of such an interview, so it's yours to bear. The practice is common among expectant mothers who want to find the right pediatrician before their baby is born. Many patients are intimidated by the prospect of interviewing their doctor, but the simple step of setting up an appointment will give you insight into how the doctor runs the office. Is the receptionist courteous or frazzled? Are you left on hold for 15 minutes? Does it take weeks to get an appointment?

3. When you finally meet with a doctor on your list, start with the basics. Where did you go to school? Where did you serve your residency? Does your specialty require you to be recertified? How often? Many doctors frame diplomas from their medical school, their state license and their certification by one of the 24 boards in one of the three-dozen specialties recognized by the American Board of Medical Specialties. Ask doctors where they trained for their specialty—a doctor who has trained with another top doctor will eagerly brag about it. Much of this information can be found on the American Medical Association Web site, **ama-assn.org,** or the site for the American Board of Medical Specialties, **abms.org.**

4. Ask probing questions. If you are seeking a specialist for a particular problem, surgery or procedure, it's important to know how many times the doctor has treated your illness or how many times he or she has performed the procedure. Chances are, you will get far better care if the doctor has treated 100 cases like yours, rather than just a few. Countless studies have shown that in medicine, quantity improves the quality of care.

Other questions to ask when vetting your doctor: Can I get seen today if I'm ill? Does your office run on time? Do you teach anywhere? (Teaching can be a sign that a doctor is keeping up with things, although it can also mean he or she has fewer days to spend seeing patients.) Ask if your doctor will communicate with you by e-mail.

The best doctors are those who encourage a patient to ask questions and who listen to their concerns. And in the end, after all your questions are answered, the best bet is to go with your instincts and to choose the doctor with whom you feel most comfortable.

THE INFORMED PATIENT: HOW TO CHECK UP ON YOUR DOCTOR

Sexual assault. Drive-by shootings. Fraud.

Though it sounds like the local police blotter, these are offenses committed by doctors disciplined by the Texas state medical board, and now their patients (or prospective patients) can read about them online.

Thanks in part to new legislation, a growing number of state medical boards are opening the books on the misdeeds of their members. California, New York and Florida recently joined Massachusetts in posting previously secret files on criminal convictions, major hospital disciplinary actions, malpractice judgments, licensing revocation and sanctions by other states' medical boards. All but a handful of states now have at least some data on the Internet regarding disciplined doctors, and are under growing pressure to add more detailed files.

The new disclosures come after decades of squabbling among consumer groups, who believe patients are entitled to as much information as possible, and physicians' groups, who say frivolous lawsuits and incomplete data can make the information misleading.

Shari Baker, a retired paralegal, has used the Internet to look up her own doctors and those used by friends and neighbors in her Petaluma, California, retirement community. Ms. Baker says the need to do such research first dawned on her several years ago, when she glimpsed her son's doctor at the courthouse where she was filing some papers for a client. After checking with the county clerk's office, she learned he was in the process of settling several malpractice suits. "We should be better informed, but we don't research our own doctors," she says. "We're usually just so impressed or intimidated by them that we don't check them out."

But though the information is now widely available, even the most savvy health consumers may find it difficult to understand. Many medical-board Web sites are cumbersome and hard to search, and they aren't updated frequently. And raw case files can be difficult to interpret once you track them down.

In the official Texas medical board listings, for example, the action against one doctor whose license was suspended was described as due to "unprofessional or dishonorable conduct and inability to practice medicine with reasonable skill and safety to patients as a result of any mental or physical condition." The real story? The doctor engaged in a sexual relationship with four patients and also admits he has a history of alcoholism. (A Texas medical board spokeswoman says the board is required to cite disciplinary actions by category codes, and sexual assault isn't listed separately. But she says the board is moving to change those requirements. While Texas doctor data "is not real accessible now, we are trying to be more transparent and consumer-friendly.")

By and large, of course, doctors aren't scofflaws. Of the more than 800,000 licensed medical doctors in the United States, there are only 2 to 3 percent whose care or conduct is substandard enough to be cited by a state medical disciplinary board, according to Public Citizen. Some doctors are disciplined for mere administrative oversights such as failing to renew their license on time. "Many of these things are technicalities, and they need to be interpreted carefully," says American Medical Association President Yank D. Coble.

But consumers have the right to know who the serious offenders are—and they haven't been able to count on the medical profession or even the federal government to give them all the information they need. Disciplinary data from a National Practitioner Data Bank launched ten years ago is by law available only to hospitals and health-care organizations. Doctors are often allowed to continue to practice despite serious infractions, and hospitals and health-care groups that are supposed to closely track the credentials of their affiliate physicians don't always do so.

"The nation's system for protecting the public from medical incompetence and malfeasance is still far from adequate," says Sidney Wolfe, Public Citizen's director of health research.

There are other benefits to having access to doctors' histories. Joy Bennett of Chicago used the Internet to look up a doctor who had treated her husband a few years ago for a workplace accident, and learned that he had been disciplined for failing to keep proper records. Had she known that at the time, she says, she believes it might have helped the couple get a better settlement in a lawsuit over the incident, because the doctor had failed to record that her husband suffered from headaches.

The biggest danger to consumers, says Quackwatch founder Stephen Barrett, are the "health hucksters"—unscrupulous phony doctors and alternative medicine practitioners whom he targets on his site. Dr. Barrett, a retired psychiatrist and a vice president of the nonprofit National Council Against Health Fraud (**www.ncahf.org**), regularly updates his lists of doctors who are prosecuted for fraud, and follows up on tips from consumers about suspicious alternative cancer treatments and dubious advertising claims. Among the phony doctors he has investigated is the notorious Gregory Caplinger, who lured patients to the Dominican Republic for a fake cancer cure. Caplinger is now serving a 14-year prison term, and faces other charges for falsely claiming to be a medical doctor.

There are numerous ways to check on a doctor's basic credentials. The American Medical Association's Web site (**www.ama-assn.org**) has a "Doctor Finder" listing 690,000 licensed physicians and their credentials. But the AMA notes that the information is submitted by doctors themselves and says it's just a starting point for getting more information about physicians' records. State medical boards, which can usually be found with a search engine, or through **www.fsmb.org,** can also provide information about the doctor's educational and specialty background. Patients in an HMO or other managed-care group can request data on credentials from the plan.

SOME OTHER TIPS TO FOLLOW

1. If you find your doctor's name on a disciplinary case, carefully read the file before making a decision to switch physicians. Some of the offenses are not threatening to patients; a doctor may have defaulted on a student loan or failed to pay a liability-insurance surcharge. Because an Internet listing may not have all the details of the case, ask your doctor why he or she was disciplined.

2. Ask your doctor for the names of hospitals where she or he has admitting privileges. Local university teaching hospitals are likely to be the most selective about the doctors admitted to the staff, and if you need to be hospitalized, you will want a doctor who can admit you to the best hospital.

3. If you have a complaint about your doctor, file it with the appropriate state agency, or federal agencies, such as the Department of Health and Human Services or the Food and Drug Administration, whose Web sites have contact information. If your complaint stems from care you received in a hospital, you can also file a complaint with the hospital's peer-review committee, which can revoke or limit a doctor's privileges to practice there.

4. Check on a doctor's reputation with people in the community, nurses and other doctors. "Ask the surgical resident who is the best anesthesiologist," says Dr. Barrett of Quackwatch. "Your family practitioner should have a mental database of who the best specialists are." But even if a doctor has been sued for malpractice, he says, don't leap to judgment. "Sometimes the doctors who get sued most often are those treating the sickest patients. There is some relationship between bad medicine and malpractice suits, but it is not enough to go on."

CHOOSING A HOSPITAL

Some doctors think the hospital you choose is just as important—and sometimes more important—than the doctor who sends you there. That's because patients often are treated by a team of "invisible" doctors, such as a radiologist or anesthesiologist, so choosing the best hospital gives added assurance about all patient care. Ask your doctor

PLAYING P.I. WITH YOUR M.D.

Ways to find out if your physician has a criminal record or other infraction:

1. **Quackwatch.com.** Operates a growing list of Web sites aimed at combating health-related frauds, myths, fads and fallacies, including **dentalwatch.org, homeowatch.org, chirobase.org** and **nutriwatch.org.**

   Reports on actions by state and federal agencies. Affiliated with the National Council Against Health Fraud, which also distributes a free weekly e-mail newsletter.

2. **Federation of State Medical Boards (fsmb.org** or **docinfo.org).** Umbrella group for all state medical boards as well as 13 state boards of osteopathic medicine. Provides Internet addresses, mailing addresses and phone numbers for state boards. Will search for disciplinary histories of specific physicians for consumers for a fee of $9.95 per report.

3. **Administrators in Medicine (docboard.org).** Free site. Contains licensing background, malpractice, criminal conviction and disciplinary information of physicians and other health-care practitioners from state government licensing boards.

4. **The U.S. Department of Health and Human Services Office of the Inspector General (oig.hhs.gov/fraud/exclusions/listofexcluded.html).** Online database that provides information on doctors, hospitals or other groups excluded from participation in federal health programs such as Medicare, due to fraud, patient abuse, licensing-board actions and default on Health Education Assistance Loans. Searchable by name or name of business; state; type of practice; type of exclusion.

where he or she has hospital privileges. Many doctors advise patients to find a doctor who has privileges at a medical-school teaching hospital. It simply requires more time, expertise and professional recommendations to win privileges at a teaching hospital. And most of us live within three hours of a major teaching hospital or an affiliate.

Many doctors suggest that for routine medical problems, a community-based hospital that is service-oriented is best, while academic hospitals are ideal for serious or rare health problems. To get a sense of the quality and service at a particular hospital, patients can visit a hospital to see if the emergency room operates efficiently, whether the hospital is kept clean and whether small items like water fountains and the floor indicators on elevators work.

Note that teaching hospitals are best avoided for elective care during July and August, when students are new and chaos reigns. It might be best to stay away in June as well, when many residents take vacation. And most hospitals are best avoided around holidays, if possible, because they tend to be shorter staffed.

How well a hospital treats its nurses can often be a sign of how well they will treat you as a patient. Ask a nurse in your doctor's office about the reputation of nearby hospitals. Your doctor may also have insights into the quality of the nursing care at a particular hospital.

The number of patients each nurse is responsible for is a key indicator of the quality of care you will get. That's because there is growing evidence that the level and quality of nursing care can have a dramatic effect on whether a patient lives or dies. A 1999 University of Pennsylvania study published in the journal *Medical Care* followed the care of AIDS patients in 20 hospitals. The study found that adding just one nurse to a patient's care rotation reduced by half the odds of a patient dying.

Doctors and nurses recommend that patients shop around when they are headed for a hospital stay. The first step is to find a "magnet" hospital in your area—that is, one that meets certain nursing standards and is certified by the American Nurses Credentialing Center, a subsidiary of the American Nurses Association. The group recognizes more than 100 health-care organizations for their excellence in nursing service. A list of magnet facilities can be found at **www.nurse credentialing.org/magnet/facilities.html.**

Studies show magnet hospitals do make a difference. A 1994 University of Pennsylvania School of Nursing study followed Medicare patients in 250 hospitals. The study, controlled for differences in physician qualifications and patient populations, found that magnet hospitals reported five fewer deaths for every 1,000 Medicare patients who were discharged. Considering the size of the Medicare population, that could represent about 50,000 fewer deaths a year.

Patients who don't live near a magnet hospital should comparison-shop by calling the patient-services or nursing-administration offices of nearby hospitals and asking about nurse-to-patient staffing ratios. There is no standard recommendation for staffing levels. Intensive-care units typically have one nurse for every one or two patients. Nursing groups argue for a ratio of 1-to-4 on general surgical units, but hospital groups often suggest staffing levels of 1-to-10. Some general floors, where patients aren't facing life-threatening conditions, may stretch nursing staffs even further. And nurse-staffing levels typically drop on the night shift.

The best way to assess staffing levels is to just do the math to see how much time a nurse will have to attend to your needs. A 1-to-12 ratio, for example, means a nurse will have an average of five minutes an hour for each patient, not counting her administrative duties. A 1-to-4 ratio gives the nurse about 15 minutes per patient. The level of nursing care a patient needs depends on the seriousness of your health problem.

Patients who fear their hospital nursing-care isn't adequate can hire a private-duty nurse or nurse's aid. But that isn't cheap and is rarely covered by insurance. A registered nurse can cost up to $40 an hour or $480 for a 12-hour shift. Nurse's aids cost about $15 an hour or $180 a shift. Many hospitals give patients the option of hiring a private-duty nurse through the hospital, but some patients may need to contact an outside agency. Have your physician speak directly with the hired nurse to make sure he or she is fully informed about your needs.

KNOW YOUR HEALTH INSURANCE

Taking charge of your health care also means knowing the rules of your health-insurance plan. The efforts of a patient to find the best doctors and best hospital care will be wasted if an insurance company won't pay for it.

The most important step toward getting the most out of your policy is to read it. Get a copy of your policy and the policy booklet often distributed to employees. The document is important because the health plan is usually held accountable for whatever it promises in the booklet, even if the fine print of the actual policy says something else.

1. Don't start reading the policy on page one, but scour it for the benefits it offers. Look for phrases like "all necessary office visits" and "medically necessary" that ultimately could limit coverage. Check under the section that describes basic facts about the plan for information about the use of specialists and other limits.

2. Study the "exclusions," "services not covered" and "conditions" scattered throughout the policy. The list of exclusions can sometimes look deceptively short but often contains broad language, such as "according to accepted standards," giving plans an opening to deny coverage. The "definitions" section is a common place for hiding exclusions. Also become familiar with the conditions imposed on the policy-holder, such as notifying the plan before going to the emergency room, so that the claim won't be denied because you didn't follow the rules.

3. **Keep detailed records and refer back to them when new records arrive so you can catch mistakes.** Most insurance problems involve simple bureaucratic mistakes, lower-than-expected reimbursements, and denials of treatments that aren't for life-threatening conditions. Although such mistakes may only be valued at a few dollars here and there, the cost can quickly add up to a substantial sum of money.

4. **If a claim continues to be denied, check with state insurance officials.** States have their own mandates about what insurance companies must cover, regardless of what the policy says. Many policies, for instance, don't cover infertility, but about a dozen states, including New York and California, require coverage. West Virginia mandates coverage for cosmetic surgery if the problem was caused by family violence. Wisconsin allows for coverage of grandchildren under the age of 18. New Hampshire and other states cover the cost of toupees for certain medical conditions.

Even people who are fairly well informed about their insurance policies can be surprised when certain services aren't covered. If your policy promises to pay 80 percent of your medical bills, know that it will only pay 80 percent of what it thinks should be charged, or the "usual, customary and reasonable charges." For instance, one cancer patient was billed $98,000 for treatment. But the insurance company decided a more reasonable amount would have been $63,000. Instead of paying 80 percent of $98,000—or nearly $80,000 of the treatment cost, the company paid only about $50,000 of the cost—leaving the family to foot the remaining $48,000 bill.

The problem is a significant one for people who choose indemnity insurance, which gives patients freedom in choosing doctors and hospitals, but holds them responsible for a portion of the bill, usually about 20 percent. Preferred-provider organizations, or PPOs, give patients the option to see doctors outside the participating network, but for a price. Instead of a small copayment, patients typically pay 20 to 30 percent of the cost of an out-of-network doctor. While maintaining the option to see any doctor you want is a good idea, you need to do your homework to find out exactly how much extra it will cost you. Often the insurance company's definition of 20 percent is far different than your own.

That's because most of the country's large health insurers that administer such plans use a tool, called the "Prevailing Healthcare Charges System," to determine usual-and-customary charges. It's a giant database containing 2.8 billion entries of what doctors charge for thousands of different procedures in more than 400 areas of the country. From that database, health insurers determine what a specific doctor should charge for a given procedure in a particular area. When a doctor charges more than that, health insurers automatically chop the bill down to a "reasonable" size before reimbursing the patient or the doctor.

Generally, patients don't learn about what their insurer will and won't pay until after the service has been performed. But patients should be more proactive.

Try to get a written estimate from your doctor of how much he or she will likely bill for the procedure. To get the most reliable information, patients should have a "CPT" code from their doctors. Doctors use the code in billing to represent a specific procedure. Getting the code in advance will help you find out exactly how much the insurance company thinks is a reasonable charge for the service.

Patients can challenge decisions through the standard appeals process, which begins with the insurer but can work its way up to state appeals boards. They also can ask doctors to reduce charges if they are out of line with what the health insurer says peers are charging. Doctor-administered drugs, like some chemotherapy and other injectible drugs, often have huge profit margins for doctors. If a doctor's fee is high, be frank with your physician about your ability to pay. The American Medical Association says doctors have an obligation to compassionately consider the patient's ability to pay.

Negotiate, but don't haggle. You aren't buying a used car. Ask if the physician will accept an in-network rate. If you must go out-of-network for a procedure because an in-network specialist is not easily available, try using this fact as a bargaining chip with the insurer to adjust your portion of the bill.

PAYING FOR IT YOURSELF

Medicine moves far faster than insurance companies, so patients who want to avail themselves of the latest in medical testing often have to pay for it themselves. But with so many new advances, it's tough to know what can really make a difference in your health and what's just medical marketing hype.

Many of the latest medical tests focus on assessing your risk for disease so you can take steps to prevent it or catching health problems before they trigger symptoms. While the screening tests often are promising, they typically lack controlled studies showing that using them really can make a difference in your long-term health. Critics also worry that widespread screening and testing of otherwise healthy people will trigger a round of unnecessary tests and risky procedures that ultimately could do more harm than good.

But that doesn't mean you shouldn't consider paying for care your insurance company refuses to cover. Screening tests are expensive, and the government and health insurers need lots of cost-benefit studies proving a particular test will save enough lives to justify the cost.

Here's a look at some emerging screening tests that you may want to ask—and pay—for yourself:

CRP Blood Test—$8 to $20. The American Heart Association says the CRP test is necessary only for patients who already show some heightened risk for heart disease. But many patients—and their doctors—are asking for the test anyway because it can signal heart disease in patients with normal cholesterol. "CRP" stands for C-reactive protein, and it's a blood test that detects coronary-artery inflammation and could signal increased risk for heart attack. The test results come back as a single number—a score of three or higher puts you at high risk, while a score below one is ideal.

Aneurysm Scan—$60–$200. This test involves a five- to ten-minute ultrasound with a handheld scanner against the abdomen. The test can spot bulges in the artery wall long before they become life-threatening. Aneurysm disease is surprisingly common—it's estimated 7 percent of men over 60 have it. But few people have even heard of it or realize they might be at risk. Aneurysms caught early can be fixed with surgery. The best candidates for screening are men and women above 60 who have a cardiovascular risk factor, such as diabetes, smoking or obesity. Everyone over 50 who has a family history of aneurysm should be screened.

Transvaginal Ultrasound—$250. This test, which is performed annually, uses a wandlike device, inserted into the vagina, to view the ovaries. There is no approved screening test for detecting ovarian cancer, which kills 14,300 women a year. The best study supporting transvaginal ultrasound comes out of the University of Kentucky, where researchers using ultrasound have an early-detection rate of 76 percent. Typically only 25 percent of ovarian cancers are caught early. Skeptics note that nine out of ten women in the study underwent surgery to remove tumors that weren't cancer. Indeed, women who get the test should know that benign ovarian cysts commonly occur in women of all ages.

Heart Scans—$250 to $500. For this test, you spend 10 minutes in a doughnut-shaped machine, which looks for calcium buildup that can signal heart disease. Although most experts don't support widespread screening, the heart scans are gaining acceptance although they are rarely covered by insurance. In particular, the tests are viewed as useful in patients at "intermediate" risk of a heart attack based on their cholesterol levels, blood pressure, age and health habits. Knowing the calcium scores of an intermediate-risk patient can help a doctor decide just how aggressive he or she needs to be in treating the patient. Many doctors think the scans aren't necessary because cheaper blood tests for CRP and cholesterol provide plenty of information to treat intermediate-risk patients.

Spiral CT Scan—$200 to $450. This annual test can find lung cancer when it is as small as a grain of rice, compared with conventional X-rays, which often don't spot cancer until it is as big as an orange. Right now, just 15 percent of lung cancers are found early. But in scanning studies, 80 percent of the cancers are caught in the early stages. The biggest problem with the tests is false positives. In studies, anywhere from 15 to 50 percent of patients scanned had unnecessary and risky lung biopsies. Patients can even request their scans be sent for review to Cornell, Mayo or Moffitt—the medical centers with the most experience reading lung scans. The scans are suggested for smokers, and former smokers 50 and over, who have smoked at least 10 "pack years"—that's a pack a day for 10 years or two packs a day for five years.

Screening Colonoscopy—$500 to $2,000. Doctors say you should be screened for colon cancer starting at age 50. But every year, 13,000 people younger than that are diagnosed with the often-deadly disease. Although studies show lowering the screening age to 40 can't be justified, some people are opting for the tests anyway and paying for it themselves.

During a traditional colonoscopy, the patient is sedated, and doctors insert a scope through the rectum to get a direct view of the colon. If a polyp is found, it is usually removed on the spot. While the test is considered very safe, there is a 1-in-1,000 chance of perforation of the colon wall, which can lead to surgery, and in rare cases even death.

While traditional colonoscopy remains the gold standard, the virtual colonoscopy is gaining acceptance. But not all virtual scans are equal. The best bet is to have your virtual scan done by a university-affiliated teaching hospital. Ask how recently the scanning equipment and software packages were updated. Some of the best research results have come from 3D scanners, although most radiologists use a combination of 2D and 3D technology. The more virtual scans your radiologist has read, the more reliable your result, so ask. Look for a radiologist who has read 50 to 100 scans and ask how many of those scans were verified by experts. The biggest disadvantage of a well-done virtual scan is that if doctors spot a problem, the patient has to undergo a second bowel-cleansing, followed by a standard colonoscopy to have the polyp removed.

Full Body Scan—$1,000 or more. The most expensive and controversial of the scanning tests, the full-body scan surveys the body, neck to pelvis, for trouble spots. The military has used the scans for years. But given the wide area being searched, doctors say it's inevitable that the scan will find something that looks suspicious and requires a sometimes invasive follow-up procedure. The full-body scans don't detect two leading cancer killers: breast cancer and prostate cancer, which can't be seen with the CT technology. They also are likely to miss small cancers of the kidneys, liver and other organs. The full-body scan also packs the largest dose of radiation. Researchers from Columbia University have reported that repeated body scans can increase a person's risk of dying from cancer by about two percentage points.

Comprehensive Health Exam—$2,000 to $7,000. This lengthy and expensive exam is essentially a one-stop shop in which patients can avail themselves of all the latest blood tests and body scans in hopes of catching potential health problems early. There's no evidence that these super-physicals make any difference prolonging patient lives, but the exams are an opportunity for a lengthy visit with a doctor, who in addition to running a number of tests offers counseling on nutrition, exercise, stress management and a range of other health issues. Typically insurance will pay for only a small portion of the overall cost.

COPING WITH A SERIOUS ILLNESS

Many people facing a serious illness are so overcome with emotion and fear that the last thing on their mind is taking charge of their health. People who wouldn't dream of letting their interior decorator make a decision without them often are willing to let doctors make life-or-death treatment decisions without asking a single question. But an informed patient can have a dramatic impact on the course of his or her own health by searching for the best specialists and the latest and most-promising treatment options.

Here are some simple steps to starting your search for medical answers:

1. Get a second opinion for *every* doctor involved. While many people know to get a second opinion before undergoing surgery or cancer treatment, most patients overlook two of the most important doctors in the process: radiologists and pathologists. A diagnosis is only as good as the doctors who read the scans and the pathologists who review a biopsy. With a cancer diagnosis in particular, virtually every decision about treatment stems from the findings of the pathologists and radiologists.

2. Recheck the lab work. And there's growing evidence to support asking for a second opinion on your lab work when cancer is suspected or diagnosed. Although serious errors are still considered rare, mistakes that could alter treatment—such as determining how fast the cancer is growing or how much it has spread—may happen as often as 20 percent of the time depending on the type of cancer, according to some researchers.

The easiest way to get a second pathology opinion is to suggest it to your physician, who will usually handle the process. Make certain the second opinion is coming from a specialist in the field rather than a general pathologist. Insurance companies often pay the $80 to $150 cost of second pathology opinions, but some may require advance notice. Asking for a second opinion doesn't require the patient to undergo another test. The slides made from the biopsy are simply mailed and reviewed by a new set of eyes. Most major cancer hospitals automatically give second pathology opinions when patients are referred from other hospitals.

The qualifications and experience of the radiologist can also make a difference, and so does the equipment he or she uses. In the case of magnetic-resonance-imaging scans, the quality of the scan can make all the difference in whether a problem is even visible on the scan. When making an appointment for a scan, patients should ask about the age of the scanner and how recently the software was upgraded. The best centers will have machines and software no more than a few years old. Patients should also ask about the strength of the machine, which is measured in a unit called a "Tesla." The best machines in widespread use are at least a 1-to-1.5 Tesla. Some manufacturers are introducing three-Tesla machines. "Open" machines, including standing MRIs, are typically just 0.5 or 0.6 Tesla. Find a radiologist who specializes in whatever field your problem falls into, such as orthopedics, pediatrics or neuroradiology.

3. Read your own medical records. In most cases, state and federal laws require doctors to provide patients with copies of their medical records, but most patients don't bother to ask. It's a mistake. Reading your medical records not only gives you specific information about your disease, but it gives you insight into your doctor. Patients reading their own records often are surprised to find details their doctor hasn't bothered to mention. The husband of one patient read his wife's medical records the night before a scheduled treatment. On the day of the treatment, he quickly realized the drugs the nurses were discussing were different from those the doctor had indicated in the patient records. He raised the issue and the mistake was corrected.

4. Find an advocacy group. Advocacy groups often have lists of specialists, send representatives to medical conferences and keep databases on current research. Search for them on the Internet by using the name of your illness. The Association for Cancer Online Resources, **acor.org,** includes 70 online cancer information and support groups, where you can tap into the vast knowledge of other cancer patients and survivors to get answers to your questions.

5. Find the best doctor for your problem. If you're sick or need surgery, you don't want a doctor who has seen one or two cases like yours during his entire career. You want to find the person that deals with your problem every day. Ask your own doctor for the name of a specialist he or she would send a family member to. Or ask a professional society for a referral or search the group's Web site for meeting agendas to find names of doctors presenting research that hasn't yet hit the medical-journal databases. You can also contact doctors listed in articles found in respected medical journals. Most articles now include e-mail addresses, and researchers can be surprisingly responsive. Talk to other patients or find online support groups to discover who other patients with the same problem think the best doctors are.

6. Tackle the Internet. The National Library of Medicine's **medline plus.gov** and the National Institutes of Health's webpage **nih.gov** both provide access to the Medline database of scientific journal articles as well as information about clinical trials, drugs and other health sources. For many people, a Google search is the best starting point in your search for medical answers. Most government and health-oriented Web sites center around published studies, but unpublished research is sometimes available on the Web sites of medical specialty conferences, where researchers may present work that isn't later published.

7. Use a professional search service. Medical search services are a little-known but powerful tool to help patients find the latest information about their disease. For between $195 and $550, they will research any health problem and provide customers with a detailed report listing standard and cutting-edge treatments, medical experts, clinical trials and alternative therapies. And while all of the information provided by the services is available on the Internet or in medical databases, finding the time to wade through it can be tough for someone battling a serious illness. A professional search service can weed out irrelevant information and offer a focused look at the latest research on a particular disease. Even so, it is important to maintain some skepticism, because the reports aren't always right. The Web site **cancer guide.org,** founded by a cancer survivor, is an excellent starting point for any medical search and also includes a list of free resources and the fee-based medical search firms.

8. Go to a medical library. Most medical libraries, which are affiliated with medical schools, are open to the public. Medical librarians often will make themselves available to teach Internet-wary visitors how to use the medical journal databases like Medline or Alt-HealthWatch, which has articles on alternative care. Some medical libraries will do free searches, while others will charge reasonable fees. Ask your doctor for the nearest medical library or call 1-800-338-7657 to find the closest medical library open to the public. A list of libraries can also be found on **nnlm.gov/members.**

CLINICAL TRIALS

The Internet has made it possible, with the click of a mouse, to locate clinical trials unknown to your own doctors. There are close to 50,000 clinical trials going on at present in the U.S. alone.

While trials can offer hope in serious illnesses where other treatments have failed, it is important to keep in mind that trials are just that—experiments on human subjects—and there are no guarantees of a better outcome.

Before enrolling in a clinical trial, patients need to consult with their doctor to answer some basic questions: Does the trial offer more hope than the current treatments available? Do the benefits outweigh the risks? They should also consider what the aim of the study is, who is sponsoring it, what phase it is in and who stands to benefit financially from it.

The informed-consent document that patients sign is critical. It should explain how long the study is going to take, what risks and discomforts there might be and how patients will be compensated for expenses. Some states require health insurers to pay the costs of clinical trials. Many trials promise free medical care, extra compensation for patients and coverage of expenses such as travel and child care.

The National Library of Medicine's **ClinicalTrials.gov** site lists more than 7,000 trials, but many privately funded trials aren't listed here. There are a few comprehensive sites that canvass the medical world for trials. CenterWatch, **centerwatch.com,** lists those sponsored by both government and industry. It also links to a clinical-trials matching service, but the site warns that such services may have an incentive to match patients with a trial that isn't as good an option as others outside their listings. The services typically work on the "bounty" model, getting anywhere from $300 to more than $1,000 for every patient they deliver to trials.

There are also lots of nonprofits that help people find trials related to specific health problems or diseases. Internet entrepreneur Lee Lorenzen started one, called **Pancreatica.org,** in memory of his brother Gary, who died of pancreatic cancer at age 45. It now has the largest compilation of clinical trials for pancreatic cancer in the world, following almost 400 drugs in all. Almost every major disease or condition now has a group of patient activists who have set up their own mom-and-pop sites or regular mailing lists to help find trials and share information with each other. Some can be found fairly easily by merely entering both the name of a disease, such as "diabetes," and the words "clinical trials" in a search engine such as **Google.com.**

ALTERNATIVE MEDICINE

No single subject in the online health arena is more fraught with dangerous and undocumented information than alternative medicine. By some estimates, Americans spend about $30 billion a year on the category known as "CAM," for complementary and alternative medicine. That's about the same as out-of-pocket expenditures for traditional doctors. (Though typically lumped together, complementary medicine usually refers to treatments used together with conventional medicine, while alternative treatments are those that replace traditional medicine altogether.) Many top hospitals are now offering "integrative" medicine centers, which blend wellness programs like massage and nutrition with medical treatments.

And in some cases, health plans and insurers are covering the treatments. A Mercer Human Resource Consulting survey of larger employers found that in 2003, 13 percent of them covered massage therapy in their largest medical plans, 7 percent covered homeopathy and 7 percent covered biofeedback, a technique in which patients use signals from their own bodies to help treat ailments.

There has been a growing effort to conduct bona-fide scientific studies on many forms of complementary and alternative treatments, and more studies are under way. It pays to do your homework; in the case of herbal remedies, for example, research has shown that some supplements may actually be harmful if taken in too high a dose or combined with prescription medications.

One of the biggest problems is a lack of quality control in the dietary-supplement industry. Unlike with drugs, supplement-makers don't have to prove a product is safe before putting it on store shelves. The independent testing firm **ConsumerLab.com** has consistently found that a large percentage of products don't contain the promised amount of ingredient or have been contaminated due to poor manufacturing standards.

To improve your chances of finding a supplement that contains the promised ingredients, look for the U.S. Pharmacopeia USP seal for products that pass its testing program. Products that passed ConsumerLab's testing may carry the CL seal. For detailed information about brands reviewed by ConsumerLab, you must pay a fee.

ACHES AND PAINS

BACK PAIN

If your doctor is still recommending traditional spinal fusion surgery to relieve your back pain, it's probably time to find a new doctor. Every year, about 250,000 spinal fusions are performed in the United States. It is a gruesome procedure. In most cases, the surgeon makes a foot-long incision to strip the muscles off the bone and expose the spine. The damaged disk, which is sometimes the

Where can people turn for reliable, unbiased information on alternative treatments? The best bets are an array of sites created by medical researchers and federal health officials.

1. National Center for Complementary and Alternative Medicine (**nccam.nih.gov**)
2. Food and Drug Administration Office of Nutritional Products, Labeling and Dietary Supplements (**cfsan.fda.gov**)
3. The National Library of Medicine (**nlm.nih.gov/medlineplus/ alternativemedicine.html**)
4. The Consortium of Academic Health Centers for Integrative Medicine (**imconsortium.org.**)
5. M.D. Anderson Cancer Center's Complementary/Integrative Medicine Education Resources (**mdanderson.org/ departments/CIMER/**)
6. New York's Memorial Sloan-Kettering Cancer Center/AboutHerbs (**mskcc.org/aboutherbs**)
7. Oregon State University's Linus Pauling Institute (**lpi.oregonstate.edu**)
8. The National Foundation for Alternative Medicine (**nfam.org**)
9. Bastyr University (**bastyr.edu**)
10. The Alternative Medicine Homepage (**pitt.edu/~cbw/altm.html**)

source of the pain, is removed. The surgeon locks the vertebrae together using rods, screws and bone fragments that allow the bones to eventually fuse. Although certain patients clearly benefit from the procedure, many don't. The surgery works, at best, 50 percent of the time, with some studies showing success rates as low as 15 percent. And the surgery itself can trigger a new set of pain problems, including the ominously named "failed-back syndrome," which afflicts as many as one-third of back-surgery patients.

But perhaps the most compelling reason to avoid traditional spinal fusion is that a number of other options are now available or soon will be. Treatments that heat the disk, less-invasive surgical techniques and bone-growth stimulators already are available. Artificial disks, already used in Europe, are being studied now in the United States and probably will be on the market in a few years. Most back problems get better with time; about 90 percent will heal within three months. But for the other 10 percent, the problem becomes chronic, painful and often debilitating.

In younger people, the disk that cushions the vertebrae is likely to be the source of the pain. Sometimes the disk is injured and bulges or tears, putting pressure on the nerve. In other cases, a weakened disk allows excessive motion, causing pain. In people over 60, the pain often is caused by degeneration of the joints in the back, due to arthritis.

Here's a look at the nonsurgical or less-invasive surgical options that may help back-pain sufferers avoid traditional spinal surgery:

1. Injections, therapy and exercise. Steroid injections, long a staple of back-pain treatment, can now be administered directly to the inflamed nerve, easing the pain of physical therapy. One of the most surprising developments in back-pain treatment is the push for strenuous exercise, something that for years back-pain sufferers have been told to avoid for fear of reinjury. Though it's often painful initially, strengthening the back muscles through intense exercise can ultimately stop the pain. Regular massage also may help. A study conducted in 2003 by a health-maintenance organization followed nearly 300 back-pain sufferers and found that those who received regular massage fared better than those who received acupuncture or general information on how to cope with back pain.

The downside: Insurance rarely covers massage, and it can cost $75 or more for a session.

2. Heat procedures. In patients with back pain due to arthritis, doctors are using radio-frequency heat to deaden nerves. In one study, the treatment worked in 85 percent of the patients, although in half the patients, the pain returned in about a year. In those cases, the treatment can be repeated. Other heat treatments are being used for patients with disk problems. If a disk is bulging, doctors can perform a nucleoplasty, inserting a probe inside the disk and using radio-frequency heat to shrink it. In patients with tears on the outside of the disk, a new technique called "IDET" uses a coil of heat around the disk to essentially melt the outside of the disk and deactivate the pain receptors. The long-term risks of heating the disks aren't yet known. And although the treatments only work on a select group of patients, doctors say the procedures already are being hyped and overused.

3. Less-invasive fusion surgery. For some conditions, spinal fusion may be inevitable. But it's still possible to avoid the traditional procedure. In certain patients, doctors can fuse the spine by inserting scopes through tiny incisions in either the back or abdomen. Recovery times are faster, and some doctors think there will be fewer long-term complications because there's less disruption of the muscles and nerves that cover the back. There's also a device for using bone morphogenetic protein, or BMP, in spinal fusion. BMP is the same protein that tells the body to heal a broken bone. In traditional surgery, doctors harvest a slice of bone from a patient's hip, or occasionally from a cadaver, that is then used to fuse the spine. Metal rods and screws hold everything in place. Now instead of installing a piece of bone and a bunch of hardware, doctors can implant a collagen sponge soaked with BMP, using a cagelike device.

Using BMP instead of screws and rods means the surgeon doesn't have to expose as much of the spine. And early studies show BMP can help bones fuse in three months compared with the six months typically needed with bone grafts. Questions remain about BMP. Doctors worry that injecting any kind of growth stimulator could speed the growth of precancerous cells, although researchers say BMP has proved safe in early studies.

4. Total disk replacement. The artificial disk has been the holy grail of back surgery. Fusion forever alters the back anatomy and limits motion, and it can place added stress on the levels above and below the fusion site. An artificial disk restores the back, as closely as possible, to its original state. In 2004, the FDA approved the first artificial disk, CHARITÉ from Johnson & Johnson, an implant that surgeons can put in place of the spongy cushions between the bones of the lower spine, relieving pain and preserving flexibility. Three more disks, with slightly different designs, are expected to become available in the next few years. Not everyone is a candidate for the implant. Furthermore, many doctors aren't trained in the new procedure and long-term data aren't yet available.

5. Back braces. A handful of new braces were introduced in the past year, designed to ease the pressure on spinal disks that are often the source of lower-back pain. The new braces are a far cry from the heavy and restrictive back braces on offer a decade ago. The old models were designed to restrict movement and immobilize the back. Not only were the braces impractical to wear, they often led to severe weakening of abdominal muscles, creating a slew of new health problems. The new models are made of lighter-weight, flexible materials. Instead of immobilizing the back, the new braces are designed to "unload" the pressure on a disk while still allowing patients to maintain a normal range of movement.

6. Prevention. It turns out your mother was right: Good posture does matter. A growing number of medical complaints—ranging from headaches and neck pain to lower back, knee and feet problems—may be solved by simple improvements in posture. Doctors around the country say they are seeing an increasing number of posture-related health problems, mostly stemming from the fact that more people are spending hours at a time hunched over computer keyboards.

Convincing patients that poor posture is the cause of their debilitating migraines or excruciating back pain can be tough. Obviously, many painful conditions are related to physical problems like arthritis or injury, but a surprising amount of pain that can't be explained by other means is due to posture, a condition known as "postural syndrome" or "postural derangement." Poor posture triggers a cascade of tiny structural changes and shifts throughout the body that can have painful consequences. The person begins to push the shoulders, neck and head forward, tilt the pelvis and shift the spine, putting added pressure on muscles and joints. Some experts are using digital photography and specially designed computer programs similar to that used by professional athletes to improve form and performance. The images graphically illustrate the odd angles and positions in which many of us have begun to carry our bodies.

To start, a few simple habits, like taking five-second breaks from computer work to stand up, stretch and take a few deep breaths, can help. To get a feeling for what good posture is, think of the military cadet standing at attention with his or her hands resting in the small of the back, shoulders and head pulled back and spine straight.

But lasting improvements will come only with regular exercises that stretch and lengthen the spine, loosen up tight hip muscles and strengthen abdominal muscles to take more load off the back.

Yoga- and Pilates-based exercises, which emphasize stretching and strengthening muscles, often are recommended to improve posture problems. Although research is limited, there is some evidence that the methods can solve back pain and other problems.

MIGRAINES

Migraine sufferers have long been told to treat their painful headaches when they feel them coming on. Now many doctors are prescribing daily drugs to prevent migraines from ever starting at all.

But stopping migraines before they start is controversial. Prevention therapy typically provides significant relief only for about half of the people who try it. While it may reduce the frequency of migraines, it rarely eliminates them entirely. And some doctors question whether the benefit is always worth the potentially high cost and the range of side effects that can be caused by some daily drugs. Patients with one or two attacks a month are likely better off with one-dose treatments, rather than preventive therapy.

Topamax showed promise in two studies of 900 patients who suffered four to eight migraines a month. These patients were given daily doses of Topamax or a placebo. About half of the patients taking Topamax reported at least a 50 percent reduction in the number of monthly headaches. The study lasted six months, but most patients who responded to therapy started feeling better in the first month of taking the drug.

Other drugs can also be used to prevent migraines. The FDA has approved the beta-blocker heart drugs propranolol (sold as Inderal) and timolol (sold as Blocadren) for use in migraine prevention. Another

SWINGING AWAY AT YOUR PAIN

A better swing will not only lower your golf score, it might reduce your back pain.

For years, golfers have viewed back pain as an inevitable part of a sport that requires constant swinging and twisting. But while chronic lower-back problems are certainly ubiquitous in golf—affecting half of amateurs and one-third of professional golfers, it's never been clear why some golfers suffer constant back pain while others rarely have a complaint.

But new research shows that when it comes to back problems and golf, the back may not be the whole problem. Instead, the problem is often due to inflexible hip muscles that limit a golfer's range of motion. While it sounds like a small detail, tight hip muscles can sabotage a golf swing—and worse, trigger a cascade of biomechanical mistakes that wreak havoc on the lower back.

The finding is significant because it suggests many golfers and their doctors are dealing with back pain the wrong way—using braces, painkillers and invasive surgical procedures to tackle the problem. But in fact, many golfers will probably get better results from a visit with a pro to learn proper swing technique, coupled with simple stretching and strengthening exercises that will enable the body to employ that technique.

The research also holds a lesson for people who don't play golf: The back itself often isn't the root cause of their pain, either. Led by a push from the sports-medicine community, doctors are finally urging stretching and strengthening of the rest of the body as a way to deal with chronic back pain.

Some practitioners are already employing such an approach. Physical therapists and sports-medicine doctors now offer "golf rehabilitation" programs that aim to deal with back pain in golfers, offering high-tech swing analysis and designing custom golf clubs that can help solve the problem.

To learn why some golfers suffer back pain while others don't, several sports-medicine researchers around the country recently studied 42 professional golfers, 14 of whom had a his-

anticonvulsant, divalproex sodium, or Depakote, also can help. Methysergide, sold as Sansert, is also approved, but it typically must be ordered from Canada because it isn't sold in the United States. No head-to-head studies have been done, but all the prevention drugs appear to work about as well as Topamax. Other drugs are being prescribed for migraine prevention "off-label," meaning they already have FDA approval for another use, but doctors also prescribe them for migraine. Tricyclic antidepressants, calcium-channel blocker heart drugs

tory of low-back pain. The researchers analyzed each golfer's range of motion and measured their muscle strength and flexibility.

The study, published in the *American Journal of Sports Medicine,* found that the back-pain sufferers had far less flexibility in their lead hip—that's the left hip in a right-handed golfer and vice versa. While it may be hard to believe a tight hip muscle is the culprit for excruciating back pain and a lousy swing, in the world of golf it makes sense.

The lead hip is the one that pivots during a golf swing, a movement that, over time, can lead to a loss of flexibility. But if the lead hip muscle is too tight, it's physically impossible to get the swing right. The torque that would normally be absorbed by the hip is instead shifted to the back, forcing it to do far more work than it should.

For golfers with back pain, the first step is to find a physician or physical therapist who understands the unique demands golf places on the body. Some will take videos of the golfer swinging a club or work directly with a golf pro to analyze the swing. A frame-by-frame breakdown not only helps identify technical problems in the swing, but it also can show what parts of the body aren't as flexible as they should be.

The doctor or therapist can measure the patient's flexibility in the hips, upper back or other muscles to determine how far below normal they may be. And the expert should evaluate the patient's muscle strength, using resistance against their own hand or by using a handheld device to measure it.

While many people think back pain happens from playing too much golf, the truth is that it also matters how technically well you play it. One study found that only 20 percent of golf injuries were due to overuse, but 77 percent were due to a technical mistake in the swing.

One of the most common swing mistakes that can trigger back problems is the reverse weight shift, in which the golfer ends the swing with most of his or her weight on the back leg instead of the front leg. For some golfers, a simple lesson with a golf pro can solve the swing problem, but for many, their bodies aren't flexible enough to make the change.

and even the wrinkle-reducing agent Botox have all been used to help prevent migraines.

One of the biggest concerns about Topamax is cost. Other migraine-prevention drugs already are sold as generics and are far cheaper. For instance, a six-month supply of Topamax costs $655, compared with just $16 for six months of generic propanolol.

Topamax's most common side effects are tingling and fatigue, but some patients in studies also complained of problems with memory and concentration. Depending on the dose, about 5 to 12 percent of the patients in the studies reported weight loss as a side effect, making it a good option for patients who gain weight on other prevention therapies.

Other migraine-prevention drugs have side effects as well. Beta blockers, for instance, can't be given to patients with asthma, and their use can make regular exercise difficult. Depakote, the other anticonvulsant used to treat migraine, can cause weight gain.

As many as a third of the nation's 30 million migraine sufferers might be candidates for prevention therapy, but many don't know it's an option, says Seymour Diamond, director of the Diamond Headache Clinic in Chicago and executive chairman of the National Headache Foundation.

Most patients use a class of drugs known as "triptans," such as Imitrex, to relieve occasional migraines. But triptans don't work for 20 to 30 percent of patients. Also, overuse of triptans and other migraine drugs can actually trigger a medication-overuse headache. Patients who have more than three headaches a month may be candidates for preventive therapies, which so far haven't been shown to trigger further headaches.

Before starting a daily pill regimen to prevent migraine, many patients will be advised to try other treatments first. Keeping a health diary to track associations between migraines, stress, foods and hormonal cycles can help. Others will see good results with biofeedback or early treatment with pain relievers at the onset of a headache.

JOINT PAIN AND ARTHRITIS

As an aging population searches for ways to deal with its aches and pains, more arthritis sufferers are turning to glucosamine, made from crushed crab shells, and chondroitin, derived from the windpipes of cows. Both are said to help rebuild worn cartilage between joints.

Long-term use of common prescription and over-the-counter anti-inflammatory drugs such as ibuprofen can have dire consequences. Side effects include indigestion, ulcers, liver damage and internal bleeding. More than 100,000 people each year are hospitalized for gastrointestinal complications associated with use of these drugs, known as "non-steroidal anti-inflammatory drugs," or "NSAIDs."

At least 16,500 arthritis patients die each year as a result of NSAID use, according to a 1998 article in the *American Journal of Medicine*. Two prescription anti-inflammatory drugs, Celebrex and Vioxx, promised fewer side effects, but as of this writing have been removed from the market.

Osteoarthritis occurs as the cartilage that acts as cushioning between joints breaks down and wears away. The result can be stiffness, aches, limited movement and severe pain. Although far from proven, the theory behind glucosamine and chondroitin is that their makeup resembles cartilage molecules, and over time they can help rebuild and repair joints.

The supplements are expensive and not paid for by insurance. McNeil's Aflexa costs about $22 for 110 tablets. Rexall Sundown's popular brand, Osteo Bi-Flex, which contains both glucosamine and chondroitin, costs $30.77 for a 110-pill bottle. In addition, because the products are a dietary supplement,

Here's a look at the types of daily treatments doctors are prescribing to help prevent migraine:

Treatment: Beta blockers
Downside: Can make exercise difficult

Treatment: Tricyclic antidepressants
Downside: Potential urination problems; weight gain

Treatment: Methysergide
Downside: No longer sold in the United States

Treatment: Calcium channel blockers
Downside: May work better than beta blockers for migraine

Treatment: Anticonvulsants*
Downside: May cause tingling, memory lapses

Treatment: Botox
Downside: Expensive; more research needed

*Includes Topamax

they aren't regulated as drugs by the Food and Drug Administration and control over the actual ingredients is limited. Although the supplements are widely viewed as safe, consumers, especially those with health problems or on other medications, should consult with their doctors. People with shellfish allergies, for example, shouldn't use glucosamine, and patients with diabetes or on blood-thinning drugs should talk to their doctors. Animal studies have shown glucosamine increases blood-sugar levels, and chondroitin is chemically similar to blood-thinning drugs heparin and warfarin.

A SCARY LINK: DEPRESSION AND HEART DISEASE

You may have one of the biggest risk factors for heart attack, and your doctor doesn't even know it.

While doctors screening for heart problems know to monitor

smoking, high cholesterol and high blood-pressure, few doctors pay attention to a potentially more serious foe: depression.

Though depression doesn't sound like something that would affect your heart health, many studies around the world show that it clearly does. Otherwise healthy patients with symptoms of depression have been shown to have as much as a 70 percent higher risk of having a heart attack—making depression almost as serious a risk factor as smoking. And depression can increase the chance of dying in the months after a heart attack by as much as 3.5 times.

More evidence about the link between depression and heart attack came from the Women's Health Initiative, the largest ever study of postmenopausal women. Among the more than 93,000 women studied, women who were depressed had a 50 percent greater risk of developing or dying from cardiovascular disease than women who didn't show signs of depression.

The study showed that even among healthy women with no prior history of heart problems, depression proved to be a significant risk factor for developing heart problems and later dying from them. It's important to note that women with severe depression or other forms of mental illness weren't included in the study, and the women at risk often had only mild or moderate symptoms of depression.

The results from the Women's Health Initiative bolster the link between depression and heart disease, but for a variety of reasons, very little is being done about it.

The biggest problem is that no study has shown conclusively that treating depression, with either therapy or antidepressant drugs, makes a difference in heart health. In a study of nearly 2,500 heart-attack patients, published in the *Journal of the American Medical Association* in June of 2004, behavioral therapy to treat depression didn't change survival rates compared with patients who received regular care.

But despite the disappointing results, the study, known as the "Enhancing Recovery in Coronary Heart Disease Patients," or "Enrichd," did produce an intriguing finding. About 20 percent of patients in the study ended up on antidepressants, either because they weren't responding to therapy or because they were in the control group and needed to be treated for severe depression. Among those patients, the risk of dying or suffering a second nonfatal heart attack was 42 percent lower.

A separate study of the antidepressant sertraline (sold under the brand name Zoloft) was designed to test whether the drug was safe to use in heart patients. While the study, called "Sadheart" (Sertraline Antidepressant Heart Attack Randomized Trial), showed the drug to be safe, the most interesting finding was the fact that the death rate from heart-related problems was 20 percent lower among patients taking the drug.

Neither study, however, proves that drug therapy can make a difference for heart patients. In the Enrichd study, patients weren't randomly given the drugs, so those data aren't reliable. The Sadheart study wasn't designed to assess whether the drugs worked—only that they were safe. There simply weren't enough people studied to make the lower-death-rate trend statistically significant.

The simple answer would be to drum up another study big enough to show whether antidepressant treatment can make a difference for heart patients. But Zoloft and many of the big antidepressants are soon losing patent protection—meaning drug companies have no financial incentive to pony up the funds for a heart study.

So, what should patients do? The first step is to take depression seriously. During your next physical, talk to the doctor about depression just as you would discuss other general health issues. Depression poses the highest risk to patients with known heart disease or a history of heart attack, so they or their family members should pay particular attention to symptoms. Most doctors are aware of simple questions that can easily screen for symptoms of depression, which include a persistent sad, anxious or empty mood; loss of interest in hobbies, sex or other pleasurable activities; insomnia; fatigue and appetite change.

Women should also be aware of the risk, because their symptoms may easily be dismissed as emotional fluctuations triggered by menopause. "Doctors need to pay attention to it and consider it as another risk factor for heart disease just like high cholesterol—and not write it off as a complaint of postmenopausal women," says Sylvia Wassertheil-Smoller, professor of epidemiology and population health at Albert Einstein College of Medicine in New York and lead author of the Women's Health Initiative depression study.

And finally, even though there's no proof yet that treating depression will make a difference in heart health, that's not an excuse to ignore it.

FITNESS

Everyone knows exercise is good for you—that's why Americans spend billions on gym memberships, home fitness equipment, personal trainers and fitness videos. But for many of us, regular exercise remains an elusive goal as we struggle to find enough hours in the day to juggle busy work schedules, school sporting events, family time and, occasionally, sleep.

But here's some good news. A growing body of research shows that it takes very little exercise to make a big impact on your health. Indeed, studies show the biggest gains in health aren't made by people who attain a high level of fitness. The biggest health boost comes when a person starts to do a little bit more than nothing.

Swedish researchers have shown that older adults who exercised only once a week were 40 percent less likely to die during the 12-year study period than those who did nothing at all. Another study showed that people with relatively low levels of fitness still were 60 percent less likely to die during the 10-year study than people who were completely sedentary.

Health experts recommend that we engage in about 30 minutes of moderately intense physical activity four or five days a week. While that may sound like a lot, consider the definition of "moderate intensity." That means walking at a "determined" pace—that can be as slow as a 20-minute mile. But if you jog, play racquetball or take part in any other activities that require more intensity, you can reduce the amount of time you exercise. The Surgeon General's actual recommendation is to get enough exercise to expend 1,000 or more calories a week; whether it takes you three days or seven days to spend those calories doesn't really matter. For a person weighing about 180 pounds, 1,000 calories of exercise is the equivalent of jogging for 25 minutes three days a week, or playing a 90-minute tennis match. Intermittent exercise during the day, like taking the stairs or parking your car a little farther away, also counts.

HOME GYMS

One way to improve the odds that you will exercise on any given day is to invest in home fitness equipment. Home exercise equipment has long had a reputation for being flimsy and space-grabbing, but lately it's getting a buff new look. Equipment-makers are increasingly incorporating features formerly found only at the health club, from added cushioning and shock absorption to wireless heart-rate monitors. Some machines have electronic personal trainers that let you program a beginner- or intermediate-level workout with motivational music and instruction from an automated voice.

Treadmills are the biggest sellers among cardio machines. But a lament with some home treadmills is that they feel wobbly, or that knees and lower backs become achy from too much pounding. Treadmills come in a range of prices—from under a thousand dollars up to several thousand—but one should expect to pay in the neighborhood of $2,000 for a machine with a solid foundation and good shock absorption.

The other hot piece of cardio equipment is the elliptical trainer—it's become popular because the climbing-walking motion puts less stress on hips and knees. Elliptical machines range from a few hundred dollars to $3,000 and up. A decent-quality elliptical generally costs at least $1,500. One thing that distinguishes the better ellipticals from the less-good ones is the stride feels very natural rather than truncated.

There's a big downside to having home fitness gear. If it breaks, it's up to the owner to make sure it gets fixed. With frequent use, a machine will likely need servicing at some point, and getting it is not always a simple process. Some customers, for example, may have to transport their machines to a service center 50 miles away.

But some manufacturers are starting to pay more attention to the durability issue. Thicker steel, longer-running motors and better-quality belts are showing up on more home equipment. It's no longer unusual to see longer warranties, even 10 years, on gym gear.

Before buying anything, it's best to visit a specialty fitness-equipment store to get a feel for the gear. For cardio equipment, take a pair of running shoes and do an actual workout in the store. (Any reputable shop will let customers do this; if yours doesn't, move on.) Make sure that the "deck" or platform of the treadmill has no side-to-side or back-and-forth movement. Determine whether the cushioning extends throughout the entire running surface or is only in isolated spots.

For strength-training equipment, as well as cardio, make sure it is easy to use—you shouldn't need an owner's manual to figure it out. Buying more than one piece of equipment at a store should give you extra bargaining power—ask the manager for a discount.

SIZING UP A PERSONAL TRAINER

Looking for a professional to whip you into shape? A growing number of people in pursuit of bigger biceps or thinner thighs are turning to personal trainers for help. With more than 70,000 trainers nationwide, finding someone is easy. The challenge is making sure they're well trained and know what they're doing.

Becoming a personal trainer doesn't require any special education or licensing. Anyone can do it. There are hundreds of organizations that offer certification for trainers, but all have different standards. Some, like the American College of Sports Medicine (ACSM), require trainers to have a health-related academic degree and pass written and practical exams; others simply require answering a few questions on the Internet. Either way, trainers can say they're "certified" and place impressive-sounding letters behind their names.

While efforts are under way to establish industry-wide standards, one professional group, IDEA Health and Fitness Association (**IDEAfit.com**), is taking an initial stab. It classifies trainers who apply into one of four groups according to their education and experience.

Spend a session with the trainer before signing up for multiple sessions. Find out about his or her education and experience. Ideally, the trainer should be certified by ACSM or the American Council on Exercise (ACE)—two of the most respected certifying organizations. Make sure the person has liability insurance and knows CPR. If you have special needs such as a disability or chronic condition, look for someone with experience in that area. Steer clear of anyone who pushes dietary supplements or espouses a "no pain, no gain" philosophy, which can lead to injuries.

The cost for a one-on-one session is typically $45–$65 an hour. Some trainers perform initial tests for body fat, aerobic conditioning, strength and flexibility. While they can be useful in determining your progress, such tests aren't essential. Before you take them, find out if they cost extra, and if so, consider skipping them.

To save money, consider sharing your training session with one or two other people. While not all trainers will agree to such an arrangement, many will. Ask about cancellation and other policies, and get it in writing.

Don't expect too much: Even the best trainer can't turn a couch potato into a triathlete in six weeks.

MAKING YOUR DIET WORK

At any given time, 30 percent of men and 40 percent of women are on a diet. But every would-be weight-loser faces a slew of powerful evolutionary forces designed to thwart even the most determined dieter. Put a new food in front of us, and we'll eat it, even if we felt full minutes earlier. When physical activity starts to burn up calories, a hunger mechanism kicks in, making us eat more. If we start to lose weight, other metabolic processes and brain signals make sure our hunger switch stays on. It seems the average dieter doesn't stand a chance.

So is losing weight impossible? Of course not. People lose weight and keep it off all the time. Exactly how they do it is rooted in a body of scientific research that teaches us the secrets of a successful diet.

One thing is clear: The basic rules don't change. The only way to lose weight is to cut calories. The diet gurus sell a lot of books by making it seem otherwise. But while a given diet plan may tell you to count the carbs or the fat, your body is still counting calories. It doesn't matter if they are carb calories or fat calories or protein calories—your body will shed a pound for every 3,500 calories you cut.

The diet that works isn't based on a single big idea. Instead, it's a set of scientifically based tools that are essential to weight loss—no matter what particular diet you're following.

Stop drinking soda. Over the course of a year, one can of regular cola a day, at 150 calories, adds up to 54,750 calories, or more than 15 pounds. But calories alone are not what make beverages so insidious. Liquid calories have the potential to do more damage in terms of weight gain because they don't make you feel as full so you end up consuming far more calories than you would otherwise.

Write it down. Most people simply can't keep mental track of caloric intake and expenditure. Many studies show dieters who religiously record what they eat lose more weight and keep it off better than those who don't keep food records.

Weigh often. Most weight-loss programs tell dieters to stay off the scale so they won't get discouraged by the slow pace of weight loss. But that conventional wisdom is wrong: A University of Pittsburgh study compared weighing habits among a group of dieters one year after losing weight. The group that got on the scales often managed to lose and keep off an average of 40 pounds, while the infrequent weighers kept off only 11 pounds.

Pay attention to portions. In one study, researchers switched a popular restaurant dish of baked ziti with a portion that was 50 percent larger. Patrons didn't notice the bigger size and ate most of the dish, consuming 45 percent more calories than when the portion was smaller. The lesson: If a dieter doesn't pay attention to portion size, the body won't, either.

Replace a meal. Counting calories is hard. How many calories was that supper you made last night? That may be one reason several studies have shown that people who replace several meals a week with portion-controlled foods such as commercial liquid diets or frozen meals have more success losing weight and keeping it off.

Monotony works. Most dieters think eating a wide variety of foods is the key to a successful diet. They're wrong. The body has different satiety quotients for different types of foods. That's why so many of us end Thanksgiving dinner stuffed with turkey, dressing and sweet potatoes, but somehow manage to find room for pie. In laboratory studies, people choosing from a variety of foods will eat 50 percent more than those given a single food.

Watch the morning carbs. Losing weight is all about calories. But sticking to a diet is all about hunger. There's growing evidence that some carbohydrates make you hungrier. The worst culprits are those found in refined grain products, like white bread, doughnuts, bagels and cereals. Your body uses them far more quickly than slow-release carbs found in most fruits and vegetables. Eating bad carbs early in the day may make matters worse by blocking the body's ability to keep blood sugar stable later in the day. One study gave 12 overweight boys oatmeal or a vegetable omelet and fruit for both breakfast and lunch. During the five hours after lunch, the oatmeal boys ate 81 percent more calories than the omelet-eaters. The science is far from conclusive on the issue. A simple rule of thumb: If you're hungry two hours after a meal, you're eating the wrong foods.

Erase your mistakes. On any given day, we make small overeating mistakes we don't even notice. A handful of potato chips or a tablespoon of salad dressing each has about 100 calories. But a 100-calorie daily mistake adds up to 10 pounds a year. Exercise is generally the only way to keep from getting fat again because it erases those small eating mistakes that are virtually unavoidable.

THE PUMPKIN-PIE DIET: HOW TO ENJOY THE HOLIDAYS AND NOT GAIN WEIGHT

Weight-loss experts have some surprising words of advice for dieters worried about holiday weight gain: just say yes.

Although the average person probably gains only about a pound from holiday eating, that weight adds up over time and represents the bulk of the 20 to 30 pounds so many of us gain by the time we reach middle age. That's why experts think correcting the eating mistakes we make during the last two months of the year can go a long way toward stemming the nation's obesity epidemic.

But surprisingly, the solution isn't to skip the holiday pies and other temptations. The trick to avoiding holiday weight-gain is to go out of your way to eat your favorite foods, paying extra attention to them, savoring and talking about foods and writing down what you consume.

The strategy runs counter to that espoused by popular diets that advocate shunning entire food groups or avoiding carbohydrates or high-fat foods altogether.

But many weight-loss experts say eating reasonable portions of holiday treats works better than depriving yourself. Numerous studies show that strict dieting or even thinking about dieting can trigger overeating. In a May 2002 University of Toronto study, half of participants were told they would be put on a diet for a week—much like holiday

WEIGHTY NUMBERS

14:	Number of calories in a potato chip
29:	Number of pounds you would gain from eating one extra potato chip a day for 20 years
19.8:	Percentage of adults who say they are obese
30.5:	Percentage of adults who really are medically obese
30:	Percentage by which people typically underestimate how many calories they eat
1,795:	Average number of daily calories successful weight-losers probably eat
24:	Percentage of U.S. adults who consume five servings of fruits and vegetables a day
510:	Number of calories in a plain Panera cinnamon crunch bagel
2:	Hours it would take a 160-pound person to walk off a plain Panera cinnamon crunch bagel
14:	Hours a 160-pound person needs to walk to lose a pound
148:	Average increase in daily calories consumed, compared with 20 years ago
140:	Calories in a regular 12-ounce Coke
10:	Diameter, in inches, of a typical restaurant plate 20 years ago
12:	Diameter, in inches, of a typical restaurant plate today

Sources: Purdue University Department of Foods and Nutrition; Journal of the American Medical Association; National Weight Control Registry; U.S. Centers for Disease Control and Prevention; panera.com; netnutritionist.com; U.S. Department of Agriculture; Coca-Cola Co.; American Institute for Cancer Research

eaters planning a New Year's diet resolution. Immediately after being told of the assignment, the participants were allowed to eat. Not surprisingly, those assigned to the dieting group ate far more than the nondieters.

It's not entirely clear how much weight most people gain during the holidays. Although it's often claimed that the average American gains five pounds or more this time of year, the actual weight increase most people experience is probably far less.

One study followed 195 workers at a Bethesda, Maryland, campus of the National Institutes of Health. During the six-week period from Thanksgiving through New Year's, the workers each gained an average of three-fourths of a pound. However, people who were already overweight or obese gained the most weight, and 14 percent of the people gained five pounds or more during the study period.

It's possible that the study group of NIH workers was an unusually health-conscious bunch and isn't representative of the general population. But the most notable finding of the study showed that more than half of the workers' annual weight gain occurred in the short six-week holiday period.

The first step to avoiding holiday weight gain is to decide which foods you simply can't live without and make a plan to eat them. People who plan indulgences in advance often end up eating less because they find it easier to skip the eggnog or chips and dip, knowing they will soon indulge in pumpkin pie or a potato pancake.

"Select them, plan to eat them and try to avoid the things that aren't that interesting to you," says Thomas Wadden, director of the weight and eating-disorders program at the University of Pennsylvania.

Dean Ornish, a well-known advocate of low-fat diets, suggests people "meditate" on foods before eating them. "I'll take a piece of really good chocolate and I'll spend five minutes eating it," says Dr. Ornish, clinical professor of medicine at the University of California–San Francisco. "If you pay attention to what you're eating, you don't eat as much of it."

While meditating on food may sound like New Age bunk, the notion is rooted in science. Studies show that people consume far more calories when they are distracted by other activities—like watching television or talking to friends. A 2002 study in the *British Journal of Health Psychology* monitored ice-cream consumption by 126 Dutch women. Researchers found the women consumed far more ice cream when distracted by a 15-minute radio program than when they were left to eat in silence.

People who focus on the foods they eat, paying extra attention to them and relishing every bite, ultimately consume less. "If you're surrounded by all this great food, then enjoy it, but really enjoy," says Dr. Ornish.

Numerous studies show that the simple act of writing down what you eat can make a startling difference in the number of calories you consume, and the practice also works during the holidays. In one study of 57 Chicago-area dieters, participants, on average, gained five times more weight during holiday weeks than in other weeks. But dieters who kept detailed food records during the holidays actually managed to lose weight during the holidays.

Writing down daily meals and snacks helps dieters see more clearly how many calories they are consuming and identifies how unnoticed calories—like a handful of M&M's grabbed from an office candy dish—can add up. It can also highlight foods that dieters would prefer to give up to make room for higher-calorie holiday foods. Several dieting diaries—some count calories while others count carbs—are sold in bookstores in the diet-book section.

Experts suggest that in addition to indulging in holiday treats, people try to come up with one or two new healthy holiday traditions—like an after-meal walk or baking low-fat versions of holiday favorites. "We have to get around the idea that special days mean eating things that are unhealthy for us," says Walter Willett, nutrition professor at the Harvard School of Public Health. "There are lots of treats that are healthy as well."

Finally, learning how to read food labels can help with controlling weight and health. Unhealthy trans fats are already beginning to disappear from many popular foods. That shift is generally good news for consumers, but it makes it more important sense than ever to know what you are eating. While some food companies have switched to unsaturated "good" fats or new high-tech oils that can boost the proportion of heart-healthy fats in a food, others are substituting highly saturated fats that aren't much healthier than the trans fats they replace.

The Food and Drug Administration has given food companies until 2006 to put trans-fat content on food labels. Trans fats are the partially hydrogenated oils used in processed foods to improve shelf life, among other reasons. The artery-clogging fats have been linked with an increased risk for heart disease and other health worries. One Harvard study found that replacing hydrogenated oils in foods with their natural-oil equivalent would reduce the U.S. diabetes rate by 40 percent.

What is surprising is the sheer number of foods that have made the trans-fat switch so far ahead of the deadline. Every snack chip from PepsiCo's Frito-Lay division is now trans-fat-free. Some margarine brands and several cereals have also made the switch—including Cocoa Puffs. And Kraft Food Inc.'s Nabisco Oreos, normally laden with hydrogenated oils, have introduced a trans-fat-free Golden Oreo cookie.

THE LOW-FAT, LOW-CALORIE CONUNDRUM

WHEN "WHEAT" REALLY MEANS "WHITE": DECONSTRUCTING BREAD LABELS

The supermarket bread aisle is packed with hearty-sounding multi-grain and wheat varieties. But many of them aren't much more than dressed-up white bread. Bread-makers use food coloring, brown wrappers and healthful-sounding words like "stone-ground," "cracked-wheat" and "multigrain" to make their breads sound more nutritious than they really are. As a result, figuring out which breads are best can be tricky.

The solution isn't to shun bread altogether—you just have to learn how to pick the right loaf. Although bread has gotten a bad rap in recent years with the popularity of low-carbohydrate diets, the truth is that certain breads are an excellent source of fiber, zinc, iron, folic acids, minerals and B vitamins. Many people don't get nearly enough fiber, which can help stave off cancer and heart disease.

Bread doesn't have to be white to be highly refined. Many "wheat" breads and "multigrain" breads sound healthful, but the first and main ingredient is the same enriched wheat flour used in white bread, with a smattering of added grains and color to give the bread a slightly different texture and look than white bread.

If you know how to read the package, picking the most nutritious bread isn't hard. Make sure the first ingredient contains the word "whole"—either whole wheat or another whole grain. The first ingredient in Arnold's Real Jewish Rye bread, for instance, is enriched wheat flour—refined rye flour is the third ingredient, and a slice contains less than one gram of fiber. But the first ingredient in Baker's Whole Grain Rye is whole rye, and each slice has nearly 5 grams of fiber.

Although "light" varieties are often recommended for dieters, remember that giving up calories can mean giving up fiber. Pepperidge Farm's Light Style 7-Grain has less than a gram of fiber per 45-calorie slice. Switching to the firm's whole-grain variety adds only 45 more calories but gives you more than triple the fiber. When comparing brands, pay close attention to serving size—labels can list fiber content for anywhere from one to three slices. Try to pick breads with at least 3 grams of fiber per serving.

A DIET OF LOW-FAT, LOW-CALORIE FOODS MAY TRICK THE BODY INTO EATING MORE

Supermarket aisles are filled with foods that have been stripped of calories, sugar, fat and carbs. But new research questions whether altering foods may actually interfere with the body's instincts and trick people into eating too much.

It has long been known that consumers consciously overeat many diet foods—remember the nation's binge on low-fat Snackwell's cookies? But what's unusual about the latest research is that it looks at the impact that regular eating of certain foods may be having on the body's unconscious, biological mechanisms for regulating food intake.

The question is whether by consistently eating sweet foods with no calories a person can eventually lose an instinctive ability to distinguish between high- and low-calorie sweet foods. Early studies have shown that babies and young children have an innate ability to judge the caloric content of foods. And while adults can obviously read labels to figure out the calories they're eating, the issue is whether sugar-free or fat-reduced foods also throw off the body's subtle, internal signals about food intake—causing us to overeat a few calories more here and there.

In the latest study, researchers from Purdue University looked at whether artificial sweeteners disrupt the body's ability to "predict" the caloric consequences of a food. The study, published in the July 2004 issue of the *International Journal of Obesity,* involved young rats who were fed a steady diet of sweetened drinks for 10 days. One group of rats consumed only sugar-sweetened beverages. A second group received an inconsistent diet—sometimes real-sugar drinks and sometimes drinks with no-calorie saccharin.

After 10 days, all the rats were given a real-sugar chocolate drink and rat chow. The rats with a history of eating both real sugar and artificial sweeteners ate three times the calories as the rats who always drank the real-sugar drink.

What does it mean? The researchers speculate that the overeating rats had received inconsistent signals about the meaning of sweet. For them, sweet sometimes had calories and other times it didn't, possibly confusing the rats' natural food-intake instincts. But the rats who always associated sweet with calories were able to compensate for sweet calories by eating less.

While rat studies can't explain the human obesity epidemic, animal studies have long given us insight into certain basic behaviors. Just as Pavlov's dogs drooled at the sound of a ringing bell, even when food wasn't present, the Purdue researchers suggest we should consider a Pavlovian approach to the obesity problem, looking at how sensory properties of foods can condition our biological instincts about eating.

The study doesn't necessarily implicate diet soft drinks; many show that people lose weight when they switch from sugared soft drinks to diet soft drinks. But the research does fuel a growing concern that processed foods may interfere with our ability to regulate how much we eat. For instance, if one day you eat a regular potato chip and another time you eat a reduced-fat version, the question is whether your body may eventually stop making a distinction between the two, causing you to slightly overeat the next time you encounter a regular chip or any full-fat food.

And at a time when bread is now low-carb, cookies and candy bars are being fused into decadent combinations and ice cream can be fat-free, it's no wonder people are getting mixed signals about foods. But the notion that we are being duped—either consciously or subconsciously—into eating more is controversial.

Human studies haven't consistently shown that artificial sweeteners affect eating behavior. One French study, for instance, showed that eating patterns didn't vary among adults who ate a yogurtlike food, whether it was sweetened with sugar or aspartame, says Adam

Drewnowski, director of nutritional sciences at University of Washington.

Part of the problem may be that adults, who have years of experience with food, are tough to study. It has been shown that infants have an innate sense of the calories they are eating. In studies, babies eat roughly the same number of calories in a sitting—eating more of watered-down formula and less of a concentrated one. Other studies have shown preschool children given standard portions instinctively eat less after a high-calorie meal, showing that, at least early in life, we use internal cues about caloric intake to control our eating.

Until we know more, nutrition and behavior experts say the rat study reaffirms how important it is to read food labels, control portion size and pay attention to obvious body signals about hunger and fullness. And the best way to avoid confusion is to eat whole foods like fruits, vegetables and fish and cut back on processed foods.

KIDS' HEALTH

Most parents would never dream of putting a child in a car without a seat belt. They would never allow a child to ride a bike without a helmet or cook on a stove unattended. And they have good reason: Accidents are the leading cause of death in young people.

But what about the things that will end up killing most of our kids once they reach adulthood? How do you protect your child from heart disease, cancer, strokes, diabetes and high blood-pressure—ailments that typically don't strike until well into middle age?

It may be hard to believe that the health decisions you make for a five-year-old today will still count when he or she is 50. But a growing body of evidence shows that childhood is actually the best time to start protecting an aging body, buckling it in for a lifetime of good health. Many studies now show that adult afflictions like heart disease and high blood-pressure clearly have their origins in early childhood. Autopsies of children who died in accidents found that fatty streaks start forming on the aorta as early as the age of three, and the damage shows up in the coronary arteries by the age of 10.

Height, for example, is mostly determined during the first five years of life, influenced by both genetics and nutrition. Bone and tooth strength—and subsequently a woman's risk for osteoporosis—is almost entirely decided by the end of adolescence, which is why calcium intake in kids and teens, and exercise in young girls, is so important. And many experts believe that if obesity occurs in childhood, when the number and size of fat cells are largely determined, a child is saddled with far more fat cells for life than she would have developed had she stayed slim into young adulthood.

Eating behavior and food preferences, perhaps the biggest determinants of long-term health, are primarily decided in childhood and adolescence. Studies show that eating habits and obesity can affect risk for premature cancer, diabetes, liver and heart disease and many other health problems. And while adults certainly have the power to change their eating patterns, much of how we eat and what we like to eat is powerfully programmed by our experiences in childhood, making us exceedingly resistant to change as adults.

Many parents, of course, already know that healthy eating habits, exercise and weight management are the keys to long-term health. The problem is, how do they make their kids follow those practices? A wholesale change in household habits seems like an insurmountable challenge in a world of supersized meals, soda machines in schools and grocery stores filled with sugar-laden kid food.

But surprisingly, influencing a child's lifelong health isn't about big changes. Hundreds of scientific studies support the notion that a series of small, subtle shifts in the way we raise our children can translate into huge advantages well into adulthood.

Luckily for parents, scientists have spent countless hours studying childhood eating habits and behavior. Here's a look at what scientific research shows are some of the small, subtle shifts in the way we raise our children that can translate into huge advantages well into adulthood:

Nutrition: Start by sitting down to family meals. Kids who frequently eat with their families eat more fruits, vegetables, grains and calcium-rich foods and drink fewer soft drinks. Limit juice consumption—juices are mostly sugar. And don't mix food and television. Studies show that kids and adults ingest more calories when distracted by TV. And families who watch television during dinner eat less fruits and vegetables and more higher-fat foods. Children are born with a preference for sweet and salty foods, but they have to learn to like everything else. And kids, like animals, have a natural protective tendency to reject an unknown taste—that's what kept our ancestors from eating poison berries. But many parents misinterpret this instinctive response to new foods.

Encourage healthy eating by stocking the fridge with healthful foods and keep putting rejected foods on the table—experts say it can take a child 15 to 20 tries before he or she will like a food. But once the cooking is done, back off. While bribes and encouragement may convince a child to eat his vegetables, over time he will develop an aversion to foods he associates with parental control. So while bribes and encouragement may prompt a child to eat a food in the short-term, over time he will develop an aversion to foods he associates with parental control, just as he would develop an aversion to a food that made him ill. And kids with lots of food rules at home binge when their parents aren't around.

Exercise: Kids who exercise are less likely to be overweight, and exercise in the teen years can affect long-term osteoporosis risk. Pick sports like tennis and running that kids can continue as adults. Purdue University researchers have shown that the most physically active kids are those who have a close friend taking part in the same activity. Parents who exercise are also more likely to have kids who exercise.

Safety: While diseases of aging will kill most of us, car accidents continue to have a big impact on life expectancy. Medical students are often told that the single biggest influence they can have on patients' health is to remind them to buckle their seat belts.

The risk of dying in a car accident peaks between the ages of 15 and 24, the age group that accounts for 36 percent of annual motor-vehicle deaths. Strict driving rules for teens can sharply reduce teen accident rates. Before letting a teen drive solo, keep a driving log, documenting 50 hours of adult-supervised driving over a six-month period, including 10 hours at night. Don't let teens drive after 9 P.M. or carry other passengers unless an adult is in the car.

SET THE EXAMPLE

At every age of a child's development, parental example remains a dominant way to influence behavior. Babies are more likely to put food in their mouths when they see a parent eat it, and toddlers, preschoolers and elementary-school kids are more likely to accept foods their parents like. Indeed, when a child refuses a food, the best strategy is for the parent to say, "That's okay, I'll eat it."

What you don't eat is important, too. Parents struggling with their own poor eating habits should consume less-healthful foods at the office, out of their kids' sight. And not buying junk food sets the example as well. "Someone is bringing the soft drinks and snacks into the home," says Barry M. Popkin, nutrition professor at the University of North Carolina–Chapel Hill. "The parents may be doing it because the kids are nagging them, but the parents are still doing it."

Children are strongly tuned in to their parents' eating preferences. A June 2004 Penn State study found that girls were more likely to be picky eaters if their mothers didn't eat a variety of vegetables. Parental preferences are the only way to explain why kids in certain cultures are willing to eat spicy foods that the body is normally programmed to reject.

Several studies show that whether a parent or family member smokes is often the single biggest determinant of teen smoking, and the vast majority of addicted smokers started the habit in their teen years. So the simple act of quitting smoking on the part of a parent can dramatically lower a child's lifetime risk for smoking addiction, cancer and heart disease.

Parents who exercise are also more likely to have kids who exercise. But parents who don't have good exercise habits can still help their kids develop them. Researchers from the State University of New York at Albany monitored 180 nine-year-old girls and their parents. While kids with active parents were more likely to be active themselves, the study also found that kids were also more active when a parent provided extensive logistical support. So a parent, usually a mother, who takes the time to learn about sports activities, sign kids up and shuttle them around can set the example about the importance of exercise, even if she doesn't exercise much herself.

HEALTH AND MARRIAGE

A slew of new research during the past few years shows that marital stress can play a significant role in a person's overall health—increasing risk for everything from chronic pain to a heart attack. A low-stress marriage can even increase survival chances when a health problem strikes.

While it's long been known that people who are married tend to be healthier and live longer than unmarried people, scientists are increasingly turning their attention to whether the quality of the marriage matters. Some of the resulting studies have shown that the risk of a bad marriage is as strong as other medical risks. Among patients who suffered congestive heart failure, those with good marriages were more likely to survive. One study linked marital distress to dangerous thickening of the heart wall, just like smoking. And while we've long known that stress is a major risk factor for many health problems, marital stress appears to be a bigger hazard than other types of stress, simply because it's so personal.

The problem is, many people aren't aware of how much their marriage is affecting stress levels. Studies have shown that arguments in couples who have been married for decades can increase stress hormones that weaken the immune system. Research has linked stress hormones with a number of health problems, making a person more susceptible to illness, slowing wound-healing and even interfering with the effectiveness of a vaccine.

The most surprising research has focused on a group of newlyweds, who, by all accounts, seemed happy, even "blissful" in their relationships. But Ohio State University researchers asked 90 couples to answer questions about their marriage, videotaped them discussing a stressful topic and took blood samples to measure hormones known to inhibit or enhance the immune system. The couples who appeared to become the most agitated and hostile in the videotapes were more likely to see increases in hormones that weaken the immune system. Levels of an immune-boosting hormone also dropped.

Years later, researchers found the couples who eventually divorced had shown significant elevation in three of four immune-weakening hormones. Because those changes were detected in newlyweds, the research shows that not only did the hormones predict divorce risk, but the study also showed that marital stress, long before it's obvious, can have a measurable impact on immune-system health.

The same researchers are now studying the role of marital stress on wound-healing. The researchers are inflicting small pea-size blisters on the arms of each spouse, studying whether positive interaction with each other can lead to faster healing by lowering the stress hormone cortisol. Stress hormones can slow the delivery of compounds that start the healing process.

MARRIAGE STRESS TEST

Here are some of the questions researchers use to assess the quality of a relationship. Lower scores indicate a higher level of marital stress.

Indicate how often the following items occur:

1 = Almost all the time
2 = Most of the time
3 = More often than not
4 = Occasionally
5 = Rarely
6 = Never

1. How often do you discuss or consider separation or divorce?
2. How often do you or your partner leave the house after a fight?
3. How often do you and your partner "get on each other's nerves"?
4. Do you kiss your mate . . .
   4 = Every day
   3 = Almost every day
   2 = Occasionally
   1 = Rarely
   0 = Never

Source: Dyadic Adjustment Scale; Graham B. Spanier

The *Harvard Men's Health Watch* newsletter examined the relationship between marital stress and heart health, highlighting a study of 72 patients who answered questions on the Dyadic Adjustment Scale, a widely used test used to assess marital stress. The study showed that marital distress was linked with a thickening of the left ventricle of the heart, as seen on an echocardiogram, just like smoking and excessive drinking. But job stress didn't have the same effect.

How much you interact with your spouse in a good or bad marriage can also influence your health. The same study found that among people in unhappy marriages, those who spent less time with a spouse had lower blood pressure than those who had lots of contact. Among those in good marriages, people who spent a lot of time with their spouse had even lower blood pressure.

But while it's clear that a bad marriage can drastically increase stress, it's not yet known whether it's better, in terms of overall health, to try to improve a troubled relationship or to get a divorce—which itself is an extremely stressful life event. Even in good marriages, the way a couple interacts appears to affect health. A Yale study asked 305 couples married an average of 43 years to name their confidant or greatest source of emotional support. Surprisingly, a couple in which a woman with children named her husband but the husband didn't name her was significantly more likely to be alive after six years than other couples, says Roni Beth Tower, now adjunct assistant professor at Teachers College, Columbia University. One reason may be that being needed, by either your children or your wife, is better for health than having someone to lean on.

AGING

Getting old used to be an inevitable consequence of—well, getting old. But now an antiaging industry has cropped up, promising that while we may not be able to turn back the clock, we can at least slow it down. Antiaging doctors use an aggressive and sometimes expensive array of tests to uncover what specialists call "biomarkers"—indicators of wellness that can range from skin thickness to oxygen consumption while exercising. These can indicate whether your body is aging faster than it should be (or slower—anything is possible). A host of other doctors, from internists to dermatologists, are adding "antiaging" components to their practices that include basic nutrition advice or aggressive hormone treatments. There's even an American Academy of Anti-Aging Medicine, a medical society, that boasts some 12,000 members. Meanwhile, chiropractors and acupuncturists are getting into this game, as well as a thriving assemblage of Internet hucksters that sell oxygen chambers, magnets and potions that claim to turn back the clock.

But alas, the medical community has debunked the more fantastic claims of the antiaging industry. The most controversial treatment involves injecting healthy adults with human growth hormone, the substance released by the pituitary gland in the brain that is responsible for growth in children and for maintaining healthy body composition in adults. Past studies have shown that growth hormone can increase lean-muscle mass, decrease fat and strengthen bone, but a recent study in the *Journal of the American Medical Association* also reveals a high percentage of dangerous side effects, from diabetes to carpal tunnel syndrome.

One of the more depressing developments in antiaging research is the discovery that eating less—a whole lot less—might actually help you live longer. The notion goes beyond the idea of losing pounds to get to a healthy weight. Ongoing studies take normal weight subjects and reduce their caloric intake by as much as 30 percent. The belief is that these calorie-restriction programs can help people stave off chronic diseases that increase with aging—such as cancer, diabetes and heart disease—or even help them live longer. No one is sure why cutting calories seems to be a path to the fountain of youth. One common theory among scientists is that digesting smaller portions cuts down on toxic by-products called "free radicals," which are considered a possible culprit in Alzheimer's disease and other illnesses that disproportionately strike the elderly.

Looking at your family history: A more practical approach to aging is to pay attention to how others have aged before you. More and more people are seeking out their family's health history, also called a "pedigree" by geneticists. As baby boomers age, they are gathering such data to gird themselves against the onslaught of such ailments as heart disease, breast cancer and diabetes that typically strike in later life. Scientific findings that link groups of genes to the predisposition for many chronic illnesses are spurring baby boomers' efforts to uncover their pedigrees.

So, what's the best way to reconstruct your family's health history? Shoot for at least three generations. Your parents, siblings and children are known as "first-degree relatives" in genetics lingo; grandparents and grandchildren are "second-degree." Go horizontally as well as vertically, including aunts, uncles and cousins. The more relatives you include, the better. Information about any ailment may prove helpful, so don't leave out illnesses because you don't think there's a genetic link. Be sure to note conditions that are potentially preventable, including high blood-pressure, heart disease, diabetes, depression and alcoholism. And include the age at which the relative was diagnosed.

Finally, include other habits that could have an impact on overall health, including smoking, drinking, eating and lack of exercise, says Robin Bennett, a Seattle geneticist who wrote *The Practical Guide to the Genetic Family History.* For family members who have died, try to pinpoint when they died, the cause of death and—at least as important— any disease or condition that led to that cause of death. Maybe pneumonia was the cause of death, but that pneumonia was really triggered by a long-term chronic illness, for example.

If you find yourself running into roadblocks, every state has a bureau of vital statistics to which you can write to get death certificates. (Unofficial copies are often cheaper and easier to get than certified copies.) As with other genealogy projects, one of the best resources is the Family History Library, run by the Church of Jesus Christ of Latter-Day Saints in Salt Lake City (**familysearch.org**).

One caveat: Death certificates, particularly older ones, can be vague and misleading. And keep in mind that medical terminology has changed through the years.

Here are some diseases for which family history increases your risk:

1. Heart disease: Risk increases with a history among your mother, father, or other relatives on either side, including bypass surgery on your father before age 55 or your mother before age 65.

2. Stroke: Twice the risk if a first-degree relative is affected.

3. Colorectal cancer: There's double the risk if you have at least one relative with the disease.

4. Type 2 diabetes: The risk increases with earlier age of onset in relatives and the number affected.

5. Cancer: Look for links among types that involve the same gene mutations, such as breast, ovarian and prostate. And don't overlook the breast-cancer history on the paternal side of your family.

It's also important to recognize when the risk of getting a disease is not necessarily heightened by family ties. The genetic risk for Alzheimer's disease, for example, decreases dramatically between the ages of 60 and 85. In other words, if you have a family member who contracted Alzheimer's after age 85, as many people do, there's little cause for worry.

Once you've compiled your family tree, you might want to get some professional help interpreting it.

Keep working: The decisions you make now about your career and retirement won't just affect your lifestyle as you age—they could very likely affect your long-term health. In recent years, medical researchers have found numerous links between health and career issues and the impact they can have on workers and their families. Studies have shown that unhappiness and stress in the workplace contribute to weight gain, antidepressant use and even how quickly a person recovers from back pain. Getting laid off even increases the chance that a child at home will try smoking.

SHAKING THE TREE

 Two resources to help you start a family health history:

1. CDC FAMILY HISTORY SURVEY
CDC.GOV/GENOMICS/INFO/CONFERENCE/
FHSURVEY.HTM

Scientists are still tinkering with this tool, but it already offers a common list of diseases and conditions that afflict many families.

2. AMERICAN MEDICAL ASSOCIATION
AMA-ASSN.ORG/AMA/PUB/PRINTCAT/
2380.HTML

Aimed at physicians, this Web site includes a family-history form much like the one you could expect to get at a doctor's office.

Given this inextricable link between our work health and our personal health, it's no wonder that the decisions we make about retirement—what is essentially our final career move—could have significant implications for our health and longevity.

While it's long been theorized that those who stay busy in their older years have better health, there has been little research to back it up. And it's never been clear whether older workers fared better because they were still working, or whether they were still working simply because they were healthier to start with.

But a long-term study of 1,000 men and women born in 1920 is shedding more light on just how much impact work and retirement can have on longevity. The participants all joined the study at the age of 70 and have been followed for the past 14 years by geriatrics researchers from the Hadassah Hospital Mt. Scopus in Jerusalem. After crunching the data at the six-year and twelve-year marks, and controlling for individuals' health at the beginning of the study, among other factors, the researchers found that it was work—whether a person kept working or retired—that emerged as a major determinant in whether a person was still alive. Among the 1,000 people studied, those who continued to work at the age of 70 and beyond were 2.5 times as likely to be alive at the age of 82 as those who had retired and weren't working at the beginning of the study.

It isn't clear from the data how long a person needs to continue working beyond the regular retirement age to reap the benefit of longevity, but it appears that the longer you continue working, the better.

While the Israeli study showed the protective benefits of work on older people, losing a job at an older age can be particularly devastating. In another study, Yale researchers followed 4,220 workers, aged 51 to 61, for six years, during which time 457 workers lost their jobs. The study, published in May 2004 in the *American Journal of Industrial Medicine*, showed that people who are laid off very close to retirement age are nearly three times as likely to suffer a stroke.

Losing a job is stressful at any age, but it can be particularly tough near retirement. Part of the reason may be that older workers have more medical concerns than younger workers, and often they are less likely to find a new job than a younger coworker.

The recent study wasn't big enough to factor in the effects of getting a new job after being laid off. But an earlier study by the same scientists showed that finding a new job did, on average, protect a worker from further declines in physical health as well as depression.

But for those workers who find themselves miserable in their jobs and can't wait to retire, the Israeli study did offer some hope. It appears that the same level of protection offered by paid work also can be obtained by doing unpaid work—essentially, extensive volunteering that amounts to a regular job. The study found that busy volunteer workers were also more likely to be alive than their fully retired counterparts.

While many retirees find meaning and purpose in helping to care for grandchildren, additional research shows that may not be the healthiest way to spend the retirement years. In the United States, about one in six grandparents have cared for a grandchild for at least six months or more. A continuing study of more than 54,000 nurses showed that retired nurses who cared for grandchildren at least nine hours a week had a 55 percent increased risk for heart attack, according to the *American Journal of Public Health.* On the other hand, nurses who cared for grandchildren but also continued working had a 30 percent lower risk for heart attack than nonworking caregivers.

Given the apparent protective benefits of work on our health, it may be worth rethinking your retirement goals. If you have a job you enjoy, don't retire simply because everybody else is doing it. If you don't like your job, consider switching to a career that brings you more satisfaction, so you can continue working for many more years. If changing jobs isn't an option, then start making plans for meaningful work—either paid or unpaid—once you retire.

HORMONES

Getting older has suddenly become far more confusing for women. That's because a controversial study called the "Women's Health Initiative" concluded that menopause hormones can be harmful, increasing a woman's risk of heart attack, breast cancer and dementia.

Many people in the health community think the WHI was flawed, mostly because it studied only one brand, Prempro, and focused on older women who started taking hormones long after menopause. But whether or not you agree with the conclusions of the WHI, the fact remains that the study has dramatically changed the way women, doctors and the government view menopause therapy.

Now doctors typically prescribe very low doses of menopause hormones and encourage women to use them for the shortest time possible. But some doctors strongly disagree with the conclusions of the WHI and are prescribing so-called bioidentical hormones that more closely resemble a woman's natural hormones. Some researchers believe patch therapies carry the lowest risk of all hormone treatments because they deliver the drug directly into the bloodstream, bypassing the liver. And many women are turning to natural remedies, forgoing drug therapy altogether.

At a time when many women have been scared away from hormone treatment, the use of testosterone therapy is skyrocketing among men eager to stave off the effects of aging. The Institute of Medicine of the National Academies said that while some preliminary evidence suggests testosterone therapy might benefit men 65 and older by improving strength, sexual function and cognitive abilities, there is a need for further trials. The concern is that the benefits aren't well documented and the dangers can include the increased risk of prostate cancer.

SEX DRUGS

Which color are men finding sexier: blue or yellow?

With two—and soon, three—drugs for erectile dysfunction in the United States, some Viagra veterans are curious to try an alternative to the little blue pill. As almost anyone with a TV set knows, the companies behind Viagra and the new yellow-hued Levitra and Cialis are waging an all-out marketing war to win over patients and their doctors.

Levitra is supposed to last a little longer (about five hours compared with between four and five) and have fewer side effects. It is also supposed to work for some patients, such as some diabetics, who haven't had success with Viagra. But now that Viagra and Levitra have been competing head to head, many doctors say they've found that there isn't much difference between them.

As a result, Levitra is making more headway with new prescriptions than in winning over Viagra users. In its first month on the U.S. market, Levitra grabbed 9.3 percent of new prescriptions for erectile-dysfunction drugs and 3.7 percent of total prescriptions, according to IMS Health, which tracks drug sales. That leaves five-year-old Viagra with well over 90 percent of market share in the United States. Yet, despite the advertising blitz, overall prescriptions for erectile dysfunction have held steady, meaning Viagra's market share has slipped—to approximately 94.6 percent in September 2004 from 98.2 percent in August 2004.

Many doctors say they are usually advising men to stay with Viagra, which is made by Pfizer Inc., if they have had good results. "People who are already on Viagra ask about it and say, 'Should I switch?' " says George W. Adams Jr., a urologist in Birmingham, Alabama. "The big difference is that Levitra works a little quicker; but is fifteen minutes important enough to switch to another drug?" The risk of switching, doctors say, is the possibility of different side effects and reduced efficacy.

Cialis—made by Lilly ICOS LLC, a joint venture between Eli Lilly & Co. and ICOS Corp.—can last more than four times as long as Viagra or Levitra, up to 36 hours. Hence its European nickname, "le weekender."

Levitra's makers, GlaxoSmithKline PLC and Bayer AG, say they aren't focusing on trying to get Viagra users to change brands. Instead they're targeting the estimated 90 percent of men with some loss of erectile function who aren't receiving any treatment. (About 25 million American men suffer from erectile dysfunction, according to the American Urological Association.) Glaxo and Bayer are focusing on younger men as well as older ones, since they say half of men over 40 experience some level of erectile dysfunction.

Some urologists cast doubt on the companies' statistic. "What they don't tell you is that it might be a one-time thing, but the other 364 days a year it does work," says John W. Weigel, a urologist at the University of Kansas Medical Center.

In Europe, Cialis is taking a huge chunk out of Viagra's sales. In Germany, Cialis now has 25 percent of the market. In France Cialis has 18 percent. By contrast, Levitra, which was launched after Cialis, has snared only 8 percent of the market in Germany, and 4 percent in France.

Robert Rozman, a 60-year-old retired math teacher and former Viagra user, was a patient in Cialis's clinical trials in Canada and says he liked its longer-lasting effects. "It takes away the pressure. The spontaneity comes back into it," he says. Adds his wife, Kathie, "We can have sex more like normal people."

Levitra and Viagra both cost about $10 per pill and Cialis is expected to retail for about the same. Some insurance companies cover the drugs, but usually only a few pills per month.

They work essentially the same. They inhibit the enzyme PDE-5, an action that causes the smooth muscles in the penis to relax, allowing blood to flow in and causing an erection. The drugs do not, however, affect libido. They require that the man be sexually excited.

But the drugs all, to a varying degree, act on other enzymes, too, which can cause various side effects. In studies, Levitra and Cialis seem to be more specifically targeted to PDE-5; that means that they may be stronger-acting and have fewer side effects. For example, Levitra and Cialis patients seem to have fewer incidents of blue-tinged vision than Viagra. Levitra users also tend to have fewer headaches than those taking Viagra.

But the new drugs have other side effects. Cialis users can experience low-back pain. Levitra can't be used by men taking certain medications for high blood-pressure and prostate conditions. Viagra also carries a precaution on its label advising doctors to be careful prescribing it to patients on similar drugs. None of the drugs should be used in combination with nitrates, substances found in heart-disease medications.

A recent study funded by its makers suggests that Levitra may help men who didn't see results from Viagra. In the study of about 500 men for whom Viagra failed at least four out of six times, 46 percent of those who went on to take Levitra were able to have intercourse successfully, compared with 16 percent of those who took a placebo. In response, a Pfizer spokeswoman says the participants "might not have been given the appropriate dose" of Viagra or received proper directions.

Also, Levitra and Cialis tend to better maintain their efficacy even when taken on a full stomach. Viagra isn't as effective if taken at a mealtime, especially if it is a high-fat steak-and-potatoes dinner.

LONG-TERM-CARE INSURANCE

Few areas of health care are more confusing than long-term-care insurance. The plans are designed to cover the costs of caring for people who are elderly or disabled, including the cost of a nursing home. Insurance companies have been aggressively pitching the coverage to people as young as their 40s, saying the longer you wait to buy it, the more expensive it gets. With the average annual cost of a nursing home at $66,000, one long stint in a nursing home could wipe out a lifetime of savings, insurers warn. However, many consumers may have trouble paying the hefty premiums for long-term-care insurance and may ultimately let the coverage drop, prompting consumer groups to recommend against the plans for most people.

But the truth is, nobody really knows whether any one individual ultimately will benefit from long-term-care insurance or whether it will end up being a waste of money. The Health Insurance Association of America, a trade group in Washington, D.C., will tell you that a person who reaches age 65 faces a 43 percent chance of entering a nursing home. That sounds like a good reason to at least consider buying coverage. But the United Seniors Health Council, an education program that's part of the National Council on the Aging, a nonprofit advocacy group in Washington, D.C., notes that half of nursing-home stays last three months or less. Overall, according to the council, a person who hits 65 has only a 23 percent chance of living in a nursing home for more than one year.

That statistic might indicate you could finance (or try to finance) a nursing-home stay on your own. The risk, of course, is that your investment strategy might not pan out the way you planned. And inflation is an important factor to consider because long-term-care costs often increase more quickly than the most common benchmark, the consumer price index. If you're on the fence, one option is to insure just a portion of the expected cost of care. That way, a couple would pay less in premiums and still take on some of the risk themselves.

Here are some things to keep in mind when you shop for a policy:

1. Before you shop for a policy, shop for an agent. Most experts advise talking to several agents. Expect to spend an hour with each at your initial meeting, maybe more if he or she wants to walk you through many details in the policies. The downside is you'll probably get conflicting advice. Grill them about their education and background. You can get started at **ahia.net.** That's the Web site for the Association of Health Insurance Advisors, a trade group in Falls Church, Virginia, for agents selling health-oriented insurance products.

2. Do your own research. Most policies have the same basic features. If you develop a cognitive impairment, including Alzheimer's disease, or no longer can perform two of six "activities of daily living," they will pay up to a certain amount for a stay in a nursing home or assisted-living center, or to provide hospice or home care (typically a smaller amount). The most important thing you're purchasing is the dollars-per-day that will go toward your eventual care. Agents typically will advise you of the average amount for your area, but there's no guarantee that will be enough. Do your own research, calling two home-health agencies, two nursing homes and two other facilities in your area to find out what they charge.

3. Pull out the spreadsheet. Deciding how many years of care to insure is a tough call. Your choices usually range from two years to a lifetime, and agents generally recommend going for the most time you can afford. The average nursing-home stay is two and a half years, and the average payout is about $130,000, according to the Health Insurance Association of America. But that doesn't take into account the years of home care often tapped before people turn to a nursing home. Some agents recommend purchasing lifetime coverage if you can swing it, particularly if you haven't hit your mid-50s. Others suggest going for coverage of six or ten years. It's worth getting your agent to open a spreadsheet and calculate how an extra year or two of coverage might affect your premium.

4. Keep up with the times. One choice, if you can afford it, is a must-have: automatic inflation protection generally compounded at 5 percent a year. Take a look at the math: With the compound option, a $140 daily benefit would be worth $371.46 a day in 20 years. With the simple inflation option, it would be worth only $280.

5. Stretching out the wait could lower the bill (for now). If you really need some wiggle room, a better place to look is the elimination—or waiting—period, which most agents liken to the deductible on your car or house insurance. Basically, once you qualify for benefits, the longer you wait to start tapping them, the better the break you'll get on your premium. Be careful: With home health-care in particular, the elimination period is an area where the language can get sticky. Some insurers include every calendar day in that countdown; others count only days when you get a visit from a care provider. So, for example, if a nurse called on you once a week and you had a 30-day deductible, it would take 30 weeks for your coverage to kick in.

6. Use add-ons sparingly. Insurance companies offer all sorts of riders to these plans, most of which would be nice perks. But some may not be worth the expense.

7. You're in this for the long haul. If your personal finances go south and you quit paying the premiums, you lose the policy. You might get a check for some sort of residual value, depending on the law in the state where you live, but there's no way you'll get anywhere close to a full refund. If you expect Social Security to be your only source of retirement income, then you can't afford the premiums.

8. Look for financial red flags. A big worry with long-term-care insurance is whether the firm will raise its rates or go out of business. There are a few questions you can ask to help screen for troubled insurers that are most likely to increase their rates. Ask your agent whether the companies you're considering have had to raise premiums on existing policies in your state. Also ask for information about their claims-paying histories. Look for firms that have been in business at least 10 years—15 to 20 years is ideal.

9. You could pay off the policy before you retire. Here's a reason for people younger than age 55 to think about coverage now: Some long-term-care insurers offer "limited pay" options through which you can pay off a policy over 10 or 15 years, or pay until you turn 65. After that, you never again have to worry about a possible premium increase, particularly when the first wave of baby boomers starts to rack up long-term-care bills. You can generally expect premiums to be two to three times what they would be for a regular policy, but if you shop around, you may find better deals.

10. Evaluating Your Health. If you're in good physical shape, you also should look for companies that go to great lengths to evaluate your health status. Some companies offer discounts ranging from 10 to 50 percent for very healthy customers. To qualify you for such a rate, an insurer typically would examine two years of your medical records.

CHAPTER TEN

EDUCATION

THE LONG HAUL

For families dreaming of sending their children to a prestigious university, the stakes have never been higher. It's trickier than ever to get into college, as the kids of baby boomers reach college age and swell the application pool. Meanwhile, tuition is soaring to record levels. The rules for saving, getting financial aid and picking a college keep changing. Even the old "safety schools"—the respectable second-tier fallback colleges that used to provide a kind of automatic safety net for even the brightest students—aren't so easy to get into anymore.

Meanwhile, funding college has grown so complex that a cadre of professional financial-aid counselors are offering to help families through the process—for a fee. With tough, new decisions to make, we'll walk you through some of the toughest new problems: when to invest in a pricey private school, how to save for college tax-free, what admissions really looks at, how to get a break on your tuition and whether it makes sense to go to grad school.

FROM PRESCHOOL TO GRADE SCHOOL

REALLY EARLY EDUCATION

With all the pressure to land kids in school, more parents are stocking up on increasingly sophisticated "prenatal education" gadgets. Now parents are being told to address their fetuses via microphone or to listen to CDs like *Ultrasound—Music for the Unborn Child*. But be aware that while research has shown that babies in utero can hear and recognize their mothers' voices, there isn't strong data showing such technology improves babies' intelligence. It may prove to be good for bonding with your child, but you should think of it as an effort to make an early connection, not a way to put your fetus on the fast track. Same goes for Baby Einstein, Brainy Baby, and other products that claim to make infants smarter. While it's good to devote energy to developing your child's brain early on, talking to him and playing games may be just as effective—if not more so—than planting him in front of a genius video.

THE COLLEGE CHASE? START IN PRESCHOOL

Today, the first step toward college begins in preschool. And getting into preschools requires new strategizing; think of it as preparation for the college race.

As more studies have produced evidence that these early years are a crucial time in setting the stage for learning, achievement-oriented parents are seeking to give kids a leg up on the competition earlier. More people can afford private schools now than 10 or 20 years ago. All this adds up to a sharp rise in applications at private preschools. And that means more parents standing in line outside the schools to pick up applications, recruiting references for their three-year-olds, enduring long interviews and prepping their kids to face the competition.

While preschools around the country vary in competitiveness, it's wise to get informed as early as possible about deadlines and application procedures. That doesn't necessarily mean applying while your child is still in the womb, but here are some things you *should* do:

1. Start looking at preschools at least a year before you think your child will be ready. If you don't, these days, you'll find yourself well behind the rest of the savvy applicant pool.

2. Think feeder schools. If you have a private grade school in mind, call up the admissions office and ask which preschools they take the most kids from and begin working to get in.

3. Start to network. If you have a friend with a child in a preschool you have your eye on, chat them up about the admissions process and whether the school has met their expectations. Parents on the inside can often help your child's admission possibilities by talking up you and your child with teachers and administrators.

4. Know the lay of the land. Maybe your kids are headed to a public-kindergarten program and thus getting into the feeder schools for that selective private academy isn't important. What *is* important is knowing precisely what kinds of choices the preschools in your area present and how they match up with your child's needs.

Among contemporary preschools, here are some options:

1. Montessori schools are an elementary-school program where children learn at their own pace, in a classroom with kids of several ages. It favors a hands-on approach—doing projects on the floor, rather than reading books at a desk. Different age levels are clumped together and children normally stay in the same class for three years.

2. Faith-based schools are in churches, synagogues or community centers; some have a religious component at their core but many eschew religious teaching for secular education.

3. Co-op preschools are schools in which parents commit to spending a certain amount of time in the classroom, often as much as two days a week. The benefit is that parents get a good idea of what's happening in the class and the fees tend to be lower. The drawback: It's hard to swing for working parents.

4. Waldorf schools aim "to produce individuals who are able, in and of themselves, to impart meaning to their lives." Children gain a sense of their physical presence through play and art before developing academic skills. Art, music, gardening, and foreign languages play a large role.

5. Reggio Emiglia is an approach based on the values of collegiality, relationships, exchange and coresponsibility. Teachers are "guides" rather than instructors. They observe and ask questions and videotape and document conversations to provide each child with stimuli for play, discovery and research.

PRIVATE GRADE SCHOOLS

In most places, grade schools encompass either kindergarten through eighth grade or first through eighth. If you're going the private-school route, some of the same issues of getting your child into a private preschool will apply. Beyond that, your child will most likely have a pre-school "record," which is where the stature of the preschool you selected and the recommendations of teachers may come into play.

There are commonsense things to consider, which can be ascertained by querying the schools you have in mind. Figure out what documentation you'll need—such as forms, test scores and immunization records. Some schools may even require references and recommendations. Determine the due dates for material—sometimes private schools have several dates: one for disclosing your interest, and one for giving them final materials. But beyond these pro-forma matters, there are other things you can do to improve admission chances.

1. Again, network. If you're trying to get into a private school, line up people you know with connections at the school to recommend your child.

2. Show a lot of interest. When you decide, let the school know how much you're interested. Contact the admissions officer politely, not just by phone or e-mail but with a snail-mailed letter indicating your interest.

3. **Remember who's applying.** It's not just your child. Admissions officers will be interviewing you and your spouse as well.

4. **Be prepared.** It seems fundamental but you shouldn't go in for an admissions interview or even a casual discussion without having thought deeply about how to articulate what makes your child special and why they'd be a good fit for the school. Just as in college, admissions officers will remember the child better if you offer a "hook"—an anecdote that tells something really unique about your child's strengths.

5. **Don't psych out your child.** Parents may be divided about whether to prepare their child for their admissions interview, which at this level is usually group play mixed with individual observation. But experts generally believe overpreparation is a mistake and may intimidate children or leave them sounding too coached. The other thing to bear in mind: Most schools say their admissions' approach is to build classes, not randomly admit individual students. Thus, it may be more important how your child fits into their mix than your child's individual "performance." With that as a variable, the best strategy simply may be to let children be themselves.

PUBLIC OR PRIVATE HIGH SCHOOL: THE $100,000 QUESTION

Even if you send your child to a public grade school, when it comes to high school, it's the $100,000 question: public or private? Thousands of families across America make huge investments in private education—or spend a lot on buying houses in expensive neighborhoods with good public schools.

But do the most expensive schools really offer more bang for the buck than cheaper competitors or highly successful public high schools? Will those moves—which often involve financial sacrifices such as driving older cars and taking fewer vacations—pay off with kids' acceptance to elite colleges?

FINDING AN IMMERSION SCHOOL

Resource: Center for Applied Linguistics "immersion directory"

Web site: cal.org/resources/immersion; lets you punch in different criteria—like what state you live in or what languages interest you—to find immersion schools near you.

Resource: The Center for Advanced Research on Language Acquisition at the University of Minnesota

Web site: carla.umn.edu/immersion; offers a wealth of information, including school profiles and research reports. (Click on the link for the American Council on Immersion Education.)

LITTLE KIDS, COLLEGE METHODS

Jeff Zucker's son Maxwell attends kindergarten in French, while his toddler's preschool is in Chinese. Linda Choppin's first-grade daughter, Michaela, gets her schooling in German every other week.

None of these children has native-speaking parents in these languages. But like a growing number of kids across the country, they are undergoing in-depth courses of study in a foreign language, often as early as kindergarten. In many cases, these pint-sized polyglots learn to read and write in their second language before they learn in English.

While some colleges and advanced high schools have long offered intensive, no-English-spoken courses, programs like these are becoming available to much smaller kids. A number of new language-immersion elementary schools have opened nationwide in recent years. Albert Einstein Academy, a public charter school in San Diego that teaches grades kindergarten through fourth grade in German part of the time, opened its doors in 2002 with 30 students, and since then its attendance has more than quadrupled.

In New Orleans, the International School of Louisiana spends 70 percent of the day teaching either in French or Spanish. Lakes International Language Academy recently opened in Forest Lake, Minnesota, where children in kindergarten through second grade will learn strictly in Spanish. At the Archimedean Academy in Miami, Florida, a public school that opened its doors in 2002, students from kindergarten through third grade spend two hours a day in Greek. Teacher Demetrios Demopoulos says most students are now trilingual—since many come from Spanish-speaking families. (Only about 10 percent have some connection to Greece, he adds.)

In all, the number of private and public schools in the United States that practice immersion has more than doubled to at least 300 in the past decade, most of them geared to the early to middle-school years.

In immersion schools, students are taught some or all of their curriculum—math, his-

According to the National Association of Independent Schools, the average tuition at private schools increased an inflation-adjusted 4.2 percent for the academic year 2003–2004, to $16,298. Tuition at several of the best-known private schools tops $25,000. And tuition figures don't tell the entire financial story. Nearly all private schools charge some variety of extra fee, whether it's for books, meals, laboratory materials or even mandatory laptop computers. The schools attribute

tory, even art class, if there is one—in the foreign language. The idea is that the sink-or-swim methodology leads to greater proficiency. "Immersion education is by far the best type of program in the U.S. for children to learn a foreign language," says Nancy Rhodes, director of foreign-language education at the Center for Applied Linguistics in Washington, D.C.

But the programs raise concerns with some parents, who question whether students can keep pace when studying science or history in a language they don't fully understand. The concerns are legitimate. Studies show that in the early grades, students in full-immersion programs trail their peers in certain aspects of English-language skills.

Some kids respond well, while others might thrive in a different academic environment. When Elena and Stuart Jewell moved to Alexandria, Virginia, in 1994, they sent their two youngest children to Rose Hill Elementary School's immersion program. While it has worked well for daughter Jennifer, 13, who now speaks and writes Spanish fluently, the family pulled their son out after about a year. "It was hindering his English," says his mother, who recalls how he struggled with his English spelling and reading. Despite the impressive progress made by her seventh-grade daughter, "maybe it's for some kids and not for others," Ms. Jewell says.

Advocates for immersion programs say some of this represents a natural trade-off—after all, the kids are using another language. But by the end of grade five, immersion students perform as well as or better than their English-educated peers in such areas as vocabulary and grammar, says Merrill Swain, a professor at the University of Toronto who has done numerous studies on immersion vs. mainstream students.

Indeed, for kids who take the plunge, there can be a long-term payoff. Studies show that students who learn a foreign language before puberty are likelier to achieve nativelike pronunciation than those who pick it up later in life. And educators say the more time students spend in the target language, the more proficient they become.

—ANNE MARIE CHAKER, THE WALL STREET JOURNAL

the rise in prices to efforts to raise teachers' salaries and other improvements. Many schools say they spend huge resources on the college-guidance process. But does it really help?

Curious about the link between money and admissions success, The Journal studied this year's freshman classes at 10 of the nation's most exclusive colleges—including Harvard and other Ivies, and places like the University of Chicago and Pomona. We tracked down the alma maters of each entering student—some 11,000 kids—and came up with a list of high schools that had graduating classes of at least 50 students and sent at least 20 of them to our chosen colleges. For each high school, we then calculated what percentage of its graduates went on to those colleges. Finally, we compared tuition costs.

Though all the high schools in our survey have outstanding reputations, the success rates at some were astonishing. The best-performing high school on our list sent a staggering 41 percent of its senior class to our 10 colleges—30 kids out of a class of 74. That school, Saint Ann's School of Brooklyn, New York, said its annual tuition of $20,500 (which isn't nearly the highest on our list) was justified in part by the personalized effort the school makes to help each student get into the best possible college.

Among private high schools, we found some surprising bargains: Germantown Friends School, a Philadelphia Quaker institution dating back to 1845, charged $16,675 in base tuition (plus an estimated $675 more for books and senior fees). But it did even better in our review than Buckingham Browne & Nichols of Cambridge, Massachusetts, where tuition ran nearly $8,000 higher.

Public schools obviously offer the better bang for the buck—assuming you don't count the high housing costs generally associated with better-performing districts. But in our survey, public schools didn't measure up to the best private ones, with the best-performing school sending fewer than a third of its graduates to our choice colleges. And a number of the better-performing public schools were small, highly selective "magnet" schools, meaning that students whose families live and pay taxes in the area don't necessarily get to attend. For example, Thomas Jefferson High School for Science and Technology, in Alexandria, Virginia, in 2003 sent 10 graduates to Harvard alone.

The colleges we looked at all had SAT scores of accepted applicants in the 1280–1580 range and an average admissions selectivity of 21 percent. Our schools were, in alphabetical order:

1. Brown	6. Pomona
2. Cornell	7. Princeton
3. Dartmouth	8. The University of Chicago
4. Duke	9. The University of Pennsylvania
5. Harvard	10. Yale

There are some notable exceptions to our list. We couldn't obtain the high-school lists for one Ivy, Columbia, or for the most prestigious school in the West, Stanford. (We added Pomona, a school with similar mean SAT scores, in the interest of including an exclusive West Coast school.) We chose to focus on enrollment, not acceptances, in the freshman classes at the colleges—in other words, the high-school graduating class of 2003. For information on students' alma maters, we relied heavily on "face book" directories that colleges generally distribute to new students. Our decision to include only schools that sent 20 or more students to our choice colleges was made to help the survey be more manageable. We also compiled the admissions data for three prestigious small colleges across the country, Williams, Amherst and CalTech, to see if our survey results would change significantly with those schools included. They didn't.

Our numbers thresholds, to be sure, excluded some small schools that had an extremely high admissions success rate. For example, New York's Collegiate School fell just below our minimum class-size requirement, with a graduating class in 2003 of 49 students. However, 25 of them, or 51 percent, went to our college picks; that would have made it number one in our study. Among the other elite schools with impressive acceptance rates that fell below our class-size cutoff were Roxbury Latin School in West Roxbury, Massachusetts, and Nightingale-Bamford and Brearley in New York.

GRADING THE SCHOOLS

If you're looking for a public school, there are a number of good resources available. In the past decade, many states have boosted the amount of data available on public-school performance. (It's harder to get data on private schools, which disagree on how much info to share.)

To find the best school, check three key statistics: standardized test scores, graduation rates and college admissions. One site, **school results.org,** serves as a clearinghouse for new state report cards on education, including data broken down to the school district and school building. Under No Child Left Behind, the new federal law aimed at improving education standards, states must report data on a range of fronts, including teacher qualifications and achievement among all major groups of students. The Web site is designed to present that

Your Tuition Dollars at Work

What do costly private-school tuitions buy in the college-admission sweepstakes, and how do public schools compare? To find out, Weekend Journal studied this year's freshman classes at 10 selective colleges—including seven Ivy League schools—and compiled a list of students' high-school alma maters (see "Behind the Numbers" for details). The survey ranked schools based on the number of students they sent to these 10 colleges divided by the high school's class size in 2003, limiting results to high schools that had a graduating class of 50 and sent at least 20 students to our chosen colleges. To find schools that delivered the most value, the survey looked at the ratio of tuition to success rate; the top 10 performers are noted with a ✔. Tuition-free public schools are denoted by a ●.

HIGH SCHOOL	CLASS SIZE	TOTAL STUDENTS SENT	SUCCESS RATE	TUITION ($)	BANG FOR THE BUCK	COMMENTS
Saint Ann's School Brooklyn, N.Y.	74	30	41%	20,500	✔	The highest success rate on our list. School has no grades; students get written evaluations.
Winsor School Boston	57	22	39%	23,800	✔	Girls' school says two-thirds of grads attend highly selective colleges.
Trinity School New York City	120	44	37%	23,475	✔	Additional fees—for lunch, parents' association dues, etc.—run about $1,250 per year.
Horace Mann School Riverdale, N.Y.	175	61	35%	24,500	✔	Upper Division Head Dr. Lawrence Weiss has just been named the new headmaster at Saint Ann's.
Phillips Academy Andover, Mass.	300	91	30%	23,400		Both President George W. Bush and his father are alums.
Deerfield Academy Deerfield, Mass.	199	60	30%	23,005		Tuition is all-inclusive; boarding students pay $29,960 per year.
Nat'l Cathedral School Washington, D.C.	73	22	30%	21,850	✔	Seven 2003 grads from this girls' school are freshmen at the University of Pennsylvania this year.
Dalton School New York City	103	31	30%	24,680		Tuition is all-inclusive; only additional fee is $75 for parents' association dues.
Hunter College High School, New York City	186	53	28%	0	●	A typical course: "Physics and (Post)Modern Culture."
St. Paul's School* Concord, N.H.	144	41	28%	31,125		Prospective Democratic nominee John Kerry graduated in 1962.
St. Albans School Washington, D.C.	81	22	27%	21,837		Tuition includes lunch, but extra fees for certain classes such as science labs, computer science or art and photography can run $75-165 per class.
Germantown Friends School, Philadelphia	88	23	26%	16,675	✔	Seniors can pay an additional $675 in fees (mostly for books).
Episcopal Academy Merion and Devon, Pa.	104	27	26%	18,800	✔	Founded in 1785 by Pennsylvania's first Episcopal bishop, the school has two chapels.
Lakeside School Seattle	111	28	25%	18,400	✔	Students (after this year's senior class) are required to have a laptop, which they can purchase from the school for about $2,200.
Sidwell Friends School Washington, D.C.	116	29	25%	20,975		This Quaker day school has a 14-acre campus in the Tenleytown section of Washington and attracts political elite. Chelsea Clinton went here.
Phillips Exeter Academy Exeter, N.H.	322	79	25%	22,800		Boarding students pay $30,000.
Hopkins School New Haven, Conn.	123	29	24%	21,550		Fifty-one percent of its senior class this year are National Merit Scholars.
Pingry School Martinsville, N.J.	132	32	24%	22,290		Eight members of the class of 2003 went to Cornell; seven went to the University of Pennsylvania.
Milton Academy Milton, Mass.	170	41	24%	24,325		T.S. Eliot graduated from this boarding school in 1906.
Choate Rosemary Hall Wallingford, Conn.	224	53	24%	22,940		School says it gives away $5.3 million in financial aid each year.
Univ. of Chicago Lab. Schools, Chicago	112	26	23%	16,125	✔	Sophomores, juniors and seniors have access to all University of Chicago libraries.
Hotchkiss School Lakeville, Conn.	148	34	23%	25,450		Students pay $350 technology fee. School is building a new music and arts center—and plans an arboretum.

HIGH SCHOOL	CLASS SIZE	TOTAL STUDENTS SENT	SUCCESS RATE	TUITION ($)	BANG FOR THE BUCK	COMMENTS
Noble and Greenough School, Dedham, Mass.	102	23	23%	24,150		This boarding and day school has a 187-acre campus and an average class size of 11.
Harvard-Westlake School, N. Hollywood, Calif.	268	60	22%	20,000		Highest number of National Merit Semifinalists in the state for the past 17 years.
Delbarton School Morristown, N.J.	118	26	22%	19,600		All-boys school is run by Benedictine monks, on a campus of almost 400 acres.
Durham Academy Durham, N.C.	97	21	22%	14,600	✔	Seniors pay a $650 activity fee covering items such as class trips, phys-ed T-shirts and commencement expenses.
Head-Royce School Oakland, Calif.	94	20	21%	20,360		$320 activity fee. Five members of the class of 2003 went to Brown; five went to the University of Pennsylvania.
Lawrenceville School Lawrenceville, N.J.	221	47	21%	24,610		Seminar-like approach here has students sitting with faculty at oval table instead of sitting in rows in most classes.
Buckingham Browne & Nichols, Cambridge, Mass.	113	24	21%	24,600		School's annual giving campaign has tripled in past decade, to $1.7 million. Students have free admission to Museum of Fine Arts, Boston.
Georgetown Day School Washington, D.C.	110	23	21%	21,472		Sent four grads each to Harvard, Princeton and the University of Pennsylvania this year, all from the class of 2003.
Fieldston Bronx, N.Y.	127	25	20%	23,900		Founded in 1878. Its early name was the Workingman's School, providing education to children of the "working poor."
T. Jefferson H.S. for Sci. and Tech., Alexandria, Va.	401	74	18%	0	●	This public magnet school has 12 labs for everything from robotics to astronomy. It's also state champion in girls' swimming and diving.
Taft School Watertown, Conn.	154	27	18%	22,500		Ten students from this boarding school's class of 2003 went to Cornell.
Ransom Everglades School, Coconut Grove, Fla.	138	24	17%	18,000		The alma mater of humor columnist Dave Barry, it's celebrating its 100th birthday this year.
Stuyvesant High School New York City	719	119	17%	0	●	This magnet school sent the highest number of students to our 10 colleges, including 21 to Harvard.
Ithaca High School Ithaca, N.Y.	336	52	15%	0	●	Forty-four members of the class of 2003 are freshmen at Cornell this year—many of them children of the college's faculty.
Scarsdale High School Scarsdale, N.Y.	278	41	15%	0	●	Guidance department has nine counselors, meaning more one-on-one attention for kids.
Roslyn High School Roslyn Heights, N.Y.	204	30	15%	0	●	School says Howard Dean's wife, Judith Steinberg Dean, went here.
Horace Greeley High School, Chappaqua, N.Y.	279	41	15%	0	●	Class of 2003 sent eight students each to Cornell and Yale; seven each to Duke and the University of Pennsylvania.
Westminster Schools Atlanta	175	25	14%	14,392		School's $75 million capital campaign helped build a new science facility, 400-seat theater and athletic facilities.
Pine Crest School Fort Lauderdale, Fla.	183	24	13%	15,350		Tuition includes books and lunch.
Millburn High School Millburn, N.J.	245	32	13%	0	●	School says Cornell has been recruiting more heavily here in past two years. Currently, 10 Millburn students are freshmen there.
Illinois Math and Sci. Academy, Aurora, Ill.	189	20	11%	0	●	The students at this boarding school run math, science and technology summer camps for elementary kids.
Boston Latin School Boston	337	32	9%	0	●	Former terrorism czar Richard A. Clarke is an alum.
Princeton High School Princeton, N.J.	260	24	9%	0	●	Location works: Twelve 2003 grads started at Princeton this year.
N.C. School of Science and Math, Durham, N.C.	257	23	9%	0	●	For the last two years, school has sent the most semifinalists in the country to Siemens Westinghouse Competition for science, math and technology.
Great Neck South High School, Great Neck, N.Y.	268	23	9%	0	●	This public school has its own observatory, plus every year it mounts a full-scale opera, with all music performed by students.
Walt Whitman High School, Bethesda, Md.	467	40	9%	0	●	Current senior class has 18 National Merit Finalists.
Bronx High School of Science, Bronx, N.Y.	604	47	8%	0	●	Our survey found 19 kids from this school at Cornell, and nine at Dartmouth.

HIGH SCHOOL	CLASS SIZE	TOTAL STUDENTS SENT	SUCCESS RATE	TUITION ($)	BANG FOR THE BUCK	COMMENTS
Staples High School Westport, Conn.	271	20	7%	0	●	Five 2003 graduates are at Cornell this year; three more are at Yale.
Paul D. Schreiber High School, Port Washington, N.Y.	290	21	7%	0	●	Sent five kids to Yale from class of 2003.
Punahou School Honolulu	421	30	7%	12,050		School was founded in 1841 by missionaries; has just expanded its center for community service.
Northfield Mt. Hermon School, Northfield, Mass.	318	22	7%	22,600		Dore Gold, adviser to Israeli Prime Minister Ariel Sharon, and the late pro-Palestinian intellectual Edward Said both went here.
Richard Montgomery High School, Rockville, Md.	363	25	7%	0	●	School has International Baccalaureate program. Students have average combined SATs of 1435
Palo Alto High School Palo Alto, Calif.	313	21	7%	0	●	Located in Silicon Valley, this school has an award-winning robotics team.
Lower Merion High School, Ardmore, Pa.	348	23	7%	0	●	Former students include Kobe Bryant, who led the school to a state basketball championship.
Lexington High School Lexington, Mass.	396	26	7%	0	●	Some students prepare for school's competitive science fair by studying with MIT or Harvard scientists.
Newton South High School, Newton Centre, Mass.	360	23	6%	0	●	School places students in internships in fields such as fashion design and antique-car restoration.
Shaker Heights High School, Shaker Heights, Ohio	356	22	6%	0	●	Takes part in a program to send students to Japan to study history, culture and religion.
Ridgewood High School Ridgewood, N.J.	345	20	6%	0	●	Four 2003 grads matriculated at Harvard this fall; four started at Yale.
Winston Churchill High School, Potomac, Md.	451	26	6%	0	●	Offers special program to let students focus on either math and science or creative arts.
Greenwich High School Greenwich, Conn.	569	28	5%	0	●	Sent six members of class of 2003 to Brown, along with five to Penn.
Newton North High School, Newtonville, Mass.	561	25	4%	0	●	Facilities include two theaters. Six hundred students participate in theater program, with ticket sales helping to defray the cost.
New Trier Township High School, Winnetka, Ill.	887	31	3%	0	●	Theater program includes two theaters and has produced stars such as Ann-Margret, Charlton Heston and Rock Hudson.
Evanston Township High School, Evanston, Ill.	780	21	3%	0	●	School has one-year international education requirement for graduation and offers classes in Japanese, Hebrew, Latin, Spanish, French and German.

*Tuition for boarding students. In all other cases, day-school tuition is listed.

information in a convenient and uniform way, so parents and policy-makers can make comparisons across districts and track student progress.

Many districts post data on the Internet; also, many local newspapers, like the *Chicago Tribune* (at **chicagotribune.com**) and the *Inquirer* (**philly.com**), offer guides to area schools and "report cards" that include scores, demographics and other info. Check schools' own Web sites. Also, look for independent sites, like New York City's **insideschools.org** to guide you through your local schools.

Charter schools are publicly funded but freed from many of the regulatory and academic restrictions on traditional public schools. Get more information at **uscharterschools.org.**

But take school districts' data with a grain of salt. The results aren't always reliable. States write their own tests and set their own passing grades, so some states show better results than others. For instance, the No Child Left Behind law charged the states with the job of defining what a good teacher is—but allowed each state to define it differently.

No Child Left Behind requires that all teachers must be "highly qualified" by 2006, and meanwhile, that schools receiving federal poverty funds must tell parents if their children are being taught by a teacher who falls short. But the law gives little advice on what makes a good teacher. It says only that teachers must hold a bachelor's degree—in any subject—and a state teaching license, and demonstrate "content knowledge" in the subject they teach.

To get a license, three-quarters of the states require their teachers pass standardized reading, writing and math tests that Educational Testing Service, which writes some of the tests, says are set at about a 10th-grade achievement level. But the states each set the passing score on their tests, which means that teachers can score at low levels. In nearly half the states, teachers don't need a college degree in the subject they teach, and in a few, they also don't need to pass a competency exam in their subject. Check your state's teacher qualifications at the local Board of Education Web site.

COLLEGE PREP: ACADEMICS AND FINANCE

THE SAT: A PRIMER

Colleges use scores on two college-entrance exams, the SATs and the ACTs, to sort through their applicants. The ACT is the leading test at schools in the middle of the country; the East and West coasts favor the SAT. Most colleges accept either one. The ACT is more curriculum-focused, while the SAT is (in theory) more abilities-focused. No matter which a student takes, he or she should be

SCHOOL RESOURCES

National Center for Education Statistics;
 nces.ed.gov/ccd
Standard & Poor's School Evaluation Services;
 ses.standardandpoors.com
U.S. Census data;
 nces.ed.gov/surveys/sdds/c2000d.asp
U.S. Department of Education; **ed.gov**
School Information Partnership;
 SchoolResults.org
GreatSchools.net; **greatschools.net**

absolutely clear on what his favorite colleges' application require-ments are.

In 2005, a new version of the SAT replaced the previous one. The old word analogies are gone, but the new exam contains more algebra and reading passages. In addition, there is a new section that tests writing skills. The test is 45 minutes longer, and the best possible score is 2400 points instead of the old test's 1600. The College Board, the nonprofit that owns the SAT, claims that changes to the verbal and math sections won't affect the difficulty of the test. The ACT also added writing tests to its college-entrance exams in February 2005. Scores on the writing exams depend on such highly subjective measures as voice, style, flow—and whether language is "competent," "ade-quate" or merely "under control."

Many colleges also want to see one or more subject tests, known as "SAT IIs," available in areas ranging from history to literature to for-eign languages.

There are a variety of ways to prep, ranging from books and com-puter programs to classes and private tutoring. There are even summer camps offering "math enrichment" and SAT prep. Practice tests for the new SAT are available in books from such publishers as McGraw-Hill Cos. Doing practice tests is essential, and many schools' basic prep courses are useful; the benefits of expensive private tutoring are less clear.

How much does a test-prep class help? An average 120 to 140 points, say the test-prep companies. But the College Board says that some of those gains come from taking practice tests, not from tutoring, and others come from the classroom learning and maturity a student picks up in the months leading up to the test. The College Board's Web site publishes studies that show that coaching adds an average eight points to verbal scores and twenty points on math. But it also pub-lishes studies that say that 97 percent of test-takers do some sort of test preparation, and it flatly advises kids not to take the test "cold."

The test companies also argue that students learn strategies, such as estimation and time-management, in test-prep classes. Princeton Review encourages just-average students to skip the hardest 10 ques-tions in any section (they're always at the end), both to give them-selves more time for the others and because they might not get them anyway.

But be sensible in the amount of time spent studying. It may not be worth spending too much time preparing for tests at the expense of grades and extracurricular activities. And some argue that the U.S. Supreme Court's 2003 University of Michigan decision upholding affirmative action has made scores on standardized tests less pivotal in admissions decisions. The court's decision allows schools to consider race, but not make decisions based on race. Schools, which once feared that any departure from objective factors such as test scores would be ruled illegal, interpret the decision as allowing them to give new weight—for any student—to subjective factors such as artistic talents.

About half of all kids take the SAT twice, and 16 percent take it three times, but almost no one takes it more than that. That's because a "true score" quickly emerges and isn't likely to improve after the third test, says SAT Director Brian O'Reilly.

TAMING TUITION

So, you're having a baby. Have you thought about college yet?

With the College Board reporting average tuition and fees of nearly $19,710 at private colleges and $4,694 at public colleges in the 2003–2004 school year, parents have to start their planning well in advance.

But if you choose the wrong savings plan, you could get hit with unnecessary taxes or your child will have to forgo financial aid for which he could have qualified.

Deciding where and how to invest will largely depend on your income, the age of your child, and your chances of qualifying for financial aid. A good place to start is to figure out how much you'll need to save. Tuition and fees at private colleges can now top $40,000 a year at big-name schools if you include living costs. At public colleges—hurt by state budget cutbacks—average charges for tuition and room and board rose 9.8 percent in the last school year (2003–2004) to $10,636, and that's almost certain to rise again, according to the College Board, an organization of about 4,500 higher-education institutions. And don't forget transportation, books and other expenses, which can add another $10,000 a year. Children born today could face college costs that are three to four times current prices, says Mark Kantrowitz, publisher of **FinAid.org,** a financial-aid Web site. States' support for their public colleges is plummeting, schools are bursting with a record

15.8 million students (2004), federal aid isn't going as far as it used to and students are needier.

Here are some helpful guidelines for parents:

1. The one-third rule: Parents should aim to save one-third of the expected college costs, pay one-third from current income and financial aid during college and borrow one-third.

2. Be realistic: The first step is to take a good, honest look at what you can afford. Scaling down costs may make a significant difference in the kind of retirement you can look forward to.

3. Include your children in the process. Try to allocate available college funds equitably among all the children. Starting college-funding conversations early also makes the kids part of the decision-making process, allowing them to ask themselves important questions, like whether it matters if they go to a name school. If the answer is yes, then the student may have to take part in figuring out how to come up with the extra money needed to pay for a top-tier school.

4. Let the kids help. Having children cover at least a share of the cost gives them more of an investment in their own education. That, however, doesn't always mean getting a job or taking out a loan. Kids can take advanced-placement courses to reduce their college requirements, or they can get grants or win scholarships.

CHOOSING A PLAN

Then it's time to pick a college-savings plan. A few good places to get acquainted with the features of these plans are **collegesavings.org,** the Web site of the College Savings Plan Network, and **savingforcollege .com,** which tracks college-savings plans. You will need to figure out whether you want to buy a plan through a broker or directly through firms such as the IAA-CREF, of New York, and Vanguard Group, of Malvern, Pennsylvania. Brokers can help you wade through the material, but they also may have a financial incentive to push certain plans.

It's important to keep financial aid in mind from the beginning, because where you invest can have an impact on your aid eligibility. Also, evaluate each plan in terms of its exit strategy—that is, what are the penalties you will incur if the child doesn't go to college. For example, you may face penalties to get a refund from a state prepaid plan or could lose up to 2 percent a year in the Independent 529 Plan if the funds' investments fare poorly. And constant changes to tax laws mean that the best savings vehicle today might not be as good later on.

No matter what vehicle you choose, remember: As kids get older, shift their portfolios to more conservative investments, so you won't face the possibility of big losses just when you need the money most.

Here's a rundown of the different options available:

State 529 College Savings Plans

These plans, named after the section of the tax code that governs them and run by the states, let you save large amounts of money tax-free, usually in mutual funds, and then later withdraw it tax-free for tuition and books. Investors have flocked to these plans since they became exempt from federal taxes in 2002: As of 2004, assets in these plans reached about $51.09 billion, according to College Savings Plan Network, a Lexington, Kentucky, research group.

The plans typically use mutual funds as their primary investment option. With the 529 plan, withdrawals are tax-free only if the funds are spent on qualified education costs, like tuition and books. Plus, there can be age restrictions placed on when the money can be tapped.

Because these plans are typically held in the parents' name, they have a relatively small effect on financial aid—though a safe tactic would be to put them in a grandparent's name rather than a parent's or a child's.

Those in high tax brackets are likely to get the biggest bang for their money, because there are no income restrictions to contribute and the plans maximize tax savings. Keep in mind, though, that under the 2001 tax law, 529 plans lose their tax-free status in 2011, though that status may be extended.

Contributions to 529 plans are subject to a gift tax if they are more than $11,000 a year if you are single, and $22,000 if you are married. But a special provision allows each parent to deposit as much as $55,000 to a child's 529 plan, with no gift-tax consequences as long as no other gifts are made in the next five years.

Potential downsides can include high fees, limited investment options and a confusing variety of fee structures. When you open up an account with the Maryland College Investment Plan, for example, you'll pay a $90 enrollment fee and then $30 annually, which is waived if your account balance exceeds $25,000 or if you enroll in an automatic-payment plan. And you can adjust asset allocation only once a year or when you change beneficiaries.

Researching the more than 80 plans now available can be bewildering. Currently, states are finalizing voluntary guidelines asking states to present their fees and expenses in standardized ways, so investors can more easily compare plans. But until the states come into line, the onus will be on investors to do their homework.

A good first step: Check out your own state's plan, which may offer you a state tax deduction for your contributions—or even a matching grant, as Rhode Island, Louisiana, Michigan and a handful of other states do. Another incentive for picking your own state's plan: A few states tax earnings and withdrawals from out-of-state plans. To find out more, call up the sponsoring states, which will walk you through all of the potential costs. Consumers can also compare plans by using the 529 Evaluator at **savingforcollege.com.**

For investors with older kids: If you're not already in a 529, beware of suddenly shifting funds into them from traditional custodial accounts, which could lead to significant capital-gains taxes. If you have capital gains and your child is only a year or two away from college, then the tax-deferred growth of a 529 plan in that short time period might not be worth the tax bite.

Also, if your child is near his or her teenage years, then you might want to wait to do a conversion. Those under the age of 14 with more than $1,500 in investment earnings are subject to the so-called kiddie tax, which means that they have to pay their parents' long-term capital-gains rate, up to a maximum of 15 percent. But wait until the child turns 14, and the bite would be a maximum of 5 percent—assuming that the child is in the lowest tax brackets. Here's one way to get the best of both worlds: Leave your custodial account alone and fund a 529 plan with new money.

529 Prepaid Plans

These state prepaid plans let you buy future tuition at local public colleges at today's prices. The plans may be worth considering if you don't want to worry about fluctuating investments and you are confident your child will attend one of your state's public schools. But budget cutbacks have forced many state schools to raise tuition, while the assets used to finance the plan benefits have dwindled with the stock market. As a result, more plans have been forced to impose fees, temporarily halt enrollment or boost prices. Moreover, payouts from these plans reduce aid eligibility dollar for dollar.

Independent 529 Plan

This prepaid plan works like the state prepaid plans, but parents can lock in tuition at a group of more than 220 private colleges at slightly discounted rates. This plan should appeal to conservative investors, families who strongly favor private colleges over public schools or private-college alumni who would like to see their kids attend their alma maters.

Although one of the big risks is that your child won't attend one of the participating colleges, you can get your money back, adjusted slightly for fund performance. Parents can also roll over the money without penalty to another beneficiary or to either a state 529 savings or prepaid plan. Like the state prepaid plans, distributions reduce your aid eligibility dollar for dollar.

Coverdell Education Savings Accounts

Formerly known as the Education IRA, the Coverdell Education Savings Accounts let families with adjusted gross incomes of up to $220,000 save up to $2,000 a year tax-free for education expenses (for single-filers, the income cap is $110,000).

These work particularly well for families who can afford to save only a little bit each month and for those who plan to use the funds to pay for private elementary and high schools. One big appeal of Coverdells is you have a lot more investment options than 529s, which allows you to hold down costs and thereby bolster returns, plus annual charges tend to be lower than for 529 plans. Also, withdrawals were tax-free before the 2001 tax law and thus, unlike 529 plans, the Coverdell's tax-free status isn't threatened by the 2011 sunset provision.

However, Coverdell savings count against you when schools award financial aid, because they are held in the student's name.

Custodial Accounts

With the latest tax cut, custodial accounts—known as Uniform Gifts or Transfers to Minors Act accounts—now deserve a second look. These vehicles have been overshadowed by 529 college-savings plans, mainly because withdrawals are taxed at the child's rate.

The new tax law shifts some additional tax advantages to custodial accounts for a limited period of time by lowering the capital-gains rate of people in the two lowest-income tax brackets. Kids over 13 years old, who tend to fall in these brackets, will be able to sell stock at a 5 percent capital-gains tax rate between now and 2007, and at 0 percent in 2008. This will benefit custodial accounts because they are the primary vehicles used to transfer securities to children. You can't transfer securities to a 529 plan.

But like all things tax-related, there are a number of restrictions on who can qualify. Younger children pay taxes at their parents' rate. Theoretically, you could get past this requirement by opening an account for a younger child as long as he or she turns 14 by the time you sell. And make sure that any stock sales won't push the child's income above the 15 percent bracket, which peaks at about $28,400, or the lowered rates won't apply.

Other big pros for these accounts: You have more flexibility to spend the money for expenses other than college tuition (as long as it's spent on behalf of the child). With a custodial account, the funds can be tapped at any time for any purpose that benefits the child, including braces, summer camp or a new computer. Also, unlike with 529s, you aren't limited in your investment choices, and mutual-fund fees and expenses tend to be lower than for 529s.

Potential drawbacks: The distributions can hurt your chances of getting financial aid. And, unless Congress acts, the cut in the dividends and capital-gains rate will disappear in 2009. In addition, once children reach the age of majority, usually 18 or 21, depending on the state, they get control of their custodial accounts, which means the money could get spent on something other than college.

Finally, custodial accounts are less appealing if you plan to buy bonds, because you will earn a lot of interest income that will be subject to income-tax rates. Instead, bond-buyers are better off opting for a 529 or a Coverdell.

Savings Bonds

Middle- to low-income households seeking a safe investment may want to consider savings bonds, such as Series EE bonds issued after 1989 and all Series I bonds. For married taxpayers with adjusted gross incomes of $117,750 or less ($73,500 for single filers), some or all of the interest earned is tax-free if used for higher-education expenses. If your child doesn't go to college, you won't be penalized for using the proceeds for something else—though, of course, you won't get the tax break. The rub with savings bonds is low returns. That's why many people will do better with potentially higher-return investments like stocks to keep pace with rising tuition costs.

Taxable Accounts

By investing money for your children in a regular brokerage account, you will have greater control, unlimited investment options and the flexibility to use the money for any purpose. Plus, the recent cut in the top tax rate on capital gains and dividends to 15 percent makes the tax bite less onerous. Like savings bonds and 529 savings plans in the parents' names, taxable accounts have little effect on how much financial aid you'll get.

"Spend-to-Save" Programs

These programs let you save for education while you shop. If you buy from one of its retail partners, Upromise (**upromise.com**) gives rebates—either by check or deposited into a tax-advantaged, 529 college savings plan. BabyMint (**babymint.com**) also offers rebates for online purchases and gift certificates. In addition, it will send a check or deposit the money into any account you specify, even a mutual fund. Family and friends can sign up for either program and contribute to your account. EdExpress (**edexpress.com**) is another option that allows family and friends to contribute. The bottom line: Your savings may be small potatoes, but it could be worth considering for things you would have bought anyway.

HOW TO GET FINANCIAL AID

How much money can you have and still qualify for financial-aid grants? Once a family earns about $100,000 a year and has about $100,000 in assets, it is generally ineligible for need-based aid at most schools.

But even if you have managed to save some money, don't count yourself out of the game. Some 22 percent of families making $100,000 or more got a grant, loan or other form of need-based aid in 2000, says a study by Harvard University Professor Susan Dynarski.

INTEREST IN LEARNING

 A quick look at the different college-savings plans available.

529 COLLEGE SAVINGS PLAN

Tax Breaks: Qualified distributions tax-free (some states may also offer tax breaks)

Contribution Limit: Up to total of about $300,000 for some plans; may pay gift taxes if more than $11,000 a year. Can donate up to $55,000 at one time.

Income Restrictions: None

Potential Sunset Changes: Earnings withdrawals will be taxed at child's rate after 2010.

Federal Financial-Aid Impact: Considered parents' assets; assessed up to 5.6 percent

Flexibility of Use: Tuition, fees, room, board and graduate school

529 STATE PREPAID PLAN

Tax Breaks: Qualified distributions tax-free (some states may also offer tax breaks)

Contribution Limit: Maximum varies by state, but plans cover, in general, up to five years of college costs.

Income Restrictions: None

Potential Sunset Changes: Earnings withdrawals will be taxed at child's rate after 2010.

Federal Financial-Aid Impact: Considered student resource; reduces aid eligibility dollar for dollar.

Flexibility of Use: For most plans, tuition, fees, room and board

INDEPENDENT 529 PLAN

Tax Breaks: Qualified distributions tax-free

Contribution Limit: Up to five years' tuition at the group's most expensive college (currently $137,000)

Income Restrictions: None

Potential Sunset Changes: Earnings withdrawals will be taxed at child's rate after 2010.

Federal Financial-Aid Impact: Considered student resource; reduces aid eligibility dollar for dollar

Flexibility of Use: Tuition and mandatory fees

And the amount of financial aid given out has been on the rise. Experts say that families whose income levels would normally make them ineligible for aid might qualify if more than one child is in college or if there are other extenuating circumstances.

There are ways to play the financial-aid game. Here's how it works:

COVERDELL EDUCATION SAVINGS ACCOUNT

Tax Breaks: Qualified distributions tax-free

Contribution Limit: Up to $2,000 a year

Income Restrictions: For single filers, $95,000–$110,000; for joint filers, $190,000–$220,000

Potential Sunset Changes: Contribution limits would revert to $500 after 2010.

Federal Financial-Aid Impact: Considered student's assets; assessed at 35 percent

Flexibility of Use: Postsecondary costs; K–12 costs, some computers

CUSTODIAL ACCOUNTS

Tax Breaks: For kids over 14, earnings are taxed at child's rate; under 14, earnings less than $750 are tax-free.

Contribution Limit: No total maximum, but may pay gift taxes if more than $11,000 a year

Income Restrictions: None

Potential Sunset Changes: Favorable 5 percent tax rate is set to expire in 2009.

Federal Financial-Aid Impact: Considered student's assets; assessed at 35 percent

Flexibility of Use: Anything that benefits the minor

SAVINGS BONDS

Tax Breaks: Interest earned is tax-free if used for qualified higher-education purposes.

Contribution Limit: Annual limit of $30,000 per owner

Income Restrictions: For 2003, for singles, $58,500–$73,500; for joint-filers, $87,750–$117,750

Potential Sunset Changes: None

Federal Financial-Aid Impact: Considered parents' assets; assessed up to 5.6%.

Flexibility of Use: Tuition and mandatory fees

TAXABLE ACCOUNTS

Tax Breaks: Up to 15 percent tax on capital gains and dividend income

Contribution Limit: Unlimited

Income Restrictions: None

Potential Sunset Changes: Favorable 15 percent rate set to expire in 2009

Federal Financial-Aid Impact: Considered parents' assets; assessed up to 5.6 percent

Flexibility of Use: Unlimited

There are essentially three different financial-aid formulas to determine how much aid you get: federal, used by all schools; "institutional," used by roughly 325 mostly private colleges; and a "consensus approach," used by 29 elite colleges.

The federal formula determines how much aid you get from the

U.S. government. The other two formulas calculate how much aid you get from the colleges themselves. Many students at private colleges get aid from both sources.

The federal formula is the most basic. Students are expected to kick in about 35 percent of their assets each year, while parents—depending on their income and other factors—are expected to contribute between 2.6 and 5.6 percent.

If you've watched your home significantly appreciate in value, you may be worried about how that "wealth" affects your college-bound child's chances for financial aid. The good news is, if you're applying for federal aid, your home equity on your primary residence isn't considered in the formula for calculating need.

The institutional formula used by most private colleges probes more deeply into your finances. Here, students are expected to contribute only 25 percent of assets and parents between 3 and 5 percent. This model does count home equity and, depending on the school, may even examine what kind of car you drive.

Still, while private colleges often consider home equity as an asset that could be tapped to pay tuition bills, it's weighed less heavily than income in the decision to award aid. Moreover, some colleges have recently decided to cap the value of a family's home in the financial-aid equation, in order to avoid penalizing a family that has a middle-class income but lives in a house that has shot up in value over the years.

The consensus approach looks at parent and student assets together and expects families to contribute only around 5 percent of them. These colleges generally won't consider home equity of more than 2.4 times the family income.

To figure out how much your family will be expected to contribute before getting financial aid, go to the EFC calculator at **collegeboard .com**. The website also has forms for requesting institutional funds.

To maximize your chances of qualifying for aid:

1. **Keep assets out of the student's name.** If you did save money in a Uniform Gift to Minor Account, most colleges expect up to 35 percent of the money in these accounts to be used each year for tuition. Since the money in the account is considered an irrevocable gift to the student, you can't simply take the money back. But you can spend it before college rolls around on education-related costs like a new computer or private high-school tuition.

2. Lower your income. Aid formulas expect parents to contribute from 22 to 47 percent of income. Parents sometimes defer bonuses to lower their income and get more aid. For the same reason, people are advised to postpone selling stocks or real estate in which they've realized a capital gain. Student income is assessed at an even higher rate than parents', so some students simply stop working just before they apply for financial aid.

3. Use your house. The federal formula doesn't look at home equity, so paying down your mortgage is a way of hiding wealth. However, home equity is counted in the institutional formula used by most private schools. One tactic: Parents take out a home-equity loan, which makes them poorer under the formula, and use the proceeds to pay off credit-card bills, which aren't counted in financial-aid calculations.

4. Don't remarry. Both the institutional formula and the new consensus approach probe the financial status of stepparents. So some divorced parents put off getting remarried until after their kid gets a diploma.

5. Update your status. If one family member lost a job late in the year or there were other reasons why the information on the application doesn't accurately reflect your current situation, keep the college up to date.

6. Do save. Don't fall into the trap of not saving at all in order to qualify. Aid is determined more by income than by accumulated assets. In reality, saving will give your child more options, not fewer.

A FASTER FAFSA

There's one simple step for boosting your aid prospects: getting your financial-aid applications in immediately after January 1. Grant money, which is need-based, is doled out on a first-come, first-served basis, starting at the beginning of the year.

The Free Application for Federal Student Aid, or FAFSA, is used to determine a family's eligibility for federal and sometimes state and institutional grants, loans and work-study programs. Deadlines for state aid may be earlier than the federal deadline.

Completing the financial-aid form does take a little preparation. Before you start, you'll want to gather together your last-year's federal

PLAYING HIDE-AND-SEEK WITH FINANCIAL AID

Here are some commonly used strategies that are legal but generally frowned upon by colleges:

1. **Minimize income.** Up to 47 percent of parental income is considered eligible to pay for school. So parents defer bonuses to keep their income low. Others sell losing stock positions to reduce their income, though only $3,000 of net losses can be taken each year.

2. **Spend the kid's savings.** The more assets the student has, the less aid he or she is likely to get. Families can legally spend custodial accounts on anything that benefits their child's education, including private high-school tuition, an SAT prep course or a computer.

3. **Keep savings in the parents' name.** A savings account in a parent's name instead of the child's can up their chances for getting aid.

4. **Quit the summer job.** Student income is assessed at an even higher rate than parents' so it often pays to keep the kid out of work the year before aid is needed.

5. **Pick your assets.** The cash value of life insurance, deferred annuities and personal property such as coin collections usually don't have to be reported on financial-aid applications.

income-tax return or documentation to estimate taxes—your W-2 wage-earning forms, bank statements and investment information. Expect to spend a few hours completing this document, whether by paper or online at **fafsa.ed.gov.** One advantage of submitting the application online is that schools will receive it faster. Still, if you're just getting up to speed on the Internet, and feel more comfortable filling out a hard copy of this form, do it on paper. Accuracy is the main goal with these applications, as errors can decrease your eligibility for financial aid.

SCHOLARSHIP STUDY GUIDE

There are more than 700,000 scholarships available annually. Start looking in the second or third year of high school, and prepare for scholarship deadlines in the spring of the junior and senior years. Keep in mind that about two dozen states offer scholarships to any of their high-school graduates who meet certain standards. Georgia's Hope Scholarships, for example, will pay full tuition at one of the state's public universities, or as much as $3,000 a year at an in-state private college, to any graduate of a Georgia high school with a B average. Many state programs don't set limits on family income. Most are renewed if a college student keeps a B average.

Some Web sites that offer free help navigating the financial-aid process.

1. **FinAid.org:** A comprehensive site that has information on loans, scholarships and saving plans. Even includes interactive calculators to help project what your child's college costs will be and how much you should be stashing away.

2. **Fastweb.monster.com:** Matches student profiles to a database containing over 600,000 scholarships. Also alerts students to application deadlines or when new scholarships are added.

3. **Collegeboard.com:** Scholarship search connects to a database containing over 2,300 scholarships, internships and loans.

4. **Srnexpress.com:** Contains over 150,000 resources, including scholarships, fellowships, internships and loan-forgiveness programs.

5. **fafsa.ed.gov:** Contains Free Application for Federal Student Aid, which any student applying for financial aid from the government needs to fill out. Online form helps ensure that no information is missing or conflicting before the applicant submits the form.

6. **wiredscholar.com:** lists thousands of scholarships and tells you which you qualify for.

GETTING A DISCOUNT ON YOUR TUITION

Don't pay full price for college. Hungry for the brightest students, many of the country's stronger universities will discount tuition even for students who don't need financial aid.

Much as banks and insurers offer special rates to their best customers, schools give the biggest breaks to their top students. Public four-year colleges, too, are offering discounts, a relatively new practice for them.

The Ivy League schools and a few others, including Georgetown University, still give aid only to financially needy students. But plenty of other nationally ranked schools offer tuition breaks to students just because they have the qualities the schools want. Parents with their high-school senior daughter on a recent visit to Lynchburg College, a private liberal-arts college in Virginia, were pleasantly surprised to learn that her status as an A-minus student would earn her an automatic $12,000-a-year scholarship if she chose to go to Lynchburg—an award based on the school's desire to attract better and better students.

Schools don't publish their discount rates, although it is possible to calculate them using information in the schools' annual reports. Georgetown, for example, lists its gross tuition and "university-sponsored discounts" in a footnote to its financial statement. But like most schools,

DO YOU NEED A FINANCIAL-AID COUNSELOR?

The aid game has spawned a corps of financial planners who specialize in moving money so it doesn't count against you in financial-aid applications. These companies offer to help parents search for scholarships or fill out federal forms, or they promote financial-aid seminars.

Trouble is, families rarely get any payoff for what can often be a sizable investment. The number of complaints about financial-aid outfits that overpromise rose 50 percent in 2002, to 482, from a year earlier, according to the Federal Trade Commission.

Indeed, some financial-aid experts question the wisdom of hiring any counselor, given the wealth of free resources available online, from extensive scholarship listings to information about various loan programs.

Paying a professional could even, ironically, reduce a family's chances of securing aid. That's because colleges may give greater scrutiny to financial-aid applications that have had

it includes in those numbers awards to graduate students, who generally receive larger breaks than undergrads. (In 2002, Georgetown said it had an undergraduate discount rate of about 18 percent.)

Another place to look is college Web sites, which often report the percentage of students receiving aid. But that number doesn't distinguish between loans and grants, or between federal money (which isn't considered in calculating the discount rate) and university money. The sites also often list the size and number of grants the schools offer, and the qualifications—grade averages, arts accomplishments, intended major.

COLLEGE LOANS AND HOW TO GET THEM

Federal student loans are the government's major vehicle for helping families pay for college, and account for almost half of all student aid. Any student is entitled to a loan, and for low-income families, the government defers interest on that loan while the student is still in school.

But those loans don't stretch as far as they once did. A freshman could borrow a maximum of $2,625 at a record-low 4.25% interest

input from a professional counselor. (The school can easily spot those applications because the counselors are required to sign them.)

Most school counselors can help families fill out forms for no charge, and many colleges, high schools and libraries run free financial-aid workshops. The Education Department operates a free hotline (1-800-4-FED-AID) for questions involving federal student aid. **FinAid.org** has a helpful section titled "Maximizing Your Aid Eligibility" that offers strategies for getting need-based aid, such as saving money in a parent's name rather than the child's. And the free scholarship search engines listed above can match student profiles to scholarship opportunities.

Good financial-aid counselors will clearly lay out what they can't do and what they can—which is mostly hand-holding and answering questions about how the process works, rather than unlocking secrets for landing aid. For more information on avoiding scholarship scams, check with the Better Business Bureau, National Fraud Information Center or the Federal Trade Commission.

rate in 2004, but that won't even come close to covering the cost of tuition and room and board at a typical state university. If parents have already reached their borrowing limits on one of the popular federally sponsored lending programs, the Stafford, they may be tempted to resort to private loans, which, in the current low-interest-rate environment, seems like a good solution. But because the rates on those loans aren't capped, a rise in interest rates would suddenly make them much pricier. Parents instead should consider the PLUS loan. It lets families borrow enough to pay for the total cost of attendance, and the variable interest rates are capped at 9 percent. Also, unlike with private loans, it's possible to lock in a fixed interest rate (through something called the "Federal Consolidation Loan Program").

If you do search for private loans, don't limit yourself to the lenders your school advises you use. Colleges tout "preferred lenders" on their Web sites, but often these lists don't include anything close to the best deal.

Seeking loans from lenders that weren't on the preferred lists, in fact, can net big savings, from about $1,000 for a typical undergraduate to more than $18,000 for a graduate student, according to Versura Inc.

The company, an independent financial-aid consultant in Washington, D.C., analyzed data on college lists at the *The Wall Street Journal*'s request in 2002.

Students ought to consider the colleges' lists as a starting point, but they should also shop around, particularly for nonprofit lenders. It may take some digging. Student loans are federally guaranteed, and they carry the same rate, initially. But where there is some leeway is in discounts on the loans' interest rates and other expenses. While some lenders take a basic approach of simply offering a one-time cash-back incentive to students who make a certain number of payments on time, others can offer larger incentives.

PICKING A COLLEGE

How do you decide?

You can take the first step from your desk at home. There are many Web sites promising to provide basic information about schools or college rankings, such as **Collegeboard.com, petersons.com** and **usnews.com.** (Beware: Don't give out personal information such as name and e-mail address to the sites, or you may wind up getting unwanted e-mail.)

The government's College Opportunities On-Line, or "Cool" site (**nces.ed.gov/ipeds/cool**) lists data about student demographics, graduation rates and tuition costs. It also includes campus crime statistics, each college's leading competitors, and details about admissions (such as how many students scored 700 or above on the 800-point SAT verbal exam). The government student-aid site (**studentaid2.ed.gov/gotocollege/campustour**) has aid-related stats for hundreds of colleges.

The College Board's website (**collegeboard.com**) is easy to use for college searches. The National Collegiate Athletic Association (**ncaa.org**) lists enrollment and graduation information on athletes. The National Association of Independent College and Universities provides links to individual colleges' self-assessment studies (**naicu.edu/Accountability/student/assesslinks.htm**).

Some sites help with comparison shopping. Tell the government's Cool site that you want an engineering program at a college with 1,500 students or fewer, no more than 1,000 miles from Washington, D.C., and it will spit out the names of 21 schools. Put a similar query to the Association of Jesuit Colleges (**ajcunet.edu**), and it will propose five of its members. But after that, any further comparison—on faculty qualifications, programs, student-faculty ratios—is largely up to you.

States also are expanding their college reporting requirements, increasingly offering data online that the federal government and commercial college-search sites don't. Florida's Board of Regents compares graduation rates among the state's public universities, and reports how many graduates from each school are earning more than $22,000 five years after receiving their degrees.

Students and parents will soon have even more data to pore through. A new higher-education law is in the works that will require universities to disclose a good deal more information than they already do. The information could include hundreds of new details about everything from price increases to job-placement rates for graduates.

What should you look for? Here are some fundamental things to ask about:

1. **Find out how many students receive aid** from the college, because that suggests the institution's commitment to its students.

2. **Check the average SAT and ACT scores of admitted students.** That will tell you if a college is a good academic fit. The Cool site breaks down each school's programs by the number of degrees they award.

3. **Ask about graduation rates and the average time it takes to get a diploma.** The latter question is particularly important because it could indicate—in the case, say, of a state school, where most students take five years—that course availability is a chronic problem. But also bear in mind that schools with selective admissions policies that attract top students are always going to have better rates than, say, state schools that are required to admit practically everyone.

4. **Ask about average class size and the number of faculty with Ph.Ds.** Another caveat here, though. These indicators are perhaps somewhat overrated, since class size alone doesn't say much about the quality of teaching, and graduate degrees are much more common than they used to be.

5. **Find out how much of the teaching load is handled by graduate assistants.** This is a better question than the one above, since it should

give you a pretty good indication of the kind of instruction you may get, especially in your freshman and sophomore years, when you'll be taking survey classes like history and sociology.

6. Are you guaranteed housing? This is a critical question unless you're going to a commuter school. Most colleges and universities guarantee dorm or other space to at least incoming freshmen and second-year students; you're often on your own after that. Parents or even students who don't feel comfortable seeking independent living arrangements would do well to keep this question in mind.

7. What's the geographic and demographic makeup of the student body? This gets at the diversity question, but it's more than that. Suppose that great middle-sized state school you have your eye on in Wisconsin turns out to have a student body in which 85 percent of the students come from the surrounding area. That could mean an empty and lonely campus on the weekends as those students go home.

PUBLIC OR PRIVATE?

Are the most expensive private schools really worth the extra money? Or might the same opportunities be available—at lower cost—from public universities?

The argument for the Ivies is that, all things being equal, a prestigious diploma offers its holder an edge in any number of situations, from applying to competitive graduate schools to seeking a promotion. A 1999 study conducted by Cornell University, the Rand Institute and Brigham Young University compared tuitions of private institutions and public colleges. The study found that tuition was about four times higher at private schools—but it concluded that the higher tuition proved a better investment when comparing the salaries earned by graduates.

But other studies show that state-school grads' salaries catch up throughout life with those of their elite counterparts—and it isn't clear whether at any point the salary differential justifies the lighter burden state-school grads face in paying off their loans. The U.S. Department of Education advises that your monthly student-loan repayments not exceed 10 to 15 percent of your monthly income. To estimate your student-loan repayments, you can use the loan-repayment calculator at **collegeboard.com**.

SCHOOL SHOPPING

 Here are some noncommercial sites to help narrow—or broaden—your college search, and some of the information they offer:

FEDERAL WEB SITES

Site: nces.ed.gov/ipeds/cool

Sample content: Who's admitted, who enrolls, tuition and other charges, biggest academic programs, graduation rates

Usefulness: Search colleges by their location, size, programs they offer and their distance from your home.

Site: studentaid2.ed.gov/gotocollege/campustour

Sample content: Detailed breakdown on how many students get aid, what kind and how much

Usefulness: Search here for details on policies like deferred and early admission, and whether the school offers honors, remedial and study-abroad programs.

STATE WEB SITES

Google your state's Board of Regents for these sites. Data varies by state.

NONPROFITS

Site: collegeboard.com

Sample content: From admissions requirements and student demographics, to computer services and social activities

Usefulness: Search for colleges by location, selectivity and major, and call up colleges with similar profiles.

Site: ncaa.org

Sample content: Graduation rates for athletes and nonathletes, by year and sport

Usefulness: Search here for national studies on gender and race of coaches, and on revenues and expenses of teams, by sport.

FEEDER MANIA

For years, the focus in higher education has been about getting into the best possible college. But for future professionals—the future doctors, lawyers and executives out there—it's all about the right grad school. So *The Wall Street Journal* decided to look at which schools are most successful at getting kids into the nation's most prestigious graduate programs, like Yale Med or Wharton.

To compile our list of the most effective feeder colleges, we researched the background of more than 5,000 students starting at more than a dozen top business, law and medical schools in fall 2003, including names like Harvard Law and the Wharton M.B.A. We factored in the class size at each of the undergraduate colleges so that small schools wouldn't be penalized.

To no one's surprise, Harvard, Yale and Princeton dominated the top of our list. But after that, we found things don't always stack up the way you might think. Four of the other Ivy League schools failed to crack our top 10 (sorry, Penn). State schools like Michigan and Berkeley came in farther down the list, and so did NYU (number 69), which trailed Kalamazoo College (number 57). And if you're looking for a college with a track record better than UCLA or Barnard, look in Minnesota—St. Paul, to be exact, home to Macalester.

For years, the emphasis has been on finding the best undergraduate college, with parents studying guidebooks and schools pumping up everything from the faculty to the cafeteria food to draw kids in. Even when they got there, students usually didn't worry much beyond taking required courses. As for who got into the Harvards and Yales of the grad-school world, Ivy Leaguers often had the edge.

They still do. Almost one out of every seven students in the 2004 fall class at Harvard Law came from, you guessed it, Harvard College. And it doesn't stop there: According to *Weekend Journal*'s survey, add in Ivy rivals Yale and Princeton, and the top three schools account for more than 750 students at our 15 grad schools, out of a pool of 5,100 openings.

Beyond the top Ivies, things tilt quickly in favor of small schools, like Williams, at number 5 in our survey; Amherst, at number 9 and Swarthmore at 10. Indeed, of our top 20 colleges, seven have a senior class smaller than 600—and only one graduates more than 2,000 students a year. Grad schools told us these small liberal-arts colleges tend to do a better job of advising their students in areas like picking courses that look good on an application. And when students work directly with professors in small classes, they tend to get better recommendation letters.

But what about state schools? According to our survey, only Michigan made the top 30, and that's with the help of Michigan Law, one of our 15 elites, taking more than five dozen Wolverines in 2004's fall class. Among the other well-known names, Virginia was 33, and Berkeley came in at 41.

Ranking the Colleges...

...for getting into Yale Med, Chicago Business and all those other elite business, medical and law schools. Below, our list of the top 50 "feeder schools," based on our count of how many of their alumni started this fall at 15 select grad programs (see "Behind the Rankings"). The rankings are based on the number of students a college sends to a grad school divided by the college's class size—our Feeder Score.

RANK	SCHOOL	CLASS SIZE	# ATTENDING	FEEDER SCORE	COMMENTS
THE TOP 50 FEEDER SCHOOLS					
1	**Harvard University** Cambridge, Mass.	1,666	358	21.49%	There's no such thing as a sure bet. But for getting into a good grad school, a Harvard bachelor's degree remains the next best thing.
2	**Yale University** New Haven, Conn.	1,286	231	17.96%	What happened to school loyalty? More Yalies (40) are going to Harvard Law this fall than Yale Law (30).
3	**Princeton University** Princeton, N.J.	1,103	174	15.78%	One of the few Ivies without its own professional school, Princeton held its first grad-school fair last year.
4	**Stanford University** Stanford, Calif.	1,692	181	10.70%	Based on our numbers, does a particularly strong job at spawning future MBA stars; med school could use work.
5	**Williams College** Williamstown, Mass.	519	47	9.06%	An up-and-comer for some time, this "Little Ivy" did better than many of the actual Ivies.
6	**Duke University** Durham, N.C.	1,615	139	8.61%	Students do well here but may take their time; only 25% of graduates here go immediately to a professional school.
7	**Dartmouth College** Hanover, N.H.	1,101	93	8.45%	Recently put its "credentials file" online to help students track recommendation letters from professors.
8	**Massachusetts Institute of Technology,** Cambridge, Mass.	1,187	92	7.75%	One of the best on our list at getting kids into business school, including more than two dozen into Harvard Business this fall alone.
9	**Amherst College,** Amherst, Mass.	431	33	7.66%	Encourages use of grad-school advising services even after graduation.
10	**Swarthmore College** Swarthmore, Pa.	336	25	7.44%	Enrollment has tripled in seven years for an honors program here that's meant to mimic grad school with small seminars.
11	**Columbia University** New York	1,652	118	7.14%	You'd think undergrads here would have an edge getting into its elilte law and medical schools. But several other Ivies sent more students.
12	**Brown University,** Providence, R.I.	1,506	98	6.51%	Sixth-ranked Ivy tilted toward law in our figures; no formal pre-law program.
13	**Pomona College,** Claremont, Calif.	362	23	6.35%	One of our bigger surprises. Nearly half of undergraduates say they're going straight to grad school, up from 32% last year.
14	**University of Chicago** Chicago	948	59	6.22%	Has 11 of its graduates at Wharton this year; its business school has new program encouraging seniors to return to Chicago for their MBA.
15	**Wellesley College** Wellesley, Mass.	585	35	5.98%	Close to the Crimson: Pre-business association has field trips to Harvard Business, where eight alums started this fall.
16	**University of Pennsylvania** Philadelphia	2,785	153	5.49%	Penn's medical school (not one of our survey schools) has the highest percentage of Penn undergrads in six years.
17	**Georgetown University** Washington, D.C.	1,666	85	5.10%	Its highest numbers were at Harvard Business and Harvard Law—12 students each this fall.
18	**Haverford College,** Haverford, Pa.	291	13	4.47%	Recently reinstated a grad-school orientation program.
19	**Bowdoin College,** Brunswick, Maine	404	16	3.96%	Now has online service to help kids compile grad-school applications.
20	**Rice University,** Houston	764	29	3.80%	President Malcolm Gillis says numbers in "surprising " findings seem low.
21	**Northwestern University** Evanston, Ill.	1,978	73	3.69%	Feeding itself: New option gives incoming freshmen in the undergrad engineering program a slot in at business grad school, too.
22	**Claremont McKenna College** Claremont, Calif.	271	10	3.69%	Aspiring lawyers could do worse: School's students landed at Chicago, Harvard, Michigan and Yale law schools.

RANK	SCHOOL	CLASS SIZE	# ATTENDING	FEEDER SCORE	COMMENTS
23	**Middlebury College** Middlebury, Vt.	660	24	3.64%	Officials say it's a "feeder" for Dartmouth's MBA, but our survey turned up only two alums there this fall (10 are at Harvard B-school).
24	**Johns Hopkins Univ.,** Baltimore	1,272	45	3.54%	Med school remains the most popular grad choice here.
25	**Cornell University,** Ithaca, N.Y.	3,565	115	3.23%	Increased funding to advise women and minorities on grad school. Spokesman disputes "lasting meaning" of our survey.
26	**Bryn Mawr College,** Bryn Mawr, Pa.	310	9	2.90%	Grad-school history: One of the first Ph.D. programs for women in the U.S.
27	**Wesleyan University** Middletown, Conn.	731	21	2.87%	Within five years of graduating, 80% of Wesleyan grads wind up at some form of graduate or professional school.
28	**California Institute of Technology,** Pasadena, Calif.	249	7	2.81%	Lighter on law than most in our top 50.
29	**Morehouse College,** Atlanta	501	14	2.79%	This all-male, traditionally black college says it has has actually scaled back student trips to top Northeast grad schools.
30	**University of Michigan** Ann Arbor, Mich.	5,720	156	2.73%	Grad schools in our survey "should pay a bit more attention to geographic diversity," honors-program chief says.
31	**New College of Florida** Sarasota, Fla.	113	3	2.65%	At this "honors college" of the Florida state schools, professors give "narrative evaluations" instead of letter grades.
32	**Vassar College,** Poughkeepsie, N.Y.	581	15	2.58%	Says it's good for future doctors, but none at Harvard or Yale this fall.
33	**University of Virginia** Charlottesville, Va.	3,213	82	2.55%	The No. 3 public college on our list doesn't have a university-wide honors program.
34	**United States Military Academy,** West Point, N.Y.	966	23	2.38%	Chief executives, Army-style: A surprising showing at Harvard Business (13 students this year) boosted West Point's score.
35	**University of Notre Dame** South Bend, Ind.	1,985	45	2.27%	Less success at medical schools than some others in our group.
36	**Emory University,** Atlanta	1,509	33	2.19%	Dean says of ranking: "Ivy begets Ivy."
37	**United States Naval Academy** Annapolis, Md.	986	21	2.13%	All business, sir: The bulk of its grad-school students ended up at Harvard, MIT and Wharton business programs.
38	**Macalester College** St. Paul, Minn.	406	8	1.97%	Less widely known than some Eastern liberal-arts colleges, it pushes internships in health-care to help med-school prospects.
39	**Brandeis University,** Waltham, Mass.	815	16	1.96%	School says it's bringing in top grad schools for admissions fair.
40	**Bates College,** Lewiston, Maine	417	8	1.92%	Taps alumni to help students get key internships.
41	**University of California, Berkeley,** Berkeley, Calif.	6,198	118	1.90%	Says its kids are accepted to top grad schools in far greater numbers than choose to attend.
42	**Barnard College,** New York	588	11	1.87%	Placed much lower than Columbia, the Ivy it's affiliated with.
43	**Trinity College,** Hartford, Conn.	485	9	1.86%	Grads of this liberal-arts school seemed to favor MBA programs.
44	**Grinnell College,** Grinnell, Iowa	337	6	1.78%	For kids interested in a specific grad program, networking program ties them with an alum who attended or worked there.
45	**Tufts University,** Medford, Mass.	1,246	22	1.77%	Far from tops in Boston, but still edged out Boston College (No. 79).
46	**Colby College,** Waterville, Maine	471	8	1.70%	Lags Maine rivals Bates and Bowdoin.
47	**Washington University,** St. Louis	1,709	29	1.70%	Made our top 50, but one of the more expensive schools on our list (tuition is $28,300 a year). Says it's "very successful" at placing students.
48	**Washington and Lee,** Lexington, Va.	413	7	1.69%	No New Haven: School made our cut—but nobody at Yale Med or Law.
49	**Case Western Reserve University,** Cleveland	729	12	1.65%	They're working on it, with new annual conference giving advice on applying to graduate schools.
50	**Reed College,** Portland, Ore.	304	5	1.64%	Sure, Carnegie Mellon—No. 51 on our list—had more students (19) get into our top schools, but Reed had slightly higher success rate.

How State Schools Did

Because our rankings are adjusted for class size, many public colleges—even ones that sent a dozen or more kids to our grad schools—didn't make the top 50. Below, a look at the top 30 state schools, including where they placed in the overall rankings.

RANK	SCHOOL	# ATTENDING	FEEDER SCORE	OVERALL RANK	RANK	SCHOOL	# ATTENDING	FEEDER SCORE	OVERALL RANK
TOP 30 STATE FEEDER SCHOOLS									
1	University of Michigan	156	2.73%	30	16	University of Calif., San Diego	16	0.41%	125
2	New College of Florida	3	2.65%	31	17	University of Calif., Irvine	14	0.39%	129
3	University of Virginia	82	2.55%	33	18	University of Vermont	6	0.36%	135
4	University of Calif., Berkeley	118	1.90%	41	19	University of Calif., Davis	17	0.36%	137
5	Univ. of Calif., Los Angeles	92	1.33%	61	20	Rutgers University	20	0.35%	140
6	Georgia Inst. of Technology	20	0.93%	75	21	University of Washington	22	0.34%	142
7	College of William & Mary	11	0.84%	82	22	Miami University (Ohio)	11	0.32%	147
8	Stony Brook (SUNY)	4	0.79%	86	23	University of Maryland	17	0.31%	148
9	Univ. of N. Carolina, Chapel Hill	26	0.74%	90	24	University of Oklahoma	9	0.31%	149
10	University of Texas, Austin	49	0.62%	101	25	University of Utah	13	0.31%	151
11	Florida A&M University	8	0.57%	106	26	University of Florida	19	0.24%	164
12	University of Illinois (Urbana)	37	0.55%	109	27	Univ. of Md., Eastern Shore	1	0.24%	166
13	Concord College (W. Va.)	2	0.51%	113	28	Purdue University	14	0.24%	167
14	Indiana University	26	0.46%	119	29	Pennsylvania State University	19	0.22%	173
15	University of Wisconsin	26	0.44%	121	30	University of Louisville	4	0.22%	174

Even if most people don't realize it, there's a bias in favor of some schools that is practically built into the system. At law schools, there's a number called "the LCM"—the LSAT College Mean, which tries to identify the students attending the "tougher" colleges (usually Ivies and small liberal-arts schools). With each new group of applicants, it evaluates schools based on their average LSAT test scores; someone with so-so grades from a high-LCM school can wind up looking better than a 4.0 student at a lesser college. It also makes a difference that many admissions officers are Ivy alums—and pick students like themselves.

We focused on 15 elite schools, five each from medicine, law and business, to serve as our benchmark for profiling where the students came from. Our list reflects a consensus of grad-school deans we interviewed, top recruiters and published grad-school rankings (including *The Journal*'s own M.B.A. rankings). So, for medicine, our schools were Columbia, Harvard, Johns Hopkins, the University of California–San Francisco and Yale, while our M.B.A. programs were Chicago,

Dartmouth's Tuck School, Harvard, MIT's Sloan School and Penn's Wharton School. In law, we looked at Chicago, Columbia, Harvard, Michigan and Yale.

Our team of reporters fanned out to these schools to find the alma maters for every student starting in fall 2004, more than 5,100 in all. Nine of the schools gave us their own lists, but for the rest we relied mainly on "face book" directories schools give incoming students. Of course, when it comes to "feeding" grad schools, a college's rate is more important than the raw numbers. So our feeder score factors in class size.

THE NEW SAFETY SCHOOLS

You may have to update your old list of so-called safety schools that top students used to fall back on. With competition for college more intense than ever, the old safeties have become unattainable, too. Kids who only a few years ago had a fighting chance for the Ivies aren't even getting wait-listed at the Vassars and Swarthmores of the world, which used to be considered second-tier schools.

So *The Journal* took a crash course in college admissions. The goal: to produce an index of the new American safety schools. A fallback for MIT, for example? Not Pomona or Johns Hopkins. Both schools now have average SATs above 1420 and admission rates only a touch more favorable than some of the Ivies. The new safety: Rochester Institute of Technology, where applications have more than doubled over the past decade.

Emory's acceptance rate dropped by more than a third over the past decade, and Williams last year rejected more than three-quarters of applicants. And then there is the University of Southern California: Once derided as the "University of Spoiled Children," it admitted just over a third of its applicants in 2004—down from 71 percent a decade ago. In many of these cases, average SAT scores have jumped significantly, about 100 points at Boston College alone over the past decade. (And that's after accounting for the upward adjustment in the SAT scale a few years ago.)

On the plus side, many of the new safety schools are gaining in reputation, thanks to recent endowment windfalls and high-profile faculty hires. Take Furman, in Greenville, South Carolina, which a decade ago was barely on the radar screen. Since then, it's spent millions

Dow Jones Safety School Index

To map out the new landscape and help students pick their fallback options, we convened a panel of five admissions counselors. We factored in everything from acceptance rates to SAT scores and divided our list into four major categories: New Ivies (former fallbacks to top schools that are now almost as selective as the Ivies) followed by three tiers of Safety Schools: Safe, Safer and Safest. While the categories are geared to top students (1400 SATs), they reflect the basic array of choices for students at varying levels. The index does not attempt to be an exhaustive list of schools.

The New Ivies (Once considered backups to Ivy League and other top schools, now selective enough to be in a league of their own)

	MIDDLE SAT RANGE	ACCEPTANCE RATE	AVERAGE GPA	COMMENT
Duke University Durham, N.C.	1350-1510	26%	n/a	Two words: Grant Hill. Once a Southern backup for Princeton, Duke has raised its profile nationally thanks to stronger academics and hoops legends like Mr. Hill.
Georgetown University Washington, D.C.	1250-1450*	22%	n/a	Guidance counselors say Georgetown used to be the classic East Coast backup. Now its acceptance rate is about the same as Dartmouth's.
Johns Hopkins University Baltimore	1320-1460	31%	3.91	Efforts to recruit humanities students have helped boost applications 70% at this science stronghold. "Previous image was a bunch of nerds," says one panelist.
New York University New York	1270-1450	29%	3.58	When TV's "Felicity" asked to film here, she was rejected. She's not the only one— NYU now turns away twice as many students as in 1990.
Northwestern University Evanston, Ill.	1290-1470	33%	n/a	The Big 10 Ivy. One plus: Its football team finally came out of the gutter. That "makes for additional exposure," says guidance counselor Joseph Runge.
Pomona College Claremont, Calif.	1360-1530*	29%	n/a	With outdoor pools and fancy dorms, it's a far cry from Harvard Square. But California's economic boom has helped spur a 33% spike in applications.
Rice University Houston	1320-1530	23%	n/a	A relative bargain. Its tuition is a third less than many other private schools—a big draw, says guidance counselor O'Neal Turner, of Culver Academies in Indiana.
Swarthmore College Swarthmore, Pa.	1370-1520	23%	n/a	No football obsession here. This school, known for students who "discuss Nietzsche over cappuccino," got *more* popular after eliminating its team.
University of Notre Dame South Bend, Ind.	1270-1425	34%	3.85	The Fighting Irish have long dominated their region but have now gained more of a national image academically. The only drawback: South Bend, says a panelist.
Vassar College Poughkeepsie, N.Y.	1290-1450	34%	3.7	A slightly safer bet. Guidance counselors place it at the bottom of the New Ivies.
Williams College Williamstown, Mass.	1320-1490	24%	n/a	Strong athletics? It's no Notre Dame, but our panel says this school's newly invigorated football and lacrosse programs have boosted its profile.

Safe (Still selective, but regarded as first-tier backup schools to the New Ivies)

	MIDDLE SAT RANGE	ACCEPTANCE RATE	AVERAGE GPA	COMMENT
Boston College Boston	1270-1410	32%	3.82	In admissions circles, they call it "the Doug Flutie effect." Applicant pool has been climbing ever since he won the Heisman.
Colgate University Hamilton, N.Y.	1270-1430	38%	3.58	After almost doubling its scholarship offerings, Colgate is seeing about 17% more applications.
Emory University Atlanta	1300-1460	44%	3.7	Coca-Cola gave Emory the real thing: money. They've spent millions lately on buildings and new majors. It's "barking up the tree of the Ivies" says one panelist.
Fordham University Bronx, N.Y.	1070-1230	63%	3.6	While it's long been a safety school for Georgetown, this "hard-charging" institution could see its acceptance rate drop to 50% in the next five years, experts say.
George Washington University Washington, D.C.	1160-1320	49%	n/a	Named for our founding father, this school has gotten its latest boost from another great American institution: direct marketing. Applications are up about 140%.
Hamilton College Clinton, N.Y.	1230-1410	39%	3.4	Applications are up 19% in just the last year. One panelist calls Hamilton "fantastic"; another says "overrated."
Harvey Mudd College Claremont, Calif.	1410-1550	46%	3.8*	Harvey *who*? Despite some name-recognition problems, admissions officer Deren Finks says applicants turn down MIT and sometimes Harvard to come here.
Tulane University New Orleans.	1220-1380	72%	3.6	Acceptance rate is still high, but it's been dropping. One reason: It's attracting more applicants from the West and overseas.

	MIDDLE SAT RANGE	ACCEPTANCE RATE	AVERAGE GPA	COMMENT
University of California San Diego La Jolla, Calif.	1310-1450	38%	4.07	This school's riding the popularity wave of the University of California system—applications are up 90% from a decade ago.
University of Southern California Los Angeles	1210-1400	34%	3.89	Once derided as the "University of Spoiled Children," its acceptance rate has dropped from 70% to 34%.
Washington University St. Louis	1270-1440	34%	n/a	Convincing Easterners to go to school in St. Louis took work. But several years of aggressive marketing have paid off.

Safer (Prestigious, but the bar here is generally a little lower than at the schools above)

	MIDDLE SAT RANGE	ACCEPTANCE RATE	AVERAGE GPA	COMMENT
American University Washington, D.C.	1130-1290	72%	3.28	The Beltway Backup. With a "mind-boggling" array of campus speakers and snazzy locale, panelists say it's a good fallback for Georgetown or George Washington.
Boston University Boston	1230-1370	49%	3.5	One current student summed it up best: "If you can't get into Harvard, at least you can see it from across the river."
Case Western Reserve University Cleveland	1260-1440	71%	3.7	It's not as geeky as it used to be, panelists say, but Case's average SAT score has climbed about 100 points over the past decade.
Furman University Greenville, S.C.	1190-1340	59%	3.6	Began to attract broader interest when it cast off its Southern Baptist affiliation in recent years, some panelists say.
Georgia Institute of Technology Atlanta	1260-1440	57%	3.7	Where the girls aren't: Less than 30% of the students here are women. But their number is rising, even as overall admission rate continues to decline.
Lehigh University Bethlehem, Pa.	1221-1397	46%	3.75	Alum Lee Iacocca has endowed a new business and engineering program, and spurred a big increase in scholarship money.
Loyola Marymount University Los Angeles	1030-1220	62%	3.32	Diversity is the buzzword here. An increase in minority admissions has helped boost the school's profile.
Pepperdine University Malibu, Calif.	1150-1350	36%	3.7	Ken Starr didn't get to go there, and neither do more than half of all applicants now. There has been a 165% increase in applications since 1990.
Providence College Providence, R.I.	1130-1300	57%	3.41	Providence has been getting gentrified (and popularized on TV), and Providence College is one beneficiary.
Reed College Portland, Ore.	1260-1420	63%	3.7	Our panelists call it a Bohemian alternative to the Ivies. "It takes a very special [read: liberal] type of student," says one.
Saint Louis University St. Louis	1060-1280	69%	3.51	Panelists say it's spent a ton of money on scholarships and renovations to lure kids away from Boston College, another top Catholic school.
Syracuse University Syracuse, N.Y.	1130-1300	58%	3.5	High-profile alums like Bob Costas, and winning sports teams, help Syracuse to take "table scraps from the Ivies," according to one guidance counselor.
University of Georgia Athens, Ga.	1130-1310	62%	3.66	"In terms of profile, they've gone from zero to 60 in three years," says one panel member. Its highly publicized merit-based Hope scholarship program has helped.
University of Miami Coral Gables, Fla.	1080-1270	53%	3.9	The acceptance rate has fallen 28% in 10 years. Chalk it up to "savvy marketing and top-notch athletics," says one guidance counselor.
University of Rochester Rochester, N.Y.	1240-1410	50%	3.61	Rochester has seen a jump in applications—but cut the number of slots in its freshman class. Result: admissions rate dropped from 64% in 1990 to 50% last year.
University of San Diego San Diego	1070-1270	49%	3.71	Food magnates Joan Kroc and Jenny Craig have donated millions—and applications soared 77% in the past decade.
Vanderbilt University Nashville, Tenn.	1240-1420	55%	3.57	"There are more kids in the Southeast than ever before—and not that many schools," one counselor says.

Safest (And if you can't get into those schools...)

	MIDDLE SAT RANGE	ACCEPTANCE RATE	AVERAGE GPA	COMMENT
Elon College Elon College, N.C.	1020-1210	61%	3.54	Wouldn't have even made the list 10 years ago, but has started recruiting outside the South. Also spending millions on facilities.
Goucher College Baltimore	1070-1290	76%	3.5	It's been getting an extra boost from kids who don't get into nearby Johns Hopkins or Georgetown.

	MIDDLE SAT RANGE	ACCEPTANCE RATE	AVERAGE GPA	COMMENT
Gustavus Adolphus College St. Peter, Minn.	1100-1350	77%	3.62	Embarked on major renovations after a big tornado ripped through campus a few years ago. And the school hasn't been shy about publicizing them.
Rochester Institute of Technology Rochester, N.Y.	1130-1300	68%	3.75	Riding the tech wave. Applications are up 114% since 1990.
Rollins College Winter Park, Fla.	1080-1260	71%	3.4	On the plus side: a lovely manmade lake. Downside: "Orlando," says one panelist, bemoaning the nearby culture.
Southern Methodist University Dallas	1060-1250	82%	3.19*	It's taken a lot of scholarship money for SMU to put its athletic scandals behind it.
St. Olaf College Northfield, Minn.	1190-1370	71%	3.7	One of the first schools to send out regional admissions recruiters. Average SATs have gone up 70 points.
University of Denver Denver	1010-1220	78%	3.1	One of two schools in the country with a formal program to wine and dine high-school guidance counselors. It's paid off: Applications are up 52% since 1990.
University of Wisconsin Madison, Wis.	1180-1350	73%	3.4	Now that it's almost impossible for nonresidents to get into Michigan, Wisconsin "is wickedly popular," says one guidance counselor.
University of Vermont Burlington, Vt.	1080-1260	80%	3.2	Vermont's done a lot of national recruiting lately. But "they're looking for kids with the money to pay," says one expert.
Xavier University Cincinnati	1030-1250	88%	3.49	Thanks, in part, to Cincinnati Reds owner Carl Linder, the school has a new basketball pavilion, student center and dorms.

*According to Princeton Review; other figures are reported by the schools. Most figures are approximate and are based on class that entered fall 2000. To account for the recentering of SAT scores, we recalculated old scores to match up with the new system.

on facilities, doubled scholarships—and seen applications jump 44 percent. Other schools have launched marketing and scholarship programs to attract top students.

DECIPHERING THE ADMISSIONS PROCESS

With competition getting stiffer, students across the country are jumping through more hoops than ever in search of a fat envelope.

College admissions were supposed to be getting easier, with baby boomers having fewer children than their parents. But people didn't count on the "echo boom," where boomers delayed having kids so long that their children are only now teenagers. As a result, while the number of high-school graduates fell until about 1994, it shot up about 12 percent over the next five years. The U.S. Department of Education projects an additional 10 percent increase in the coming decade. The competition is also tougher because so many parents of the 90s could afford everything from fancy summer schools to SAT prep for their kids. And there's another problem: Critics say some schools are trying to gin up more applications so that their well-publicized rejection rates will seem higher. A big piece of this has been the Internet, which allows students to churn out dozens of applications.

Given the gridlock at top colleges, what actually helps kids get in? Here are a few tips we culled:

1. Play the oboe and play it well. The old ideal of the football player–Latin scholar–thespian is passé. Many schools now prefer to see a lot of talent in a specific field, though exactly what they're looking for varies. Colleges are looking for a well-rounded class, not well-rounded kids: They need some math geniuses, actresses, and a tuba player.

2. For women, play a sport. The reason: Title IX of the education law, mandating that colleges attempt to offer varsity athletic slots and scholarships in numbers proportionate to their male and female enrollments, or face penalties. That has many colleges hunting for enough women's sports and competitors to offset football, where the NCAA permits 85 scholarships for every roster.

3. Move to Iowa. Don't laugh: Schools prefer a geographically diverse class. But school officials say they can spot a fake right away: families that use vacation or relatives' homes as their address. A spokesman for Swarthmore says the admissions office would check with an applicant's high school if it had any doubts.

4. Get a life. Flip as it sounds, this was the strongest message we heard. Some schools are urging kids to stop frantically amassing extracurriculars—or even take a year off. A survey by the National Association for College Admission Counseling found that extracurriculars ranked ninth in importance, behind grades in college-prep courses (first), teacher recommendations (sixth) and even the interview (eighth).

5. Demonstrate interest. Sometimes prospective students with SAT scores and grades well above the average are turned away if they haven't bothered to interview with the school. The judgment: They won't come if accepted. Spurning them is a way to manage the "yield rate"—the percentage of accepted applicants who then enroll, used by college guidebooks, bond-ratings agencies and prospective faculty as a measure of the college's appeal. To lower the risk of being rejected by a safety school, make contacts with the school—arrange interviews

THE DEMISE OF THE GPA

Many colleges increasingly don't place much weight on grade-point averages. The problem is that GPAs—always somewhat erratic because curriculums differ so much—have in some cases become almost meaningless as high schools experiment with ways to measure students. Some high schools give extra weight to grades in more difficult or advanced-placement courses. Other schools are either loath to measure students at all with traditional grades.

To try to cut through this hodgepodge, colleges around the country are coming up with their own formulas to recalculate each applicant's GPA. One strategy—used by Emory University and the University of California system, among others—is to drop the pluses and minuses alongside letter grades. (So a B-plus in trigonometry becomes a B.) Another approach is to disregard the applicant's entire freshman year of high school. Some schools, like Georgetown University and Haverford College in Pennsylvania, now go a step further—throwing out the GPA altogether and relying instead on the student's class rank. In the past couple of years, Johns Hopkins began recalculating GPA by throwing out "nonacademic" courses like art or music, unless such a course shows academic rigor, as in advanced-placement art history or AP studio art.

The upshot is that it is now often impossible for students to assess the admissions power of their grades unless they know the system used by each college they are applying to. Colleges say that in most cases GPAs wind up dropping after the recalculation. So for some high-school students, a 4.0 might be worth far less than they thought. The high-school transcript of a student with lots of pluses next to his grades could mean more to Johns Hopkins, for example, which takes those shades into account in its recalculation.

In addition, since colleges like Emory don't give credit in their formula for difficult courses, it may not make sense for a student already taking a decent dose of APs to overload on them and risk a low grade.

Of course, none of this means that high-school grades don't matter. Many colleges continue to look more favorably on applicants who take challenging classes, even if they don't factor that into their GPA formula. And, of course, good grades can improve students' odds of getting academic scholarships and grants.

Still, students should ask colleges point-blank whether and how they do the recalculations. In the case of courses such as art or religion, which may not be counted in the GPA formulas, students can ask their high-school counselors to write a letter vouching for its credibility as a rigorous course. It carries sway with some schools.

and campus overnight visits and let them know when you visit, even if it's just for a day.

6. **Spend a summer with us.** A growing number of schools, like Brandeis and Harvard, are trying to get to know potential applicants by offer-

ing summer programs. Some let high-school kids take college courses and earn college credit.

7. Take Advanced Placement courses—college-level courses—with optional AP exams. AP courses have standardized curriculums and national tests—making it easier for administrators to compare students against each other. Plus they're more challenging. AP tests can also allow students to place out of a language requirement or to place students in harder courses. There are more than 30. If a high school doesn't offer AP courses, a student can go to colleges or community colleges to take harder courses.

Bonus Tip: Keep your paper trail. Students should keep a copy of everything, including notes or e-mails from admissions offices, personal ID numbers and passwords and cancelled checks. At every step, from taking the SAT to filling out an application, keep the student's name consistent (Kate versus Katy). Make sure colleges received all supporting documents.

BUYING YOUR WAY IN

To attract prospective donors, colleges sometimes bend admissions standards to make space for children from rich or influential families. A big donation—or the prospect of one—doesn't guarantee admission, but it does put applicants on the priority list of the college's fundraising, or development, office. The question for many parents is: How big is "big"?

The price for special treatment rises with the college's endowment. Educational consultants say a five-figure donation—as low as $20,000—is enough to draw the attention of a liberal-arts college with an endowment in the hundreds of millions. That's a relatively modest sum compared with the $140,000-plus parents pay for four years of tuition and housing. At an exclusive college, it can take at least $50,000 with some assurance that future donations will be even greater. At the top-25 universities, a minimum of $100,000 is required; for the top 10, at least $250,000 and often seven figures. Parents who aren't that flush can compensate by pledging stock or a portion of their estate through various deferred-giving arrangements.

At Duke University and some other colleges, names of these "development applicants" are brought to the attention of the admissions office, which typically has reviewed the applicants already without regard to wealth—and may have tentatively rejected them. These students are then judged by admissions on a lesser academic standard—not whether they can excel, but whether they can graduate. Still, admissions may turn them down. At some institutions, that decision is final. At Duke, if development and admissions can't resolve a case, the student's fate is referred to the provost. Even when turned down, development applicants are often treated with kid gloves. Duke and other universities sometimes encourage them to reapply after a year at another college or school.

The development edge for children of prospective donors is a separate factor in admissions from the better-known boost for alumni children, often known as "legacies." But since major donors tend to be alumni, the two preferences often overlap. At some schools, the development and alumni offices may provide separate lists of priority applicants to admissions; elsewhere, the lists may be combined.

College administrators are reluctant to discuss such preferences. But when pressed, Duke and others argue that tuition alone doesn't cover the cost of education, while donations underwrite scholarships, faculty salaries and other expenses. They also say they admit only students who can flourish.

Educational consultants say it's a good idea for parents to pave the way early. Donate at least $2,500 to $5,000 annually—even sporadically—to the favored school even before the child is old enough to apply. Development offices look kindly on consistent givers, in part because the influential *U.S. News & World Report* rankings use the percentage of alumni who donate as an indicator of student satisfaction. And a philanthropic track record boosts hope for future donations.

The extent of an applicant's legacy preference depends on the family's current prosperity as well as its history of giving and service to the college. Service may include

TIPS ON BUYING YOUR WAY IN

1. **Give.** $20,000 is enough to draw the attention of a liberal-arts college. At top-25 universities, a minimum of $100,000 is required; at top-10 schools, from $250,000 to $1 million.

2. **Be Tactful.** Parents should work through an intermediary—such as a friend on the college's board—to speak to the development office about the family's interest in contributing.

3. **Hint Broadly.** List a parent's occupation as "private investor" or "founder," or give the home address of an estate.

4. **Express Yourself.** Suggested topic for admissions essay: "How I learned the value of philanthropy at an early age."

committee memberships, fund-raising, interviewing prospective students and other volunteer duties.

If the parents are big donors to their child's secondary school—preferably five figures—that school's development officer may be willing to alert a university counterpart to the family's philanthropic track record. It's even more effective, but also more time-consuming, to join the prep school's board. Another relevant connection: if a parent is employed by or sits on the board of a corporation or foundation that the university hopes will donate.

A BACK-DOOR ROUTE TO COLLEGE

Community colleges are emerging as a surprising back-door route to admission to top universities. Long maligned as places for students who can't cut it at a more-rigorous campus, two-year colleges in a number of states are becoming official feeder schools to highly competitive public universities. In California, for example, students who complete two years at an accredited community college are guaranteed admission to one of the state's four-year schools (though they may not get their first choice). Other community colleges are raising their academic standards, making it less of a leap for elite universities to consider their graduates when they apply for transfers.

A number of community colleges are striking agreements with big universities to make transferring easier. At Blinn College in Brenham, Texas, some students are guaranteed admission to Texas A&M University if they meet certain grades. Some universities promise to give transfer applications extra attention. The University of Virginia says it gives less weight to the high-school transcripts of applicants who complete two years at a community college. In some cases, applications from local community-college students are actually accepted at a higher rate than those from high-schoolers. Some universities explicitly tell students who didn't make the admissions cut to try again after attending a community college.

Of course, the student experience is often very different between two- and four-year schools. Virtually all students at community colleges are commuters, leaving campus life short on clubs, sports and other extracurricular activities. And many of the students are more interested in getting enough credits for a particular license or job.

But at the very least, the growing clout of community colleges offers a new way to approach application season. Now, instead of settling for a more obscure four-year school or taking a year off to reapply, you may be able to take the community-college detour. Ask for statistics on how easy it is to transfer, and find out how well community-college transfers do compared with students already enrolled.

THE NEXT STEP: COMPARING PACKAGES, APPEALING AN OFFER

After you hear from schools, there is a great deal you can do to jockey for a better deal—you can appeal a rejection and tease out a better financial-aid offer.

When you receive offers, take the time to sift through them to make sure you're maximizing the amount of aid. If you're disappointed with a school's offer, you may be able to sweeten the deal. Although colleges usually cringe at the word "negotiation," most are open to taking another look at your offer if you've got good reasons for requesting a review—particularly if the student in question has stellar credentials.

Your aid will typically consist of a mixture of scholarships, grants, loans and work/study programs. At the most basic level, you'll want to subtract the aid award from the total cost of attendance to arrive at your bottom-line expenses, otherwise known as your "family's expected contribution."

In order to make direct comparisons across offers, you'll need to strip out any awards that aren't based on meeting specific financial criteria, such as unsubsidized Stafford loans and PLUS loans, which more schools are rolling into their aid packages.

Another way to compare offers is to compute the cost of just the gift aid, such as grants and scholarships. Subtracting that aid from education costs is another way to measure your out-of-pocket expenses.

If you find large discrepancies between offers, it's possible that the school offering your teen less money may be missing information. In that case, you may be able to improve your package by appealing your aid offer.

A "professional judgment review" is the process by which colleges can make adjustments to students' aid packages in cases involving unusual circumstances. If a parent loses his or her job, for example, the financial-aid office can decide to use estimated-income information for the award year instead of the actual income figures from the base year. It's best to send supporting documentation—ideally from independent third parties—along with your request for review.

About 47 percent of all professional judgment reviews resulted in increases in students' total aid awards, according to a 2001 survey conducted by the National Association of Student Financial Aid Administrators. Moreover, 40 percent of four-year private colleges and 32 percent of four-year public schools said they were willing to make changes in aid packages based on new information provided by students and their families. A handful of schools may even match other offers, usually from schools that the college considers to be its peers.

Even if you don't get more aid, there may be other ways you can improve your offer. Students who see their aid package reduced because they have a lot of outside scholarships can ask the aid office to reduce the amount of loans before the grants are touched.

Take full advantage of any scholarships and grants, since you don't have to pay back those funds. If you must borrow, exhaust federal loans first, since interest rates are low. And keep in mind that even after you accept an aid award, you can always reapply for aid throughout the academic year.

THE DREADED WAIT LIST

All colleges wait-list applicants, meaning if perhaps enough people who were actually admitted to the school decline or drop out, you might still get in. But many students who end up on the wait list—particularly if it's the college they're dying to get into—are crushed. And it is true: For the vast majority of wait-listers the list is a dead end. Still, for students who are still pinning their hopes on a certain college, there are things you can do to improve your chances of getting off the list and into school:

1. **If you're put on a wait list, send a concise letter expressing interest in attending**—and pass along any impressive senior-year grades, new awards or achievements the admissions office didn't know about. Getting a favorite teacher to dash off a fresh letter of recommendation may also score some points.

2. **Don't appear desperate.** Applicants who land on the wait list shouldn't call or e-mail the school more than once a week, and parents

shouldn't call at all, college counselors say. A campus visit can help, but be low-key about it.

3. Students who are on more than one wait list need to be careful. Playing schools against each other can backfire. They may communicate with each other.

4. Finally, be prudent. Don't pin all your hopes on getting selected from a wait list. Accept an offer elsewhere; you can change your mind later.

APPEALING YOUR REJECTION

Each year, thousands of rejected students get a second shot at being admitted to college, thanks to an option increasingly available at many state and private schools. It's called an "appeal," and most colleges aren't especially eager to let you know about it.

Public universities are more likely to have formal appeals processes, as they receive state funds and are more accountable to the public than private colleges. A number of private schools also consider appeals. They include Georgetown and Brown universities, though they tend to mention it only as a last resort when rejected applicants or their parents call to complain. The number of appeals granted varies widely from school to school, from zero in a typical year at Duke to fully one-third of the total requests submitted at the University of Minnesota–Twin Cities.

Colleges vary in their appeals protocols. The University of Michigan, of Ann Arbor, Michigan, posts information about its appeals process on its Web site. Other schools, such as the University of Texas at Austin, simply ask for a letter of appeal from the student, accompanied by any supporting documentation, such as any outstanding grades they haven't already submitted and perhaps a fresh letter of recommendation. In addition, some personal matter that may have affected academic performance, such as a personal tragedy or illness, could make a difference at many schools.

THE "WINK" LETTER: USING IT AS LEVERAGE

In increasing numbers, colleges are wooing their top choices with notes of praise and hints of acceptance letters and scholarship money to come. The idea is to win their affections by getting them some good news before the competition does. This courtship, which can take place up to several months before formal acceptance letters hit students' mailboxes, comes in various forms: everything from "likely" letters—which tell students that they're likely to get admitted—to "love" letters, or handwritten notes from admissions offices complimenting a student's essay or some other aspect of the application.

Most Ivy League schools generally send out such letters only when pursuing an athlete who may be getting sports scholarships from non-Ivy institutions. The Ivies are bound by a rule that requires them to mail out acceptance letters no earlier than April 2. But in some cases, the "likely" letters don't outright admit the applicant, they just hint at it.

All of this presents high-school seniors with some new options as they're shopping around. Some students use their letter as leverage to get more aid from a second choice. Still, students who get promises of acceptance as well as scholarship money should be careful not to accept too soon. Wait until the other schools send their offers and then fax them the original offer from the likely letter and see if they can match it or do better.

GRAD SCHOOL

WHEN TO GO AND HOW TO TACKLE THE COST

Going back to school midcareer often involves financial sacrifices that affect the whole family. Still, there are things you can do to make it more manageable.

Calculate your need. The first step is to figure out how much money you'll need to attend school, how much debt you can reasonably afford to carry and, most important, how much time you anticipate being without a regular paycheck while you pursue that degree. To figure out how much debt you can shoulder, **FinAid.org** offers calculators that will crunch the numbers for master's and doctoral candidates.

To get a feel for how long you'll be out of work, contact a financial-aid counselor at the school of your choice and discuss your goals. Determine whether it's feasible to attend night school and continue to work. Also, many fields of study require extended internships. Ask for guidance on how well these jobs pay, if at all.

Now add in all the collateral costs: Will you need more child care? Will your commuting costs increase? Will you have to pay for your own health care? When you total it up, sticker shock may ensue. But relax, there is funding available to help ease the burden.

1. Search for financial aid. One big mistake most adult students make is assuming they make too much money to get financial assistance. (For tips, see our section on college scholarships.)

2. Ask your current employer. More companies are adding tuition-assistance programs to their benefits packages in an effort to attract and retain top talent. Some 81 percent of 960 companies surveyed offered some type of tuition-assistance plan in 2002, according to outsourcing and consulting firm Hewitt Associates in Lincolnshire, Illinois. But beware of strings. Many employers require assurances that you're enhancing your current skills, not training for a new career. And a growing number of companies are adapting the military's take on higher education: You sign a contract that says if your employer pays two to four years of higher-education costs, you'll continue working at the company for an equal or greater number of years.

3. Unionize. If you, a spouse or a parent is part of one of more than 40,000 labor unions, you may be eligible for additional tuition-assistance programs, grants or scholarships.

4. Consider loans. Despite low interest rates on federal student loans, many professionals may not be able to take advantage of them due to government loan limits. Many postgraduate students rely on private alternative loan programs from commercial lenders, such as Citigroup and American Express. But these programs typically charge a percentage point or two more than federal loans.

Tip: Leave that nest egg alone. Education is a long-term investment in yourself, so it might seem like a no-brainer to tap your 401(k) to pay for it—whether you stay with your current employer or not. But borrowing from your retirement savings should be your last resort. And don't forget, you have to be able to pay it back quickly—typically within five years—or you'll get hit with personal income taxes and a 10 percent penalty on the money.

DOES AN M.B.A. PAY OFF?

Traditionally, the M.B.A. degree has guaranteed students a fresh start in a new career. But now with so many graduates competing for so few jobs, recruiters can afford to be very choosy. They are less inclined to take a risk with a career-switcher when there are plenty of M.B.A. graduates with past experience in their industries or job functions.

Many potential M.B.A. students are even questioning the degree's value, and fewer are applying to business school. Why, they wonder, should they invest more than $100,000 in a degree that no longer ensures them a lucrative new career?

Even some M.B.A. types are starting to question the bottom line: One Stanford professor concluded that a business degree often didn't mean truly higher pay, but instead effectively got M.B.A. graduates treated as a few years more senior for compensation purposes. And big loans may be a crushing burden.

However, the Graduate Management Admission Council surveyed 4,700 graduating M.B.A. students worldwide in 2002 and found an average salary increase of 64 percent from their last full-time job before school. For students in the United States, the average salary rose 54 percent to $77,000 from $50,000 pre-M.B.A.

Recruiters and career-services directors advise students not to be too ambitious. The best strategy: Change either your industry or your job function, but not both.

Carefully check out your business school's recommendation with potential employers, and keep an eye on the ball. Once they're admitted to business school, career-changers don't have a minute to waste these days. They can't rely any longer on the career-placement office and on-campus recruiters. Instead, it's all about hustle and ingenuity. Students must choose an industry and job function to focus on even before they crack open their first textbook. Then the hard work starts—networking with alumni, cold-calling prospective employers and figuring out which skills are most transferable from their past work life. Getting the right internship is a critical first step. Some

M.B.A. graduates even take unpaid internships to help fill the void on their résumés.

Some students try executive M.B.A. and other part-time programs, which cater to mid-career executives. The part-time programs, which typically last two years, allow executives to continue working full-time. Classes often are taught on weekends, and some programs include course work via the Internet. To retain their most promising managers, companies have been quite willing to sponsor employees in such programs, which charge as much as $115,000 for the two years.

ENTER THOSE SCHOOL COMPETITIONS

In the tough job market for those with M.B.A.s, many recruiters say the edge in landing jobs and plum internships increasingly belongs to students who have participated in business-school case competitions. These are typically contests sponsored by a school or an organization for teams of candidates for a master's in business administration who have to solve some sort of business dilemma in a certain time frame. There is usually a cash prize—and a chance for students to schmooze and network with company executives. The competitions give students the chance to solve "real world" problems. That is why more recruiters are also using them as a way of identifying top candidates, business schools say. Companies want hires who can hit the ground running at a time when employers don't want to spend money on training.

For more information on the top M.B.A. programs, please see *The Wall Street Journal Guide to the Top Business Schools, 2004.*

ONLINE EDUCATION

CYBER-CLASSROOMS

The Internet is particularly useful for working people with long hours and family obligations, who can't deal with rigid course schedules at universities and colleges. Most students use the Internet to complete graduate degrees they need to win a promotion, take a few courses to fill in gaps in their résumés, bone up on the latest technology, improve their management skills or finish the continuing education required by their professions.

SOURCES FOR COURSES

International Centre for Distance Learning; icdl.open.ac.uk. The U.K.-based site lists 31,000 courses at 1,000 colleges around the world. The site is affiliated with Open University, a program encouraging lifelong learning.

Cyberu; my.cyberu.com. Lists online classes, training programs and degree programs from colleges, universities and training providers around the world.

MindEdge; mindedge.com. Includes both online and traditional in-classroom courses from universities, colleges, training programs and learning Web sites.

Western Governors University; wgu.edu. Lists courses from universities, colleges and training organizations around the country.

WorldWideLearn; worldwidelearn.com. Lists courses from universities, colleges and training companies around the world.

The good news: a growing number of rich and satisfying courses. Many institutions offer accredited degree programs, from Stanford University in California to Seton Hall University in Orange, New Jersey. And many more colleges simply offer lists of classes, both accredited and nonaccredited, that students can participate in over the Internet. For instance, the University of Phoenix Online caters exclusively to working professionals and offers 90 percent of the degree programs found at the institution's brick-and-mortar campuses.

Despite the Internet's reputation as a cheaper alternative for just about everything, it isn't always less expensive to go to school online. The cost can range from nothing for the basic science-related courses offered on **WebMD.com** to $95,000 in tuition and assorted fees for the Duke M.B.A. global executive program at Duke's Fuqua School of Business.

The bad news: Finding the right class can be a monumental research task. The term "online education" is used to describe everything from semester-long seminars to 20-minute tutorials. Some so-called courses are little more than how-to articles served up on webpages, offering little or no teacher contact. It's important to know what your goals are and to read course materials carefully.

Seek out classes with a detailed syllabus, an experienced professor and a high level of interactivity. Many course providers provide a sample lesson: Use these demonstrations to see what you're getting. Some sites and course directories will refund your tuition if you're not satisfied, so be sure you understand the site's policy before enrolling.

Before you sign up, read the course's technical requirements carefully. Online students usually need ready access to a good computer, and a fast Internet connection. Make sure the site provides an e-mail or 800 number for technical support in case you have problems connecting or downloading course software.

Be aware that often students never actually meet professors or classmates. Many programs offer little in the way of such student services as job placement, internships or counseling. So above all, online students must be disciplined and self-motivated.

Also, be aware that the growth of Internet courses has caused an increase in diploma mills issuing fake degrees. It's helpful to seek out accredited programs to ensure the college's academic quality and financial solvency. The Council for Higher Education Accreditation Web site (**chea.org**) lists regional accreditation organizations.

CHAPTER ELEVEN

LIFE IS A TIGHTROPE

BALANCING WORK AND FAMILY

Trying to balance family and work isn't just a daily exercise—it's hourly: Your son has a play date that ends at 6:00, but just as you're leaving to pick him up the client you've been waiting all day to hear from finally calls. It's hard enough when everything is running on schedule, but when children get sick or you have to travel for work, the stress can be overwhelming.

What makes the juggling act even more challenging is the psychological battle, sometimes called the "Mommy Wars," being waged through books with titles like *Home-Alone America* (the cover shows a woman in a business suit with a clinging toddler at her leg) and *The Mommy Myth,* whose thesis is that society has its ways of punishing working mothers. Studies about how behavioral problems in children who were in day care and how working moms can make children more assertive only add fuel to the fire.

When one parent stays home, it's also a major life change for the one who continues to work. Imagine volunteering to give up nearly half your household income, sell your toys, forgo vacations of the kind your friends enjoy, and work as if three or four lives depended on your next paycheck. Jobs are no longer nine to five, robbing you of time at home. The spouse at home can feel isolated and need more emotional support. And many solo breadwinners battle feelings of resentment, fear and frustration over their heavy loads while trying to meet expectations of being sensitive parents and spouses at home. On the other hand, the child-rearing benefits of having a parent at home can be huge. Families save on things such as child care, convenience foods, and commuting and clothing costs for a working woman. Also, many couples believe the setup simply makes their families run better.

The evenhanded approach is to acknowledge that there is no right way or real answers, only trade-offs. And that's when it's important to remember that while divvying up time for everything that's happening in your life is a challenge, having both work and family is also a blessing in that it gives your life balance. In that spirit, think of it like walking a tightrope: stay flexible. Here are some basics for maintaining that equilibrium:

1. **Begin by finding your center.** Know what you want and what you don't want and act accordingly. If you know you want to grow your career but also want to see your toddler every day, don't accept a job that requires travel 50 percent of the time and don't stay attached to a boss who demands 24/7 attention. If, on the other hand, you want to run your own business and you're married to a workaholic, accept that your children will likely spend more time with your nanny than with either you or your spouse. If you're single, don't take up the slack for colleagues with families who expect to be first out the door. Take time

for your friendships and interests outside of work. You don't need to have kids or a spouse to need balance.

2. Learn to know and respect your energy level. Some people only need four hours of sleep each night and others need seven. If you only need four hours, maybe you can write poetry or train for a marathon between 4 A.M. and 7 A.M. But if you need seven hours, try to get that much rest, and stop feeling like a slacker. Balancing is about having and doing the most you can—and enjoying yourself in the process.

STARTING AND RAISING A FAMILY

It's a truism of parenthood that you won't know how you truly feel about balancing work and family until you hold your newborn in your arms. And whatever you feel then is bound to change again when your baby starts preschool or when you suddenly land a dream job.

Still, you shouldn't wait until after childbirth to think about how you plan to balance work and family and what you expect of your spouse. Premarital education programs are adding this topic to their training materials and some couples are negotiating prenuptial work-and-family balance agreements. **You should at least have a discussion with your partner about your expectations.**

If you are a dual-career couple, you might agree to both avoid jobs that demand workaholic hours, or to plan on the lower-earning spouse switching to flexible time or part-time work once you have kids, or to take turns making each of your careers a priority.

Some Topics for Discussion

1. **How many work hours are too many?**
2. **What do you expect of your spouse when it comes to sharing housework and child care?**
3. **Will you transfer for a job, and if so, whose job and how often?**
4. **What will you do if one of you is laid off?**

For help talking over these issues, three organizations offer good premarital exercises to help couples assess their values: Foccus, 877-883-5422; Life Innovations, at **lifeinnovations.com** and the Relate Institute, Utah, at **relate.byu.edu.**

BEING SMART ABOUT YOUR RIGHTS

Start planning your family leave from work early in your pregnancy. Begin by learning your rights. The federal family leave law allows 12 weeks unpaid leave to new parents, plus a continuation of health benefits during a leave and a guaranteed return to the same or an equivalent job. Here are things you need to know:

1. **To qualify, you must work for an employer with 50 or more employees or at a location with at least 50 employees within 75 miles.**

2. **Your employer can deny you leave if you haven't worked there for the last 12 months and for at least 1,250 hours in the past year.**

3. **You also may be ineligible for protection if you are among your employer's top 10 percent of employees based on pay.**

4. **The law also doesn't protect you from being laid off during or after family leave if your job is eliminated because of cost cuts.**

LIFE AFTER BABY

Physicians and psychologists recommend that new parents, and especially mothers, take adequate time off from work for their own physical and mental well-being. Mothers who take at least three months off after childbirth show 15 percent fewer symptoms of postpartum depression after they return to work, compared with mothers who take six weeks or less, according to a recent study by the National Bureau of Economic Research, Cambridge, Massachusetts.

Since few companies offer paid family leave, you need to plan financially for time off. Patch together as much vacation time, sick days and other paid time off as your employer allows and save that for your leave. To build up savings, you could also temporarily decrease 401(k) contributions, or set up a credit line.

If your company has a short-term disability policy, new mothers usually are eligible for six to eight weeks of full or partial pay. If you live in New York, New Jersey, Rhode Island, Hawaii or California, you may be eligible for disability pay from the state. And don't rule out negotiating paid leave from your employer. If you are highly valued, your employer may agree to provide at least some paid time off in order to guarantee your return.

Then again, you may have a boss who pressures you to shorten your leave or keep working from home—even though under the law you are entitled to uninterrupted time off. Stretched thin by layoffs or dependent on your contribution, some bosses try to convince pregnant employees that they will sacrifice a promotion or be denied a comparable job unless they take just minimal time off and rush back to work. Or they call new mothers at home, requesting that they participate in conference calls and other work. Here are strategies to cope with that:

1. Learn to set limits. Start by anticipating and offering solutions to your boss's potential objections and concerns.

2. By your fifth or sixth month of pregnancy, develop a plan for how your work can be handled while you are on leave.

3. List jobs and projects that can be set aside until you return and others that can be delegated. Then get your boss and coworkers to agree and even put the plan in writing. You may have to make some trade-offs— offering, for example, to take on some extra work from coworkers on your return to give them a breather.

SETTLING DISPUTES

If you are covered by the federal family leave law and believe you have been denied leave or discriminated on the job because of taking it, you may have cause for filing a suit. It isn't easy to sue your employer, however. Employment-discrimination charges are hard to prove and often get dismissed. Even if you win, you may find yourself blackballed from other jobs. Still, if you think you've been treated unfairly, you should seek legal help.

HELPFUL RESOURCES IN PLANNING AND MANAGING A LEAVE

1. *Family and Medical Leave in a Nutshell,* by Kurt H. Decker. A consumer's guidebook to federal family-leave law.

2. *The Best Friend's Guide to Maternity Leave,* by Betty Holcomb. This book lays out strategies for arranging childbirth leave, including paid leave, and coping with the transition back to work.

3. *The Job-Survival Hotline 800-522-0925:* run by advocacy group 9to5, National Association of Working women and staffed by counselors who can provide information on family-leave laws in your state.

4. *Workoptions.com:* This Web site offers help planning and requesting flexible work setups that may help you arrange a gradual return to work.

Here's where to turn during a family-leave dispute:

1. **The Labor Department Wage and Hour Division (wageandhour.dol.gov): Regional offices field complaints under the Family and Medical Leave Act.**

2. **National Association of Working Women (800-522-0925): Organization operates job-survival hotline staffed by trained counselors.**

3. **National Employment Lawyers Association (nela.org): Members devote half their practice to representing employees' state bar associations.**

THE HARDEST ISSUE: FINDING GOOD CHILD CARE

How and by whom your children are cared for while you are at work will determine much of what they experience in their first years of life. It also will affect your job performance. If you spend most of your day worrying about whether your child is safe and well cared for, you won't be very effective or happy at work.

Consider child-care options before you give birth, even though you probably won't be ready to make a final decision. Visiting centers and family day-care homes and interviewing prospective nannies takes time, which you will be short of when you are first caring for an infant. And you don't want to spend all your leave searching for child care.

For help sorting out options, contact the National Association of Child Care Resource and Referral Agencies at **childcareaware.org**. They'll connect you to referral agencies in your area and also provide information on how to choose quality child care.

Quality as well as costs vary widely, depending on type, geographical region and the experience and reputation of the providers. Average prices are roughly $6,000 to $10,000 a year for child-care centers, $3,600 to $8,000 a year for a family child-care home and $18,000 to $35,000 a year for a nanny who takes care of your child in your home.

Your selection will be based on what you can afford and what is available where you live. But costly child care doesn't necessarily guarantee high quality. The $400-a-week nanny who provides the convenience of in-home care isn't worth the cost if she ignores or mistreats your child. One-to-one attention is invaluable for young children, but only if it is loving attention.

If you decide to search for a day-care center, what will matter most to your child isn't shiny toys or computers but how he or she is treated every day. It's the touchy-feely intangibles, things that you may not immediately see on a visit to a day-care center. Teachers who offer constant support with words of praise ("That's great, you did such a wonderful job"), who can help two-year-olds resolve a fight without making either of them ashamed and who give kids information that helps them feel safe ("When we play in the playground, no one can push or shove") will help your child thrive in day care. Teachers who communicate poorly and spend most of their time criticizing kids and ordering them about can cause emotional harm.

If intangibles matter so much, how can you assess day-care choices? Here are some tips:

1. **Spend time in a center you are considering and do as much observing as possible.** What do you see and hear? How are other children treated and what do they seem to be experiencing? Check your own observations by talking with other parents whose children are enrolled.

2. **Carefully assess the tangible qualities.** Classroom ratios of one adult for every three or four infants, four to six two-year-olds and seven to ten three-year-olds are recommended by the National Association for the Education of Young Children, a Washington, D.C., accreditation group. How many children are crammed into a room is also important. A day-care room, for example, with 36 toddlers and nine caregivers is bound to feel chaotic and overwhelming for your child. The association recommends groups of no more than six to eight for infants, eight to twelve for two-year-olds and fourteen to twenty for three-year-olds.

3. **Know the teachers.** What's the experience and longevity of teachers? How do they seem to get along? The last place you want your child is in a center full of quarrelsome, inexperienced caregivers.

4. **What is the turnover among children**? Do they tend to stay for several years or is turnover rapid, which could signal problems?

5. **Be sensible about the location.** How far is the day-care center from your home or place of work, and what are its operating hours? Do

BELLY TALK AND WOMB MUSIC: DOES IT WORK?

Eager to get her fetus on the fast track, a pregnant woman recently sent an e-mail to anthropologist Sallie Han. Ms. Han is studying what she calls "belly talk," the phenomenon of parents-to-be talking to their yet-to-be-born children. Proponents claim that reading books and playing music for a fetus give it a head start educationally. The woman who sent the e-mail wanted to know how she could "maximize" her baby's time in the womb.

As parents, we're hammered by experts telling us that we shouldn't wait too long to have crucial conversations with our children about drugs, sex, war and death. We're encouraged to talk to them in adult language even when they are infants, so we can build their self-esteem and widen their minds. But this chattering to offspring is increasingly beginning just moments after conception.

Store shelves have been filling up with more sophisticated gadgets that help parents speak to their still-unborn kids. The BabyPlus Prenatal Education System, at about $150, takes fetuses through a 16-week course on rhythmic sounds. Its marketing pitch: "You're never too young to learn. (In fact, you don't even have to be born.)" The WombSong Prenatal Sound System ($50) lets parents address their fetuses via microphone.

"More parents want to give their kids a leg up," says Ms. Han of the University of Michigan's Sloan Center for the Ethnography of Everyday Life. "Belly talk is a symptom of the anxiety we have today about parenting."

Parents are no longer just cooing to their unborn kids. One California obstetrician has started a program called "Prenatal University," where parents follow a detailed conversation regimen to stimulate their fetuses. And a range of other products—from the book *Prenatal Classroom* to the CD *Ultrasound—Music for the Unborn Child*—insist that fetuses can be intellectually enriched.

That's news to Anthony DeCasper, the University of North Carolina at Greensboro psychologist whose research helped give birth to the belly-talk movement. During the 1980s, he began conducting studies with a feeding apparatus that belly-talk enthusiasts dubbed "the suck-o-meter." It allowed newborns wearing headphones to select a voice by sucking either faster or slower. Most babies chose their mother's voice over a stranger's, and newborns who heard *The Cat in the Hat* while in the womb preferred that book to others.

Dr. DeCasper's research shows that babies in utero hear and recognize their mothers' voices. But others have overstated the results of his work, using it to advocate for "prenatal education" and "fetal-stimulation" devices. His take on belly talk: "It won't make your baby smarter, healthier or better." In research circles, studies that claim otherwise are considered very controversial. And overseas—where belly talk is far less prevalent than in the United States—there is some eye-rolling over Americans' fetal expectations. Dr. DeCasper worries that belly-talk devices could damage babies' hearing. He also wonders whether belly-talking parents will consider themselves failures if their kids turn out to be average.

Last week, I visited a yoga class for pregnant women in Ann Arbor, Michigan. Most of the nine women I met weren't sure belly talk helps their fetuses educationally, but they do it because it feels good to say loving things. One mom-to-be told me she reads the newspaper aloud. Another's husband gives "music lessons" to their fetus—from Beethoven to Pink Floyd—through headphones. The baby seems to move to the music, she says. Karen Germano told me she was two weeks overdue with her last child, so she kept talking to her tummy, saying, "Come out, little one." She believes her baby heard her and complied. Amy Higgs said she doesn't feel inhibited talking to the baby, except sometimes while riding a public bus.

Some grandparents-to-be—having never belly talked when they were expecting—are uncomfortable with the concept, the women said. Today's husbands also vary in their enthusiasm for the practice. A woman at the yoga class said her husband finds it weird and cannot get beyond "Hi." But in Ms. Han's new study, one husband pressed his lips close to his wife's navel and, speaking slowly to be understood, said: "I love you."

Ms. Han finds that parents-to-be are often torn between their urge to get started as early as possible on the parent-child dialogue and their fears that they're pushing their kids too hard. Some worry: If I don't belly talk, could it lower my child's Apgar score at birth, or his SATs later? Will overzealous prenatal reading foster a love of literature or turn my child away from books?

This is misplaced energy, argues psychologist Gordon Neufeld, coauthor of *Hold On to Your Kids: Why Parents Need to Matter More Than Peers.* Belly talk might help Mom and Dad feel like they've bonded with their kids, but it's more crucial that children grow up feeling attached to their parents, he says.

At the yoga class, those women who already have older children said they've cut back on the belly talk this time around. They're busy talking to toddlers, or trying to talk to their teens. They hope their not-yet-born children will flourish even without this prenatal attention.

Dr. DeCasper is reassuring. "The irony is that you don't have to talk to your fetus to have it exposed to language," he says. "In the normal course of daily life—when you talk to your husband, your sister, the mailman—those speech sounds reach your fetus."

But whether a mother is cooing a love song or thanking the mailman, he says, "the fetus doesn't know the difference."

—JEFFREY ZASLOW

PRE-NATAL PRATTLING: PRODUCTS FOR PARENTS WHO WANT TO CHAT WITH THEIR YET-TO-BE-BORN KIDS

Deluxe First Sounds Gift Set, $49.95; both parents can listen (and talk) to baby simultaneously.

The BabyPlus Prenatal Education System, $149.95; fetuses receive a 16-week regimen of rhythmic sounds.

WombSong Prenatal Sound System, $49.99; talk or sing into the womb via microphone; listen via stethoscope.

these match your work schedule? The seemingly loving, caring place you've found simply won't do if getting your child back and forth presents a logistical nightmare.

6. What's the center's attitude toward you? Are parents encouraged to visit the center whenever they want, to nurse or be with their children? Does the center welcome parental involvement in activities or in setting policies?

THE NANNY CHASE

If you think evaluating a child-care center is difficult, the nanny challenge can be downright daunting. A teacher at a day-care center looking after your child as part of a class of 10 is one thing. But nannies often become "part of the family"—or at least they move into your home for part if not all of the day. Their one-on-one relationship with you and your child is fraught with an extra measure of prospect and peril.

There are several routes to finding a nanny. A main one: nanny agencies. For parents seeking live-in or full-time child care in their homes, nanny agencies generally charge an application fee plus about 10 percent of a nanny's first-year salary. For this, the better ones are supposed to perform the following tasks:

1. **Interview you extensively to get a keen sense of your particular needs and the kind of person you are looking for, whether college-aged au pair or an older Mary Poppins type.**

2. **Interview, from their roster of candidates, applicants who seem best suited to you and your child's needs.**

3. **Conduct extensive background checks on potential applicants.**

4. **Provide you with a choice of candidates to consider.**

Tip: Alas, not all agencies are created equal and experience shows that some don't perform the exhaustive background checks on their pool of candidates that might catch serious problems. So if possible, seek an agency that belongs to the Alliance of Professional Nanny Agencies, a professional group that requires members to do rigorous background checks and meet other standards.

THE NETWORKING OPTION

If you want to avoid the cost of an agency, seek referrals from friends who've had good experiences. If their children are school-age, they may be ready to pass on a nanny. Or their nanny, who likely circulates with other nannies, may know someone looking for a new job.

You can also place an ad in a local paper, or scan listings on the Internet. Postings for nannies on **craigslist.org,** which has free bulletin boards in 23 cities that list everything from jobs to personal ads, have been rising steadily. Other sites such as **4nannies.com** charge a fee to contact candidates who post résumés.

Caution: Ads and online boards draw many good candidates but they also attract job-seekers who can't pass a background check or be placed by agencies because of incompetence. You may want to see a résumé before you decide whether to do an in-person interview, or at least do some screening on the phone, asking the applicant about past experience. You may also want to schedule an initial interview away from your home and not bring your child with you to that first meeting.

THE INTELLIGENT SNOOP: INTERVIEWING AND BACKGROUND CHECKS

Whether or not you use an agency, you should thoroughly interview references yourself for every past child-care job and verify education and non-child-care employment. And unless you use an agency that provides written documentation, you should do a background check, including Social Security and criminal records. This requires the applicant's written permission and also a lot of work on your part because you need to check for criminal records in every place where the applicant has lived.

An easier route is to hire an agency that specializes in background checks. They typically charge $125 to $250. There are also many Web sites that do background searches for less money.

Here's where to turn for help when conducting a search:

USSearch.com: offers a range of background and reference checks, including a nanny-screening service, for $39.95 to $119.95.

ChoiceTrust.com: checks a proprietary criminal-records database, court records and Social Security number, for $57.98.

MyBackgroundCheck.com: conducts and certifies background checks at the request of job applicants, for $24.95 to $76.95.

Apnaonline.org: Web site of Alliance of Professional Nanny Agencies, which lists members that must comply with its standards.

International Nanny Association: nonprofit group that includes background check agencies. Call 888-878-1477.

GIVING YOUR NANNY A SPIN

It helps to try out your child-care arrangement at least two weeks before you return to work. Even if you can't afford or don't want to start full-time child care, many centers will allow you to leave your baby for a few mornings or afternoons to get used to the surroundings. That also gives you a chance to familiarize yourself with the routine, get to know the teachers better and become used to the idea of leaving your child in the care of others. The same goes for family home-care centers. And nannies should be willing to do some babysitting before they begin full-time duty and before you return to work.

THE VIDEOTAPE DILEMMA

Is it okay to videotape your nanny?

It's not something every parent wants or needs to do to guarantee that their nanny is doing a good job, but it is legal to do in common areas of your home. Beyond the law, there are right and wrong ways to do it.

Here are the do's and don'ts:

1. **Install the camera before your nanny starts work.**

2. **Level with your nanny.** It helps, if you've used monitoring before, to simply explain that this is part of your system and isn't an act of suspicion directed at her or him personally.

3. Put the camera or cameras in public rooms only; avoid bathrooms or the nanny's bedroom.

4. Avoid secret monitoring. Many a good and responsible nanny has quit after discovering hidden cameras, considering them to be a breach of privacy and trust.

5. Stick to video only. Federal and state law generally requires the consent of another person before you audiotape a conversation. You could be running afoul of the law.

The Good News: Nannycam vendors estimate that 40 to 70 percent of nannies are dismissed after hidden cameras are installed, most often for minor offenses such as loafing or benign neglect rather than outright abuse. Furthermore, prices for in-home surveillance have dropped dramatically in recent years. Prices for a very basic camera offering remote computer access start at $130 for the Xcam2, by X10 Wireless Technology, Kent, Washington. **SpyWorld.com,** Carson City, Nevada, sells a higher-resolution camera hidden in a clock or smoke detector for $360, while Mommy Track, by Cenuco, Boca Raton, Florida, is $499 and transmits images that can be viewed over a cell phone, PDA or computer.

WORK LIFE: TAKE THIS JOB AND LOVE IT

Most of us work because we need the income. If you're also lucky enough to have a job you like, you'll have a much easier time balancing work and family. If your work is stimulating and rewarding and you like the people you work with, you won't be venting job frustrations at home, and you'll be more emotionally available to your children and spouse. You'll also feel less guilty about leaving your children each day.

In fact, studies show that what has more impact on children than the amount of time parents spend at work is how much parents' work tensions taint home life. Parents whose jobs lift their self-esteem and pay them enough to afford good child care have better-adjusted children than those parents who are unhappy about their work. So before you decide that juggling a job and family is too stressful, make sure it's not your particular job that is driving you nuts.

HOME ALONE: CARE FOR OLDER KIDS

Child-care needs change as your children grow. But children need supervision for many years, at least until they are mature and responsible enough to feel confident at home alone, rather than lonely and afraid. For most kids that doesn't happen until they are at least 10 to 12 years old. Many teens aren't ready to take care of themselves in their parents' absence, or need help to get to after-school sports and other activities.

If you're a middle-class parent of a school-age child, you're probably patching together a variety of child-care arrangements—from after-school-center care to tutoring sessions, and lessons to part-time babysitters. You may arrange flexible scheduling so you can pick up your child from school one or two days a week.

The decision about whether a child is ready to be left alone should be made one child at a time. He or she should be able to do simple jobs such as fixing a snack. He should know how to handle accidents or emergencies and whom to call for help. A parent should be able to trust the child to come home after school, to follow rules, do homework and use his time wisely. If your child does stay alone after school, you should also communicate with him from work. Schedule regular afternoon phone calls to check on homework assignments and activities and to chat about her day.

Remember, too, that a child who does fine on his own at, say, 13, may need more supervision at 14 or 15. Teens face more crises and social pressures, such as drug and alcohol use, and may need adult supervision more than a 12-year-old. Be prepared to adjust your work schedule and be more present at home when your children are teens, or hire babysitters.

FINDING A FAMILY-FRIENDLY COMPANY

How do you get behind a company's façade and find out what it's really like to work there? While selling yourself to a prospective employer, here are some things to be alert to:

1. **Watch for nonverbal signals.** A person uninterested in you during an interview is likely to be uninterested in you as an employee.

2. **Listen to what prospective employers say. Words matter.** Good bosses respect employees. Watch out for interviewers who are sarcastic, make demeaning remarks about other employees or make you feel apologetic or defensive about yourself.

3. **Wait to raise questions about work/life balance and your own family needs until you're sure an employer is interested in you.** Then ask neutral questions, such as "What's a typical workday like?" and "Is everyone on the same schedule?"

4. **Try to uncover the values that drive management.** Ask about the department's proudest accomplishment. If this elicits tales of all-nighters or your prospective boss boasts about marathon hours and not seeing his kids for weeks on end, be forewarned.

5. **Ask to talk with current employees or find former employees willing to level with you.** What do they say about the work culture and what's expected in the way of overtime, night and weekend work? How much flexibility is there to set one's own schedule?

6. **Remember that whatever a company's written policies, family-friendly practices are local, not global.** A company that is a great place to work in one department can be a nightmare six cubicles away. Some bosses demand constant face-time and dislike subordinates who leave or arrive earlier than they do; others value the quality and quantity of their employees' work, rather than where or at what hour of the day or night it is done.

BONUS TIPS

How to handle the child-care query: Most employers want to know how job candidates will juggle family and work responsibilities—but they face potential discrimination charges if they ask directly. If an interviewer asks you what kind of child care you have, instead of describing your child's day-care center, say, "I assume your concern is, am I a reliable employee, and I can assure you that I am."

If you're pregnant: Pregnant job candidates should be up front about their situation. If you conceal that you're expecting and then announce this after landing a job, your new boss is likely to feel that you were underhanded and can't be trusted. By contrast, if you state in an interview that you're pregnant and that you can manage the job well, you will be seen as honest and open.

MAKING A CURRENT EMPLOYER MORE FAMILY-FRIENDLY

Change happens at different ways at different companies. While starting an ad hoc work-family network can get you fired at one company, it could advance your career at another.

When seeking flexible scheduling, try to tie your wishes to business needs and show how changes may boost productivity. Say you want to get home by 6:30 each night, but find that you can't possibly complete your work in time to do that because much of your day is spent in meetings where little is accomplished. Suggest to your supervisor that a reduction in meetings and fewer interruptions during the day would allow you to get more and better work done.

Flexible scheduling runs the gamut from starting and leaving work an hour earlier than most employees, to compressing a 60-hour work week into four 12-hour days, to telecommuting from home once or twice a week. Some companies have formal flex policies, while others expect employees to negotiate them individually.

Here are some guidelines that will make it easier to get flex time:

1. **Do your job well and enthusiastically.** You stand a better chance of getting what you want if you consistently turn in excellent work and are willing to do extra during pressured times than if you turn in average or less-than-average work and are always the first one out the door.

2. **Try banding together with other employees.** You may have more clout negotiating family-friendly practices if you approach them as a group. That way everyone gets equal treatment and you can make sure your office is staffed as needed.

3. **Respect coworkers.** If they cover for you when you need to pick up your kids from day care or get to a doctor's appointment, you should fill in for them when they need or want time off.

WORKING FROM HOME

Telework from home is becoming common, thanks to high-speed connections to the Internet and research showing that teleworkers spend more time on job tasks than their counterparts in the office. As a result, more supervisors are doing it at least occasionally and allowing their employees the same convenience. If you aren't a factory worker, retail salesperson or customer-service employee chained to a desk, you may be able to negotiate at least some telecommuting from home—once a week, for instance, or on school snow-days when you lack child care.

PART-TIME

Is a part-time job worth it? The biggest pitfall is that you could reduce the hours you're expected to work—and your pay—but end up with no corresponding change in your workload. So it's critical that you negotiate job demands along with compensation and scheduling *before* going part-time. Otherwise, it's a recipe for being forced to squeeze five days of work into three, for three days' pay.

Here are some helpful rules to making part-time work for you:

1. Communicate often with bosses and managers. Be aware that they often assume that part-time employees lack commitment and the desire to advance.

2. Keep in close touch with colleagues when you're not in the office. Remember: The office grapevine, though it sprouts lots of useless information, can also bear crucial knowledge. You don't want to find yourself out of the loop on important issues.

3. Don't miss crucial meetings, even if they fall on your day off. The very supervisors who may have approved your part-time arrangement will most certainly notice your absences.

RETURNING TO WORK

If you've dropped out of the labor force for several years to raise kids, you may have more difficulty than you anticipated trying to jump back in. Résumé gaps don't go over well with employers who are keeping staffs lean and trying to hire only employees who need no job training or hand-holding. With advances in technology, women, as well as men who have taken even a few years off, may have fallen behind or feel out of touch. And the job-hopping of the last decade means that many of your old professional contacts, mentors and networks are dispersed.

You may be forced to take a low-level or low-paying "starter" job on reentry and then work your way up.

But there are clever ways to better position yourself for reentry.

1. **Be strategic about the volunteer work you do while out of the workforce.** Choose leadership-oriented work rather than, say, making cookies for the school bake sale. If you're in marketing, help produce a brochure for a school or community program.

2. **Keep abreast of your field.** Read industry journals, retain memberships in professional associations and stay in touch with former colleagues.

3. **Keep your skills current.** If you've been an accountant, consider doing accounting for a nonprofit organization. You can also try to land seats on nonprofit boards, where you will be called on to review personnel and finance matters (and also have a chance to make valuable contacts).

4. **Refresh your network and your networking skills.** Even if you've let all your old work alliances slip, tap into people you know well in other contexts.

5. **Try applying to smaller companies.** A smaller, entrepreneurial firm may be more opened-minded about a stay-at-home mom's skills than big corporations with a somewhat set hiring policy.

6. **Investigate nonprofit groups.** Since they often rely on volunteers, they may have more respect for a résumé filled with school and community volunteer work.

7. **Finally, check out the Occupational Outlook Handbook from the Labor Department's Bureau of Labor Statistics (bls.gov/oco/home.htm).** It lists accreditation requirements for different professions, along with salary ranges and professional organizations that you can contact.

THE BIG MOVE: AVOIDING THE RELOCATION BLUES

Moving for a job can sometimes be the path to career greatness, but it can also, especially in the short-term, be a stressful semi-disaster for you and your family. If you're asked to relocate for a job—or forced to make a move after you lose a job—be prepared to negotiate hard for the transfer package you want, remembering that there is often a direct correlation between the generosity of your moving benefits and ease of your transition. Many employers have cut back in recent years, but a boss wanting you to relocate is often willing to negotiate perks on a case-by-case basis. Along with moving allowances, make certain to ask for the "softer" supports that can help your family: counseling; job-finding help for a trailing spouse; multiple house-hunting and school-search trips and time off to get settled.

Here are some resources for relocating families:

SchoolMatch.com: The best source of school-by-school test scores, student-teacher ratios, per-pupil spending and education level of residents.

USConsumerConnection.com: Free SchoolMatch data, plus real-estate price information and trends.

HomeStore.com: Free city-by-city cost-of-living calculator and crime-rate comparisons.

BestPlaces.net: Free city comparisons on climate, transportation, crime, public services, taxes and demographics.

THE JUGGLING ACT

ARE YOU AN INTEGRATOR OR A SEQUENCER?

The answer should help you figure out how to best juggle all the disparate parts of your life: career, marriage, kids, extended family and friends, community and creative interests, sports and hobbies.

If you're someone who negotiates multimillion-dollar business deals on your cell phone while bathing and feeding your baby or watching your daughter play soccer, you undoubtedly are an integrator. Multitasking is easy for you. In fact, you feel anxious when you aren't checking your office voice mail while cooking dinner for your family.

If, on the other hand, handling two or three different activities at once gives you a headache, you're probably a sequencer. When you're at work, you don't want to research summer camps for your children. And when you're playing with your toddler or trying to help your kids with homework, you hate being interrupted by business calls. You're better off unplugging your phone and BlackBerry when you get home

HOW TO LOOK LIKE A WORKAHOLIC

What if you can't persuade your boss to stop demanding that you work 24/7? Learn to look like a workaholic while still maintaining a life.

Here are some tips for making your boss think you're slaving away:

1. **The well-timed appearance:** If your boss always works on Saturday mornings, show up at the office and make sure that you're seen. You'll leave the impression of being very diligent. Attend all the required meetings and make yourself heard. If you telecommute from home, a targeted blitz of e-mail or phone calls on issues important to your boss will make an impression. So will regular, well-timed visits—even if they're short.

2. **The well-timed disappearance:** A rising star at a management-consultant company disappeared every afternoon at 3 P.M. to do errands or go to the gym, but was always at his desk every evening between 5 P.M. and 8 P.M. His bosses noticed he was always working late—and never realized he was gone for two hours in the afternoon.

3. **The computer smoke screen:** Program your computer to change the material on the screen every few minutes, so if your boss stops by it will look as though you just stepped away for a moment.

4. **Marry your BlackBerry:** Carry it absolutely everywhere so that you can convey the impression that you're *never* out of touch.

5. **Mimic the boss:** Bosses who are workout fiends usually look charitably on employees who show up at the gym when they do. This means you can probably extend your lunch-hour gym break and not lose work points. Some workaholic bosses make other exceptions: They'll knock off early to get to their kids' school plays and sporting events. You probably won't get docked for doing the same.

6. **The late-night e-mail ruse:** When you log in at 3 A.M. and send a memo to a colleague or boss, no one will know you really got up to nurse your baby. You will look like a true workaholic.

and focusing exclusively on your family for several hours, then logging on again later at night to check office messages.

Most of us are a blend of both styles. And to some extent your style is shaped by work and family demands, and not entirely in your control. If you're a single parent, you have to multitask more since you can't hand off your child to a spouse when you're suddenly interrupted at home by a work call. And if you're in a job that requires 24/7 contact with clients and employees around the globe, you have to blend home and work.

Both styles can lead to productive work and home lives, assuming you follow a few commonsense guidelines.

For Integrators

1. Learn to chill: If you're an integrator and your spouse is a sequencer, don't expect her to be pleased when you answer your cell phone at dinner or bring your laptop on vacation. Negotiate reasonable limits on your integrator tendencies.

2. Limit multitasking to times when it is truly productive. Planning a staff meeting while on the treadmill is fine. The same task attempted during a family barbecue is going to turn out badly anyway. Don't go there.

3. Know your multitasking limits. If you feel brain-dead from juggling too much, resist doing more than two tasks simultaneously.

For Sequencers

1. Take it easy on yourself. Sequencers are notorious perfectionists who feel compelled to complete each task flawlessly, often without interruption. That's frequently a recipe for failure.

2. Learn to prioritize, and budget your time. Make lists and give lower priority to mundane tasks. Resist the tendency, for example, to spend the entire day fixing some annoying bug in your spreadsheet program while that critical report your spreadsheet is supposed to churn out goes undone.

3. Compartmentalize. Admit you are a bad juggler and can't answer e-mails and concentrate on that long-term report at the same time. Set aside e-mail time and report time and don't mix the two.

ELDER CARE

You never know how or when an elder-care crisis will strike. Maybe your elderly parents have spent many healthy retirement years, enjoying their independence and ability to care for themselves. Then suddenly one of them has a stroke, or dies, while another falls and is incapacitated and your help is needed. This is where planning for the inevitable is so critical.

THE VALUE OF HOMESPUN KNOWLEDGE

Here's an idea for synergy: You can make what you learn at work work at home. And you can apply the lessons of home to work.

More and more smart working parents are learning to share with their children what they do on the job as a way of helping them understand the work world—and the value of interpersonal relationships—better. And those same parents are using their parental skills to better manage employees and get along with colleagues.

One approach: At home, don't lecture your kids about how to start or advance a career or ask for a raise. They don't want lectures and will likely tune you out. Instead, talk about problems and how you overcame them or are trying to. And talk about "good guys" and "bad guys" you deal with at work.

One mother related how her boss ordered everyone to work all weekend on a crash project and then on Monday announced all the extra work was unnecessary—and blamed them for misunderstanding him. "So what should he do better next time to be a better boss?" she asked her kids.

Her daughter replied: "Not pass the buck and cover his butt."

Another manager involved his school-age kids in an advertising campaign his company was launching to try to win back business from a rival. The kids came up with ideas and slogans and learned a lot about business.

At work, use the insights you gain as a parent. The different personalities of your children can help you identify the different strengths of employees and the need to provide individual attention to each. Your kids don't like it when you scream at them or bark orders. They probably respond a lot better to praise than criticism. So will your employees and work colleagues.

And you know what it takes to get your kids to confide in you—a lot of listening and little judging. The same goes for employees.

Here are some guidelines to make this inevitability as painless as possible:

1. Find out what kind of care your elder wants before he or she needs it. You don't want to be having this discussion at some emotionally fraught time or when a severely ill parent is incapable of communicating.

TIME IS HONEY

You love your kids and you may even love your job. But remember, life is richer than that. The experts tell us that a more balanced approach—taking time to nourish your marriage, friendships and individual interests—will pay dividends elsewhere. You'll be a more interesting, less frazzled parent; you'll get in the habit of chronically recharging your batteries for your job. We know you're busy, but here are some no-nonsense tips for squeezing time out of airtight schedules:

1. **Spend some time with your spouse each week separate from children**—a lunch date, dinner date, gym date. Couples who devote time exclusively to each other have fewer marital problems, which in turn is a bonus for their children. So don't think of time apart from the kids as taking something away from them.

2. **Get together with a few close friends once a month for dinner**—a reading group discussion, or to attend a sports event.

3. **Use several hours each week to replenish your physical, emotional and spiritual energy.** Go on a long walk or bike ride, visit an art museum, exercise, attend a religious service. Do what you value and what is fun.

4. **Treat yourself to a personal trainer who comes to your house once or twice a week, saving you trips to the gym.** Or find a gym adjacent to your office, or create one at home.

5. **Dare to try something you've always dreamed of doing**—mountain-climbing, photography, designing a Web site, learning how to sew. Following your dreams will give you new energy and broaden your life.

6. **Learn to delegate and let go.** Maybe your spouse doesn't cook the meat loaf or take care of the car repair the way you do. Unless you learn to accept that and enjoy his or her efforts, you will be on perpetual overload, and angry about it.

7. **Eliminate things you think you should or ought to do.** If you really want to bake cookies for the school bake sale during a pressured work week, go ahead, especially if doing so may relieve job stress. But don't bake just because you think you should in order to look like a "good" parent. Buy store-bought cookies and take a breather. The same goes for taking on extra projects at work just to prove you can handle anything. Don't believe that doing more than everyone else will necessarily get you ahead. It's more likely to lead to burnout and an inability to handle what is crucial.

8. **Stop trying to be a super mom, super dad, super boss, super employee.** They don't exist. Aim for being as good as you can be. That is more than good enough.

2. **If your relative is the independent-minded type with strong objections to nursing-home care, strongly suggest that they get a long-term home-care policy before they become frail or ill.** Such policies, while expensive, cover at least some of the cost of at-home health-care providers.

3. **Consider the legal issues well in advance.** Think about getting your parent to delegate a power-of-attorney to you or a sibling, to handle their affairs during a crisis. This also requires you to know in advance your parent's wishes about emergency situations—what would they want done if mentally incapacitated, for example? Would they want to consider being kept on life support? Powers-of-attorney come in two types: The most common is "durable," meaning that it remains valid after the signer becomes incompetent. An older person can also opt for a "springing power-of-attorney," which takes effect only when certain conditions are met—when the person is certified incompetent, for example. Twenty-seven states also allow special "health-care proxies" that some attorneys see as more flexible than straightforward powers-of-attorney.

4. **Know where to locate your elderly relative's key documents**: his or her will; Social Security card, life, health and home insurance policies; tax returns and savings; credit-card and real-estate records. This will save you an enormous amount of time and frustration when and if your parent's estate goes to probate.

5. **Be realistic about the role you can play.** Many families in America still take in elderly parents to live with them in their declining years. But what if you're one of those families where both spouses work long hours from necessity and you're already struggling with a child with special needs? In such a case, whatever your emotional attachment, you may be better off seeking other solutions.

6. **Remember that elder-care decisions often require family collaboration.** Be proactive: Identify up front the health and ethical issues and the individual values and preferences of your siblings or other relatives who may be involved. Look for conflicts among relatives and try to resolve them before a crisis occurs. Determine who should decide. Then choose a course of action and evaluate the results.

7. **Be aware that you face hard choices.** For example, say your mother can no longer drive safely and refuses to stop driving. If she has an ac-

THE ONE PROMISE YOU SHOULD NEVER MAKE

In proud or emotional moments, many of us make grand promises to our kids, our parents, our spouses, our bosses. But there are some promises you should simply never make, lest harsh realities make you a liar in the end.

Mia Herschel vowed years ago that she would never put her mother in a nursing home. "My mother would say, 'Promise me you will never put me in a place like that. Kill me first!'" and Ms. Herschel assented, she says.

But Alzheimer's disease afflicted her mother in her late 60s, and her symptoms soon made it unsafe for her to live independently. Ms. Herschel, on a doctor's advice, arranged for guardianship and placement of her mother in an assisted-living facility. Now 70, her mother is expected eventually to move to a nursing home.

Ms. Herschel, of Lake Zurich, Illinois, wishes things had turned out differently, but takes comfort in knowing "I did the best I could." She says she will never ask her daughter to make promises about long-term care: "If I do, I've asked my husband to punch me or something."

Keeping promises has grown harder in the past decade as the burdens borne by families—health care, education, care for the aged—have grown heavier. Double-digit gains in the costs of all three, plus a 38 percent increase in the over-85 population, according to the Census Bureau, are overwhelming families. Accelerating corporate change, from restructurings to outsourcing, has made breadwinning a high-stakes gamble.

For me, this calls to mind an apocryphal tale about the fiery composer Igor Stravinsky. Known for writing ridiculously difficult passages into his works, he created a violin interlude so formidable that a violinist came to him and declared it impossible.

"Of course," the composer is said to have replied, "I don't want the sound of someone playing the passage. I want the sound of someone trying to play it."

Perhaps that's what we should strive for in family life—the sound of someone trying. I promise to try my best . . . to keep the family homestead, to care for you in old age, to provide enough money, to raise you in a happy home. I will try. That is all that is within my power.

—SUE SHELLENBERGER

cident or winds up lost and frightened, you have an ethical obligation to face the situation squarely with her. One woman broke the news gently by saying, "I don't want you to hurt yourself and I don't want you to hurt someone else." She cushioned that blow by keeping her mother's car tuned up and using it to drive her on errands, telling her, "This will always be your car."

ELDERCARE.GOV: Provides help finding a local aging agency near a loved one

CAREMANAGER.ORG: Provides a directory of geriatric-care managers

BENEFITSCHECKUP.ORG: Helps find government programs offering financial assistance

CAREPLANNER.ORG: Offers help finding type-of-care options

CAREGIVING.ORG: Assigns quality ratings to eldercare books, videos and Web sites

CAREGIVER.ORG: Posts a downloadable "Handbook for Long-Distance Caregivers" and other resources

NADSA.ORG: Provides listings of the National Adult Day Services Association

NAHC.ORG: Provides help finding home-health agencies

NFCACARES.ORG: Lists elder-care resources

FINDING THE RIGHT CARE

The growing importance of elder care as a national health-care issue has made it an industry of its own. There are lots of resources these days to help you find the right help, place or situation for your elderly parents or other relatives. Here's where you can start:

1. **Many employers have resource-and-referral services to help you find long-term-care arrangements.** Ask at work if yours does.

2. **Hospitals, senior-citizens centers, churches and nonprofit groups** such as local Alzheimer's associations chapters are often excellent sources. Check them out.

3. **Build a support system that includes your elder's neighbors, clergy, friends, doctors, accountants and other advisers.**

4. **Use the Internet to locate information and help.** Above are some Web sites that can help locate services or provide support for caregivers of elder relatives.

IN-HOME CARE

Close to 25 percent of the nation's caregivers to elderly or disabled relatives live with the person they are caring for. Steep costs for long-term care are driving this trend as much as family ties.

You may feel responsible, relieved and also gratified if you take in an aged parent. The experience may strengthen bonds between your parent and your children. But it also may cause a resurfacing of old tensions with your parent, conflicts with your spouse and children and burnout.

Your spouse may resent the intrusion and new time-demands on you. Your children may feel neglected or resentful of an aged relative who requires lots of care. And you are likely to suffer from exhaustion, especially if your elderly parent keeps you up most of the night.

Here are some ways to prevent home care from becoming a nightmare:

1. Anticipate these and other problems and address them quickly when they surface. Ignoring them or letting them fester is a recipe for disaster.

2. Your spouse is key. Unless a spouse is willing to share at least the commitment of caring for an elderly parent in your home, think twice about this arrangement.

3. Even with your spouse involved, don't go it alone. Even the most patient of caregivers need breaks now and then. Consider bringing in part-time help, or even arrange for a temporary stay for your elderly relative in a nursing home to ease your burden. And consider one of the fairly new wrinkles in elder care: adult day-care centers.

THE BRAVE NEW WORLD OF ELDERCARE

 Technology, which is changing the landscape in so many industries, is making inroads in elder care, too. Here are some facilities and companies that offer a glimpse at what's already here:

Granny on the Internet: Southland Suites, an assisted-living facility in Lake City, Florida, uses video cameras in public areas like dining rooms and courtyards to transmit broadcasts that families can monitor over the Internet.

Gramps wired: Pleasant Bay Nursing & Rehabilitation Center, Brewster, Massachusetts, is building assisted-living units that will offer residents senior-friendly e-mail and Internet access and will use e-mail to keep family members informed of their relative's health and well-being.

Nursing Eyes and Ears: ResourceLink, Iowa City, Iowa, installs small cameras and TVs in elderly patients' homes that nurses use to check in with patients.

THE SCOOP ON ADULT DAY-CARE CENTERS

These provide daytime oversight for frail, demented or disabled elders. Based in a variety of settings, from churches to community centers, some programs offer activities, personal care and recreation. A growing number also provide medical care, nursing and rehab services. In some cases, they have been shown to improve elders' health and well-being and they can postpone or even eliminate the need for a nursing home. And, of course, they have the advantage of allowing family caregivers to keep working during the day.

To find a center, ask your family doctor or contact your area Agency on Aging, identifiable through an elder-care locator at 800-

677-1116 or **eldercare.gov** or through **nadsa.org.** If you still can't find a center, seek help on **info@nadsa.org** for suggestions on lobbying legislators to increase programs in your area.

Once you find a center, you must persuade your elderly relative to go, often a difficult feat. Schedule a visit yourself, telling your relative you are curious, and invite him or her along. You might also try calling day care by another name. One senior calls his center his "club," which has made going there far less humiliating.

Adult day care costs an average of $1,200 a month. That compares to roughly $2,000 to $3,000 a month for a home-care aide, an average $2,379 a month for an assisted-living facility and an average $57,765 a year for a semiprivate room in a nursing home. Most long-term-care insurers pay for adult day care and Medicaid funds can also be used in most states for elders who qualify.

CHAPTER TWELVE

FINANCING YOUR LIFE

THE NEW REALITIES

During the Roaring 90s, investing was almost too easy. It sometimes seemed that everyone in the stock market could stop worrying about paying for retirement or for much else. Want to sleep late, play golf, lie on the beach, ski, travel, collect art? No need to save or sacrifice. Just jump into your stock of choice and—presto!—you soon would have the money you needed.

The crushing bear market of 2000–2002 brought many people back to reality, if only by forcing them to wait additional years before retiring. And it left them with a problem. If casino-style investing no longer was the secret to financial security, what was? And if the stock market could crumple, how about the real-estate market or the bond market?

It turns out that there are smart ways and dumb ways to save, invest, borrow, finance a home or put aside money for retirement. Perhaps not surprisingly, many run against normal intuition. Most important, saving and investing aren't a short-term bet that you win or lose in a matter of months. They are a long-term proposition that you should be working on over a lifetime.

Tip: The biggest mistake most people make—amateurs and professionals alike—is to watch markets closely and invest based on month-to-month swings.

THE RADICALLY CHASTENED WORLD OF SAVING AND INVESTING

ASKING THE RIGHT QUESTION

One big reason people make mistakes is that they ask the wrong question when planning how to finance their retirements. That wrong question is: How can I make the most money? That mentality produced the market bubble and the bear market.

Perhaps the hardest thing for an investor to do is to stop thinking about dollar signs and think instead about stock fundamentals. If you follow your instincts, you will often invest based on emotion and greed—and probably pay a penalty for it. To retire comfortably, you need the equivalent of a financial firewall—some rules to prevent yourself from doing that.

We'll admit that the Roaring 90s clouded things by spoiling people. Many investors came to believe that a 20 percent annual gain in their portfolios was the norm. By 2002, at the market bottom, polling showed that expectation had fallen to just 5 percent. Then stocks recovered and people came to expect 10 percent returns. Just as quickly, that rally faded and 7 percent seemed reasonable. In other words, notes *Wall Street Journal* columnist Jonathan Clements, "the answers rise and fall with the stock market."

One way to avoid getting caught in this short-term thinking is to stop asking how much, and ask instead: when?

How soon do you need to tap the money you're investing? If you plan to use the money in two or three years, you probably don't want to risk stocks' volatility—you'll want to lean toward bonds and other stable dividend-producing investments. Over long periods, stocks tend to rise more than bonds, but in a short period, say one to three years, they can fall 20 percent or more.

OF BEACHGOERS AND CONTRARIANS

But if you are younger and aren't planning to use the money for 20 or 30 years, or if there is part of your retirement hoard that you aren't planning to touch for a long time, then putting the money in bonds probably is a terrible idea. The best strategy is what one financial adviser calls "go to the beach" investing. You pick a mix of stocks—big and small, foreign and domestic. You spread your money among them. And you go to the beach and forget the short-term swings.

One irony is that if you are saving money every month and putting it into the stock market—say through your company's 401(k) retirement plan—it can be just fine if the stock market drops in value. That isn't the way it feels, of course. When stocks fall, the temptation is to sell and hide, but at that point you need to ignore your emotions and do just the opposite.

Why buy at such a scary time? Because you aren't investing for the next year or even for the next 10 years. You need to be thinking 20, even 25 years out, and that strategy involves staying diversified, picking up cheap stocks, and benefiting from the market's historical tendency to rise over long periods of time. Easy to say. Not easy to do.

Indeed, people who worry about short-term market swings tend to do the opposite, buying stocks when they seem strong and then selling in a panic after they fall. They do the same thing with Treasury bonds and real estate. Studies have shown not only that ordinary people do this, but that pros (who also have emotions) do it, too, timing the stock market and making exactly the wrong choice at the wrong time. We'll say it firmly: For almost everyone, trying to time the market is a losing strategy.

That's one reason that some experienced investors prefer index funds, which simply track the performance of broad groups of stocks, rather than trying to pick individual winners or invest in funds managed by humans trying to do that. And the implicit strategy of such funds is a word you need to keep in mind: "balance."

HOW TO STAY BALANCED

The basic principle is a fair one: Stocks go up over time, but in the process, they dip and soar. If you buy only when they are soaring, you are buying high. If you also buy when they dip, you are buying low. Since you can't know whether they are poised to rise or to fall, you need to keep buying regardless.

Average stock gains over the years, with inflation taken out, work out at a pedestrian 7 percent, according to a long-term study by Professor Jeremy Siegel at the University of Pennsylvania's Wharton School. Assuming this trend isn't going to be upended anytime soon, it's foolish to try to attain 20 percent annual gains. Over a 15- to 20-year period, it's entirely likely that you will see years when the market gives investors 20 percent gains and also 20 percent declines. Ignore that and remember to snatch up those bargains when the market is falling and avoid the temptation to buy when only the bull is raging. This is how, over the years, you can build an impressive portfolio.

The going-to-the-beach metaphor, however, has its limits. As with any vacation, you can't stay at the beach permanently. Your portfolio is dynamic, and just like your body and your car, it requires a regular checkup.

Let's say you've decided to put 70 percent of your money in a mix of small, large, domestic and foreign stocks and 30 percent in a mix of government and corporate bonds. And suppose during the year gone by, stocks have gone up 10 percent while bonds have gone down 10 percent. Now your bond holdings have slipped to 26 percent and stocks have picked up the lost ground. What do you need to do?

The opposite of what comes naturally. Don't buy more of your winners. Put your portfolio back in balance.

Why? First, a theory analysts call "reversion to the mean." That's simply the tendency of high-flying stocks to come back down to earth by weakening in the future. Second, if your original strategy was based on a portfolio mixed for long-term growth or short-term safety and your objective is unchanged, then steer back to that mix. Another Wall Street cliché: Don't chase your winners. Stick to your plan.

Two key words to remember are "diversify" and "rebalance." Since small stocks typically don't show the same gains as large ones, and foreign ones don't do the same as domestic, you need to rebalance that mix, too, as well as your bond mix.

To avoid a capital-gains tax, you preferably would do this by buying more of the stocks and bonds that have been weak, rather than by selling your winners. If the balance has shifted a small amount and the only way to adjust it is to make sales that would create capital gains, it may be cheaper to wait. Don't overtinker.

STAYING UNCONFUSED

To build a winning portfolio, you need to mix together the right combination of stocks and bonds. But oftentimes, it's investors themselves who get mixed up.

Much of the blame, I believe, lies with conventional financial wisdom. Consider the four portfolio-building guidelines below.

All four guidelines are extremely popular—and they're all seriously flawed.

1. Gun for growth. Younger investors are frequently advised to load up on stocks of rapidly growing companies, especially technology companies. Good advice? I don't think so.

Contrary to popular belief, growth companies—as a group—don't generate superior long-run returns. In fact, history suggests that the best returns come from buying "value" stocks, many of which appear to have poor growth prospects.

Because value stocks are so suspect, they trade at cheap prices compared to current earnings or corporate assets. But with expectations so low, good news can mean startling stock-market gains.

Don't get me wrong: I am not arguing that younger investors should overweight value instead of growth. Rather, I think it is foolish to go overboard on any sector. Faced with all the uncertainty over which investments will perform best, I favor building a globally diversified stock portfolio.

Which brings me to a somewhat radical notion. Suppose you are age 25 and you think you can get the optimal mix of stock-market risk and reward by owning, say, 45 percent large U.S. stocks, 20 percent small U.S. companies, 5 percent real-estate investment trusts, 25 percent developed-foreign-market stocks and 5 percent emerging markets. If that mix is optimal at age 25, I would argue that it is probably also the right mix at age 65.

But what about changes in your risk tolerance as you grow older? I wouldn't fiddle with your mix of stock-market sectors. Instead, I would react to changes in your risk tolerance by changing your portfolio's mix of stocks and bonds.

2. Act your age. The standard advice, of course, is that we should boost our bond holdings as we grow older. But in reality, our risk tolerance doesn't always decline as we age.

"Youngsters are often much more risk-averse than old folks, because they aren't accustomed to the market's volatility," notes William Bernstein, an investment adviser in North Bend, Oregon.

Indeed, your stock exposure in your 60s may not be much lower than it was in your 20s. But this isn't just about risk tolerance. It's also, once again, about owning the optimal mix of investments.

As every investor quickly learns, bonds often perform well when stocks are suffering, and vice versa. Result: By buying both, you can build a portfolio that delivers a more attractive combination of risk and return.

If you run the numbers, you find 100-percent stock investors can trim their portfolio's overall price gyrations—without hurting returns—by moving 10 percent into bonds. Similarly, 100-percent bond investors can boost performance without increasing risk if they shift 25 percent into stocks.

In practice, the range of recommended portfolios is usually far smaller. Investment advisers typically suggest that retirees maintain at least 40 percent in stocks, while aggressive investors are usually told to cap their stock exposure at 80 percent. And many investors, both young and old, will end up somewhere in between, with maybe 50 or 60 percent in stocks.

3. Take twenty. To build a well-diversified portfolio, all you need is 20 stocks. Or so says one of Wall Street's most popular rules of thumb.

There is some logic to this advice. If you own 20 carefully selected companies, your stock portfolio shouldn't perform much more erratically than the broad market.

Volatility, however, isn't the only measure of risk. There is also the issue of "tracking error," the chance that your 20 stocks will earn returns that are far better—or worse—than the market.

Let's say you earn 6 percent a year, while the broad market clocks 8 percent. Doesn't sound like a big difference? On a $10,000 investment over 20 years, you would amass $32,071. But if you had notched the market's return instead, you would have accumulated $46,610, or 45 percent more. The lesson: To be diversified, you need far more than 20 stocks.

4. Invest for income. Retirees are frequently advised to load up on high-dividend stocks, like utilities, real-estate investment trusts and dividend-paying blue-chip companies. But that isn't a strategy I would recommend.

Partly, it's because you will have a lopsided portfolio. It is the same problem that young investors face when they overweight growth stocks. If you overdose on dividend-payers, you are making a big bet on one part of the market—and it could turn out to be the wrong bet.

The advice to buy dividend-payers, however, also reflects muddled thinking about how to generate income in retirement. Remember the old axiom that you should "never dip into principal"?

Believe me, it's alive and well. Many retirees are wholeheartedly committed to spending only their income and never touching their capital.

"You often see older individuals advised to tilt their portfolios toward income-producing securities," says Mr. Bernstein, the investment adviser. "But that's ridiculous. It's total return that matters, not income."

In other words, you should aim for decent overall portfolio performance, whether those gains come from dividends, interest or price appreciation.

But what about generating income? You can always raise cash by selling some of your stocks and bonds.

With that in mind, I typically advocate that retirees maintain a cash reserve equal to five years of spending money, with this money parked in short-term bonds and money-market funds. As retirees spend down this cash reserve, they should look to replenish it, by selling some of their stocks and riskier bonds.

If stocks fare well in a particular year, they can sell from that side of their portfolio. But if shares are suffering, they can leave their stocks alone and instead top up their cash reserve by unloading some of their riskier bonds.

—JONATHAN CLEMENTS

AVOIDING THE FEE-FOR-ALL

Even with the radically chastened landscape, many investors can't help yearning—and trying—to surpass those 7 percent a year gains. Yet, while we don't have a crystal ball, the economic landscape ahead, at least until the aftereffects of the 90s' stock bubble wear off, actually indicates average gains could be less than that.

Why? Because the late 90s' gains were well above average and, except in Lake Wobegone, the laws of mathematics dictate that the stock market can't turn in above-average returns every year.

On top of that, the succession of happy economic trends that began in 1982 may be just about played out. Interest rates, whose steady two-decade decline was one of the main motors of the stock market and the bond market, have begun to rise again. The government deficit may not decline soon. The need to pay for rising military costs has made economists wring their hands over the risk of inflation and even, in a throwback to the painful 1970s, stagflation—inflation and sluggish growth together.

In addition, baby boomers will be withdrawing more and more from their stock and bond portfolios as they retire, and spending more and more on medical care. Fidelity Investments' chief operating officer Robert Reynolds has called the financing of baby boomers' retirement "the largest do-it-yourself project in the history of this country." Even if the nation avoids stagflation, it's hard to imagine a fresh period of falling rates, falling deficits and falling inflation.

What can investors do to compensate for the possibility of mediocre stock performance? If you're young, buy. If you're older and need more money before you retire, there is a tempting solution, recommended by many stockbrokers: Pick the winners of the future and buy those. Alas, this solution has failed almost everyone who's tried it; indeed, it's a recipe for buying high and selling low.

The best ways to get through a period of sub-par market performance are neither easy nor painless. But here are some we can recommend:

1. **Curb some of the luxury spending habits you may have developed in the bull market.**

2. **Seek out no-load mutual funds**, which don't charge an up-front fee. Buying broker-sold funds that charge fees means giving up a percentage of your investment before it even begins to work for you.

3. **If you must buy a broker-sold fund, avoid those known as "B shares,"** which charge no up-front fee, but assess big annual expenses and charge big commissions when they are sold. A and C shares are less sneaky. A shares charge an up-front fee, while C shares assess high annual expenses.

4. **If you already own broker-sold funds, learn how you can sell them without fees.** A few broker-sold fund companies allow people to transfer money from one broker-sold fund to another without paying a fresh commission, through something called an "NAV transfer." Your broker may not mention this, since it doesn't generate a fee, so you might need to ask.

5. **Avoid mutual funds that assess heavy operating fees.** The average actively managed fund charges a whopping 1.5 percent a year for managing your money. Index funds often charge less than 0.2 percent. In a world of slack market growth, saving 1.3 percent a year on fees can make a big difference. Over time, it can have a huge impact on your savings, whether stock growth is slack or not.

6. **Avoid funds that trade heavily.** Every one of those trades takes a brokerage fee, which holds down the fund's performance, even though it probably doesn't show up in the accounting.

7. **Finally, take a hard-eyed look at what you're paying to your financial adviser or your broker.** Suppose you have put aside $1 million for retirement and you withdraw 5 percent a year. You will receive $50,000 a year. If your broker or adviser is taking 1 percent a year and your mutual fund is charging 1.5 percent, Wall Street is taking $25,000 a year from you—half of what you are making yourself.

    Bonus tip: Be wary of "chasing performance"—the mutual-fund equivalent of chasing stock winners. That means you should avoid funds that posted the biggest gains in the previous year. Mutual-fund companies love to advertise their big-gainers in an effort to make you buy them. But remember the rule: The stock or fund that was up 200 percent last year is simply unlikely to continue to rack up such gains.

Another way to get through a period of sub-par market performance is also one of the most painful: Put more aside in savings, which in most cases will mean sacrifice. Older baby boomers, those born between 1946 and 1955, have a median net worth of only $146,000, including the net value of their homes, according to a study done by AARP, the Washington, D.C.–based seniors group. Some will receive pensions from employers. But that net-worth figure is a slim one to retire on. It suggests that too many people may have been relying on their stock gains to finance their retirements, and that some may wind up working longer than they thought they would.

PICKING A BROKER

All too often, brokers and financial planners aren't qualified, charge too much and give self-serving advice.

But things are getting better.

As I see it, the financial-advice business is plagued by four huge problems. Two of the problems have been largely ignored. But the other two have been the subject of fierce debate over the past two decades—and, amazingly, the good guys seem to be winning.

Nonetheless, buying financial advice remains a treacherous endeavor.

Looking to hire a broker or planner? Never lose sight of these four issues:

1. **Wrong Pitch.** For years, brokers collected clients by touting a single, compelling fantasy: We can help you beat the market. There was just one problem: Most brokers couldn't deliver.

To make matters worse, as brokers devoted their energies to investment management, they tended to overlook other areas of their clients' finances—areas where they really could make a difference. After all, it's hard to pick market-beating stocks and mutual funds. But it is fairly easy to help clients save enough, purchase the necessary insurance, trim taxes, plan their estates, buy the right-size home and get a low-cost mortgage.

As advisers came to realize that they could better serve clients by taking a broader view of their finances, many set up shop as financial planners.

The big brokerage firms, of course, still dominate the advice business. But it looks like the financial planners have won. These days, not only do brokers style themselves as "financial consultants," but many also have taken to selling market-tracking index funds, a clear sign that the beat-the-market fantasy is on the wane.

In all this, there's a lesson for investors. If you use an adviser and you want to get your money's worth, make sure the adviser is helping with all facets of your finances, rather than just tinkering with your portfolio.

2. Feeling Conflicted. Many advisers continue to get the bulk of their compensation by collecting commissions on the investments that their clients buy and sell.

Still, the emergence of financial planners has been accompanied by a move away from commissions and toward fees.

Some fee-charging advisers levy annual retainers or hourly fees. But most charge a percentage of a client's account value, with the client paying maybe 1 percent a year, equal to $5,000 on a $500,000 portfolio.

Paying fees isn't necessarily cheaper. But it does remove some nasty conflicts of interest. When advisers collect commissions on every trade, they have an incentive to push high-commission products and to prod clients into buying and selling, even if these trades aren't in the clients' best interest.

Fee-only advisers, by contrast, don't have these dangerous incentives. Because they get a percentage of a client's portfolio, these advisers have the same goal as the client—to make the portfolio grow.

Even so, not all conflicts of interest are removed. For instance, a fee-charging broker or planner might discourage clients from using a chunk of their savings to pay down debt, because this will shrink their portfolio and thereby reduce the adviser's fee.

But I consider that to be a relatively minor drawback. For investors, paying a percentage of assets is clearly less dangerous than paying commissions. And it's clearly the direction in which the business is moving.

Financial planners may have led the way. But, once again, the big brokerage firms are following. Major brokerage firms now offer programs where you can get your portfolio handled for an asset-management fee.

3. Amateur Hour. The move toward financial planning and toward fees is, I believe, a marked improvement. But we are still a long way from nirvana.

Unfortunately, there are two other drawbacks, neither of which gets a lot of attention.

First, the advice business doesn't have widely accepted ethical and educational standards. Indeed, many brokers and planners have had little formal training, and certainly nothing approaching the education that is expected of doctors and lawyers.

Consider the certified-financial-planner designation. I consider the CFP designation to be a basic requirement for anybody in the financial-advice business.

To qualify, you need three years' work experience, you have to meet various education requirements and you have to take a two-day exam. Yet hardly anybody bothers. There are well over two million insurance agents, brokers and financial planners in the United States. But only 45,000 are CFPs. Want to locate a certified financial planner? Go to **cfp.net** online.

4. Highly Charged. Even among CFPs, there is one subject that is all but taboo. Which brings me to the second, unaddressed issue: Financial advisers charge too much.

We have had lousy stock-market returns in four of the past five years. And I am not sure things will get better anytime soon. If you own a balanced portfolio of stocks and bonds, I figure you might earn 5 or 6 percent a year over the next decade.

Knock off 1 percent for mutual-fund annual expenses and 1 percent for an adviser's fee, and suddenly you are looking at an after-cost annual return of just 3 or 4 percent. Factor in taxes and inflation, and you may not make any money at all.

What to do? Slashing investment costs would certainly help. But that notion is an anathema to many on Wall Street. Advisers are determined to collect their 1 percent of assets each year, whether through fees or commissions.

But if you pay that sort of money, you will be hard-pressed to earn decent long-run returns.

—JONATHAN CLEMENTS

WHERE TO INVEST:
MAKING GOOD CHOICES

The bursting of the 90s stock-market bubble has driven some people out of stocks altogether. Some are trying real estate. Others look out a few years ahead and think bonds are the best bets. Alas, the choices facing investors aren't unlimited and no particular investment is immune from ups and downs. The question of whether real estate might be the next bubble has already been written about extensively in the pages of *The Wall Street Journal*.

We think the most useful thing here would be to lay out the alternatives to 90s-style stock investing and give investors a handle on how they might approach each.

UNDERSTANDING THE CHOICES

Bonds

One widespread misconception is that a bond fund is the same as a bond, and doesn't decline in value if it is held to maturity. A bond fund ordinarily doesn't have a maturity. Bond-fund managers buy and sell bonds, just as stock-fund managers do. If the bond market falls, bond funds generally fall, too. In that way, they are more like stocks than bonds.

A Treasury bond or a money-market fund is a pretty safe investment, but real estate and bond funds can fall in value just like the stock market. And corporate bonds—junk bonds in particular—always have the risk of default.

Buying individual bonds is more complicated than buying a bond fund. Over long periods, bond funds tend to act like bonds, so the big problem is for someone who is planning to cash out in a relatively short period. Individual investors can buy Treasury bonds directly from the government at **treasurydirect.gov**. Corporate bonds can be bought at **internotes.com, direct-access.com** and **smartnotes.com**. Fees or minimum-purchase requirements may apply.

To avoid the risk of bond funds, some 401(k) plans offer a "stable value" fund or a guaranteed-income contract, which provide a predictable annual appreciation and are unlikely to decline in value.

Retro-Play: Dividend-Paying Stocks

Another idea that is regaining popularity is dividend-paying stocks. Thrown on the trash heap in the 1990s, when fast price growth was considered the only important objective, the idea of dividends has enjoyed a resurgence. After bond yields fell to historic lows, some investment advisers began pointing out to clients that they could get a better yield with some stocks. Even Microsoft began paying a dividend.

Dividends are especially useful for retired people, parents of college students and others who need to spend some of their investment income. The trouble with dividends is that they are taxable each year, unlike price gains, which are taxable only when stock is sold. And companies can reduce dividends or eliminate them. Some stocks offer a high yield (dividend as a percentage of stock price) because the company is in trouble and the stock has tanked. But if the company isn't in trouble and is just out of favor, a high-yielding stock can be a smart investment, generating both a dividend and a possible stock gain.

Variable Annuities

A possible risk for investors, especially older investors, is something often marketed as a conservative investment: the variable annuity. A variable annuity is simply a mutual fund, or group of mutual funds, wrapped up in an insurance policy. It looks attractive because it is tax-deferred and, should you die early, your heirs will receive an insurance payment. But because of high annual expenses, variable annuities can be the worst of both worlds.

Someone headed for retirement will have to pay taxes as soon as he or she begins withdrawing money, and often would be better served by an IRA, a 401(k) or a standard taxable mutual fund with low expenses. Variable annuities typically are marketed to older people, but ironically, they may be most advantageous to the young, who will be less likely to need the money soon and therefore will benefit from the long-term tax deferral. **Tip:** A variable annuity isn't the same as an immediate-fixed annuity, under which an insurance company or other institution agrees to pay you an annual income for a fixed up-front price. That can be more attractive for retirees.

Handling Your 401(k)

If you are like most people, you probably will change jobs several times before your working life is over—and if so, you need to be careful how you handle the money you have in your company's 401(k) retirement account.

You have four choices for your 401(k) if you change jobs:

1. **Leave the money in the old 401(k) plan.**

2. **Move it to a new one.**

3. **Put it in an Individual Retirement Account.**

4. **Cash out.**

Which you choose can affect your taxes and your investment options.

With all the stress of changing jobs, 401(k) accounts aren't the first thing on most people's minds, but they shouldn't rely on their old employers to do the right thing. Companies have been known to make mistakes. They hold on to money that was supposed to be rolled into a new account, close accounts that weren't supposed to be closed, transfer money to taxable accounts or mail checks directly to former employees, instead of to new retirement accounts. Money that leaves your old 401(k) needs to get into a new retirement account within 60 days or it is subject to taxes and to a 10 percent early withdrawal penalty.

For most people, cashing out is an error. Assuming that you don't make that mistake, which of the other options is best?

RELATIVE MERITS OF THE OPTIONS

1. Staying put: If you are happy with your old 401(k), and if your old employer will allow it, it is tempting to leave the money there and avoid the hassle. But your old company may hit economic trouble or be acquired, making it complicated to recover the money when you retire. And you may forget the old account.

2. Moving it to your new company's 401(k): The benefit here— your money is all in one place and thus easier to manage. If you're an inexperienced investor who doesn't like keeping lots of records— and assuming your new employer has good 401(k) investment options—this probably makes sense.

3. Moving it into an IRA: If you're an experienced, active investor and don't mind keeping extra records, an IRA can offer some advantages. In an IRA, you aren't limited to the investment options offered by your company's plan. You can invest in just about any stock, bond or mutual fund. That permits you to seek the lowest mutual-fund expenses and acquire as broad a group of investments as you wish. The account also can be left to a beneficiary after your death, and he or she can withdraw the money gradually. If you die with money in your 401(k) and someone other than your spouse inherits, your employer probably will insist on cashing out the money immediately, creating a sudden tax hit. Later, if you take a new job with an enticing 401(k), you usually will have the option of rolling an IRA into the new plan.

But IRAs have drawbacks, especially for the undisciplined. There is a temptation to speculate with the money, instead of leaving it alone. And you can't take the money out of an IRA without penalty until you are 59 and a half, while your 401(k) money is available when you are 55. (If you want to force yourself to save longer, however, an IRA might be preferable.) First-time home-buyers can withdraw money penalty-free from an IRA for a down payment, while money from a 401(k) can be withdrawn only as a loan.

SOME SNAGS TO WATCH FOR

1. Some firms that manage 401(k) plans make it hard for people to transfer money to new 401(k) plans or IRAs. They may insist on mailing you a check instead of sending the money directly to the new plan. If so, to avoid tax-withholding, insist that the check be made out to the new 401(k) or to the IRA's trustee, and not to yourself.

2. Some smaller plans make distributions only once a year, and about 7 percent allow you to close your account only once a year. This may force you to delay transferring the money until the distribution date.

3. Watch for technicalities. If, through an error, your old plan mails your 401(k) money to you directly, to a taxable account or to the wrong place, the IRS gives you 60 days from the closing of the old account to resolve the problem and transfer the money to the right place without incurring taxes or penalties. But if the money is mailed directly to you or to a taxable plan, your old plan may have withheld 20 percent for taxes. You can reclaim that when you file your tax return after you put the money into a retirement account, but in the mean-time, you must put the full amount into the new retirement account. You must temporarily make up the 20 percent with your own funds to avoid taxes and a penalty on that amount. If you miss the 60-day window to fix things, you can file an appeal, but that process can be costly and there is no guarantee the IRS will rule in your favor.

Tip: Regardless of how you structure your old 401(k) money, one of the most elemental rules of saving is that you should participate as much as possible in your company's 401(k) unless the available invest-ment choices are truly awful. Most people don't have the discipline to save money every month without a structured plan. And most em-ployers match a certain percentage of the money you invest—that is free money that no one should pass up.

TAXES AND ESTATES

One way to beat the IRS is to die broke, but that is a timing trick that most people won't achieve. Tax law is constantly changing, making it hard for any but the most dedicated tax avoiders to keep up with it. And you need to beware of going to extremes: The IRS regularly dis-allows some of the most "creative" tax shelters, causing financial and legal pain to those who set them up, even on the advice of a certified expert.

Here are a few basic ideas that people have found useful in tax- and estate-planning:

1. **Give up on your losing stocks and look for capital losses.** That $2 dot-com stock you bought for $115 a share may come in handy after all. If you have a capital gain in another stock, consider selling losers to offset the gain. Then you can think about where you really would like to invest the money.

2. **Remember that money left to a spouse generally isn't taxable,** but there is a limit on what you can leave to other beneficiaries tax-free. (The amount is scheduled to vary, over time, from $1 million to $3.5 million and then back to $1 million, and those numbers could change.)

3. **Consider giving before you die.** You can give as much as $11,000 a year tax-free (the amount is subject to revision by the IRS) to

anyone. You and your spouse together can give $22,000 each year to each of your children or to another beneficiary. Some people have gone so far as to give children money and then ask them to use it to support their parents in their dotage. Some even have set up legal contracts and annuities between parent and child. But that can backfire by straining family ties. It is risky to give away money you think you may need later. And be careful of shooting the beneficiary in the foot, if the person isn't really ready to manage a sudden cash windfall.

4. You can give appreciated stock instead of cash. You have the same $11,000 limit, $22,000 for a couple. The stock then goes to the child or other beneficiary at the current price, not the (presumably higher) price that will apply at your death. If you give the money to a child in a low tax-bracket, the child can sell the stock and pay a capital-gains rate as low as 5 percent. But beware of the "kiddie" tax, under which children aged below 14 pay tax on unearned income above a certain level at the same rate as their parents. That tax would apply to dividends as well as capital gains.

5. If your net worth exceeds the exemption, you might not want to leave everything to your spouse. In the short run, it isn't a problem: Anything your spouse inherits is free of estate tax. But once the spouse dies, his or her heirs likely will owe tax. One way to avoid that is to leave part of the estate directly to other heirs in the form of a trust. You can designate the assets for the use of your spouse, to revert to the other heirs on the spouse's death. But watch out: If you have remarried and your current spouse isn't related to your children, there can be a fight over the management of the trust, or even over its ultimate destination on the spouse's death. Even if you think your spouse and children are close, beware of putting them at odds.

6. If your will is several years old, take another look at it. Was the lawyer an estate expert? If not, consider asking your financial adviser, your insurance agent, your accountant or the local bar association for the names of lawyers who are. Before you meet to revise your will, prepare a list of goals, assets and intended beneficiaries. Ask yourself whether you want to leave the same share to the same people. Your family has probably changed; children or siblings may have married, divorced or had children. Their financial status may have gone up or down. You may have designated beneficiaries, custodians or trustees in whom you no longer have confidence or who have died. Your small estate may have grown so much that your bequest no longer is tax-free or you may no longer want a child to receive it all in a lump sum.

TRUSTS AND OTHER IDEAS

Your lawyer may be able to suggest simple trusts to deal with some of these questions. But if you create a family trust, be careful whom you designate as trustee. State laws have jacked up trustees' responsibilities to maintain diversified portfolios, and your trustee could face liability if things go wrong. And if you designate a bank or a law firm, you have no guarantee that the friendly person you know there will still be there when you die. Here are some other basic rules:

1. **Be sure you have properly designated and updated the beneficiaries** for your retirement accounts, life insurance and jointly owned property, none of which typically is governed by your will. You also may want to create a durable power of attorney or a health-care power of attorney, permitting others to make decisions for you if you become incapacitated. You can create a living will, outlining what kind of life-prolonging measures you want or don't want.

2. **Consider a living trust.** Assets in a living trust go directly to heirs designated by the trust and avoid probate, saving you legal expenses. If you own homes in two states and want to avoid probate in one of the states, you can put that home in a living trust. But be sure that the cost of setting up trusts, and revising them as situations change, doesn't exceed the legal fees and taxes you are trying to avoid. And consider another risk: If a child is living in a home that you own partly or fully, be sure that the home's value won't be subject to inheritance taxes. Also be sure that you don't run the risk of dying insolvent with such a home-ownership arrangement: Your share of the home could be attached by creditors, putting your child in a bind.

3. **Consider paying off your debts.** In some states, legal fees are based on your gross estate, not your net estate. Say you have $1 million in assets and $300,000 in debt. By paying off your debt, the gross value of your estate could be reduced to $700,000 for purposes of legal fees.

4. Avoid illiquid assets. Real estate, art and coin collections can be hard to value and hard to sell to pay taxes and legal fees. Unless you have a sentimental attachment to them, consider turning them into something more liquid when opportunities arise.

5. Don't surprise or confuse your heirs. A contested will can make legal fees skyrocket. If you make clear decisions, tell your heirs exactly what to expect, and if you make it explicit in your will, you reduce the risk of a legal fight.

BORROWING MONEY

THE MORTGAGE REFINANCE GAME

When interest rates are falling, refinancing seems like a no-brainer. Depending on how much lenders are competing and how much they are prepared to waive in closing costs and legal fees, even a drop in rates of half a percentage point can make it worthwhile to cancel one fixed-rate mortgage and create a new one.

When rates stop falling, there still are times when refinancing can make sense—but here, things get more complicated. Suppose you missed the chance to refinance at rock-bottom rates, but your home has appreciated and you can get a longer-term loan with a rate similar to the one you already have. It is tempting to refinance for the home's new value, just to get more money. Or you could refinance to buy a larger home, on the assumption that it will appreciate in value and make a good investment.

But keep in mind that your total interest payment depends on how much you owe, not just on the rate. If you take a new loan, even at the old rate, think about whether you will still be making payments after you retire.

What's more, there is no guarantee that home values will rise. Housing values have defied gravity for years in many parts of the country, leaving people with the impression that real estate can't decline. It is true that if your house declines in value, you can just live in it and wait for its value to rise. But that assumes that you never will need to realize the home's value or move to a new location, and that you can continue paying the property taxes and mortgage payments if they go up when the home value doesn't.

Over the past 30 years, home values have risen 6.1 percent a year, barely exceeding the 4.9 percent average inflation rate. And that doesn't count the cost of property tax, maintenance, insurance and interest. People who think their homes have risen sharply in value may not be taking everything into account. And some people who refinance use money to pay for home improvements that, depending on how well they are done, may or may not increase the home's value. If you borrow to the hilt and your house falls in value, you can wind up with a loan that is higher than the resale price of your home.

Another thing to watch out for: When rates are volatile, lenders sometimes offer loan applicants the opportunity to "lock in" a rate for 30 to 60 days until the loan's closing. But they may charge for the service, and if paperwork or processing delays push back the closing, the lock-in can expire or the price can rise. Borrowers need to find out a lender's policy on such situations in advance—including the policy if the lender blames the delay on a third party, such as a title company. The borrower then needs to keep a close eye on the loan's progress, and be prepared to become a pest if a delay crops up. If the lock-in agreement isn't in writing, an unscrupulous lender may try to ignore it. One way to speed things up is to schedule your closing for the middle of the month; closings for home purchases typically are at the end of months, a time when it can be harder to schedule lawyers, title companies and others.

FLOATING VS. FIXED

If you decide that a new loan is the right thing for you, you need to decide whether to borrow fixed-rate or floating-rate. The choice isn't always obvious.

When rates are falling, people tend to opt for fixed-rate mortgages, in an effort to lock in the low rates. But when rates start to rise, people tend to favor floaters because rates for new fixed mortgages tend to rise before rates on floating loans do.

Why? Fixed rates generally are tied to the rates on 10-year Treasury notes, while floaters are tied to shorter-term rates, and long-term rates tend to rise sooner than short-term ones. So not only are adjustable-rate mortgages lower to start with, they tend to move up more slowly.

But once you sign a mortgage contract, a fixed mortgage won't move up, while a floater will keep moving along with market rates. And choosing a multiyear loan based on your guess about where rates are headed can be risky. Professional traders have a hard time predicting rates; you probably will have a harder time. Before you choose which is best for you, look at what the contract says about how much the adjustable rate can rise, and whether there is an upper or a lower limit. Then ask yourself whether the lower rate you get to start with on an adjustable mortgage offsets the risk that it will rise later.

Floaters got a big boost from Federal Reserve Chairman Alan Greenspan's comment early in 2004 that, since interest rates generally fell for years through the middle of 2003, homeowners could have saved a bundle by taking adjustable mortgages. Trouble is, it is hard to imagine rates falling much below the 45-year lows hit in 2003. The yield of the 10-year Treasury note got close to 3 percent that year, and some adjustable-rate mortgages got down to the 4 percent range.

No one can predict rates, but history dictates that, from 45-year lows, they will almost certainly rise. If they do, adjustable-rate mortgages look more risky. At a 4.2 percent annual rate, a borrower pays just $2,240 a month on a mortgage of $450,000 that adjusts annually, counting principal and interest, according to HSH Associates, which supplies consumer information on loans. But as recently as March 2000, the rate on such a mortgage was almost 9 percent, and the monthly payment at that rate is nearly $3,500. For someone who takes the adjustable mortgage in an effort to stretch and afford a more expensive house, that kind of increase can be a real burden.

People who don't want to risk taking a floating rate but want to hold down their interest payments sometimes go for a 15-year fixed-rate mortgage. Because it is so much shorter than a 30-year loan, that kind of loan tends to carry a lower rate. It also has lower total interest costs, because you pay interest over half the period. Trouble is, it also requires larger monthly payments, because you pay off the principal faster.

Some borrowers try to get the best of all worlds with hybrid loans that are fixed for the first three to ten years, and then float. Those tend to carry higher initial interest rates than pure floaters, but lower rates than fixed mortgages. The risk is that if market rates rise, the rates on these mortgages can jump suddenly once they begin to float.

Different lenders have different restrictions on how much the rate can rise after the fixed period ends, and it is important to check that in advance—it can be as much as five percentage points in the first year, and more later. Some borrowers figure that if that happens, they can refinance. But that can be a mirage: There can be a penalty for refinancing, and if you choose to refinance after rates rise, the refinancing itself will be at a higher rate. However, if you sell your house within a few years and pay off the loan, such a loan can make sense.

Tip: Be wary of banks' marketing efforts. During periods of rising rates, lenders tend to push floating-rate mortgages through direct-mail come-ons and even billboards. They emphasize the low initial rates, without playing up the risk of higher rates later. Some offer loans whose rates can change monthly, making them particularly risky for borrowers. Some of these loans look even better because they allow borrowers initially to make only minimal payments. That can turn such loans into time bombs. If rates rise suddenly, the unpaid interest can leave borrowers actually owing more than when they started.

If the only way you can justify the house of your dreams is to find a floating-rate mortgage with the risk and most of the payments pushed off into the future, ask yourself whether it is worth it.

HOME-EQUITY FINANCING: OF LOANS AND LINES

An alternative to a straight mortgage refinancing is a home-equity loan or line of credit.

Home-equity loans generally provide lump sums for fixed periods at fixed rates, like a second mortgage. They have fallen from popularity in favor of home-equity lines, which usually are cheaper and more flexible. Home-equity lines permit borrowers to draw and repay amounts at will up to the total amount of the line. The interest bill depends on how much you have out at any time, and interest on the first $100,000 of a home-equity line typically is tax-deductible.

The risk with this kind of borrowing is that, as with an adjustable mortgage, the rate can balloon if market rates rise. And some banks are willing to provide home-equity lines and loans that, together with the first mortgage, exceed the borrower's actual equity in the home. That is enticing as long as rates are falling and home values are rising, but if rates start to rise and real-estate values fall, it can leave borrowers in over their heads.

But, especially when rates for fixed mortgages are rising, people turn to home-equity lines as a way to raise additional cash while keeping the existing mortgage terms. In some cases, lenders have offered home-equity lines at rates below prime, which is hard to refuse—unless prime begins to skyrocket. A good rule of thumb with home-equity lines is not to borrow amounts that you would have trouble repaying if the interest rates became burdensome.

Tip: Rates on home-equity lines tend to adjust monthly, and unlike a floating-rate mortgage, there typically is no cap on the amount the rates can rise.

Some economists worry that consumers are overusing home-equity lines. A task force of the Office of the Comptroller of the Currency found in 2003 that lenders had loosened their lending standards and needed to sharpen risk-management practices.

Anyone considering a home-equity line should shop around. Fees, closing costs, legal fees and rates vary sharply among lenders. And some lenders charge annual fees, early termination fees and "non-usage" fees for people who don't draw down their lines enough.

CONTROLLING CREDIT-CARD DEBT

One of the most fundamental rules of borrowing is: Don't borrow on your credit card. Take a home-equity line, mortgage a child, but avoid credit-card debt, with its double-digit interest rate. Everyone knows this rule. Few observe it.

One reason for the lack of self-discipline is that banks flood people's mailboxes with come-ons for new credit cards offering the chance to add on more debt. It is hard to say no, especially if your other borrowing opportunities have dried up. But that is precisely when you need to stop borrowing.

Among the most popular cards being marketed are those that offer cash rebates, including some that offer rebates only during months when you carry a balance and pay interest. Carrying debt on those cards is a bit like letting someone pick your pocket if he promises to give some of the money back.

And that is just the start. Some credit-card issuers offer low interest or no interest for life on balances transferred from other cards. Sounds unbeatable. But these offers typically come with provisions that the attractive rates will be cancelled or large penalties assessed if you are late with payments or fail to make a minimum payment. Or the card may include heavy interest rates on new charges—which can't be paid off until you pay off the old balance.

Others card issuers offer seemingly impossible-to-refuse loans, with zero interest for the first six months or longer. Why is this a bad idea? The card issuers are counting on most people being unable to repay the loan after six months. The standard advice on such deals is that they are good only for people who are disciplined about repaying debt. And those are the people least likely to need the loan. More likely to take such a loan are people who think they are disciplined, and aren't.

Even if you don't borrow on your card, you may still be overpaying. Less than 15 percent of cardholders pay annual fees, for example. If you are still paying an annual fee, ask yourself whether the service justifies the cost. If you don't pay an annual fee, pay close attention to the other fees. Card issuers are boosting fees for late payments or for purchases that exceed your limit. To help them assess such fees, they are cutting the time limit they give customers to pay their bills before they start charging interest and late fees. And if you are getting close to the credit limit on your card, don't assume that your card company will automatically disapprove purchases above the limit. The issuer makes more by approving the purchases and then charging you a fee for exceeding the limit.

CHAPTER THIRTEEN

SHOPPING

THE NATION'S NEW SEX?

If shopping is our nation's new sex (just think about *Lucky Magazine*), then throw away your *Kama Sutra* and check out our guide to spending. The number-one thrill in shopping is getting a bargain, and there are some fairly straightforward—though often neglected—fundamentals. The first thing to remember, says Paco Underhill, CEO of shopping consultants Envirosell Inc., is to **shop in the morning,** when you are less tired and have the whole day in front of you to make other choices. Never shop hungry, always make a plan for your "accessories" (spouse, children, dog), pay with debit or cash and try to recognize the difference between shopping and therapy.

THE SAVVY SHOPPER'S TIPS FOR GETTING A BARGAIN

1. It never hurts to try to negotiate. Most people don't, but you'd be surprised at how often the price is up to the manager's discretion. Of course, it is futile to try to talk down milk at the grocery store or get 10 percent off on a busy Saturday; so pick a time when the store is empty. Try it at small, upscale shops rather than large chains.

2. Get to know the manager. This also works well at smaller, more upscale stores. Here it is important to realize that smart shopping isn't always about getting the best price—it is also about getting exactly what you want. If you become friendly with the manager, even providing your e-mail address for targeted sales, your wants and needs will become more familiar. So if you buy a certain item a lot, do it at the same store every time and introduce yourself to the staff.

3. Learn to recognize the cost of convenience and work out your own formula for when it makes sense to drive farther for something cheaper and when it doesn't. Too often shoppers don't do any research before they head out—they just go to the closest place that sells what they want; on the other hand, you may want to rethink whether it's worth it to pay $5 more for gas to save a few dollars on toilet paper.

4. Finally, consider buying used. It's not just cars where that can make a huge difference in price; it's everything from cameras to pressure-washers. The stigma on used goods has virtually disappeared, thanks to the advent of everything from eBay to Target.

TRADITIONAL SHOPPING OUTLETS

DEPARTMENT STORES

At mainstream department stores like J.C. Penney Co. and Macy's, every event from Veteran's Day to "Pre-Thanksgiving" becomes an excuse for a storewide sale. But the perpetual promotions have sucked the value out of the offers. Department stores often play a game called "high-low" retailing, where clothing is sold at deep discount for a short period of time and then returns to the full price when the promotion ends. Since most states have laws requiring stores to sell at full price at least some of the time, the shops often keep prices high in the early part of the week, when traffic is slowest, making Monday and Tuesday often the worst time to shop. Sale activity often starts on Wednesday and continues through the weekend. The bottom line about shopping at most of these stores: **Only buy on sale.** The massive amount of merchandise sold at a discount has conversely inflated the full prices.

Other tips:

1. **Look for consolidation sales.** Most department stores hold these events twice a year (often in February and July). They gather up the season's unsold merchandise for one big mega-sale that travels from outlet to outlet. (Watch for ads, or phone the store for the timing of these things.)

2. **Keep an eye out for "rejected special orders"**—items that customers special-ordered but never picked up.

3. **Finally, don't hesitate to give your phone number to salespeople and ask them to alert you to sales or unusual merchandise.** You don't have to be a big spender to get that treatment, you just have to be loyal.

CHAIN APPAREL STORES

At stores like Gap; Ann Taylor; Limited, owned by Limited Brands Inc.; J. Crew and Bebe, there's a key time to land deals: Wednesday through Friday. Since the stores see the heaviest traffic on weekends, merchandisers use the beginning of the week to analyze that sales data and determine what isn't selling well. They get markdowns in place by midweek.

A number of stores have specific days when they reduce prices nationwide: At Eddie Bauer, it's Wednesday. At J. Crew markdowns typically happen on Thursday. Banana Republic and Gap are constantly getting in new merchandise, so the discounts continue until the clothing is gone, but the first price cut is often the deepest.

HIGH-END STORES

When a change purse can cost $2,800, there's little pretense when it comes to pricing. These stores, like Barneys, Bergdorf Goodman and Saks discourage bargain-hunters by using sales sparingly, and keeping their customers accustomed to paying full price. Barneys has just two sales a year, one in February, the other in August. Sales usually start on the eighth of the month. Neiman Marcus has four brief sales a year—the first one is in January.

The only other way to get a deal? Ask for one. Customers report these stores are increasingly willing to barter, or offer quiet deals, like waiting to charge a customer's credit card until after an item goes on sale.

RESALE SHOPS

Not long ago, resale or "consignment" shops were second-floor repositories where frumps and college students picked over the out-of-style frocks wealthy women retired from their closets. But some of the more haute consignment shops are honing strategies for attracting trendier, and wealthier, shoppers. They don't pay for inventory—consignors bring the goods and split the proceeds 50-50—so overhead costs are low. Owners have more pricing flexibility. Assortments change daily. Hint: Go during season changes, when wealthy women like to clean out their closets.

SAMPLE SALES

These sales are held by top designers to make back some of the money they spent putting together sample outfits to show to store buyers.

The items, plus overstock and cancelled store orders, are sold to the public, but the affairs are kept hush-hush in order not to anger retailers. The result is that most sample sales are patronized primarily by fashion "insiders" who have connections to those running the sales. It's a great way to buy clothes for the season that's happening when you shop, but there are some things to keep in mind: Most sales are final; many don't have dressing rooms, so wear something you can try on clothes over easily; go early and avoid lunchtime shopping and always call ahead. For a list of sample sales in New York, and more sample sales tips, go to **theinsider.com**, click on "New York City," "saving a few bucks" and "sample sales." In Los Angeles, check out "Billion Dollar Babes," a clothing sample sale that offers $200 Platinum memberships that include early admission and a separate dressing room.

FLEA MARKETS

A Web site, **fleamarketguide.com**, means you can now get a listing of markets large and small throughout the country. You click on a state to find the markets there. But don't get lost in the crowd! The site is kind of like a flea market itself. Check out the wholesalers' links if you want to know where flea-market dealers get those dolphin lamps.

OUTLET STORES

Some department stores have developed separate chains out of clearance items. The Nordstrom Rack stores feature original merchandise along with unsold goods from Nordstrom's full-price stores; Boston's Filene's department store gave birth decades ago to a clearance center, Filene's Basement; Neiman Marcus has its Last Call stores, located in outlet malls from Arizona to Michigan; and Dillard has clearance stores in places like Kansas.

THE ART OF GETTING WAITED ON

With stores getting more colossal than ever, it can be hard to get help. Here are some tips for minimizing the aggravation:

1. **Look for telephones or other in-store service assistances.** For example, Lowe's has buzzers in its stores to summon a staffer. Some stores owned by Toys "R" Us have phones scattered around that you can pick up and ask for help.

2. **Try shopping-mall name stores that have freestanding branches:** Rents are generally cheaper and operating costs can be significantly lower because the retailers don't have to pay shared utility costs for common areas. And since shoppers are more likely to go to a freestanding store for a specific item, sales per square foot are typically higher than in mall-based stores. The standalone stores appeal to busy people who say they don't have time to spend browsing through a mall.

ⓘ Designer labels are increasingly popping up in outlet malls. For a complete listing, check out **Outletbound.com.** Here's a list of some of the best:

1. **Yves Saint Laurent:** Locations include Secaucus, New Jersey, and Desert Hills Premium Outlets in Cabazon, California.

2. **Tod's:** Locations include Desert Hills Premium Outlets in Cabazon, California; Orlando Premium Outlets in Orlando, Florida; Fashion Outlet of Las Vegas in Las Vegas, Nevada; Woodbury Common Premium Outlets in Central Valley, New York. At the Desert Hills store, new arrivals come in once a week, usually on Wednesday.

3. **Loro Piana:** Locations include Woodbury Common Premium Outlets in Central Valley, New York. New shipments come in every month or so.

4. **Carolina Herrera:** Location includes Woodbury Common Premium Outlets in Central Valley, New York. There's no set delivery schedule. Shipments are sporadic.

5. **Prada, Miu Miu:** Locations include Desert Hills Premium Outlets in Cabazon, California; Woodbury Common Premium Outlets in Central Valley, New York. There are two big deliveries a year at the Cabazon store. Deliveries are timed so fall outlet goods ship around the same time as fall regular-price goods.

6. **Giorgio Armani General Store:** Locations include Desert Hills Premium Outlets in Cabazon, California; Orlando Premium Outlets in Orlando, Florida; Woodbury Common Premium Outlets in Central Valley, New York; Manchester Designer Outlets in Manchester, Vermont.

GARAGE SALES

Been to a tag sale lately? If not, you're in for a surprise. Thanks to everything from eBay to the *Antiques Roadshow,* this once humble weekend tradition has fast become a front-lawn standoff between fortune-seeking sellers and bargain-hunting buyers. Nobody, it seems, wants to sell anything—even Grandma's old trash can—for less than $25. In some towns, the number of sales themselves has dropped. And all those friendly buyers, who were once content to putter their weekends away at sales, have turned into eBay sharpies, snatching up tag-sale finds just to "flip" them in online auctions.

So savvy tag-sale browsers have changed tactics: While yard-sale gospel says you have to hit a sale first thing in the morning in order to find the best stuff, some veterans are starting to wait until the end of the day. The reason? That's when some of the sales' high-priced goods finally have to come down. Some suggest doing "homework" on tag-sale goods before hitting any sale. And others claim you can even make a living out of people's junk, because the Internet has widened the scope for reselling those 25-cent T-shirts and ashtrays from garage sales.

GOVERNMENT SALES

The federal government sells everything from cars and planes seized by Customs, to carpets, computers and clothes auctioned by the U.S. Treasury, to surplus scrap metal from the military. Many states (and state universities) sell extra stuff like camcorders and pressure-washers and generators on eBay.

The best way to find out about all these different sales is to go to the Web site **firstgov.gov/shopping/auctions/surplus.shtml.**

THE SCIENCE OF PRICING

In recent years there's been a shift in pricing, with many companies starting to use the same computer programs used by airlines to analyze customer buying patterns and help stores determine when to launch discounts. The good news: So far, the new programs have delivered a clear message to retailers to start markdowns earlier. But consumers increasingly need to beware of "bundling," where companies cut prices on one item to lure you into buying a related product at a steep markup. One example: Retailers might discount a $199 home-theater system but make up the margin on accessories like a $49.99 surge protector or a $119.99 connection kit.

Here's a power shopper's guide to taking advantage of the new pricing schemes:

COMPACT DISCS

Looking for a deal on a new release? Hit the stores now. If a CD is released on a Tuesday, prices could rise as early as Sunday. That's generally the case with new CDs at chains like Best Buy Co. and J&R. The deep early discounts sometimes even drop below the wholesale cost. Not every chain adheres to such a rigid pattern: Tower Records, among other stores, keeps prices low as long as the CD remains a best-seller. And there are exceptions. Some mega-groups have it written into their contracts that their albums won't be sold at a deep discount right after the release. Also, buy used CDs—but only if you can return them if something's amiss.

ELECTRONICS

Price competition is fierce on DVD players and digital cameras and many retailers offer deals simply to draw traffic, often selling them at close to cost. The spring is the best time to shop, as manufacturers begin to roll out their new lines in March and April—and start discounting last year's models to clear the shelves. Historically, Hewlett-Packard Co., Kodak, Nikon and Fuji Photo Film Co. have all

GROCERIES:
THINGS SUPERMARKETS WON'T TELL YOU

They're the three words supermarket shoppers have become obsessed with: "You just saved." That is the phrase increasingly being chirped by grocery-store clerks these days amid the rapid proliferation of supermarket club cards. These programs are calculated to appeal directly to your inner penny-pincher: Swipe your membership card in the checkout line, and the next thing you know a receipt prints out saying something like, "You just saved $21.83." Message: You are being rewarded with deals so special, they are reserved for members only.

But how much cash are you really saving by shopping at a supermarket that has a card, instead of a non-card store? To find out, *The Wall Street Journal* went shopping at both types of stores and talked to a range of card experts. We found that, most likely, you are saving no money at all. In fact, if you are shopping at a store using a card, you may be spending more money than you would down the street at a grocery store that doesn't have a discount card. We learned this the hard way, by going on a five-city, shop-till-you-drop grocery spree. In each city, we shopped at a store using its discount card, and afterward went to a nearby grocery store that doesn't have a card, and bought the same things. Then we rolled up our sleeves, unrolled our receipts and crunched the numbers. In all five of our comparisons, we wound up spending less money in a supermarket that doesn't offer a card—in one case, 29 percent less.

The bottom line: Sale prices—which were once available to all shoppers—are now mostly restricted to cardholders in stores with cards and are called "card specials." In our experience, items not covered by card discounts tended to be more expensive than at nearby non-card stores. As a result, we paid more at card stores than at non-card stores.

cut prices at that time. As always, the rule with electronics is, prices constantly fall as models age.

VIDEO GAMES

Video-game makers capitalize on the fact that kids aren't patient. Games are priced highest when they are first released and drop in regular intervals during the next year, when kids' attention shifts to the new hot product. For those willing to wait, the price drops like clockwork. Typical games have an average shelf life of 12 months. During

SIGNS OF THE SHOPAHOLIC

How do you know if you're a compulsive shopper? Some telltale behavior:

1. **Preoccupation with shopping. You need a shopping "fix" and it's constantly on your mind.**
2. **It results in debt.**
3. **It results in family or marital discord.**
4. **You often buy things that go unused.**
5. **You like to shop at least once a week.**

that period, there are three price cuts, of $10 each, in three- or four-month increments. By the end of the 12 months, they hit the bargain bin at $19.99. In addition, the entire video-game market works on a five-year cycle, tied to the release of new PlayStation2 game consoles. The price on newly released games starts to fall in the third and fourth year of the console life span.

SHOPPING ONLINE

BARGAINING IN CYBERSPACE

It's pretty simple (or it should be) to find what you want in a brick-and-mortar store: You ask, and somebody can point you to what you're seeking.

Most online stores still use only the most rudimentary search software, but if you have patience and use common sense, you can get much better deals through the Internet than at the local mall—plus a wealth of research and reviews about almost any product you could want to buy.

WHAT A DEAL

A handful of bargain-basement Web sites (see "Online Bargain Basements" on p. 429 for a complete listing) buy unsold wares such as high-end bedding, designer clothes and electronics from retailers and

DO YOU NEED A PILL TO STOP SHOPPING?

Deborah Rodriguez sometimes gets headaches from trying to resist the temptation of clearance sales. Once, she came home with six packages of clothespins even though she didn't own a clothesline. But recently, she found a new way to rein in her shopping urge. After taking the antidepressant Celexa as part of a Stanford University study, she says that she was less driven to shop. Things may start looking up for more people like Ms. Rodriguez.

"Compulsive shopping" is increasingly being looked at not just as a silly habit or a source of tiffs between spouses, but as a mental disorder. New studies indicate that antidepressants may help, while a budding movement to get compulsive shopping formally recognized as a medical problem could convince more insurers to cover treatments.

Behind much of this is a growing tendency in the psychiatric community to view as treatable a variety of problems that were once considered lifestyle quirks (such as nervousness about going to parties or addressing a boss). In the case of compulsive shoppers, Forest Laboratories Inc., maker of Celexa, has funded three studies so far that test whether its antidepressants may help reduce the amount of time people spend obsessing about shopping or prowling the stores. While larger and more rigorous trials are needed, early results suggest that Celexa has some benefits.

All this is heating up a debate in the psychiatry world: Should compulsive shopping be a formally recognized disorder with its own listing in the *American Psychiatric Association's Diagnostic and Statistical Manual of Mental Disorders,* the bible of mental illnesses? Impulse-control-disorder experts who are involved with revising the manual's next edition say they are already planning to come up with a stand-alone definition and diagnostic code for the behavior. That would be a big boost for antidepressant-makers, since many insurers are currently reluctant to cover

manufacturers, then resell them at deep discounts online. Internet-based sellers can function with extremely low overhead by selling directly to consumers, and can also save shoppers the hassle of bumping elbows at discount stores.

Some big retailers are getting into the act themselves: Sharper Image, RadioShack and Dell Computer all auction liquidation items on **eBay.com;** even **Amazon.com,** the largest Internet retailer, is buying liquidated products to resell as part of its efforts to keep prices low.

But sometimes there are obvious reasons why the leftovers didn't sell in the first place, like odd color combinations or unusual sizes. Another

treatments for compulsive shopping. Without a separate classification, the problem "is generally not perceived by the public as a serious issue," says Donald Black, a professor of psychiatry at the University of Iowa who has also studied compulsive shopping. Most insurance companies say, "It's an unproven condition of questionable validity and we're not going to pay for it."

The notion that compulsive shopping can be considered a medical disorder is a recent development. In the past, serious cases of compulsive shopping were typically considered symptoms of other mental problems, such as bipolar disorder or serious depression. Some critics don't see any reason for that to change. Darrel A. Regier, director of research at the American Psychiatric Association, expects a rigorous approval process before a new classification can be published. "I don't think there's been sufficient evidence to warrant consideration for compulsive shopping as a mental disorder," he adds.

But proponents of the idea say the category could include everyone from those who can't resist a sale to people who have trouble paying their bills. It's a "significant public-health problem" if you take into account the number of people who have trouble controlling their credit cards and debt, says Susan McElroy, a professor of psychiatry at the University of Cincinnati, who has published criteria for diagnosing compulsive shopping. One study published in the *Journal of Consumer Research* estimates that between 2 and 8 percent of the U.S. population are compulsive shoppers or "at risk" of becoming one.

So how do you know if you need a pill to stop shopping? Psychiatrists agree that plenty of people can take pleasure in shopping without getting into trouble. "If you like to shop and you're not running up a debt, it's not interfering with your marriage and you're not getting fired from your job," then it's not a problem, says Eric Hollander, a New York psychiatrist who will be involved in revisions for the next diagnostic manual. But when a person's shopping "significantly interferes with their functioning, then it's a disorder," he adds.

---

downside of off-price Internet shopping: shipping fees that sometimes get tacked onto your order. Then there are the sometimes Draconian return policies. If the sites allow returns at all, they don't make it easy, charging return fees and shipping. The Web site **eValueville.com,** which buys from department stores such as Bloomingdale's, doesn't allow returns, period.

Customers should also take the "retail" prices listed alongside the discounts at many sites with a grain of salt—since many products on the liquidation market are discontinued, the retail prices aren't always an accurate reflection of an item's current value.

SHOPPING? IT'S MY JOB—REALLY!

On the breezy patio of the Silver Lake Golf Course in Staten Island, New York, Jennifer Voitle was hard at work. "Cheers," she said, hoisting a frosty Corona with lime. Tanned and relaxed after playing a few holes, she finished up the beer and ate a cheeseburger. The golf and burgers were all part of the job, as were the strict instructions from her boss to "consume at least one alcoholic beverage."

Her morning jobs were equally trying. She went dress shopping, stepped into a bank to cash a check and visited a Saturn dealership to look at new cars. After golf, she was headed to Manhattan for dinner at a nice Italian restaurant. All these activities were paid jobs. Her total earnings for the day: about $300. "Can you believe they call this work?" she said.

Jennifer Voitle has mastered the Freebie Economy. A former investment-bank employee who was laid off two years ago, Ms. Voitle has found a new career in the arcane world of dining deals, gift certificates and "mystery shopping," where companies pay her to test their products and services. She gets paid to shop, eat at restaurants, drink at bars, travel and even play golf.

She gets free gas, free groceries and free clothes. When her car breaks down, she gets paid to have it repaired. She can make $75 for test-driving a Land Rover, $20 for drinking at a bar and $25 for playing arcade games (she keeps any winnings).

Golfing is her latest passion, and in addition to playing on courses around the country free of charge, she gets free food and drinks and gifts from the pro shop. Weekend trips to Hawaii and Mexico? "I don't pay for anything except occasional meals," she says. She does much of her work on a free handheld computer. "My friends tell me I should just get a job," says Ms. Voitle, who is slim and blond and gives her age as "somewhere over 30." But, she says, "most full-time jobs out there don't make economic sense."

Ms. Voitle never planned on becoming a freeloader. A trained engineer and financial expert, with four advanced degrees and a gift for numbers theory, Ms. Voitle worked for years

---

It's also possible to get deals online by using special retail codes— just go to one of the following Web sites: **naughtycodes.com, currentcodes.com, dealhunting.com** and **discountcodes.com.** Users scroll down the menu to find stores, then enter the store's discount code to complete a purchase. For the most part, retailers don't seem to mind this code-sharing practice, saying it's a way for folks to find out

as a number-cruncher for Detroit's auto factories. Her real dream was to make it big on Wall Street. In 2000, she got her break when Lazard LLC, the storied investment bank, hired her to analyze fixed-income derivatives in the firm's asset-management business.

Single, with a salary of more than $100,000, Ms. Voitle bought a house in leafy Baldwin, New York, complete with a pool and gym. She spent weekends golfing, traveling or playing with her cats—Continental and Northwest. In the fall of 2001, she was laid off. With thousands of other investment-bank workers losing their jobs, Ms. Voitle couldn't find any financial work. Last summer, her unemployment checks ran out and both her electricity and phone were shut off. "I woke up one morning and said, 'That's it. I have to start looking for money, wherever I can find it,' " she says.

Trolling the Internet, she discovered an ad for mystery shopping. "I thought, 'This looks too good to be true,' " she says. Mystery shoppers get paid to sample a company's service or products and write a report on their experience. For companies, mystery shopping is a popular way of checking on quality.

For Ms. Voitle, it was a quick source of cash and freebies. Her first assignment was a Pathmark grocery store, where she received free groceries and $10 for a quick report. She worked her way up to gas stations, clothing stores and restaurants. She quickly discovered that the best-paying mystery-shopping jobs were for upscale businesses like banks and high-end car dealers. She earns $75 for test-driving a Land Rover, compared with about $30 for a Ford.

Volume is critical. On any given day, she will mystery-shop gas stations, grocery stores, golf courses, clothing stores, casinos, hotels, insurance companies and restaurants. She even gets paid to shop for apartments and interview for jobs.

Beyond mystery shopping, Ms. Voitle also collects gift certificates, travel deals, two-for-one coupons and cross-promotional deals. She does detailed cost-benefit analyses of most of her deals. She's always on the lookout for what she calls "freebie synergies," or combining multiple deals to get more value. Before she sets out each morning, she plans a detailed travel route to make sure she hits the greatest possible number of stores.

---

about deals; in fact, many retailers work directly with sites like this to promote discounts.

Another approach is simply buying something online and then signing up for special promotions and e-mail alerts—sometimes you don't even need to buy something. Some of these deals can be found on bargain-hunter sites such as **DealHunting.com, ShoppersResource.com** and **QuickToClick.com,** which post coupons and discount codes. Discount codes are also posted on sites such as **TrendyLA.com** (click on "Discount Shopping") and **Passwird.com.**

Some shopping sites claim to search the Internet for the cheapest price out there. Known as "shopping 'bots" (short for "robot"), these services—**DealTime.com, MySimon.com, Bargaindog.com, Saleseeker.com** and **PriceGrabber.com**—search prices at hundreds of online retailers so you don't have to click all those pages yourself. Google's Froogle price-finding tool claims to scour the entire Internet for deals, whereas many other sites search only merchants with whom they have advertising relationships. Longstanding rivals are adding bells and whistles; most now offer tax-and-shipping calculators to make price comparisons easier.

Online coupons are another saving device. Delivery methods vary, but most demand some pertinent information used for market research and then let you print the coupons directly from manufacturers' Web sites. The Web sites include **CoolSavings.com** and **Freestuffcentral.com.** Another site, **ValuePage.com**, requires only a zip code and e-mail address. You can find classified ads for any newspaper in the country online. That's a great way to locate anything from cars to furniture to a pet tiger. Or you can go to an online classified site like **classifieds2000.com** or **freeclassifiedads.com.**

Another way to save (and get items faster) is to pick up your online purchases instead of paying for shipping. From Best Buy Co. to Circuit City Stores Inc. to Recreational Equipment Inc., an increasing number of retailers are touting in-store pickup—a sort of drive-thru window for people who shop on the Internet. Home delivery of a 250-pound kayak, for example, typically costs $85.

But in-store pickup doesn't always mean you can get your items instantaneously. The key to making it work is asking how much time it will take to arrive at a nearby branch before you buy.

What's really great about the Internet is the free, unbiased product advice based on what other Internet denizens say about certain merchandise. For that, check out:

1. **Myproductadvisor.com.** On this site you say what features are important to you and get recommendations based on your preferences. For example, if you're looking for a digital camera, the Web site asks you whether you're more interested in taking high-quality action shots or

long-distance shots; whether you want to be able to produce large prints suitable for framing or smaller photos for a scrapbook; which editing features are important to you—and so on. The questions get very detailed, but if you're impatient you can just skip straight to the recommendations at any time.

On this screen you get a list of all the recommended products, with prices, photos and descriptions, and you can see side-by-side comparisons of the ones you're interested in. The information you submit is completely private: The company just uses the aggregate data as a kind of survey to show manufacturers what consumers are thinking. It charges the manufacturers for access to this information, meaning the service is free for consumers. You don't have to give any personal details to use the site.

2. Consumer-action.org. Run by the agency Consumer Action, it reminds you of your rights, and reports on cases of fraud. It also helps you figure out how to buy a range of products.

3. ConsumerReview.com. This website is actually a portal to a number of more specialized sites that are owned by the same company, such as **audioreview.com, photographyreview.com** and so on. It relies on reviews and ratings posted by other users of the site. Many of the reviews are long and quite detailed. You can sort the products in each category alphabetically, by price, by rating or by number of reviews. There's also a forum where you can post questions or comments about a product. You can read all the content free without giving any information; if you want to post messages or write reviews, you have to sign up, but that's also free. The site makes money from advertisements and from offering sponsored links to companies, but the reviews and ratings are submitted by users.

4. Epinions.com. Like ConsumerReview, Epinions lets people post reviews and rate products on its site, so that you can then read what other people are saying. You can search by brand and price, and by other criteria specific to that product. If you're looking for a camcorder, for example, you can narrow it down by recording format or zoom capability. After you've read the reviews on a product, you hit "compare prices" to get an instant comparison of the prices offered for that product at different stores across the Internet. The site is free to use, and the ratings and reviews come from other consumers.

Epinions merged with price-comparison company **Dealtime.com,** and all Epinions reviews are now on the combined **Shopping.com** site.

5. **Consumerworld.org.** A way to keep up to date on all consumer issues, including news quickies on everything from the latest scams to recent government regulations. The site also gives product reviews, price comparisons and links to consumer agencies.

6. **Internet news and use groups.** We recommend caution here. Some expert sites may prove their worth—professional photographers shopping for a particular high-end digital camera can tap the knowledge and experience of others who've used such a camera, for example. But for the general consumer, there's so much disorganized, biased and misguided advice on these newsgroups and discussion boards that it's easy to spend all day and end up more confused than when you began.

KEEPING SAFE AND SECURE ON THE INTERNET

The most important (and most obvious) advice about shopping online is to make sure the site you're buying from is secure—one that scrambles credit-card numbers. And check to make sure the site has a mailing address and phone number to contact in case there's a problem.

Panic about using a credit card online has diminished since the early days of the Internet, in part because credit-card issuers have made online shopping safer. One big step: offering virtual account numbers, or substitute card numbers, which typically have the same number of digits as a regular credit-card number.

First find out if your credit-card company offers the service; if it does, sign up and register your card at the company's Web site. You may have to download software to your computer or come back to the site to get a new disposable account number before each purchase. In general, the number can be used at only one merchant, whether for a single purchase or for a service with a recurring monthly charge. Virtual account numbers, however, can't be used for all transactions, since some require the actual credit card to be presented to claim purchases; the single-use number, by its nature, doesn't appear on your credit card and is typically linked to your account only through the issuer's system.

Even with a safe credit card, you can still get duped by unreliable Web sites that sell different products than advertised—or just take your money and run. But there are a couple ways to check them out first.

ONLINE BARGAIN BASEMENTS

Where to find off-price deals on everything from Prada bags to Olympus cameras:

WEB SITE: BLUEFLY.COM

Description: A designer-shopper's bonanza, with clothing by high-end designers, including Gucci and Prada

Return policy: Ninety-day money-back guarantee

Shipping: $7.95 flat fee no matter how large the order

WEB SITE: OVERSTOCK.COM

Description: A massive off-price site with a wide selection of everything from jewelry to toasters

Return policy: Charges a $4.95 fee for returns; 15 percent restocking fee for electronics

Shipping: Flat rate of $2.95; $50 charge on oversize items

WEB SITE: SMARTBARGAINS.COM

Description: An easy-to-navigate online warehouse that includes luggage, TVs, kitchen appliances and designer shoes

Return policy: Returns accepted for any reason for 30 days

Shipping: Flat rate of $6.95, no matter how much you order

WEB SITE: EBAY.COM

Description: The world's largest Internet bazaar. Some companies, like Sharper Image, sell excess or reconditioned inventory on the site.

Return policy: Depends on the seller

Shipping: Varies by seller

WEB SITE: EVALUEVILLE.COM

Description: Auctions leftover goods from retailers that have included Bloomingdale's on eBay. Very erratic selection—no frills, but dirt cheap.

Return policy: No returns

Shipping: $5.95 on first item; rate drops on additional items

1. Trustmarks: Watch for these Internet equivalents of the Good Housekeeping Seal of Approval. One of the best-known trust marks is that of **BBBOnline.org,** a service of the U.S. Council of Better Business Bureaus, based in Arlington, Virginia. To earn BBBOnline's "reliability seal," a merchant must meet requirements, including

INTERNET SHOPPING BECOMES MORE TAXING

 A growing number of Internet shopping sites are starting to charge sales tax, but there are still some holdouts. Here's a look at who charges and who doesn't:

RETAILER: **WALMART.COM**

Where it charges sales tax*: All states with a sales tax

Why: Recently expanded sales-tax collection so it can offer more combination services, such as in-store pickup of online orders.

Comment: Similar pricing at **Walmart.com** and Wal-Mart stores, although **Walmart.com** has a better selection in some categories, such as big-screen TVs.

RETAILER: **GAP.COM, OLDNAVY.COM, BANANAREPUBLIC.COM**

Where it charges sales tax: All states with a sales tax. Some clothing and footwear are exempt in Connecticut, Massachusetts, Minnesota, New Jersey, New York, Pennsylvania, Rhode Island and Vermont.

Why: Conveniences like in-store returns of online merchandise mean Gap has long collected sales tax for purchases from all its Internet stores.

Comment: Free shipping on **Gap.com,** where prices are the same as Gap stores; applies only to orders over $75

RETAILER: **TOYSRUS.COM**

Where it charges sales tax: All states with a sales tax, except Arkansas, the District of Columbia and Wyoming

Why: Company began charging sales tax recently in all states where it has stores so that customers can return Internet purchases in stores.

Comment: Site often has deals not available in its stores, not to mention serenity compared to the chaos of the store aisles.

RETAILER: **STAPLES.COM**

Where it charges sales tax: All states with sales tax, except Hawaii

Why: The office-supply retailer says it's legally obligated to collect sales taxes because the Web site is integrated into Staples' operations.

Comment: Customers can still get a good deal if they order at least $50 worth of goods, qualifying for free shipping.

RETAILER: **BESTBUY.COM**

Where it charges sales tax: All applicable states, doesn't deliver to Hawaii

Why: Web site collects in all states where Best Buy has stores.

Comment: Merchandise prices are the same in stores, but with a free-shipping offer on all Internet purchases, consumers aren't paying more for online convenience.

RETAILER: **SEARS.COM**

Where it charges sales tax*: All states with sales tax

Why: Sears store and Internet operations are tightly integrated, opening up **Sears.com** to sales-tax liability.

Comment: With shipping charges, Internet customers will pay more online. But between 30 and 40 percent of **Sears.com** customers pick up their Internet orders in stores to avoid delivery charges.

RETAILER: **DELL.COM**

Where it charges sales tax: Texas, Tennessee, Florida, Ohio, Kentucky, Nevada, North Carolina, Pennsylvania, Idaho

Why: Charges sales tax in any state with a Dell call center, manufacturing plant or other physical outpost

Comment: **Costco.com** sometimes sells models at prices below Dell's. **Costco.com** charges sales tax in 30 states, to Dell's nine, though.

RETAILER: **BARNESANDNOBLE.COM**

Where it charges sales tax: New York, New Jersey, Tennessee, Nevada, Florida, Massachusetts, Pennsylvania, South Carolina, Wisconsin

Why: Limited sales tax because the Web site remains separate from the retail company, but it still collects in states where it has a physical presence.

Comment: Cheaper than most Barnes & Noble stores, since discounts on books are usually steeper; free shipping on orders of $25 or more.

RETAILER: **AMAZON.COM**

Where it charges sales tax: Washington State, North Dakota, Kansas

Why: Only collects sale taxes where it has headquarters and a customer-service center

Comment: Very limited sales tax, steep discount, plus free shipping on orders over $25 means most items are cheaper at Amazon than at stores.

*Delaware, Montana, New Hampshire and Oregon don't have sales tax.

promptly responding to consumer complaints, agreeing to dispute resolution at a consumer's request and agreeing to a code of business practices. BBBOnline and other services also have seals that indicate a site's privacy policy meets certain requirements. And VeriSign Inc., based in Mountain View, California, provides a trust mark that indicates a site has obtained a digital identification card that provides some assurance that the site isn't an impostor and will protect credit-card and other personal information as it's transmitted to the site.

2. Consumer Feedback: Sites like BizRate.com, DealTime.com and **ResellerRatings.com** show what shoppers have to say about a broad range of retail sites, by rating stores and posting shopper comments. Some have refined their ratings to allow consumers to review specific aspects of retail sites, like the speediness of delivery or whether a product met expectations. Generally speaking, store ratings that stem from a larger number of reviews are more reliable than those compiled from, say, three shoppers. If you're browsing on eBay, take a look at the Feedback Forum, which allows buyers and sellers to rate their experiences transacting with each other.

3. And finally, make sure you pick a safe password; they're very easy to crack if they're simple. For example, using a family name—which is what more than half of respondents in several surveys have confessed to doing—is like an open invitation to access your private data. The longer and more complex your password, the harder and longer a hacker will have to work to crack it. So make full use of the tools offered. If the program or Web site allows you to have a password that's 14 characters long, use them all. If you're allowed to use capital letters and other characters, do it. It's the difference between "johnbrown" and "j()7*n_b50%N." Change your passwords every few months, don't use the same password for multiple accounts and never give a password to anyone. Store them on your palmlike device if you like, but remember that even in a well-encrypted file, all your valuable stuff is just one password away from being accessed.

SOME MORE PASSWORD TIPS

1. Begin with mnemonics or acronyms. You could use the title of your favorite song or movie, or the name of your favorite football team, as a starter. Avoid things like your birthday, your place of birth or your kids' names. What you want is something that you know a lot about, but not something that other people can find out about you. How do you turn a movie title into a password? Well, if *The Year of Living Dangerously* is a favorite film, you could take the first letters of the title and use them in conjunction with the initials of its two main stars, Mel Gibson and Sigourney Weaver, to create the password "tyoldmgsw."

2. Now turn some of your letters into numbers, punctuation symbols and capitals. Try turning the "o" into a similar-looking zero, the "l" into a one and the "s" into a five. That would give you "ty01dmg5w," which is a lot better and still easy to remember since the numbers are similar to the letters they've replaced.

3. Add a finishing trick or two. Sadly, the people who write hacking programs are on to techniques like replacing letters with numbers, so your password is still a bit vulnerable. So try capitalizing the family-name letters, alter the "0" to similar-looking bracket marks () and move the numeric characters one key to the left on your keyboard. If the Web site or program you're using allows it, try using such less-common characters as "OA" or "y." These can be entered by having the number lock key on, holding down the "Alt" key, and then pressing the appropriate code on the number pad to the right of your keyboard.

PRODUCTS FREQUENTLY BOUGHT ONLINE

Drugs

An e-mail message from an Internet pharmacy blares: "Your VALIUM prescription is ready." "Get Valium, Xanax, Prozac and more ON-LINE!!" Its Web site touts that "it has never been easier to get the drugs you need," and suggests customers start by clicking on the drug they want. The e-mail come-ons are inescapable, and their message is clear: It's easy to get prescription drugs online. But is it a good idea—not to mention legal? And is it really as easy as they say?

The answer to all those: yes and no. There are reputable Internet pharmacies out there that provide drug shoppers with a measure of convenience and privacy. The best use the Internet to provide information about drug interactions and will e-mail customers if a drug they ordered has been recalled, or a cheaper, generic version has become available. Some also sell drugs for less than brick-and-mortar pharmacies, which is important for people without drug coverage.

However, there are dangers in ordering drugs online. Some sites ship substandard drugs. Others may not adequately check for drug interactions. Sites that prescribe drugs without a physician's consultation may offer pills that are dangerous for certain individuals, such as those with compromised immune systems. Furthermore, two Internet-pharmacy offerings—cheap drugs from Canada-based online pharmacies and prescriptions obtained online without actually seeing a doctor in person—skirt the edge of legality.

The following is a look at the issues involving online pharmacies, and the good and the bad ways the Internet is helping fulfill a health-care need.

1. **Safety.** For most people thinking about buying prescription drugs online, the primary concern is safety. Is the online pharmacist reliable, and will there be someone there to help them with any special needs? Some things to look for are seals from boards of pharmacy in the states where the pharmacy does business; posted policies about prescription verification and customer support and the usual common-sense signals of a reputable e-merchant, like a professional-looking site and a posted address or phone number you can call to reach a human being.

The surest way to choose a safe online drugstore is to look for the Verified Internet Pharmacy Practice Sites, or VIPPS, seal, which shows a druggist has been certified by the National Association of Boards of Pharmacy, a national group in Park Ridge, Illinois, representing the 50 state pharmacy boards, as well as some outside the country. To be included in the program, a pharmacy must pledge to facilitate patient-pharmacist communication and provide safe storage and shipment for its drugs, among other criteria. The program also confirms the pharmacies' state licenses and inspects their facilities.

2. **Savings.** An indisputable advantage of shopping online: It's more convenient to compare prices among Internet pharmacies than among the brick-and-mortar kind. Internet pharmacies say they can offer savings because of the centralized warehousing for fulfilling orders and the efficiencies of scale. The biggest bargains come from Canada (with Web site names like **canadapharmacy.com, canadadrugs.com, affordablerx.com**), thanks to government price controls. But there's a

hitch: The Food and Drug Administration bans the cross-border shipment of drugs into the United States. It sends warning letters to overseas pharmacies and alerts the Customs Service to watch out for packages from them. At the same time, the FDA has made it clear that its enforcement efforts are targeting overseas pharmacies that ship drugs to the United States, and not individuals importing non-narcotic prescription drugs.

3. Privacy. For shoppers whose utmost concern is privacy, the benefit of online shopping is indisputable. Instead of dealing with a pharmacist face-to-face, alongside other customers, online shoppers can submit their prescriptions by fax or have the Internet store's pharmacist call their doctors. As for the confidentiality of the information being exchanged, Internet pharmacies employ similar security procedures as most other e-commerce sites. **Drugstore.com,** for instance, makes sure employee access to the data is on a need-to-know basis.

The company also employs the current security industry's "best practices," which include regular security audits. What's more, **Drug store.com** contracts with outside "white-hat hackers" to probe its network for weaknesses and try to compromise it by any means possible. Advocates of online pharmacies argue that the Internet can extend privacy and anonymity to the prescribing of drugs as well. Rather than go to the doctor's office about a prescription, some online services offer prescriptions using an electronic questionnaire, which a doctor working with a site will review and if needed write a prescription.

FOOD

Whether it's German gingerbread, French foie gras, Spanish squid ink for *arroz negro,* or even *pomodori pelati* for a plate of perfect papal pasta, you'll find it on an astounding number of sites selling gourmet foods online.

Start with **GourmetSleuth.com,** based in

VERIFIED INTERNET-PHARMACY PRACTICE SITES (VIPPS) APPROVED BY THE NATIONAL ASSOCIATION BOARDS OF PHARMACY

1. accuratepharmacy.com
2. AdvanceRx.com
3. AnthemPrescription.com
4. rxrequest.com
5. Clickpharmacy.com
6. cvs.com
7. drugstore.com
8. Eckerd.com
9. Familymeds.com
10. medcohealth.com
11. careforlife.com
12. rxwest.com
13. teldrug.com
14. walgreens.com

Los Gatos, California, for guidance, and just plug in what you're looking for. A couple other good sites: **Petrossian.com** and **IGourmet.com.** Buying across borders can be tricky, in part due to export regulations on some food products.

And many delicacies can be found locally, of course, shielding you from language barriers, import-regulation headaches and shipping costs. Shipping charges—one of the main things that keeps more people from buying food online—can be mitigated if you use the buddy system. Find a friend in your office or neighborhood who wants to order from the same site as you, and split the shipping costs. And don't forget, looks can be deceiving. Some of the most attractive, professional-looking sites can have comparatively high prices or lack the selection found on plainer sites.

RATING SOME INTERNET MUSIC STORES

Legal music downloading is slowly gaining traction. More and more companies are offering online music stores, and the number of songs available at most of them has now crossed 500,000.

Apple Computer, the first to offer a good legal download service, is still the leader, by far. Its iTunes music store has sold more than 50 million tracks since April of 2004. Nobody else is even close.

But recently, two other big names have launched their own music download stores to challenge Apple and to stake a claim before Microsoft jumps into the business. One is RealNetworks, long a leader in digital audio. The other is Wal-Mart, the giant retailer. We've been testing the new RealPlayer Music Store and the Wal-Mart music download service, and comparing them to the iTunes store. Our verdict: thumbs-up to Real, but thumbs-down to Wal-Mart.

Wal-Mart's service, which is available under Music Downloads at **walmart.com,** has just one thing going for it: price. Unlike the other major legal services, which charge 99 cents a song, Wal-Mart charges 88 cents.

But that 11-cent savings comes at a steep cost. Wal-Mart's download service is much clumsier, slower and more complicated to use than any of the other major services. It shows a fundamental cluelessness about how digital-music lovers like to buy and play music.

Apple, Musicmatch and now Real embed their music stores in music jukebox software, which also handles your existing music collection.

This software manages your playlists, imports music from CDs, burns your songs to custom CDs, and transfers music to portable players.

But Wal-Mart's service is just a Web site, with no jukebox software. Buying music there is like buying garden tools. You have to go through a laborious process involving shopping carts and checkout procedures.

At Apple's store, you buy songs with a single mouse click, and at most others, two mouse clicks is the maximum. But in tests of the Wal-Mart store, it took at least eight steps to buy a single tune, and then you have to fire up a separate program, Windows Media Player, to play the music. And before the music plays, the Media Player tells you it has to "Acquire a license." The whole process is annoying.

Also, unlike other major download sites, Wal-Mart doesn't include album art with its songs. I'd rather pay 11 cents more per song than endure the deficiencies of the Wal-Mart service.

By contrast, the RealPlayer Music Store is quick, slick and designed for music lovers. It is a part of Real's latest jukebox program, RealPlayer 10, which can be downloaded free at **real.com.**

Both Real's Web site and the RealPlayer software have been overhauled to make them simpler and easier to use. In the past, I have criticized Real for being overly aggressive and intrusive, plastering its icons and links all over your PC. But in the new music store and jukebox software, Real has dropped this approach. It politely asks if it can place icons on your desktop.

The Real Player store organizes music brilliantly, sorting songs into more than 500 subgenres, and offering loads of intelligent commentary on the genres and artists. For instance, at Apple's store, there's one "Country" genre. But in Real's store, you get 15 subgenres of Country. If you click on one of them, "Traditional Country," you get another eight categories, including "Square Dancing" and "Yodeling."

Buying any song takes just two clicks, and you can reduce that to one click by changing an option setting.

Also, the song files Real sells are recorded at a higher quality level than the downloads of the other major legal stores—192 kilobits a second, compared with 128 kilobits for Apple's songs and 160 kilobits for songs on Musicmatch. This makes for better sound if you have discriminating ears. But there's a price. Real's song files take up about 50 percent more space on your hard disk than the identical songs purchased from Apple.

Another big advantage for Real: Its jukebox program is the only one I know of that can play all the major copy-protected formats used by the competing download services as long as you are on a computer that is authorized for playback by those other services. For instance, I downloaded Sheryl Crow's "The First Cut Is the Deepest" from the Apple, Real and Wal-Mart stores, and only Real's software could play all three versions.

But there are some drawbacks to the RealPlayer store. It sells songs in its own proprietary format, which only one portable music player, the Creative Nomad Zen Xtra, can play back. Apple's downloads also play on just one portable device, but it happens to be the iPod, which is by far the most popular player. Wal-Mart's downloads can be played on numerous devices.

The process of setting up playlists or searching for music is clumsier in RealPlayer than in iTunes. And, unlike Apple and Napster, Real doesn't include historical Billboard charts, a very handy tool for finding music. Also, in the new RealPlayer software, album art doesn't always show up, and when it does, it's displayed as a tiny, blurry image.

But, all in all, the RealPlayer Music Store is a winner. It's not as good as Apple's iTunes store, but it's a worthy competitor.

WEDDING HELP ONLINE

For wedding-gift shoppers, the Internet offers particular advantages. With a few clicks, you can track down where the couple is registered without having to ask them directly, and it saves trips to the mall to find the requested items. And an added bonus for couples: Creating registries at multiple stores has never been easier, since your guests can often find your registries all in one place on sites like these:

1. WeddingChannel.com. This site lets you simultaneously search for registries at over a dozen national retailers, including JC Penney, Macy's, Bloomingdale's and Crate & Barrel. When you get on the site, go to the box at the right. Type in either the bride's or groom's first and last name, and it will pop up a list of possible weddings, their dates and links to stores where they've registered. Click on the one you want to check out, and it'll bring you directly to the couple's registry at that store. Most online retailers offer gift-wrapping for a few dollars and you can get the gifts shipped to you, or to the couple directly. If you feel limited by the couple's gift choices, the site offers advice on other gifts to purchase in your price range.

2. Felicite.com. You probably won't find the couple's registry on this site unless they told you about it first. The site, which caters to all sorts of gift-giving occasions, including baby showers and graduations, lets couples create their own registries, and often supplies nontraditional gift requests—for example, cash donations to the "honeymoon fund" or a favorite charity. All the requested gifts, regardless of where they're sold, are listed in one full list. A nice option for guests: You can give as much as you want and contribute partially or fully to gifts. So even if you can't afford the $20,000 speedboat the couple yearns to get, you can give $50 or $100 toward the boat's purchase. However, on cash gifts, the site says it charges a 4.9 percent transaction fee. The site also lets couples build their registries from an unlimited number of stores. Couples can leave descriptions, explaining to guests why they're requesting certain gifts.

3. TheKnot.com. This comprehensive wedding-planner's site includes a database for guests that links to online registries at over 30 national retailers, including Kohl's, Marshall Field's, Target, and Linens 'n Things. When you get to the home page, click on the "gifts & registries" button near the top. Then, under "wedding guests," it lets you type in a bride's or groom's name, wedding date and location—though you often only need a name. It will then list retailers and couples who are registered at those stores. You click on the link and it redirects you to their registry at that store. The site also offers extras such as linking to personal wedding sites that have photos, information about the ceremony and reception and a way for guests to R.S.V.P. online.

STAYING FASHIONABLE

Fashion can be intimidating, to say nothing about mercurial. But there is help out there. A plethora of shopping and fashion Web sites give everything from tips on how to buy the latest Pumas even when they're not yet sold in the United States to whether those Pumas are really something you want to wear.

1. **Dailycandy.com** sends e-mails about new offerings in fashion, describing itself as "like getting an e-mail from your clever, unpredictable and totally in-the-know best friend." The site has city-specific info for New York, Los Angeles and Chicago, but there's also an "everywhere" e-mail, and one for kids' stuff. Many cities have their own versions of Daily Candy—just hunt around.

2. **Gurl.com** has (along with advice on everything from relationships to religion) bulletin boards that focus on shopping and fashion, with headings like "Where can I get . . . a ruffled skirt."

3. **alltheparties.com/intheknow/fashion** provides the latest news stories about fashion trends.

STAYING CLASSIC

Not everyone wants to buy the latest trend. Knowing a few simple rules and sticking to basics make it possible to be a stylish power-dresser—even on a budget.

TIPS FOR MEN

1. **Shirts.** Look for fine-combed cotton, lightweight with a tight weave and a close-cut fit. Sartorially inclined men should choose shirts with French cuffs—an upturned cuff that can be secured either with cuff links or buttons, with sleeves that dip about a centimeter below the wrist bone. The collar should be fitted, and hug the neck snugly with a tie. If you can slip a finger in the neckline, it's too loose. There's one proviso with cutting costs: Get a high-quality silk tie and loop it into a Windsor knot—the classic, triangular knot—to balance the look, otherwise you'll look like a salesclerk.

2. **Suits.** The classic suit is single-breasted, lined, three-button, wool— the equivalent of a four-wheel-drive car that will take you anywhere. Can you save cash and go ready-made? Sure, but make sure you test-drive the jacket. It should hug you smoothly and rest cleanly on your shoulder. No puckers, no bumps. A cheaper fabric that works is Micro-fine, a wool-Lycra mix that helps give a better fit. Other suit mantras: The length of the sleeve should cover the wrist and reach just over the root of the thumb. Only about a centimeter of shirtsleeve should show

past the jacket. And three is the magic number, for the minimum number of suits an executive should have: black, navy blue and pin-striped.

3. Pants. To go with the jacket, wear durable pants: pleated at the front, for comfort, and European-cut—which means the pant has three buttons, with a tab on both sides of the hip. Pull the tab over to the button farthest away and you reduce waist width by almost four centimeters. Undo after a full lunch. With this feature you can extend your pant life to accommodate weight fluctuations. Sadly, the European cut is rarely found on ready-made pants. As for length, trousers should be long enough that socks don't show while walking, while cuffed trousers should rest with a slight break on the top of the shoe.

4. Shoes. Here's what you need to know about good shoes: The leather rounded-toe Oxford lace-up with hand-sewn welting is the most comfortable. Welting—where a strip of material is hand-stitched between the sole and the upper part of the shoe—is essential for enhancing flexibility. It also makes the shoe easier to repair, since cobblers can easily rip and replace, compared to ready-made shoes with glued and molded soles directly attached to the upper. Stitches done by hand are looser than machine-made ones, allowing contours to stretch over time and accommodate feet. If you can't afford custom-made shoes, buy ready-made shoes elsewhere and bring them into a store to have welting put in. This costs about a third of the price of a handmade pair. If you are shopping for even cheaper shoes, keep it simple. Have a staple of black and brown Oxford lace-ups, the standard that steps out well with any suit—whether it's pin-striped or carries a cuffed pant.

BETTER CLOTHES FOR BIGGER GUYS

When it comes to men's clothing, the big-and-tall business may be bigger than you think.

Nearly 65 percent of Americans are overweight, turning plus-size clothing into a strong seller at retail outlets from Kmart to Nordstrom and for names such as Ralph Lauren and Versace. In all, big-and-tall has become an estimated $6 billion business, representing more than a 10 percent share of the total men's market.

Much of the action is coming from online and catalog buyers— which makes sense, given that shopping at home is always more comfortable. Casual Male, the nation's largest big-and-tall chain, says sales through its online catalog were up 50 percent during the past year, while Big Tall Direct, an online offshoot of a Dallas retail chain, has seen a 38 percent increase.

The rub: Because weight distribution varies widely from one big customer to the next, it can be tough for shoppers to find a good fit without trying items on. Though I'm at the slimmer end of the target audience—men's plus-size waist sizes generally range from 42 inches up to 80—I volunteered to shop for five outfits, sight unseen. I posed the same scenario to phone reps at different vendors: I wanted a "business casual" ensemble for an informal meeting with a client, and asked each one to suggest a sport coat, slacks and dress shirt. To help me judge my new duds, I enlisted Palm Beach, Florida, tailor Antonietta Incristi.

When my gear arrived, I found fits that were all over the map— from stylish to clownish. Most disappointing was the $190 ensemble from KingSize, a division of catalog company Brylane and one of the industry's most prominent names. As soon as I showed the outfit to Ms. Incristi, she did her best imitation of a chattering canary: "Cheap, cheap, cheap." The wide-leg pants were so ridiculously oversize they left me feeling like Bozo's understudy. The hopsack blazer had the dubious distinction of being too tight and too loose in different spots. (Its green color—dubbed "forest"—added insult to injury.) But while fit is an individual matter, my tailor said the blazer was so poorly cut, it is doubtful it would work for anyone.

In some cases, the clothing was top-shelf, but the fit wasn't. Kaufman's Tall & Big Shop, a Colorado retailer that sells online, sent me a $420 outfit that included a sharp blue-gray patterned wool sport coat. But despite the phone rep's optimism that it would fit—she suggested a slightly longer size than I normally buy—it was tight around the upper arms. Still, the company won kudos for the most stylish shirt; slate-blue with a sheen, this $38 private-label model had a slimming effect.

Eventually I found a couple of winners in the fit department. Both Casual Male and Big Tall Direct picked ensembles that seemed almost tailored to my specifications—in large part because, unbeknownst to me, the companies sent me nearly identical hopsack blazers from the same manufacturer, Hardwick. The rest of the items were hit-and-miss: My $260 tab at Casual Male yielded some classy charcoal pleated wool slacks that were nicely creased and just the right weight for year-round wear, but the sport chambray shirt was soft to the point of appearing shabby. ("The shirt is cheap," Ms. Incristi said, back in canary mode.)

With Big Tall Direct, the opposite was almost true: My $210 bought me a respectable Oxford dress shirt, while the graphite-gray dress slacks seemed bargain-basement—a polyester/wool blend in which the polyester (65 percent) was too obvious for my tailor. Still, I give Big Tall Direct the nod for Best Value, because I thought its rep was among the most knowledgeable and helpful.

For Best Overall, I pick Rochester Big & Tall, a company that emphasizes the designer end of the plus-size spectrum. True, when I called, the catalog seemed to be out of many items. But the rep eventually suggested an outfit that ran about $370—a silk twill three-button blazer and pants ensemble from Axis, with a dress shirt from DKNY. It was a stunner of an outfit, casually cosmopolitan in styling and downright luxurious in feel, and it put to shame the drab big-man's garb I was forced to wear years ago. When I told Ms. Incristi the jacket was the slightest bit snug around the waist, she said not to worry. It could easily be altered—or better yet, she suggested, I might lose a couple of pounds.

—CHARLES PASSY

TIPS FOR WOMEN

1. Jackets. No other item in a woman's wardrobe can make her look as sexy and powerful as a jacket. And it's not brain surgery. All you need for a durable classic: a simple double-breasted jacket in a reliable fabric, preferably a wool-mix blend. No pockets, for a seamless look. Length? Just touching the hip, any shorter and it will date quickly. What distinguishes girls from the boys: the all-essential nip at the waist. Another must: lining, to add structure and shape, with no pucker and well-joined seams. Aside from the usual blacks and blues, creams and whites give a fresh, sharp look. Don't want to look like a doctor? Get one with details, such as a metallic clasp or textured fabric.

2. Pants. The key feature to look for is a flat front and back darts to accentuate your bottom. Very important: The rise—the distance between the pants' waistline and crotch—should be centered just slightly below the belly button. Any lower and you'd need to be built like Britney, any higher and you'll look frumpy. Want a snugger fit? Look for two-way stretch fabric, but remember: dry clean only, to preserve the fit. As for cut, a slight flare can be flattering for taller folk, but a straight leg suits everyone and never dates. Pants should be long enough so that when seated, the hem shouldn't ride past the ankle-bone.

3. Skirts. Trends may come and go, but there are two must-have matte-black skirts that should figure into any working woman's wardrobe. The skirt arsenal: the straight pencil style that hugs the body from waist to knee, and either an A-line or bias cut shaped with a gentle swing at the knee. Paired with different accessories, both should take wearers from day to night. A favorite cut is the bias: Since the material is cut at a diagonal, it drapes fluidly across the hip and stomach and flatters most figures. Details that can distinguish a sober skirt from one with va-voom: textured grosgrain ribbon trim at the waist, or rich plum-colored lining. An essential element for any skirt is a good-quality lining in natural fibers such as silk or cotton. Man-made polyester fabrics don't let your skin breathe, so sitting all day with your legs crossed gets sticky. As for fabric, triacetate—a medium-weight, high-spun synthetic fabric—is good for year-round wear. Another versatile bet is lightweight wool.

4. Shoes. Unlike men's footwear, there is no enduring woman's shoe, and no pair is worth wearing after its third year of use. Nonetheless, within that time frame, working Cinderellas should have at least one pair of black calfskin closed-toe pumps with an elegant arch and pointed toe. A tapered point is vital, since a boxy toe makes ladies' legs look thick. If your toes need more wriggle room, get a slightly more elongated shoe that will taper out past the toe line. One example of a classic, comfy but pretty pump is the evergreen Ferragamo Vara pump—a low-heeled, gently rounded shoe with a signature bow on top. Lastly, forget flat shoes; ladies should rise above the occasion.

SIZE MATTERS: MAKING THINGS FIT

Try everything on before you buy. It's long been the bane of a shopper's existence—finding clothing that actually fits. The numbers on the labels are increasingly meaningless as designers and retailers play to vanity and their own customer demographics in determining the length of an inseam and width of a waistline.

A modern study of the size and shape of Americans hasn't been done before. In fact, the clothing sizes used by many apparel companies are measurements that were originally derived from U.S. military and government research conducted back in the 1940s, when Americans were more svelte as a population and not as ethnically diverse.

While apparel manufacturers refer to these government-issued body-measurement tables, there is no law or regulation requiring them to strictly adhere to the charts. Each company can subjectively interpret how big and wide a size six should be and, as a result, today's sizes are all over the map. There's a pervasiveness of "vanity sizing," whereby a woman who is a true size six might find herself comfortably fitting into a size two. (The problem is more pronounced with women's clothing than men's.) And many companies have developed their own in-house sizing scales to fit the frames of people who they think are their core customers.

Add to that the confusion caused because sizes are represented by different numbers in different countries (a woman's size 8 in the United States is a size 10 in the United Kingdom, a 36 in Germany, a 42 in Italy and an 11 in Hong Kong), and it's little wonder what's written on a size label is almost meaningless. (**Tip:** you can check out **onlineconversion.com** for figuring out size conversions in other countries.)

VIRTUAL MODELS: A FIT OVER ONLINE SWIMSUITS

Finding a swimsuit that fits is tough enough under ideal circumstances. Just try doing it over the Internet.

Retailers are scrambling to make it easier to shop for clothes online these days—and with good reason. While online retail still accounts for only 2 percent of total sales for major retailers, it's growing fast. For instance, the clothing retailer Guess? says its Web site already pulls in enough money to rank as one of the chain's top five "stores" in terms of sales.

As a result, retailers are going to great lengths to improve the online experience, revamping Web sites with features that attempt to make it easier to size yourself up. Lands' End, for instance, is one of several offering a "virtual model"—you simply answer questions about your appearance, from hairstyle, to the shape of your face, to

THE INSIDE DIRT ON
STAIN-RESISTANT FABRICS

Since the days of Lady Macbeth, people have been battling the same frustrating reality of human existence: tough stains. Now clothing companies are pitching a solution for those damned spots. From JC Penney's machine-washable men's suits, to Lands' End's stain-resistant Teflon-coated chinos, retailers are bolstering their fall lines with technology-enhanced clothing designed to repel spills, thwart wrinkles and avoid visits to the dry cleaners. While fashionistas might scoff at the notion of functional fashion, the latest generation of products are often indistinguishable from their natural-fiber counterparts. Instead of spraying on a waxy finish, the new versions blend or bake the materials into the cloth. Result: You don't feel like you're wearing a rain slicker.

But does this stuff work? To find out, *The Wall Street Journal* borrowed some of the official stain tests used by major detergent-makers and also subjected the wrinkle-free claim to the tightly packed suitcase test. Our findings: Don't throw away your dry cleaner's phone number just yet. Most of the stain-resistant items initially put on an impressive show by causing liquids to bead and then roll off the garment. While that makes for a neat party trick, the stains often settle in for good if you let them sit.

whether you wear a beard (men only). Then the software creates a likeness of you, which you can dress as you choose.

We decided to put the new features to the test with one of the toughest articles of clothing to buy—a new bathing suit. More than half of women surveyed need to try on six or more suits before finding one they like, according to a recent survey by DuPont (which took an interest because it makes Lycra). Still, it's not so unusual to shop for a swimsuit online. Retailer J. Crew, in fact, says its shoppers online are more likely to buy swimwear than shoppers in its stores.

But there are obstacles. For one thing, retailers refuse to abide by a single, uniform sizing chart. Two of the five Web sites we tried offered only three sizes: "small," "medium" and "large." One of the two wouldn't let us mix-and-match a different-sized top and bottom.

By far the best service came from Lands' End. Its "Swim Finder" categorizes suits by body shape and whether they purport to lengthen

A FASHIONISTA'S DRY-CLEANING TIPS

The first question most people have for their dry cleaner is: When will my clothes be ready? But Betty Halbreich, a personal shopper at Bergdorf Goodman in New York for over 27 years, wants to know how recently the cleaning fluid was changed. If it's more than a week old, it can leave clothes dirty and discolored, she says.

Ms. Halbreich, who frequently deals with dry cleaners in her job, also brings her own plastic hangers (wire hangers can ruin shoulders), and asks that sleeves be stuffed with tissue. As soon as she gets home, she yanks off the plastic wrap, to let the clothes breathe. When she gets food or wine stains on a garment, she never tries to scrub them out herself—that can leave permanent rings. She takes it to the dry cleaner as is.

Still, she's careful not to dry-clean her clothes too frequently. (It wears them out faster, she says.) When she can, she spot-cleans just-worn collars, cuffs and necklines with a washcloth and a cleaning fluid like Everblum.

legs or deemphasize the waist. It has a special category—"anxiety zones"—to help people find a suit style that masks their least-favorite body part.

When we called the customer-service hotline to double-check measurements, an attentive rep suggested the best size for me. The resulting suit fit perfectly (though the color I wanted was temporarily on back order). Lands' End's virtual model is fun to play with. After picking a suit, clicking the "try on" button takes you through a registration process, which creates the model based on the physical description of yourself. But while the virtual model does help visualize what the clothing looks like, it won't help you decide what size to order. (You have to use the site's other tools for that.)

JCrew.com organizes its suits similarly to Lands' End, and also offers illustrations that try to explain why some swimsuit shapes tend to flatter certain body shapes. It doesn't have a virtual model— but the customer rep on the phone was quick and helpful. After a brief discussion of our needs, she confirmed the size I needed. When the suit arrived, it fit properly.

Guess? provided the least hand-holding. It offers only three sizes, then it hides its customer-service 800 number on the "help" page; most other sites list it more prominently. We had to simply hope that a "medium" would fit. (It did, sort of.)

Other retailers could learn a lesson from Victoria's Secret, which uses standard bra sizes for many of its bathing suits—which some other retailers do sporadically or not at all. As a result, the suit fit well, although it didn't quite look the same on us as it did in the photo of the Victoria's Secret model.

Girlshop.com, an online-only retailer, offered perhaps the best selection—oodles of suits in all kinds of groovy prints. But for the suit we wanted, its sizing services were the least helpful. The suit also came only in small, medium or large—with no chart to help decide which would be the best. We called the customer-service rep, who suggested that old standby, medium. It ended up being far too small.

Girlshop's chief executive said we happened to pick a suit brand that tends to run small. The site is working on providing more sizing charts, she said.

ACKNOWLEDGMENTS

First of all, this book wouldn't be possible without the extremely smart and talented reporting staff of *The Wall Street Journal,* and the reporters and editors of the Weekend and Personal Journal sections in particular. A big thanks to Paul Steiger, Joanne Lipman, Amy Stevens, Edward Felsenthal, Tom Weber and Eben Shapiro for easing the process. The guidance provided by Steve Adler and Roe D'Angelo was invaluable, as was the assistance of Daniel Nasaw. Thanks also to John Mahaney and Annik La Farge at Crown. Finally, the biggest debt is owed to Ken Wells, editor extraordinaire, who pulled it all together.

INDEX

ABOUT THE AUTHOR

NANCY KEATES has been a reporter and editor for *The Wall Street Journal*'s Weekend section since 1996, covering travel, art, home trends, technology, health, restaurants and shopping, as well as education and family issues.

Before joining *The Journal,* Nancy spent three years as Johannesburg correspondent and bureau chief for AP-Dow Jones, the international arm of the Dow Jones newswires. She then moved to Washington D.C., covering international trade and finance, including the World Bank, the International Monetary Fund and the White House, as well as the Treasury and Commerce Departments.

Nancy holds a B.A. in government from Cornell University and an M.B.A. from George Washington University. In addition to frequent appearances on both CNBC and the Fine Living Channel, she has been a guest on NBC's *Today* show and *The News with Brian Williams.* She is also a popular radio and panel guest, discussing travel and other topics.

She and her husband, David Siker, a physician, live in Portland, Oregon, with their two sons, Vaughan, 5, and Theodore (Teddy), 3.